WINNERS AND LOSERS

PRINCETON STUDIES IN
Political Behavior

Tali Mendelberg, Series Editor

Winners and Losers: The Psychology of Foreign Trade, Diana C. Mutz

The Autocratic Middle Class: How State Dependency Reduces the Demand for Democracy, Bryn Rosenfeld

The Loud Minority: Why Protests Matter in American Democracy, Daniel Q. Gillion

Steadfast Democrats: How Social Forces Shape Black Political Behavior, Ismail K. White and Chryl N. Laird

The Cash Ceiling: Why Only the Rich Run for Office—And What We Can Do about It, Nicholas Carnes

Deep Roots: How Slavery Still Shapes Southern Politics, Avidit Acharya, Matthew Blackwell, and Maya Sen

Envy in Politics, Gwyneth H. McClendon

Communism's Shadow: Historical Legacies and Contemporary Political Attitudes, Grigore Pop-Eleches and Joshua A. Tucker

Democracy for Realists: Why Elections Do Not Produce Responsive Government, Christopher H. Achen and Larry M. Bartels

Resolve in International Politics, Joshua D. Kertzer

Winners and Losers

The Psychology of Foreign Trade

Diana C. Mutz

PRINCETON UNIVERSITY PRESS
PRINCETON AND OXFORD

Published by Princeton University Press
41 William Street, Princeton, New Jersey 08540
6 Oxford Street, Woodstock, Oxfordshire OX20 1TR

press.princeton.edu

ISBN 978-0-691-20303-4
ISBN (pbk.) 978-0-691-20302-7
ISBN (e-book) 978-0-691-20304-1

British Library Cataloging-in-Publication Data is available

Editorial: Bridget Flannery-McCoy and Alena Chekanov
Production Editorial: Debbie Tegarden and Mark Bellis
Cover Design: Karl Spurzem
Production: Brigid Ackerman
Publicity: Kate Hensley and Kathryn Stevens
Copyeditor: Jay Boggis

Cover Credit: Shutterstock

This book has been composed in Adobe Text and Gotham

10 9 8 7 6 5 4 3 2 1

CONTENTS

FIGURES

PREFACE

This book was supposed to have been completed before Donald Trump took office. That book would have addressed a relatively low-profile political issue, how the mass public decides where it stands on international trade. With Trump's candidacy and subsequent election, this turned into a much larger project. By choosing foreign trade as one of his signature campaign issues, Trump raised the profile of this issue tremendously, creating turmoil in both mass opinion and elite reactions.

As a result, this topic has become far more interesting as an academic subject. It is also far more important as a political issue. Unfortunately, the dynamics of opinions toward trade also became far more puzzling after Trump's election. Had I stopped then and sent things off to press, what I had observed would have been far easier to explain. But it would not have withstood the test of time. No one wants to write a book whose theory is out of date almost immediately after it is published. So, in retrospect, the book comes closer to offering a thorough understanding of mass trade opinions as a result of having slogged through the baffling dynamics of trade opinions throughout Trump's presidency.

As someone who is not trained as an economist, I approached trade as a lay person might. I had always assumed—and found to some degree—that trade opposition was borne of empathy for the victims of trade, the unfortunate people we hear about on the news whose factories are closed and livelihoods thus devastated. I say "hear about on the news" because most Americans are not employed in import-competing lines of work. Given that most of us are employed in non-tradable sectors of the economy, we learn about this problem through sources other than personal experience.

My own early sources of information gave me mixed feelings. I grew up in the state of Indiana at a time when the steel and automotive industries in the northern part of the state were experiencing massive layoffs. Whole communities were decimated by factory closings that were widely blamed on international trade, and particularly on competition from Japanese car manufacturers.

Many years later, as a scholar studying public opinion in American politics, my colleague Ed Mansfield re-introduced me to this interesting issue as a topic of academic research. What surprised me most was how differently international relations scholars and students of American politics viewed the public's knowledge about trade and the likely bases of their policy attitudes. The kinds of calculations political economists attributed to average Americans did not mesh well with what I knew about levels of voter knowledge or the usual bases for forming opinions on policy issues. International relations scholars clearly had a lot more faith in the expertise of the mass public than scholars of American politics did. But the types of evidence they marshaled to make their cases were also quite different, making it difficult to reconcile such starkly different conclusions.

The initial studies that Ed and I pursued out of our mutual interest in this topic laid the groundwork for what later became this book. Without his encouragement and expertise, I would never have taken on this topic at all. That said, he bears no responsibility for the conclusions herein.

As happens to me with many topics, as I learned more about the origin of mass trade opinion, my own views changed. First, travelling internationally to less economically developed countries made my mental images of inequality far starker than what I had seen in the US. There was poverty, and then there was extreme poverty. Few will argue with the claim that trade has helped the world economy, expanding the size of the global middle class.[1] Around the globe, people have benefitted and levels of worldwide poverty and inequality have dropped. Nonetheless, among Americans, trade's effects on domestic inequality tend to be the more salient concern. So, while I continued to find trade's negative effects on American jobs off-putting, I became increasingly cognizant of the positive aspects of globalization and the beneficial consequences of international markets.

Further, the results of my studies did not paint as well-intentioned a portrait of trade opposition as I had anticipated. First, it was not the people losing jobs who were most upset about trade as had been widely assumed. I had thought that in addition to concerns about displacing US jobs, those opposing trade would be concerned about its environmental impact, and about problems such as child labor and unsafe working conditions. Those concerns were out there, to be sure, but only to a very small extent. Instead, what I found was that it was all about us, that is, all about the US getting what Americans see as its fair share of the international pie. This seemed like a bizarre perspective from one of the richest countries on earth.

In one of our early studies, Ed and I found that domestic ethnocentrism—differences in how positively Blacks, whites and Latinos in the US judged their own group relative to other racial groups—was the best predictor of trade opposition. Those who didn't like racial outgroups, didn't like trade. In another experimental study, people's judgments indicated that no amount of job gains for trading partner countries could justify the loss of even one American job in most Americans' eyes. In another study, white Americans supported trade with dark-skinned countries systematically less than trade with light-skinned countries. And countries without the same language and cultural customs were also deemed less worthy. On and on it went. I thought I was studying an economic issue, but people's views were less about the bottom line than about what kind of people they viewed as deserving.

When the culture within a country encourages favoring co-nationals in a supposed competition against citizens of other countries, I'm afraid that it brings out the worst in people. For that reason, I end this book with some practical suggestions for approaching discussions of trade with mass publics. There are many legitimate reasons to favor or oppose international trade, but appealing to Americans' competitive instincts and their desire to dominate other countries and "win" against the competition are not the most admirable. While economic self-interest is easily justified, racism and ethnocentrism give trade opponents a bad name. When people are keen to support trade only if it allows them to take advantage of countries that are not like them in terms of being well-off, white, and Christian, then trade opposition loses some of its nobility. In short, the roots of opposition to trade were not as rational and well-meaning as I had assumed.

During the writing of this book, I have incurred a huge number of debts. For funding that made much of this data collection possible, I am grateful to the Guggenheim Foundation and to the Andrew Carnegie Foundation for their support of this project. At the University of Pennsylvania, the Christopher H. Browne Center for International Politics and the Institute for the Study of Citizens and Politics also made important contributions. Penn undergraduates Veronica Podolny and Ivy Hunt helped with preparation of the manuscript. My graduate students were heavily involved in many of the projects that ended up in this book, and I could not have handled such large volumes of data without them. I give special thanks to Laura Silver, Eunji Kim, Kecheng Fang, and Amber Hye-Yon Lee for their contributions. Kyle

Cassidy helped with preparation of the figures and tables. The series editor, Tali Mendelberg, and my editor at Princeton, Bridget Flannery-McCoy, both provided valuable encouragement in taking on this controversial topic.

Finally, I thank my husband, Robin Pemantle, who is neither an economist nor a political scientist, for being precisely the right kind of person to read many drafts of these chapters. As another kind of outsider, his advice was extremely valuable in conveying what did, and did not, make sense as I pulled this book together.

Just as I was concluding this book, COVID19 descended upon the United States. Some are predicting that it is yet another nail in globalization's coffin. My own, far more optimistic, view based on this research is that while economic hard times in the near future may temporarily turn people inward, COVID19 brought to the forefront of public attention the need for global cooperation in order to address the world's most pressing problems, that is, problems without borders. Toward that end, it is incumbent upon the US to provide global leadership, including a new image of trade as a path to enhanced international cooperation.

Diana Mutz
Haverford, PA
November 2020

WINNERS AND LOSERS

1

Beyond the Conventional Wisdom

Kevin Watje manufactures garbage trucks in Iowa. He knows a lot more about international trade than most Americans because his company gets the steel it uses in its trucks from China. Trump's trade war with China has made obtaining materials much more expensive for his company. Yet when a reporter interviewed this Trump supporter about his views on trade, he remained steadfast in his support for both Trump and his trade policies, suggesting that we "got to do what we've got to do." When asked about this larger goal, he described his quandary:

> I get it, there is an imbalance of trade, and that needs to be dealt with. And I support him in that, but we just want to make trucks out here, O.K.? And I understand it needs to be done, and I support his efforts, but I think it's been adding a lot of stress to our company because of these tariffs and how it's disrupted our supply chain.[1]

Pressed further by the reporter about why he supports a policy that is personally hurting him and his company, Kevin explains,

> There's men and women that go to war and put their lives at stake. And we're Americans, we all ought to fight this fight with our president. And we're not risking the things that soldiers do to keep our future safe and prosperous. So, I think it's a small price to pay. I think we ought to stand in there and help him.

Kevin may be unusual in his level of knowledge about how he and his company are affected by trade, but the way in which he thinks about where he stands on trade is more commonplace. It has less to do with how he is personally affected by the policies in the short term than about broader, often symbolic long-term objectives.

This book examines how Americans decide what they think about international trade. Some scholars question whether they even think about it at all. But in the twenty-first century, globalization of the world economy is difficult to ignore. People know that products and services come from all over the world, that globalization is an inevitable fact of everyday life. But is this development something they welcome or something they view as best avoided, if at all possible?

From the initial conversations about trade that I had with everyone from neighbors to participants in random national surveys, three general observations emerged, themes that seemed to me to contradict much academic thinking about mass opinion on trade. First, for most Americans, globalization is something happening "out there," away from their everyday lives. Unlike Kevin, most do not see themselves as an integral part of this narrative. For example, a consistent majority of Americans say that their families' personal finances are unaffected by international trade in either positive or negative ways.[2] While I'm certain that economists and policymakers would beg to differ, it is nonetheless striking that most Americans see it that way.

Second, when people talk about what they like about international trade, they seldom talk about economic principles. For economists, there are two standard reasons that trade makes sense as a mutually beneficial enterprise.[3] One logic, credited to Adam Smith, is that specialization saves everyone time and money.[4] People can produce more things of value if each person does one thing instead of trying to do everything for themselves. By trading for other things that they need, production is more efficient, and everyone gets more of what they need than they would working on their own. I have once, and only once, made my own butter. It was interesting, but highly inefficient relative to buying it at the store.

A later extension of the logic in favor of free trade is more complex. In his theory of comparative advantage, David Ricardo argued that international trade was mutually beneficial due to differences in countries' capacities to produce goods. A country does not have to be best at anything to gain from trade, but mutual benefits occur when countries specialize in things they are *relatively* better at, even though they may not have an absolute advantage in those areas. I find that even college-educated Americans are not thinking about these logics when asked about international trade. They lack confidence in their understanding of the expansive and complicated range of large-scale interactions constituting the international economy.

When average Americans who favor trade articulate its benefits, these virtues are notably absent. For example, even among those who are enthusiastic about trade, few wax poetic about the wonders of the invisible hand, the efficiency of market specialization, or even the lower cost of consumer goods. And not a single individual mentioned the importance of trade relationships to the liberal international order, a common refrain among political scientists. This is not to say that these ideas are completely absent from their reasoning, but they speak a different language about trade from that of economists and political scientists.

A third observation is that despite limited economic knowledge, people do, nonetheless, hold opinions about international trade, even quite strong opinions in some cases. People are not so much misinformed as they hold alternative, lay theories about how international trade works. But again, contrary to what much of the academic literature suggests, these opinions are seldom expressed as a matter of personal economic costs and benefits. Instead, the mass public's views are rooted in their understanding of the psychology of human interaction, projected onto their nation's relationship with foreign countries. The way ordinary Americans think about trade is very different from the way economists and policy wonks think about it.

Previous work on how people form attitudes toward trade has focused almost exclusively on people's *economic* reasons for supporting or opposing trade. Consequently our understanding of public opinion has been incomplete. This book addresses that gap by focusing on the lay theories and internal logic the public uses to make judgments about international trade.

I begin by briefly rehashing what we thought we knew about how the public formed its opinions on trade. I then outline an alternative framework that has emerged from my observations over fifteen years of studying the American public. Fortuitously, this time period happens to have been a particularly tumultuous time for American attitudes toward trade, thus shedding light not only on how people form their views, but also when and why they change them.

The Conventional Wisdom

There are two well-known theories that have been offered to explain the origins of mass opinions on trade. Both focus on individuals' pocketbooks and how they are personally affected by trade. According to the Heckscher-Ohlin model, trade preferences depends on a person's skill level and what kinds of products their home country produces most efficiently. In a high-skill country like the US, highly skilled people should favor trade, and low-skill individuals should oppose it. An alternative theory, known as the Ricardo-Viner model, suggests that people base their opinions about trade on the industry in which they are employed. If their industry benefits from trade by exporting goods, they favor it. But if their industry must compete with foreign imports, they will oppose international trade.

Such highly rational expectations are common in economic analyses, but they seem much less plausible from the perspective of what we know about American political behavior. Situations in which people have been found to express self-interest-based policy preferences are known to be rare. They are limited to simple, straightforward issues, or to populations of especially sophisticated people.[5] Trade policy does not fit that mold well. As an economic issue, trade is complicated, abstract, and multi-faceted. There is a lot for people to consider and potentially synthesize, particularly when trade has simultaneous positive and negative effects on people as workers, as employers, and as consumers. As one study recently concluded, "The sheer complexity of the global economy makes it difficult for economic actors—and the scholars who study them—to predict how policies would affect material interests."[6]

Nonetheless, it is not difficult to convince people that there is merit to theories rooted in self-interest, and not only because economists have widely endorsed this idea. Media coverage also promotes this idea as a "natural" reaction to the loss of jobs that is caused by trade.[7] Apparently humans have a well-documented psychological tendency to overestimate the impact of self-interest on *others'* attitudes and behaviors,[8] even when they are not personally influenced by it. In the context of international trade, this means it is easy to sell the idea that opinions boil down to how it affects people's pocketbooks.

Why have alternative explanations for trade preferences been so slow to emerge? My best guess is that this is because people seldom find what they are not looking for. Initially the economic studies supporting self-interest-based interpretations were exclusively aggregate-level analyses based on measures of collective behavior within geographic units of some kind. When scholars turned to individual-level survey data to test these theories, some findings still seemed supportive of skill-based self-interest because education level was equated with skill level. Education consistently plays a role in promoting support for international trade.[9]

Studies of individuals as well as analyses of geographic aggregates agree on the importance of education in predicting trade preferences. Higher levels of education are directly related to support for open trade, even when taking characteristics such as income into account. Where these studies disagree is in the interpretation of what the relationship between education and trade support means. When economists are interpreting this evidence, education is often viewed as an indicator of a person's job skills. Political psychologists, in contrast, are likely to note that education is associated with a wide range of potential explanations for trade preferences, including many that have nothing to do with whether trade threatens a person's livelihood. For example, low levels of education are terrific predictors of negative attitudes toward outgroups, whether domestic or international. Low levels of education also support the tendency to see the world in an "us versus them" framework.

Survey data ultimately made it possible to distinguish among these various interpretations of education. People could be asked about their industry of employment, as well as their skill levels, and this could be matched with official data on how industries were affected by trade, as well as with occupational wages. The overall consensus from these studies is that personal economic self-interest plays little, if any, role in people's opinions on trade.[10] With the exception of varying interpretations of education's impact, relationships between labor market attributes and trade policy preferences do not hold up in US survey data.[11]

Indeed, the behavioral revolution in international relations increasingly suggests that inferring ordinary people's preferences based on complex economic models can lead scholars astray. Thus a second wave of studies of trade opinions has pursued a variety of alternative, largely non-economic explanations. This book attempts to pick up where the early explanations left off, focusing on explanations for trade preferences that have surprisingly little to do with economics and far more to do with basic human psychology.

To be clear, the fact that personal self-interest matters little to trade preferences does not imply that Americans are altruistic or that the economic impact of trade does not matter to them. When contrasting self-interested and "sociotropic" predictors of trade preferences, that is, how a person believes he or she is affected by trade as opposed to how he or she believes the country *as a whole* is affected, scholars have at times equated sociotropic impact with altruism.[12] This characterization overlooks the fact that there are many reasons that people base their policy views on perceived national impact, reasons that have nothing to do with altruism as traditionally understood. Rooting for the home team to win is not an altruistic act.

Although personal economic interests may not predict trade preferences, perceptions of how trade affects *national* economic conditions, that is, sociotropic perceptions, matter a great deal.[13] People's perceptions of the national-level impact of trade may or may not be accurate, but these perceptions are key to understanding their opinions on trade policy.[14] Regardless of how selfless or selfish one might be, it is simply much easier for people to connect policy decisions made in Washington to those policies' collective national consequences than to connect events in their daily lives to decisions made in Washington. Surprisingly, even something as gut-wrenching as losing a job is widely viewed as a personal rather than a political problem; unemployment is seldom a cause for a change in political attitudes or behavior.[15] Far from being a default reaction, politicizing personal economic experiences is difficult and uncommon.

This is surprising to many because personal experience is such an easily accessible source of information. But the process of politicizing personal experience involves multiple steps, any one of which can break down the process. In the case of international trade, first, ordinary people need to be able to formulate accurate assessments of how trade affects their personal incomes and purchasing power. Second, they must attribute these effects to actions (or inaction) by government leaders. Finally, they must link the personal economic consequences of trade to support for specific policies. What is depicted by some as a "puzzling disconnection between material interests and policy preferences"[16] does not seem puzzling or even unusual to those who study how ordinary Americans form policy preferences. Across a wide range of issues beyond trade, evidence of self-interested policy preferences is uncommon.[17]

Most Americans have a difficult time figuring out when a policy aligns with their personal financial interests. There are some exceptions, of course, but trade policy does not seem likely to be one of them. It is very difficult to observe directly the positive and negative effects of trade on individual American lives. With the exception of when a person knows that he or she has lost a job due to trade, this is a complex calculation.[18] The effects of trade on the lives of people overseas are even more difficult for Americans to observe.[19]

The progression of research on how people form attitudes toward trade closely parallels the progression in studies of how the national economy affects voting. Initially, the idea that people voted their pocketbooks was considered a "self-evident truth."[20] But as individual-level data became more widely available with the advent of representative national probability surveys, serious questions were raised about this interpretation.[21] When family financial self-interest did not predict voting behavior as had been anticipated, some explained this by saying scholars simply had not measured self-interest properly. Others suggested that perhaps it was group-based financial interests that mattered.[22] But neither of these approaches did much to resolve the inconsistency between aggregate patterns that seemed to support the idea that people voted their pocketbooks, and individual-level evidence suggesting that they did not. This disjuncture was resolved to some extent by the concept of "sociotropic" economic voting. People did not vote on the basis of how they themselves had been affected economically, but they did vote on the basis of how they thought the nation as a whole had been affected.

Studies of trade preferences have followed a very similar path. In contrast to the lack of evidence that personal financial self-interest drives attitudes toward trade, there is clear evidence that the perceived collective effects of trade on the country as a whole matter a great deal to people's policy preferences.[23] Here, as in many other policy domains, sociotropic perceptions, that is, beliefs about the impact of trade policy on the country as a whole, are more easily linked to policy preferences. What is unique about international trade is that in forming opinions, one can potentially consider not only its perceived effects on one's own country, but also its perceived effects on trading partner countries. In this sense I have termed it doubly sociotropic because people may consider trade's impact on trading partner countries as well as its impact on the US.

Conceptualizing a Global Economy

It is easy enough to criticize Americans' lack of formal knowledge about economics and international trade. But it is worth taking a step back to remember that the sheer idea of a *national* economy is highly abstract, and only a recent phenomenon. One hundred years ago, people did not talk about something called the "national economy." Unlike the national anthem, or the American flag, there was no national economy until social scientists imagined it into existence in the wake the Great Depression. Indeed, 1934 was the first time the US government had a quantitative indicator of how things were going in the country as whole, something they initially dubbed "National Income." Before that, concepts like GDP were not a part of public consciousness.[24]

Today it seems as natural to talk about how "the economy" is doing as it is to discuss sports scores. We forget that economies are highly abstract entities, reified at regular intervals by economists and journalists. We don't see them or touch them, and we rely a great deal on experts to tell us in what shape they are in. Few people would have enough personal exposure to the extensive American economy to assess how it is doing across this large country were it not for regularly released government statistics.

If the notion of a national economy is abstract, then an international economy is even more incomprehensible. Global trade has brought about relationships on a scale and at a level of abstraction that was previously unimaginable. Because these relationships are indirect and typically mediated by complex international markets, they are extremely abstract and difficult for most of us to wrap our heads around. What's more, when these abstract entities seem distant and divorced from everyday life, people may feel the lack of control that naturally comes with not understanding how distant processes work.

Because humans are guided by a psychology that is deeply rooted in concrete, face-to-face, interpersonal interactions, our thought processes are poorly suited to comprehend large-scale, complex systems such as international trade. To deal with this problem, people often try to extend what they know about human interaction to understand international interactions, an approach that does not always serve them well.

Relationships and interactions on scales beyond our comprehension lead to some predictable responses. One is to simplify the target of our consternation down to something concrete that we do feel we can understand. When someone tells us that balancing the federal budget is just like balancing the family checkbook, then we are reassured by the familiarity, even if it is misleading.[25] Likewise, the stories we tell one another about trade can influence the attitudes we form, regardless of their veracity. Whether the stories are about foreigners stealing our jobs or about poisoned dog treats from China, once these ideas are reduced to compelling narratives, they can spread quickly.

Such narratives and metaphors encourage people's sense that international trade is a source of risky relationships, unlike relationships with people we can see, hear, and know firsthand.[26] After all, we tell children at a young age not to speak to strangers, let alone to have "relationships" with people in far-flung countries. Distant relationships are naturally seen as less trustworthy and reliable than those close to home. Thus globalization runs headlong against the grain of much of basic human psychology, asking us to trust distant, impersonal, and dissimilar others, and to cede the control we may feel over at least our immediate environments.

For someone who has never thought much about whether trade is beneficial or harmful, intuition based on everyday experience is a natural starting point. Americans begin by forming lay theories about how their day-to-day lives are influenced by trade.[27] Given an admittedly challenging task, this approach seems like a reasonable way for people to try to grasp the highly abstract concept of participating in a global economy. Indeed, one major theme running through this book is that people react to trade relationships in much the same way they do other relationships in their lives.

Competition versus Cooperation

If their opinions are not based on economic considerations, then how do Americans think about trade? The most basic difference that comes through when Americans talk about trade is whether they view it as a form of cooperation or as a source of competition. One recent observer characterized the kind of people predisposed to be unfavorable versus favorable toward globalization as either "drawbridge up" or "drawbridge down" types:

> Do you think the bad things will all go away if we lock the doors? Or do you think it's a big beautiful world out there, full of good people, if only we could all open our arms and embrace each other?[28]

The former, "drawbridge up" types, tend to be distrustful of people beyond their borders, and fearful of being taken advantage of by others. They believe cooperation is for suckers. These are people who tend not to trust strangers and especially do not trust foreigners who seem very different from themselves.

"Drawbridge down" types, on the other hand, come out of central casting for the old Coca-Cola commercial featuring a multicultural chorus of young people from all over the world gathering on a mountaintop to sing, "I'd Like to Teach the World to Sing in Perfect Harmony."[29] Of course, this characterization is overly simplistic and definitely corny. But as I describe in the chapters that follow, this warm feeling is an important part of why people who favor trade feel so positively about it.

Nonetheless, most Americans appear to view trade as a form of international competition. In a 2013 address, the economist Paul Rubin lamented this fact, noting that introductory textbooks on economics in the US mention competition eight times more often than cooperation.[30] Of course, most

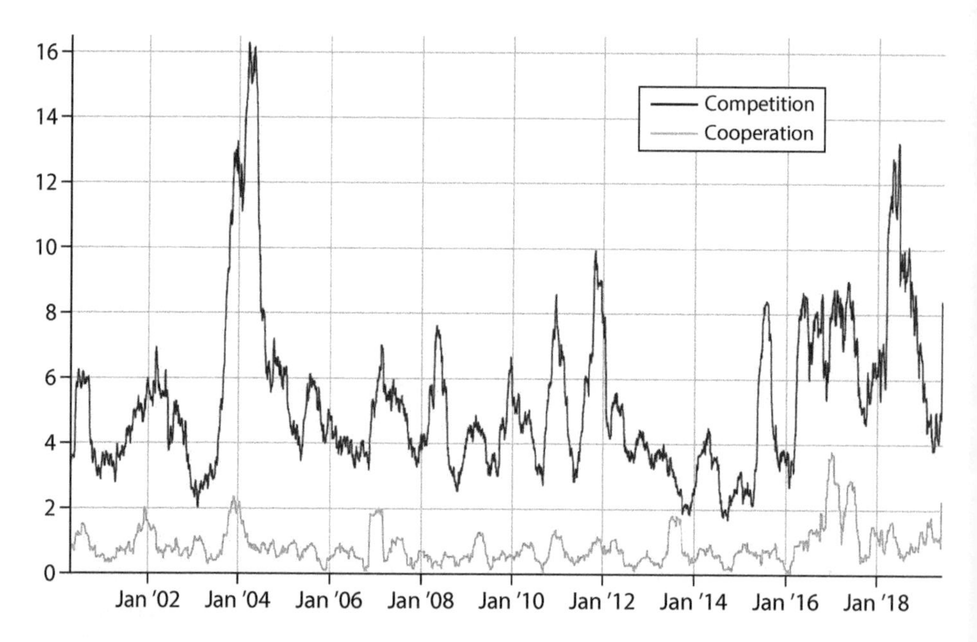

FIGURE 1.1. Extent to Which Trade Is Mentioned in Conjunction with Competition and Cooperation in Major US Newspapers, 2000–2018
Note: Lines represent the rolling average of the number of mentions of trade within the same article as either the word "competition" or the word "cooperation," or their variants. Numbers are based on a batch download of all articles mentioning trade in major US newspapers included in the Nexis database, after extracting those articles that use this term in other contexts.

Americans do not read economics textbooks anyway. But this raises the question of which of these perspectives—the cooperative or the competitive one—dominates in popular discourse? To provide a quick answer to this question for the US, I downloaded a large quantity of text from an extensive database of major US newspapers from 2000 to the present, including all articles that met specifications indicating that international trade was being discussed in some capacity.[31] I then plotted how many times articles mentioning trade co-occurred with the word "competition" versus "cooperation" over time, including variants of these words.

The findings in Figure 1.1 suggest that trade is overwhelmingly mentioned by the press in conjunction with competition, far more often than in conjunction with cooperation. Although this is admittedly a quick and dirty assessment of the emphasis on competition versus competition, regardless of the terms I used to specify these ideas, competition always dominated cooperation. Whether this coverage simply reflects the pre-existing emphasis of policymakers or helps to shape the competitive emphasis among the public remains to be seen. But competition clearly dominates thinking about trade in the US.

The tendency to emphasize a competitive framing of trade may be responsible for many of trade's negative connotations for Americans. Whereas cooperation sounds highly moral and laudatory, and implies a win-win situation, a policy rooted in competition sounds to many like a dog-eat-dog, cut-throat situation that results in one group dominating another.[32] A policy that creates winners and losers is inherently more dangerous than one rooted in cooperation.

What is ironic about this characterization is that when economists refer to trade as a policy that creates "winners" and "losers," they are referring to the distributional consequences of trade, that is, winners and losers in different lines of work *within the home country*. For example, in the US, businesses and industries that export products generally benefit, as do employees in those lines of work. But industries that cannot compete in the global marketplace may go out of business, thus creating "losers" and unemployment among people in those industries. In contrast, when the public at large thinks about winners and losers due to trade, they are more likely to think of a competition involving the US and a trading partner country, one in which winner and loser countries must ultimately emerge.

Winners versus Losers

In the US, a common way people understand trade is by means of a competitive sports metaphor.[33] The US Department of Commerce has encouraged this framing, for example, by featuring a photo of a basketball game over a discussion of the US trade agenda.[34] The whole point of a competition is to determine a winner and a loser, and many Americans see trade as precisely that: a competition between nations that the US must either win or lose, with national pride on the line.[35] Still others view it through the closely related Darwinian metaphor of survival of the fittest. In this view, trade compels intense competition between nations, making us leaner and meaner and better at what we do. But ultimately America must destroy other economies or be destroyed, because only the strongest survive, at least so the argument goes.

When talking to Americans about trade, I was at times transported to episodes of one of my kids' favorite shows on The Discovery Channel: *Animal Face-Off.* This program featured hypothetical battles between animals, frequently animals that would never encounter one another in real life or who do not compete for resources due to differing territories or diets. A computer-animated fight scene nonetheless allowed them to duke it out until one or the other was eaten alive, drowned, crushed, or hurled off a cliff.

However illogical these programs may be, Americans love competition, particularly when their side wins.[36] Indeed, cross-national studies demonstrate that Americans believe in the merits of competition more than any other industrialized country in the world.[37] The problem posed by globalization's rise is that Americans no longer see themselves as the sure-fire winners of this competition. Instead, they fear themselves to be potential losers in an inter-country competition. It is in this sense that Americans today complain about whether there is "a level playing field." For most members of the mass public, a desire for "fair trade" does not indicate a concern about treatment of overseas labor or the environment; instead, it means they believe the game itself is unfair, and thus they may "lose" this competition by no fault of their own. Indeed, politicians frequently reassure the American public by telling them, as the Democratic platform did in 2012, "If the playing field is level, Americans will be able to compete against every other country on Earth."[38] Therefore, if Americans are not "winning" in this global competition, and China is gaining ground in a zero-sum game, it must be because of a faulty playing field. The 2012 Republican platform similarly advised that, "American workers have shown that, on a truly level playing field, they can surpass the competition in international trade."[39]

Many of the statements Americans make about trade suggest that they believe we must dominate or be dominated. To hear some tell it, when we engage in trade, we risk our very autonomy as a nation and as human beings. As one person expressed a common refrain, "The way things are going, we will all work for the Chinese one day." Thirty years ago, it was Japan that was rumored to be buying Yellowstone National Park.[40] More recently, one American pondered, "I wonder if some day we will sell California to China."[41]

Notably, the disclaimer for *Animal Face-Off* warns, "Since the fights are created artificially, results in real life may vary." Likewise, I am unaware of any Chinese efforts to buy California, although President Trump did recently attempt to purchase Greenland.[42] He also argued that Americans would need to learn Chinese if his challenger were elected.[43]

Whereas economists view trade as a form of cooperation for mutual benefit, the public sees it as a high stakes competition that the US could lose. For those who see global interconnections as threatening, a trade negotiation is just another episode of *Sperm Whale versus Colossal Squid* (spoiler alert: Sperm Whale wins).[44]

The increasing concerns about trade witnessed in the contemporary political environment have a lot to do with public attention focused on the rise of China. It is not that Americans oppose the idea of trade per se; but many see trade as benefitting "them" at "our" expense, and China is now perceived as a much stronger country than it used to be. If Americans could be assured that they would come out on top in what they conceive of as an inter-country competition involving trade with China, then they would be fine with it. Trade has essentially become another weapon to use in a great power competition.

Ingroup-Outgroup Dynamics

Once an enterprise becomes "us versus them" in people's minds, there are well-known psychological processes that kick into gear. In particular, when relationships are viewed through the lens of competition rather than cooperation, people assume a defensive posture, and the psychology of intergroup competition comes to the forefront. Given the strong emphasis on competition in discussions of trade in the US, the most useful psychological theories for understanding Americans' trade preferences come from studies of domestic intergroup relations and ingroup-outgroup dynamics. Thus throughout the book, I draw on psychological constructs to identify who is most likely to view trade through a competitive versus a cooperative lens. These measures do not ask about people's opinions on trade at all, but instead identify individual differences tied to tendencies toward ingroup favoritism.

For example, in some studies, I use social dominance orientation (SDO), an index developed to tap how appropriate a person thinks it is for some groups in society to dominate others.[45] Being high in SDO means a person prefers hierarchy to equality. A sample item from this index asks people to agree or disagree with statements such as, "Superior groups should dominate inferior groups." Those high in social dominance naturally care a lot about being on the dominant, winning side of competitive contexts like trade.

SDO is known to correlate strongly with authoritarianism,[46] that is believing in the importance of obedience to authority, which is measured in a totally different way, asking about the kinds of child-rearing practices people favor. For example, people are asked which is a more important quality to instill in children, independence or respect for their elders? Both authoritarianism and SDO are known to be tied to ethnocentrism, that is, racist beliefs and attitudes. More important for my purposes, they also have implications for trade when it is viewed as a competition between ingroups and outgroups.[47] Likewise, national superiority, a sense that one's own nation is better than other nations, is tied to ingroup favoritism and trade preferences.[48] In slightly different ways, each of these tendencies identifies people who see their ingroups as superior to an outgroup. Although these are all distinct concepts, they overlap a great deal. What they share is the tendency to think in black and white, "us versus them" terms.

Since a major distinction in Americans' views of trade is whether they view it primarily as cooperation or competition, I also include scales developed to identify highly-competitive versus less-competitive individuals. Some people can't walk away from a game of checkers without establishing a winner and a loser, whereas winning is less of a motivator for others. People also vary in whether they see competition as a beneficial or a destructive force. One widely-used question asks people if they think competition is harmful and brings out the worst in people, or whether competition is basically good because it stimulates people to work hard and develop new ideas. Competitiveness intensifies ingroup favoritism, and Americans are uniquely strong believers in the value of competition. For this reason, I also identify those who view trade in "zero-sum" terms with respect to its impact on jobs. Those who view job gains in one country as tied to job losses in another country can be said to view trade's impact as zero sum.

In the context of trade, public perceptions of threat from outgroups play an important role in this story. The outside threat was Japan in the 1980s, whereas China is seen as the enemy today. Perceptions of threat can trigger ingroup favoritism and negative outgroup attitudes among those most susceptible to it. For example, theories of authoritarian "activation" posit that when individuals with certain authoritarian traits "perceive that the moral order is falling apart, the country is losing its coherence and cohesiveness, diversity is rising, and our leadership seems (to them) to be suspect or not up to the needs of the hour, it is as though a button is pushed on their forehead that says 'in case of moral threat, lock down the borders, kick out those who are different, and punish those who are morally deviant.'"[49]

In other words, for people sensitive to threat, ingroup favoritism can be intensified by threat. For example, "China bashing" rhetoric can elevate people's sense of anxiety and focus them on a threat and the need to confront that enemy.[50] This constellation of closely related characteristics—social dominance, authoritarianism, national superiority and ethnocentrism—all strengthen ingroup favoritism. They are important to understanding mass opinions on trade because trade preferences are heavily influenced by ingroup favoritism.

What is especially noteworthy is that these are all also characteristics tied closely to education levels. Less-educated people are higher in authoritarianism and social dominance orientation. They also tend to be higher in ethnocentrism and to hold more discriminatory views toward outgroups. Less-educated Americans are also higher in their sense of national superiority. The important role of education in predicting support for trade is thus subject to numerous alternative interpretations beyond its potential to represent a worker's skill level.

As documented in the many studies that follow, whether one sees trade as a cooperative endeavor or a competitive threat does not, by itself, determine whether a person supports trade or opposes it. If trade is viewed as cooperation, people are generally favorable toward it as a means to better relationships and more peaceful international relations. But if trade is viewed as a competition, whether people favor it or not depends on whether they think "we" or "they" are winning. Competitions are naturally more popular when the home team is seen as winning, and more unpopular when it is perceived to be losing.

A Psychological Perspective on Opinions toward Trade

My central purpose in this book is to bridge a gap in our understanding of the causes and consequences of American attitudes toward international trade. It is not intended to be a treatise on why one should or should not support free trade, nor is it an analysis of the positive and negative economic consequences of trade. I leave those tasks to economists. Instead, it is an attempt to understand why mass opinion toward trade appears to have been on a rollercoaster over the last twenty years, with support rising and falling by double-digit percentages during short periods of time, and changing partisan alliances—all leaving one to wonder what could possibly account for this turmoil in mass support.

The book is also a plea for economists and political scientists who study public opinion and voting behavior to pool their considerable resources. Both groups study public reactions to trade and their influence on politics and policy. But their depictions of how the public operates in this realm could not be further apart. Based on aggregate-level evidence, economists generally conclude that Americans understand how trade affects them and hold political leaders accountable at the ballot box for the effects of trade on their personal financial well-being. In this view, trade opinions simply reflect democratic accountability for the economic consequences of trade. Political scientists using survey-based evidence present a starkly contrasting picture suggesting that people seldom understand their position in the international economy, and that whatever understanding they have is unlikely to be connected to their vote choice. This book alone cannot definitively reconcile this evidence, but my hope is that it will stimulate a dialogue that can bring these two versions of reality closer together.

Why It Matters

At the time I began writing this book, many felt that understanding public attitudes toward trade was of little importance. Trade policies were made by elites, after all, and the public did not pay enough attention to trade for their opinions to matter to elites. Since the 1970s, a largely pro-trade consensus among elites had kept globalization moving forward without much fear of public reaction.[51] But that has changed. Since the 2016 election, trade and globalization have received increasing attention, thus making them more salient as potential election issues than they have been in the last several decades.

In the latter part of the book, I explore two consequences of trade opinions for American society. Electoral consequences are typically first on people's minds, and my evidence suggests that such effects can occur, although they are not as common as has been assumed. Even when trade features prominently as an issue in voting decisions, it is but one of many issues. Most importantly, there is little if any evidence of political accountability for trade's impact. Even when trade opinions help to change people's votes, these opinions are not reflections of how individuals have been helped or hurt by trade policies.

Secondly, I present evidence that public attitudes toward trade have social consequences. America's cross-national relationships affect how Americans think and feel about groups of people different from themselves, both domestically and overseas. When politicians decide to whip up frenzies of anti-trade sentiment for possible electoral gain, this affects everyday interactions in a diversified America. Likewise, when they opt to promote a sense of solidarity and inter-country similarity, this has implications for how people in a diversified America treat one another.

The way elites portray international trade and the way the public talks about it are central to the quality of intergroup relations in the United States. Because the public tends to think about international trade the same way it thinks about small-scale social interaction and exchange, this relationship turns out to be a two-way street. Just as attitudes toward foreigners and people of other races or ethnicities affect attitudes toward international trade, the way that Americans are encouraged to view international trade—as a competitive threat or as an opportunity for cooperation with often dissimilar others—can change their attitudes toward "others," both global and domestic.

Chapter Overviews

In the chapters that follow, I use a wealth of survey and experimental data to explore the ways in which these central themes influence American reactions to trade. When trade is viewed as a form of cooperation, it is regarded as fundamentally different from when it is viewed as a form of competition. And even among those who similarly view it as a form of competition, it matters whether they see their nation as winners or losers in this competition. Although my focus is primarily on American mass opinion, I use parallel studies of Canadian and American public opinion toward trade to illuminate how the way in which a country thinks about itself can alter the dynamics of trade preferences.

Whenever possible, I draw from the respondents' open-ended comments to illustrate my quantitative findings. These verbatim comments are shown in italics throughout. Although I have left the respondents' capitalizations intact to reflect their own emphases, I have occasionally corrected spelling and added punctuation to their comments to avoid distracting readers from my central purpose in including their thoughts. More detailed analyses pertaining to findings in each chapter are included in chapter appendices linked to each chapter. Those interested in the original sources of data discussed throughout will find descriptions in the appendix. Throughout the text there are references to figures and tables for supplementary analyses included in an online appendix. A link to this appendix material can be found at press.princeton.edu/books/winners-and-losers.

Chapter 2 provides an overview of how Americans think about and express their views on trade in their own words. I find that there is an internal logic to their beliefs, even if it is not the same logic that economists or policymakers might offer. While relatively few Americans are familiar with the economic case for free trade,[52] this lack of knowledge plays at best a minor role in influencing their trade preferences.

In Chapter 2 I also ask Americans to explain, in their own words, what they like and dislike about trade, both in term of its impact on the US, and in terms of its impact on other countries. There are, after all, many dimensions to this issue that might motivate the public. Trade both creates jobs and takes them away. It can be good or bad for the environment. The treatment of labor has been argued to improve as a result of trade, while in other contexts trade is blamed for promoting sweat shops and child labor. Consumers may perceive both prices and the quality of goods to be influenced by foreign trade. Some may view it as a source of ongoing conflict between nations, whereas others argue that trade relationships are a primary reason that countries avoid going to war against one another.

Interestingly, people's views on the many dimensions of trade's impact were not as nuanced as one might expect. People seemed to either like trade or dislike it, and they perceived its consequences for the US and trading partners countries either to be entirely salutary or as all bad. The one important exception is trade's influence on job availability, where the same Americans who see trade's impact on the US as one that takes away jobs tend to see its impact on other countries as one of creating jobs. I find little consensus among Americans as to why one should support international trade, but there is strong consensus on why one should oppose it: its impact on American jobs.

Chapter 2 suggests that what scholars view as a highly complex economic issue is not so complicated when considered by ordinary Americans. Instead of complex economic calculations involving import competition or labor market differentials, trade is supported or opposed for largely expressive and symbolic reasons such as high levels of nationalism,[53] racial prejudice,[54] competitiveness,[55] and the general desire to "win" and dominate others.[56] Slogans such as "Foreigners are stealing our jobs" epitomize the simplistic way trade is typically presented to the public, as an appeal to ingroup loyalty and "taking care of our own." When trade opponents claim that "buying American" is a form of patriotism, or that jobs that have gone overseas are rightfully "ours," this emphasis on loyalty to the home country becomes clear.

Chapter 3 addresses the relationship between partisanship and trade preferences. Almost all controversial issues in American politics are divided along party lines, with Democrats largely on one side, and Republicans on the other. But American attitudes toward trade are unusual in this regard. Partisanship has not consistently predicted trade preferences over time. In fact, the positions of Republican and Democratic partisans on trade has flipped during the course of just the last fifteen to twenty years. From the 1990s through roughly 2008, Republicans and Democrats in the mass public had largely indistinguishable views on trade. After Barack Obama's election, Democrats in the mass public became more favorable toward trade and globalization than Republicans. But once Trump was elected, Republican views on trade became far more positive.

Such large swings on policy preferences in short periods of time underscore the malleability of opinions on international trade. In Chapter 3 I use the emphasis on trade as a form of competition to explain how that came about. I suggest that people did not dramatically change their minds about the value of these international relationships so much as their views of trade as cooperation versus competition underwent dramatic change. Among those who viewed trade as form of competition, trade as a form of dominance appealed to Republicans in a way that trade as cooperation did not.

In Chapter 4, I get to the heart of the importance of viewing trade preferences through the lens of human psychology. Because trade is widely viewed as a competition by the American public, it matters a great deal how much one feels they are a part of the home team. Because people reason about trade relationships in much the same way they reason about human relationships more generally, ingroup and outgroup sympathies play an important role.

I use a nationally-representative survey experiment to examine two distinct forms of ingroup favoritism that influence American attitudes toward trade. The first, and least surprising, is that Americans value the well-being of other Americans more than the well-being of people outside their own country. The more surprising finding is that Americans are no more supportive of a "win-win" trade policy than they are of a policy in which the US wins the same number of jobs, but our trading partner countries lose jobs. In other words, "winning" this competition is important to people; mutual benefits are not necessarily their goals.

Those Americans who care about "winning" at trade prefer policies that benefit the ingroup and *hurt the outgroup* over policies that help both their own country and trading partner countries. In other words, for a policy to elicit mass support in the US, it is important not only that the US benefit, but also that it hurt the trading partner country so that the US achieves a greater *relative advantage*. This study highlights the difficulty of judging what "fair" trade might look like in the eyes of Americans.

In Chapter 5, I go beyond examining people's overall attitudes toward trade to better understand why trade preferences are not constant across potential trading partner countries. Why are Americans fine trading with some countries, but not others? The mass public may lack a nuanced understanding of trade, but they nonetheless have views that vary according to *the specific country* with which their country is trading. Isn't this inconsistent? At the very least it seems implausible that these opinions vary due to complex calculations based on how their finances will be affected by trade with Mexico as opposed to Canada.

I find that people make judgments about trading with other countries the same way they decide with whom to trade sandwiches at lunch: whom do they trust? For better or worse, trust is rooted in many dimensions of similarity between people. Likewise, similar countries are deemed more worthy trade partners as well. I use an experiment embedded in a national survey to systematically alter many different types of country similarity in order to assess their effects on willingness to trade with other countries. I find that Americans are reliably more supportive of trading with countries that are similar to the US than with countries perceived to be different, regardless of the particular dimension of difference.

Interestingly, using similarities as the basis for supporting trade contrasts with one of the key reasons trade is supposed to be mutually beneficial; at least according to the Ricardian logic in favor of trade, specialization is advantageous because each country can produce whatever it produces best,[57] and then trade with other countries for other necessities. In other words, trade is advantageous because of the inherent *differences* among countries, not because of their similarities. Nonetheless, the public is more likely to support trade with other wealthy western countries that are just like the US.

Given the important role of ingroup favoritism and trust in influencing support for trade, it is natural to wonder how trade preferences are related to other forms of ingroup favoritism. In Chapter 6 I examine how racial and ethnic minorities in the United States feel about trade and how whites' racial attitudes enter into considerations involving international trade. Minority groups such as African-Americans and Hispanics tend to have lower incomes and lower levels of education, so they are more vulnerable to economic downturns and to potential job dislocations due to trade. Likewise, their occupational skills make their jobs more likely to be displaced by trade. All of these characteristics suggest they should generally be more opposed to trade than whites.

On the other hand, as members of low-status groups in American society, Blacks and Hispanics are less prone to prejudice and outgroup animosity than are whites. The extent of white Americans' prejudice toward minority outgroups is consistently greater than the animosity minority groups feel toward majority whites. These differing levels of ethnocentrism turn out to matter to trade support. As detailed in Chapter 6, for most of the last fifteen years, minorities have exhibited more *positive* attitudes toward trade than whites, thus highlighting the need for theories that take into account characteristics that go beyond economics.

The results in this chapter suggest that minorities reason differently about trade than majority whites. For example, even when the so-called winners and losers from a given trade agreement are known, minorities are more likely to value the gains to trading partners than are whites. Ingroup favoritism is a stronger force when majority whites reason about trade than when minorities do. As the US becomes a "majority minority" country, these differences will matter. When trade is framed as a form of cooperation for mutual benefit, minorities tend to hold more favorable views of trade than whites. But they hold more negative views of trade when it is framed as a competition with winners and losers.

This chapter suggests that the future framing of trade by political elites is likely to influence the kinds of people who form coalitions supporting or opposing trade. Trade as a competition with winners and losers is less likely to attract minority support. The findings in this chapter also foreshadow the ways in which the politics of white grievance is inextricably tied to the politics of international grievance. Just as many white Americans have come to believe that minorities are now taking advantage of whites, the idea that the US has been taken advantage of by the rest of the world has simultaneously gained credence. In both cases, powerful groups/nations claim to have been taken advantage of by less powerful entities.

In Chapter 7, I delve further into one of the more depressing earlier conclusions, the finding in Chapter 4 that Americans care little, or not at all, about how people in other countries are affected by international trade. Ingroups and outgroups play such a persistent role in human behavior that it is tempting to interpret these findings as mere human nature. Of course, people care about their compatriots more than foreigners in other countries. However, by replicating the exact same survey-experiment described in Chapter 4, but this time on a Canadian sample, I show how ingroup loyalties need not necessarily lead to negativity toward outgroups. In a culture with far less emphasis on competition, these same patterns are not necessarily inevitable. Although Canada is more trade-dependent than the US, Canadian citizens exhibit many of the same beliefs and hold roughly the same levels of misinformation about trade as Americans. However, my survey-experimental findings suggest that there are important differences that stem from the fact that Canadians view trade in less competitive terms. Unlike Americans, Canadians are more supportive of "win-win" trade agreements than of agreements in which they achieve greater dominance over trading partner countries by gaining at others' expense.

Chapters 8 and 9 examine the impact of Americans' most important sources of information about trade, the mass media. Coverage of trade in the US media, like coverage of the economy more generally, tends to emphasize negative news over positive news. Media appear to play an important role in informing people's sociotropic perceptions of trade's impact on the country as whole. But even more importantly, mass media tend to frame discussions of trade's impact around sympathetic individuals who are victims of trade. Using an experimental design embedded in a national survey, in Chapter 8 I demonstrate how this prominent media framing of trade influences public support.

In Chapter 9, I examine the role of media coverage in assigning blame for job loss. News media have emphasized trade as the major source of manufacturing job loss. Likewise, the American public perceives most manufacturing job loss to be due to trade, when in fact more job loss has resulted from automation.[58] Again using an experimental design embedded in a representative national survey, I show that by altering a single news story about one man's job loss and attributing it to automation rather than trade with China, I can reduce anger about job loss, change attitudes toward trade, and make Americans less likely to think that manufacturing jobs can be brought back.

Even though losing a job is economically traumatic regardless of the cause, the personification of job loss as something caused by foreigners as opposed to machines leads people to believe it is more socially acceptable to make derogatory statements about Asians. This finding, in combination with additional findings in Chapter 12, underscores the dangerous link between denigrating outgroups through trade bashing and promoting racial intolerance and discrimination.

Chapters 10 and 11 address a topic studied by both economists and political scientists, the potential impact of trade on electoral politics. One of the chief reasons that people care about mass opinion toward trade is that they believe it can affect election outcomes. Drawing on panel data from 2008 to the present, I explore the potential for trade to matter in people's presidential vote decisions. Because most Americans' voting preferences are predetermined by partisanship long before any given election campaign occurs, very few issues have been documented to make such a difference, so this is a high bar. This is also where economists and political scientists butt heads most often, with economists using aggregate-level evidence to argue that exposure to import competition changes election outcomes, while political scientists who study electoral behavior are less convinced. As many as four different theories have been offered for a variety of proposed relationships linking trade to voting behavior, but findings have been inconsistent. In addition, trade support is subject to change depending upon which party is in power at the time, a pattern I refer to as "party-in-power" effects. Panel data document a consistent increase in trade support among co-partisans when a new party comes into power. This pattern complicates efforts to hold political leadership accountable for any negative impacts from trade.

My own panel analyses of Americans voters in the 2008, 2012, and 2016 elections suggest that trade has only recently attained the status of an issue likely to impact elections. Before 2016, Americans did not perceive any clear differences in trade support between the two parties, and thus had little means by which to hold political leaders accountable for the impact of trade on jobs, whether locally or nationally. In Chapter 11, I suggest that the 2016 presidential election was unique in that trade as an issue clearly benefitted support for Donald Trump in ways that immigration and other issues did not. But most importantly, these two chapters call into question the common narrative in economic analyses suggesting that citizens' voting patterns hold political leadership accountable for the economic impacts of trade on their lives and communities.

In Chapter 12 I draw on multiple experimental studies to examine what happens when people purposely attempt to change others' trade preferences. These findings provide insight into what kinds of appeals are most likely to work and which are not. Two studies strongly support the theory that increasing perceived interpersonal similarities is the easiest route to increasing support for trade, far more than making economic arguments. To increase trade opposition, efforts to increase the perceived threat from trade were effective, but these efforts had noteworthy consequences that went beyond encouraging people to be more opposed to trade. Encouraging negative attitudes toward foreign outgroups has unintended consequences for intergroup relations in the US, encouraging discrimination against Asians, regardless of whether they are Asian-Americans or foreigners.

Chapter 13 summarizes the lessons learned from these many studies for knowledge about what drives American trade preferences and what the consequences of these views are. As debates about globalization continue, it is increasingly important to understand trade preferences as a function of psychological forces. Viewing trade as a purely economic issue leads to very different conclusions about how to proceed, regardless of whether one is for or against trade.

The concluding chapter also speculates about the future of public opinion toward trade and globalization more generally. Given the unusual malleability of mass opinion on trade, much about the future of globalization depends on how future leadership chooses to frame this issue. If it is seen as a means to peaceful relationships and cooperation, it will be far more popular across both parties than if it is cast as an ongoing competition between countries. Although a competition that the US is supposedly "winning" by dominating other countries also can be popular among highly competitive Americans, trade-as-domination is not a sustainable position for a country. In the long run, who would be eager to engage in a trade agreement with a country that is openly doing so for purposes of gaining a relative advantage over the other country?

I conclude that the widely acknowledged backlash against globalization leading up to Trump's election was less a function of individuals who had been personally hurt by trade than of general anxiety that the national ingroup as whole was losing status relative to other countries. Likewise, the surge in support for trade during Trump's administration was not due to improvements in the lives of those formerly impacted by trade.

The fact that policy opinions were not tied to self-interest does not make it any less important that so many people lost jobs and/or experienced depressed wages as a result of trade. Improving the strength of America's safety net for workers displaced by trade will be essential to American confidence that trade is good for the country as a whole. But to forestall future backlashes requires renewed confidence in America's status in the world. Despite President Trump's claims to the contrary, trade wars have no winners, and the American public has borne the brunt of the fallout from increased protectionism.

2

At Face Value

WHAT AMERICANS SAY THEY LIKE AND DISLIKE ABOUT TRADE

The problem with abandoning dominant theories about the origins of trade attitudes is that one is left empty-handed. If people do not form attitudes toward trade based on how international trade has affected their personal economic situations, then where do these views come from? If they form opinions on the basis of how they perceive the nation as a whole to be affected by trade, then where do those perceptions come from?

Some have questioned whether average Americans actually have views on this complex issue. The claim that Americans have "remarkably vague views on the question of free trade"[1] has led some to worry that surveys are picking up "non-attitudes," that is, efforts to satisfy the request for an opinion by providing a random answer, but without truly holding an opinion. My own surveys as well as those from several other organizations provide little support for this concern. When simple, straightforward questions about trade are asked, people have opinions and can express them in a reliable way.[2] And if asked to explain why they feel the way they do, they can do so. But when economic terms such as tariffs, balance of trade, and so forth come up, many no longer understand the question.

Some of the most widely used academic surveys, such as the American National Election Studies (ANES) and the International Social Survey Program (ISSP), are less than ideal in how they have asked about trade. In the

ANES, for example, there is a single question about trade that has been asked since 1986. In the post-election interview, respondents are asked:

> Some people have suggested placing new limits on foreign imports in order to protect American jobs. Others say that such limits would raise consumer prices and hurt American exports. Do you favor or oppose placing new limits on imports—or haven't you thought much about this?

The most common response to this question—at times as high as 60 percent—is that respondents "don't know" or "have not thought much about it." This result has been used to argue that most Americans simply do not have opinions on this issue. However, concurrent surveys asking about support for international trade in more straightforward ways have produced lower to non-existent levels of non-response.[3] For example, when respondents are asked whether they favor or oppose the federal government in Washington negotiating more free trade agreements, fewer than two percent have difficulty answering.[4]

The unusually high rate of non-response with the ANES question is likely to be a function of how the question is worded rather than of a public without opinions. Based on the usual standards for survey questions, this question has a number of problems. Perhaps most confusingly, the question is a double-negative. In this case, "favoring limits" means opposing trade, whereas "opposing limits" means favoring trade. One could be forgiven for finding this question difficult to parse. Further, one could be excused for not necessarily knowing that this was a question about international trade given that the word "trade" is never mentioned. Instead this question requires an understanding of what imports and exports are, and an understanding that foreign imports are what another country calls their domestic exports. International trade is, indeed, a complex issue. This question does not make it any easier for respondents to understand precisely what is being asked.

In order to answer, one must also accept the terms that the question offers in its two options. In other words, one must believe that limiting foreign imports will save American jobs, and one must accept that the benefits of trade are strictly for consumer prices and exports. These are clearly not "facts" believed by all Americans.[5]

Another frequently used trade question asks respondents how much they agree or disagree with the statement that their country "should limit the import of foreign products in order to protect its national economy."[6] This question wording equates limiting imports with protecting the national economy. For those who accept this argument, it might not be problematic. But for those who reject it, it is unclear how they should respond. Protecting the national economy sounds like a worthy idea, but what if a person believes a trade war puts the national economy at risk? Scholars using this measure argue that this is often the way protectionism is defended in political discourse, which is certainly true. But ideally survey questions on support for trade policies should not incorporate specific arguments for supporting or opposing trade from either side.

Even when survey questions are balanced in terms of including arguments on both sides of the trade debate, they have limited their focus to economic arguments. For example, one common question asks, "Generally speaking, do you think that US trade policy should have restrictions on imported goods to protect Americans jobs, or have no restrictions on imported goods to enable American consumers to have more choices and the lowest prices?" With this question framing, there is no possibility that restricting imports might cost Americans jobs. Instead, the question pits protecting jobs against lower consumer costs, arguments that are not, as it turns out, of equal strength in the minds of Americans.

Ideally one would want a measure of trade opinion that was not influenced by specific arguments for or against trade. In a perfect world, we would have a whole battery of questions about trade that would enable us to know if people have well-formed, consistent views on this topic. Good survey measures should, at a minimum, be consistent across multiple questions asked at any given point in time and reliable by statistical standards. To study mass opinion on trade, we need to first be certain we can measure it.

Measuring Public Opinion on Trade

In order to be certain that my measures of public opinion on trade represent true underlying attitudes, I have asked as many as five or more different questions tapping support for international trade within a single representative national survey. These questions were designed to be simple and straightforward, and to avoid providing arguments either for or against international trade. The first question I posed was, "Do you think government should try to encourage international trade or try to discourage international trade?" A second question mentioned NAFTA as an example of a trade agreement since it was the most high profile of trade agreements in the US at the time: "Do you favor or oppose the federal government in Washington negotiating more free trade agreements like NAFTA?"

Although economists will be quick to point out that one could favor free trade in principle, yet not like NAFTA in particular, I find little evidence of such nuanced views among the mass public. Regardless of which trade agreement one asks about, or how one asks about it, people's responses are very strongly correlated. A third question was phrased in terms of globalization: "Do you believe that globalization, especially the increasing connections of our economy with others around the world, is good or bad for the United States?" Some might argue that globalization encompasses more than just international trade, but again, this appears to make little difference when asked in terms of our economic connections with other countries. A fourth question addressed how people feel about the World Trade Organization, the only international organization that deals with the rules of trade between nations: "Do you have a very favorable, somewhat favorable, somewhat unfavorable or very unfavorable opinion of the WTO, the World Trade Organization?" Although the WTO has been controversial, to be sure, I found that mass opinion lacked subtlety. Instead, people's attitudes toward international trade and the organization that regulates it seem to be all of one cloth.

In one of my early studies, a fifth question was not initially assumed to measure people's underlying attitudes toward international trade, and instead addressed foreign direct investment (FDI), though not in those explicit terms: "Should foreign companies be encouraged or discouraged from investing in the United States, for example, by building one of their factories in this country?" Because inwardly-directed FDI brings jobs into the US, whereas trade is widely feared to take jobs out of the country, I had assumed this item would not hang together with the other four. However, I was wrong.

These five questions, each measured on four-point scales, were tightly inter-correlated.[7] Contrary to my initial assumptions, the question tapping attitudes toward inward foreign direct investment was just as strongly correlated with the trade questions as the trade questions were with one another. This pattern is noteworthy for two reasons. First, it suggests that Americans' attitudes on these questions are part of a single underlying attitude construct. Regardless of the particulars in any given question, people tend to be either drawbridge-up or drawbridge-down types when it comes to trade and economic globalization.

Second, this pattern foreshadows some of the discoveries to come, namely that opposition to trade is not, in fact, strictly about job loss. Attitudes toward inwardly-directed FDI and support for international trade are strongly positively correlated, even though the former brings jobs into the country, while the latter is assumed to cause job loss. What these items share is involvement with foreign countries, not a connection to job loss. As later chapters demonstrate, people's attitudes toward foreigners and foreignness turn out to be a significant component of attitudes toward foreign trade.

Another pattern worth noting is that unlike responses to the ANES question, these questions all have high response rates. The percentage of people who said they did not know or who refused to answer ranged from 2.6 in response to the first, most simple, question, up to 4.9 percent for the WTO question. In short, most Americans know how they feel about international economic connections to other countries.

In Their Own Words: The Basis of Trade Preferences

In order to avoid forcing my own theories onto my data, I started out by asking people open-ended questions. What are the most salient reasons that people give for liking or disliking international trade? To answer this question, I began one representative national survey that was administered in 2013 by asking, "Do you think government should try to encourage international trade or try to discourage international trade?" Of just over 3000 respondents, under 3 percent could not answer this question, suggesting that they did, indeed, have a sense of whether this was a good or bad policy to pursue. Next, I asked them to explain, in their own words, why they favored or opposed trade. Assuming people have insight into why they feel the way they do, what reasons would they give?

There are many potential dimensions of international trade that might motivate the public to form positive or negative views. Beyond its impact on jobs, some argue that trade produces a "race to the bottom" in environmental standards, while others argue that it improves the environment. The treatment of labor has been argued to improve as a result of international trade, but in other contexts, trade has been blamed for promoting sweat shops and child labor. Consumers may perceive both prices and the quality of goods to be influenced by foreign trade. Some see it as a boon to the American economy, whereas others see it as the source of its certain ruin. Those focused on war and peace may view it as a source of relationships that can prevent countries from going to war against one another. Others, such as President Trump, have pronounced it a national security threat.

To get a sense of how the mass public understands trade, I drew on people's open-ended answers in response to a follow up question asking,

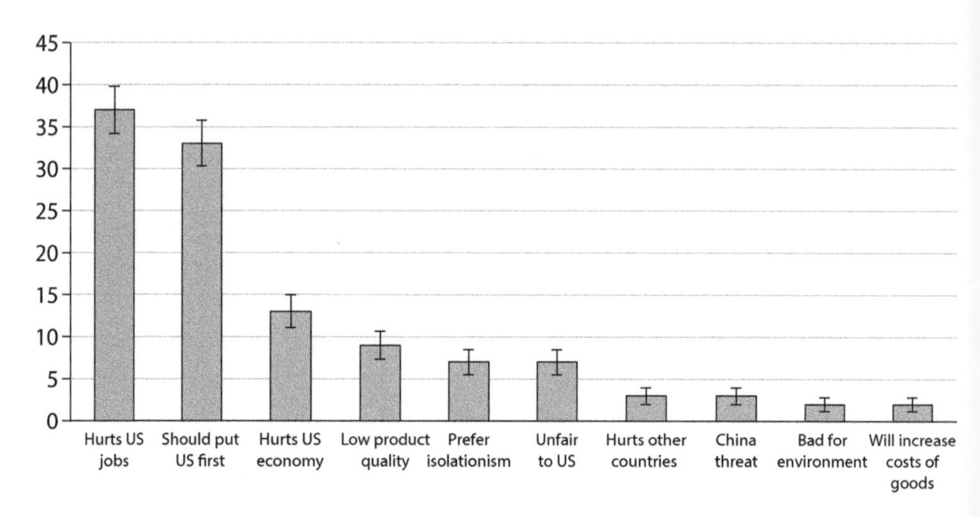

FIGURE 2.1. Percent of Respondents Mentioning Specific Reasons for Opposing Trade
Source: US Trade Survey-Experiment, 2013–2014 (GfK Ltd.). Bar heights represent the percent of those respondents opposing trade. Respondents could offer more than one explanation for their view.

"Why is it that you think trade with other countries should be [encouraged/discouraged]? Please explain." The answers to these questions were later coded for up to five potential explanations per person. Answers ranged from the very general and abstract ("It's good for the economy") to the highly specific ("It hurts the quality of pet food."). They were later organized into broader categories representing the top ten types of reasons that were given for favoring or opposing trade.[8,9,10]

As shown in Figure 2.1, the results of this bottom-up process suggest that American opposition to trade is overwhelmingly centered on the issue of job loss. Thirty-seven percent of respondents who disliked trade mentioned job loss—the highest percentage of any category—and frequent references to foreign countries "stealing our jobs" made it clear that this was the central objection. Respondents repeatedly emphasized the idea that the key to having more jobs for Americans was to oppose trade and buy more products that are American-made:

We should be making things in America to keep Americans in jobs.
We need jobs here!
We need to try to stay with made in America and support our own nation and its people and jobs in this country.

Because for some reason we stop making stuff in the US and getting most of everything from outside—if we could start making and having other countries buy off the US, we could have jobs available.

Exporting jobs overseas through agreements like NAFTA hurts American workers, reduces the quality of products in the US because other countries don't have to follow US regulations.

All of our trade is coming in and not much going out. Our jobs are lost as we are not making anything anymore. Everything I pick up is made in China.

The second, almost as frequently mentioned reason for opposing trade was loyalty to one's co-nationals and "taking care of our own." As shown in Figure 2.1, putting the US first was indistinguishable in popularity from hurting US jobs as a reason to oppose trade. These statements were often vague with respect to how reducing trade would help Americans, but the gist was that trade is something that "we" do for "them," not a source of mutual benefits. In this respect it overlaps with the "Unfair to US" category in Figure 2.1. Although this was 2013, long before Donald Trump's presidency, Americans already spoke of putting America first as a reason to avoid international trade. Trump's "America First" slogan was not even on the horizon, yet public responses already reflected a great deal of trade opposition based on the argument that loyalty to one's country demands opposition to trade:

We need to keep America first and foremost.

Take care of our own needs and boost economy.

Profits from industry should be used & invested in our own interest FIRST. If we have excess—then help others.

We need to take care of the American people. . . . .poor homeless jobless.. need to take care of ourselves.

Why can't we take care of our own people before we spend so much to other countries. while we have so many people right in the USA going without food and very poor living conditions?

Take care of our own.

I'd like to find things made in America. I want to support our own.

We need to take care of our own country and buy American products not foreign.

I think we should take care of ourselves and mind our own business.

Because we need to build our economy and create jobs here in America.

Think of ourselves first.

Job loss and putting America first covered the overwhelming majority of reasons people gave for opposing trade, and in some cases they were combined to suggest that obviously the way to put America first is to oppose trade and thus save US jobs. Other themes, such as low product quality and the general idea that trade hurts the American economy, hovered at around 10 percent of respondents, but most alternative explanations were endorsed by single digit percentages of Americans. One category, the idea that trade is "unfair" to the US, was unclear with respect to whether it referred to jobs or some other consequence of trade. But if the idea that trade does not benefit America as much as it benefits other countries were considered in the same category as "putting America first," then together these two explanations alone would account for the most respondents who opposed trade. The message, loud and clear, is that trade is opposed not only because it is linked to job loss in people's minds, but also because it is seen as violating norms of ingroup favoritism when it comes to how one should treat their fellow Americans.

Trade advocates, on the other hand, demonstrated far less consensus as to why trade is beneficial. First, a larger proportion of these respondents were unable to provide any explanation for why they favored trade, despite repeated attempts to prompt them. Among trade opponents, 21 percent of people offered no valid reason that could be coded; among trade advocates, fully 37 percent of respondents offered no reason as to why they thought trade was good, despite equal amounts of prompting. At least as of 2013, the reasons one might oppose trade appear to be far more accessible and widely articulated than the reasons one might favor it.

As shown in Figure 2.2, even the most popular explanation, that trade helps the US economy, was endorsed by only 22 percent of pro-trade respondents. To the extent that there is a consensus among advocates as to why trade is beneficial, it is somewhat vague and abstract. A few mentioned bigger markets for American-made products, but few could go beyond the positive generalization that trade was good for the economy.

The second most frequently mentioned reason for favoring trade was the increased availability of products. This explanation was repeatedly expressed in highly concrete terms involving access to products that Americans would not otherwise have:

To receive the important products we need, which might be less accessible in the US.

People like other countries' products and should be able to get them.

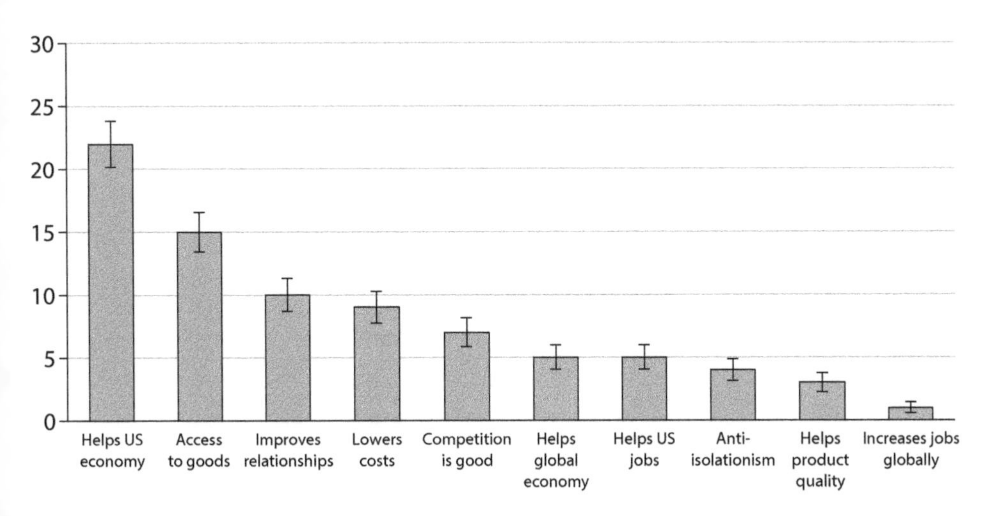

FIGURE 2.2. Percent of Respondents Mentioning Specific Reasons for Favoring Trade
Source: US Trade Survey-Experiment, 2013–2014 (GfK Ltd.) Bar height represents the percent of those respondents favoring trade. Respondents could offer more than one explanation for their view.

Having items available that are bought from other countries helps everyone.
It allows countries access to seasonal goods year long.
To gain access to materials a country may not have available to them.
Because it provides us with items not available in this country.
US citizens should have access to all the products of the world, not just to products of this country.
It is a good way to assess new technologies invented by other nations. It also gives the US access to resources unavailable in the US. We get access to different products/services/technologies.
Makes products from around the world more accessible to the average consumer.

The third most popular explanation for favoring trade was because it is good for our country's relationships with other countries. I was frankly surprised to see this idea mentioned as often as it was. It is a popular argument in international relations, to be sure. But to hear so many people express this sentiment in their own words was notable. Responses were replete with references to the quality of "relationships" and to "friendliness" among countries. Whereas the idea that trade promotes more peaceful relations might seem obvious to scholars, academic journal articles are not where the mass public obtains its understanding of trade, nor is this an argument articulated frequently by elites.

However, if one assumes that people think about trade between nations in largely the same way they think about trade between individuals, then this idea is intuitive. In interpersonal relationships, we sometimes engage in trade with others—such as buying our colleagues' daughters' Girl Scout cookies—not so much because we truly want or need the cookies, but to be friendly and supportive. To call these mere economic transactions is to miss their significance. By engaging in trade, we solidify our relationships with others. Likewise, large numbers of Americans see trade as beneficial simply because it strengthens our relationships with other countries:

Increases mutual trust between nations.
It opens communication between countries & provides for better relations.
Encouraging trade goes hand in glove with a more sophisticated, global way of viewing our place in the world and hopefully leads to less enmity and divisiveness.
It is good to be friendly.
Creates good will.
Well for the most part I think it helps bring about civil conduct between different nations and helps to bring about solidarity among the world.
I believe positive relationships with other countries will grow with mutually beneficial international trade agreements.
I feel that it will help perhaps to heal some of the issues between some countries.
It helps globalization and to secure relationships amongst countries worldwide.
Trade encourages good relations with other countries.
It may have the effect of bettering relations.
I think that it would help with the relations between countries.
Relations between different countries will become better as a result.
Because not trading with other countries would give the US a stigma of being unfriendly.
Forge important bonds between nations.
To trade with other countries helps with getting along with others.
Good relations which always is a plus, for any country!
Because it would bring more unity with different countries.

Good for relations between countries.

International trade not only fosters the exchange of physical goods but also encourages friendly relations between nations and spreads innovative ideas from one country to another.

In addition to friendliness for purposes of better relationships, some respondents explicitly linked economic interdependence to strategic advantages in dealing with other countries:

Trade creates jobs and jobs raise the standard of living. With higher standards of living comes a higher chance for peace since countries have something to lose.

I think it allows a peaceful way to influence countries that might not have the best intentions for our future.

Intertwining economies are a great deterrent to war.

To aid in good relationships with other countries and also to develop means of leverage when it is necessary.

Trade with other countries help us to solidify a friendship which the United States may need at a later date.

They have the opportunity to build an alliance with other countries for support, goods, and other aid.

Plays a role in national security in that a robust trading partner is more likely to remain either allied with the US or neutral.

Finally, some respondents explicitly linked trade to preventing war. The recurrent themes in their comments were mutual interdependence, cooperation as a means of preventing war, and promoting peace.

International trade strengthens the economic bonds between nations and lessens the chance of war.

Less likely to go to war because of the disruption war would cause on their bilateral trade relationships.

To make the world safer by making countries depend on each other for their survival.

International trade also provides a strong stimulus for international cooperation and conflict avoidance. While there is no fail-safe war aversion tactic, international trade can provide a strong reason for countries to work together.

Trading among/between countries increases interdependence and can discourage wars.

Trading with other countries is important, because trading is better than war.
It is good for foreign relations and to prevent wars.
More peace among nations.
Wars are less likely if countries need trade with each other.
Helps world peace.
Peace with other countries.

What respondents are suggesting is what is known in political science as the "liberal peace" or "democratic peace" thesis. Scholars generally agree that "democracies are less likely to fight wars with each other."[11] There is less agreement as to why this is the case, but one prominent explanation is that this occurs because democracies foster economic interdependence through trading relationships. According to this theory, trade leads to greater peace among democracies either because war is too economically costly with a trading partner, or because trade simply encourages better relationships among countries.[12]

As expressed by the mass public, this perspective had little to do with democracy leading to trade relationships and promoting market economies. Instead, trade was seen as a direct means of encouraging positive, peaceful relationships even with non-democratic countries such as China. As one respondent explained it, "Keep your friends close and your enemies closer." In other words, trade was viewed by some as a potential alternative to democratizing as a means of fostering peace with other nations. In their view, the benefits of economic interdependence could extend to non-democratic countries as well. These respondents saw trade relationships as an alternative means of promoting peace and improving relationships, even with one's enemies.

Although not all respondents were clear on why they thought trade would diminish the prospects for war, far more people mentioned the benefits of better relationships than mentioned the economic advantages of avoiding war with a trading partner. As described by ordinary Americans, the idea that international trade is good for relationships often sounds similar to intergroup contact theory. In social psychology, it has long been argued that contact among people from different groups improves their relationships. In the real world these benefits are often contingent on characteristics and contexts in which the interaction takes place.[13] Nonetheless, the consequences of intergroup contact are typically positive, encouraging greater mutual understanding and accommodation.[14] But because trade seldom involves a great deal of face-to-face contact among people from different nations, it is somewhat surprising that so many people think it should have the same kinds of benefits:

It helps that people get to see the result of how other people live and value.
Lowering trade barriers simultaneously promotes greater interactions with other countries and can bring countries closer together.
Makes people & countries interdependent; more likely to know each other, less likely to hate or dislike someone based on prior biases.
Opening up trade may also open up other aspects of understanding and communication with other nations.
Promote mixing of cultures.
International trade encourages teamwork and cooperation, and can help make the world a better place for everyone in it, rather than just the citizens of a single country.
More international trade will lead to a better understanding between countries of both cultural and ethnic qualities.
Can't be stuck in a bubble.
Because we would like to have communication with the other countries.
Helps maintain cooperative relations between countries, spreads knowledge about and relationships with different cultures.
Those countries that trade together have greater cultural awareness and sensitivity to each other.
The global world is shrinking and we need to get along with everyone.
We should get along with everyone and spread what each part of the earth has to offer.

Although Americans may not have thought a great deal about why trade is good for US relationships with other countries, they concur that these improved relationships are beneficial. This is in sharp contrast to the idea that trade restrictions and increased tariffs are necessary for reasons of national security. In fact, only 6 people out of 3170 mentioned a national security risk associated with trade. Far more Americans perceive trade as a boon to national security and to peaceful international relations. When President Trump argued that "Economic security is national security," and suggested that tariffs against key allies would strengthen US national security, he advanced an argument that runs counter to people's intuitive sense that friendly, allied nations trade with one another. Moreover, tensions between countries naturally escalate when one dubs the other a national security risk and threatens to implement tariffs as a form of retaliation.

The main reason many economists think that average Americans *should* favor trade—the lower cost of consumer goods—was mentioned by surprisingly few trade advocates. This pattern of results is consistent with research showing that third-party observers believe that self-interested motivations matter a lot more to people than they actually do.[15] The lower cost of consumer goods manufactured overseas is an obvious reason one might support trade. Further, the lower cost of goods from overseas could be known through personal experience without needing complex economic knowledge. Nonetheless, less-expensive products were mentioned as a benefit by only 10 percent of trade supporters, usually in combination with either product quality or the broader availability of goods facilitated by trade:

Competition, cheaper prices, exchange of technology. It helps their economy and also helps us get things at cheaper price.
The products from overseas have quality that is often as good as that produced in the USA and is cheaper.
Will encourage lower prices and more selection and provide a market for our goods.
Variety of products and prices.
To pay materials for cheaper prices.
It increases the quality of products and keeps prices low.
More products, more variety, less expensive.
It can mean less expensive products for Americans to purchase.

Because the lower cost of consumer goods is supposed to be one of the key reasons Americans support free trade, it is particularly surprising how limited public awareness is of this fact. Outside of the open-ended reasons given for supporting trade, respondents in the survey were also asked, "Has international trade increased or decreased the cost of consumer goods in the US?" and given three possible response options. Forty-four percent of Americans were aware that trade decreases the cost of consumer goods. Others believed that it had no effects (25%) or that it increased the cost of consumer goods (28%). So even when asked about something simple and straightforward, levels of economic knowledge are not high. This bedrock assumption of economics is clearly not as obvious to average citizens as one might think.

When I presented this finding to some economists, they were astounded that it was even possible to imagine that trade increased the cost of consumer goods. What were people thinking? To shed light on why people might believe this, follow-up telephone interviews were conducted with a random subsample of respondents who claimed that trade increased the cost of consumer goods. Three types of explanations came out in their responses. First, some respondents talked about transportation costs, and how much it costs to fly to places such as China. They reasoned that the same product made in China would cost more because one would need to add in the costs of transporting it from China to the US. If it were made next door, those costs would not be incurred, therefore trade increases the costs of consumer goods. Americans are familiar with transportation costs, perhaps more so than differential labor costs across countries. Plane tickets to China are, indeed, expensive, so this misperception is understandable.

A second type of explanation emphasized government intervention and the idea that "we subsidize" foreign products. As one respondent put it, consumer goods from other countries are more expensive "just because of the taxes they put on it, just because of the import export fees." In this case, some kind of tariff appears to be blamed for higher consumer costs, although it is unclear if Americans believe these tariffs are placed on goods by the US or by other countries.

Yet a third type of answer suggested that consumer products (and particularly electronics) from overseas were more expensive because they were more sophisticated than what was actually desirable. In response to a question asking how trade increases the cost of consumer goods, one respondent answered, "I don't know it has increased. What has increased is technology, it's not so much that the merchandise has increased [in cost], it's the technology that goes into the products."

To summarize, there is no clear consensus among trade supporters as to why it is good. Other than a general sense that it helps the economy, the main attractions appear to be obtaining products that are not available in the US, and improving relationships with other countries. But even when combined, these two explanations do not account for even a third of those who support trade. Despite being better educated than those who are opposed to trade, trade supporters are less likely to have explanations for their views at the ready. Trade opposition, on the other hand, is heavily concentrated on two rationales: the fact that trade displaces American jobs, and that it demonstrates a lack of loyalty to Americans over foreigners.

Do People Understand Their Positions in the Global Economy?

Economists often point to the kinds of sentiments expressed above as evidence of a public that simply does not understand that trade is a "win-win" policy that benefits all trading partners. Otherwise, why would it be seen as disloyal to one's country to favor trade? Of course, to say that people have opinions on an issue is not to say that those opinions are well-informed. The reason that self-interest seemed like an ideal basis on which the public could form opinions on trade was precisely because it required little expertise other than knowledge of how one's personal financial situation was being affected by trade. This sounds easy enough, yet understanding one's position in the global economy is not as simple as one might think. I learned this when attempting to construct an indicator of whether a person's industry of employment is positively affected by exports or negatively affected by imports. This task—essentially figuring out whether individuals are trade "winners" or trade "losers" based on their jobs—turned out to be quite difficult. The difficulty occurs because these two activities, importing and exporting, often characterize the very same industries.

On the one hand, it makes perfect sense that firms engaged in the global economy as exporters are also likely to import goods from elsewhere as part of global supply chains. On the other hand, the rhetoric of trade "winners" and "losers" belies the complexity of how Americans are affected by trade, even when one limits this definition to strictly how they are affected as workers. If one attempts to incorporate how they are affected as consumers as well, this task becomes extremely complicated.

Is there evidence that people are aware of global connections within the industries in which they work? In one study, Ed Mansfield and I asked all currently or recently employed respondents an extensive set of questions about their occupations and where they worked. In addition, they were asked four questions about their perceptions of their place of employment and its ties to the international economy:

> "As far as you know, does the place or business where you [work/worked most recently]
> . . . export parts, products, or services to other countries?
> . . . import parts, products, or services from other countries?
> . . . supply products or provide services for other companies that import or export products, parts, or services from other countries?
> . . . outsource some of its work to workers in other countries?"

Responses indicated that 21 percent of respondents thought they were employed by a business that exports, 31 percent by a business that imports, and 31 percent thought their business was part of some kind of supply chain. Only 14 percent thought the place where they worked outsourced to workers in other countries. Interestingly, the same people tended to perceive all kinds of international ties to their workplace, with each item (importing, exporting, etc.) positively correlated with every other.[16]

Perceptions of importing and exporting, for example, produced a strong positive relationship.[17]

Thus the problem with sorting out "winners" and "losers" is not solely a function of workers' fallible perceptions of their ties to the international economy. Importing and exporting are also confounded in the real world. Based on official industry-level measures, the same industries that export also tend to import. If one matches each respondent's industry of employment to official data, indicators of Import Competition and Export Orientation are strongly positively correlated in a representative sample of American workers.[18] This obviously muddies the interpretation of who the winners and losers are since people are often both. For people to act on their winner versus loser status would require respondents to know whether their own industry gains more from exporting than it loses from import competition. This is an extremely high knowledge bar for the average American.

Reporting that one's place of work exports is positively correlated with actually being in an export-oriented industry,[19] suggesting some awareness of export-orientation. But import perceptions, the basis for most of the negative attitudes toward trade, are weakly correlated with actual importing.[20] It appears that workers have some sense of whether they are connected to the global economy through their industry of employment, but for them to be able to accurately differentiate themselves as winners and losers in the global economy is unlikely.

Of course, it is possible that they are unaware of being trade winners or losers by virtue of their industry, but still know whether they benefit or are harmed by trade based on their occupational skill level. Using average occupational wage as a surrogate for skill level, Ed Mansfield and I found that when their reported occupations were coded using official data about "outsource-prone" occupations, their perceptions were barely correlated at all with actual risk levels.[21] And counter to expectations, those in low-skill occupations were less likely to say the place where they work outsources than those in higher-skill occupations.[22] So, although low-skill workers are more likely to be affected, they are less aware of this threat. Collectively, this evidence casts doubt on workers' abilities to accurately identify themselves as economic winners or losers from trade.

General Economic Knowledge

People's own work situations and the personal effects that trade has on their lives provide a difficult basis for forming trade preferences, in part due to unrealistically high knowledge demands. But one might expect general knowledge about trade's effects and about the functioning of the economy to be more relevant, particularly to sociotropic perceptions about whether trade is good or bad for the country. Education is known to be the most reliable predictor of trade support, but it is by now widely accepted "that the effects of education on individual trade preferences are not primarily a product of distributional concerns linked to job skills."[23] Perhaps instead, higher education contributes to people's economic expertise by familiarizing them with the standard economic arguments in favor of trade.

To examine this possibility, Ed Mansfield and I once asked a random sample of Americans whether they had taken an economics course.[24] We also asked them whether they thought economists believed that free trade was good or bad for the economy, regardless of their own views. The results of our analyses suggested that taking an economics class had at most a marginal impact on support for trade. Likewise, people who believed that economists favor trade were only marginally more supportive of trade themselves. What's more, including these variables did little to reduce the impact of education on trade preferences, thus suggesting that this was not the key mechanism by which education was influencing trade preferences.[25]

To get around the problem of people projecting their own opinions onto economists' views, we also asked people about economic knowledge that was not directly tied to trade. This made it possible to evaluate whether the economically knowledgeable are more likely to favor trade, while lowering the likelihood that their opinions on trade are being projected onto economists, thus producing a misleading relationship between the two. To evaluate whether those who are more economically knowledgeable are more likely to support trade, I asked two questions borrowed from the National Economics Challenge, a competition for high school students that is sponsored by The Council for Economic Education. Each was a multiple-choice question with three possible answers. First, respondents were asked, "If the U.S. dollar increases in value, then <u>U.S. exports</u> to other countries are likely to increase, decrease, or stay the same?" Second, respondents were asked, "If the U.S. dollar increases in value, then <u>U.S. imports</u> of goods from other countries are likely to. . . . ," with the same three response options.

These are relatively difficult questions. Further, the pattern of results makes it clear that people either understood the questions and knew the answers or they did not. There were disproportionate numbers of people who answered neither question correctly (35%) or both correctly (38%), with fewer in between (27%). As expected, those with higher levels of education scored higher on average than those with less education.[26] In addition, those with higher levels of economic knowledge were more likely to support trade, even after controlling for a large number of other predictors. But accounting for economic knowledge did not eliminate or even weaken the power of education in predicting trade preferences.[27] Thus education matters to trade preferences, but not because it conveys greater economic knowledge that changes people's views on trade.

Understanding How Lay People Think about Trade

The American public is not well informed about economics or about how they themselves are affected by trade. This combination begs the question of where their views come from. The terminology used in people's comments provided some important clues.

One theme that emerged in the comments of both trade advocates and trade opponents was the idea that the United States had a debt or deficit as a result of international trade. Given frequent references in public discourse to the trade deficit, this should come as no surprise. Moreover, to think that a deficit is a bad thing seems perfectly logical and intuitive. After all, when one runs a deficit in a business, it means one is losing money. Open-ended comments from Americans used the terms deficit and debt interchangeably:

Too much debt.
Sell them our stuff to get out of debt.
Because if we buy American made products, we keep the money in our own country and perhaps help decrease our country's debt.
Because we are too in debt. We need to use our products from America to keep the money in America so that we can get out of this recession.
I think it contributes to our national debt.
The key to eliminating this debt or deficit is widely understood to be exporting US goods.

These kinds of views are widely espoused in popular discourse on trade: "In the international trade area, the political rhetoric is almost always about how we must *export,* and what's really good for America is an *industry that produces exports.* And if we buy from abroad and import lots of goods from countries like China, Japan and Mexico, that's supposed to be bad."[28] This understanding of trade is pervasive, even among trade supporters. Among trade advocates, respondents were quick to differentiate their support for trade in principle, from trade that increases deficits:

Trade is essential to the economy. Not trade DEFICITS.

While trade with other countries in most cases is desirable, the gov. should always keep in mind that we should not carry a deficit because of it.

Trade is a two way street. We need to balance the number of imports and exports to maintain a good level of job creation in our country.

We need to sell our products as well as purchase products from other countries for balanced trade.

We are importing more than exporting. So we should discourage trade until its equal.

I think we should promote American made products; I'm not saying no to trading with other countries, I just think it should be reduced, especially with our nation in such debt.

I think that is a good idea only if USA products get focused on. We can't have us receiving stuff from other countries and them not receiving an equal amount from us in return.

Hoping international trade would allow us to export more goods. Nations like China, Russia don't import a lot of our goods. There has to be a balance.

It's good for the economy to have goods coming and going as long as we don't have a trade deficit.

There has always been trade since day one of our world but if we have high trade coming in but not as much going out it is not balanced.

Trade should be done in moderation/balance.

I do not believe in protectionism. We should not isolate ourselves from the rest of the world. Nor should we have a tremendous imbalance of trade. There needs to be a balance.

Trade opponents are far more strident in their discussion of trade deficits, suggesting that a trade *imbalance* is directly responsible for job loss in the US. Although no one attempted to explain precisely *why* a trade deficit should translate to fewer American jobs, these two phenomena were widely assumed to be causally related:

All of our trade is coming in and not much going out. Our jobs are lost as we are not making anything anymore.

Too much coming IN and not enough going OUT. . . . .jobs in America have been LOST..because of this.

We need jobs here in US—if we don't trade, maybe manufacturers would bring back work to the United States.
To have more jobs here, and because of the trade imbalance.
There is lack of balance in trade, with foreign exports flooding the U.S. at the expense of U.S. production and jobs.
Trading outside our own country decreases employment within our own country.
Ross was right, there was a GIANT SUCKING SOUND as the jobs left this country when NAFTA was forced upon the American people.

Some trade opponents expressed resentment about how trade affects "us" versus "them," just as in the "America first" arguments. From their perspective, trade is a form of foreign aid, benefitting "them" directly at "our" expense. Rather than lifting poor countries out of poverty, trade is conceived of as lowering Americans' standard of living as a means of creating greater global equality:

The global economy and the international banking system is a load of shit meant to help 3rd world countries and "even the playing field." I'm an American; not a Kenyan or Chinese. My country comes first. My people come first. Not everyone else. I used to live in the greatest nation in the world until Left-wing cry-babies decided -everyone- needed to be equal.
We should go back to tariffs on their products and tax the blazes out of American companies that ship our jobs overseas. Our middle class has taken the worst hit ever on wages. We are expected to work hard for long hours to live in poverty like the 3rd world countries do.
The US gets the short end of the stick.
Because it always seems the scales tip in the other countries' favor.
Because the goods we get back aren't as good as the goods we send over.
We are being fleeced.

Although these responses were volunteered in 2013, long before Trump took the national political stage, this appears to be precisely how President Trump understands the idea of a trade deficit. As he put it, "Our trade deficit with China is like having a business that continues to lose money every single year. Who would do business like that?"[29] Further, many Americans see their compatriots as treated unfairly by international trade: "In the words of Donald Trump, we are getting 'hosed,' 'ripped off,' 'crushed,' and 'killed' by our trade partners who then laugh at us as they supposedly steal our jobs."[30]

When the notion of fairness came up in people's comments, it was not in the same sense that the "fair trade" movement concerns itself with fair wages and the treatment of overseas labor. Instead, it was about feeling that America was being treated unfairly. As one respondent put it, "America gets the shit end of the stick. (Unless you own the Business)."

Extensive concerns about trade deficits and the trade imbalance are generally eschewed by economists. As Adam Smith famously noted in 1776, "Nothing . . . can be more absurd than this whole doctrine of the balance of trade." The fact that imbalance is still widely believed to be problematic is testimony to its intuitive appeal. "Balance" certainly sounds like something one should want. And colloquially speaking, a "trade" seems fairest when the same amount of goods goes back and forth. Even Americans who registered pro-trade preferences often qualified their views by saying trade was good, except when it led to debts or deficits. Spending more money than one makes understandably seems irresponsible to most Americans; it sounds just like overdrawing one's bank account. Further, many respondents conflated the trade deficit with the US national debt, which is money primarily owed to Americans, not to foreigners.

Most economists, in contrast, see the trade imbalance as irrelevant to the availability of jobs or to the economic health of the nation as a whole. To average Americans, this does not seem logical. The economy can be booming when the deficit is high, and in poor shape even when the deficit is low. This occurs because multiple forces influence the size of the trade deficit. For example, government spending increases the deficit. A booming economy also increases the deficit because it means Americans have more disposable income with which to buy things from overseas. The exchange rate is also a contributing factor.[31]

Some economists have expressed concerns about the trade deficit, but typically only if it persists over too long a period of time or becomes far larger than it is now. Some worry about it due to how it may affect mass opinion; they fear the trade deficit may drive a populist backlash toward trade in mass opinion, which could affect policymakers. Still other economists worry that a US trade *surplus* could be dangerous to the stability of the world economy by lowering global economic growth.

Regardless, there is widespread agreement among economists that whether trade is "balanced" with any individual country is irrelevant to a country's economic well-being and the availability of jobs. Trade deficits do not correlate with unemployment, for example. A balance with respect to a specific country has more to do with what those specific countries trade with one another. However, this notion persists, perhaps because of the idea that trade must produce "winners" and "losers" in some sort of head to head face-off in which "trade deficits mean you lose, and surpluses mean you win."[32]

Concern about bilateral balance is especially pronounced with respect to the US-China balance of trade. Because many Americans find China threatening, this trade imbalance has become the focus of the greatest public attention. The trade imbalance with China has become a rallying cry for protectionist policies because it is seen as akin to being dominated by China in the eyes of many Americans.

Given that the trade deficit has little to do with the country's economic condition and that governments cannot directly control the size of the trade deficit in any case, Americans' obsession with the trade deficit is unlikely to lead them to support policies with the desired economic effects. In particular, the hope that tariffs and trade restrictions can bring back high-paying manufacturing jobs is misplaced.[33] Instead, our trading partners simply turn to other countries to do business. Once again, by shrinking our conceptual understanding of the international economy down to the size of our own bank accounts, people may be misled.

Dimensions of Trade Judgments

As noted, international trade is liked and disliked for more than purely economic reasons. Indeed, trade is such a complex issue that there is the potential for people to hold highly nuanced views on this policy. One might believe trade is good at lowering the costs of consumer goods, for example, but bad for the environment and for underpaid workers overseas. Or one might believe it improves the quality of products in trading partner countries, while lowering the quality of products in the US. In order to understand more than simply the summary opinion formed by Americans, I asked directly about trade's impact on seven different outcomes. These included its effects on working conditions, on the environment, on the availability of jobs, on the cost of consumer goods, the quality of products, on national security, and on corporate stock prices. Many of these types of impacts were drawn from Jagdish Bhagwati's (2004) book, *In Defense of Globalization*, in which he outlines the popular arguments against trade and globalization as well as the major arguments in favor of it.

Unlike many controversial issues, however, trade can be evaluated based not only on its effects on the US, but also based on how it is believed to affect trading partner countries. Thus for each of these seven dimensions, people were asked whether they thought trade helped or hurt the US, and whether

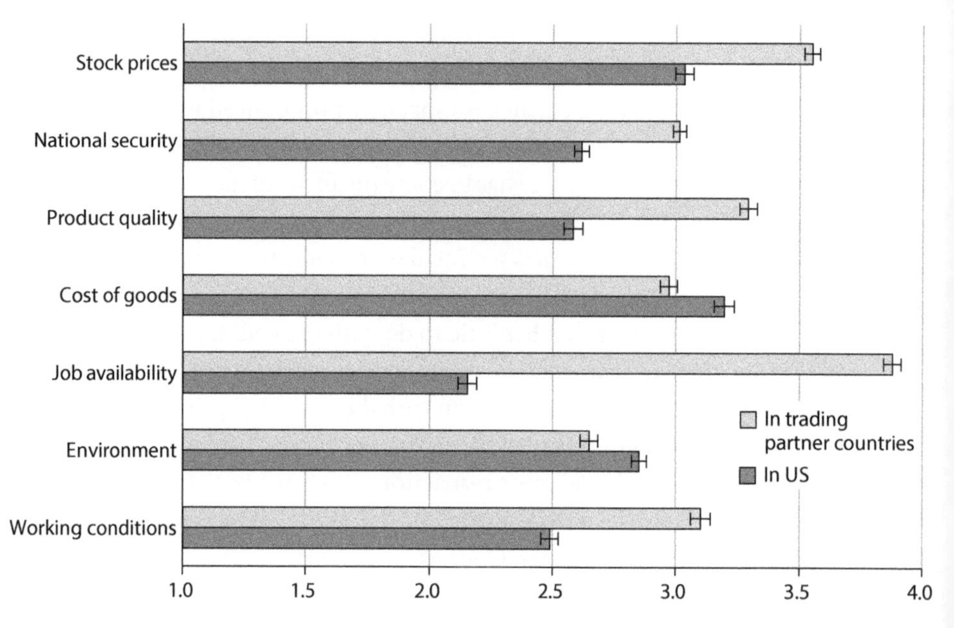

FIGURE 2.3. Perceived Benefits of Trade for US and Trading Partner Countries
Source: ISCAP Trade Survey Experiment 2013–2014 (GfK Ltd). Bars represent the extent to which respondents perceived trade as improving each specific dimension on a 1 to 4 scale, that is, improving national security, decreasing costs, improving product quality, etc. The midpoint (2.5) represents a mean value indicating neither positive nor negative consequences.

it helped or hurt trading partner countries. For example, respondents were asked, "Has international trade helped or hurt the quality of products available in [the United States/trading partner countries]?" and "Has international trade increased or decreased the number of jobs available in [the US/trading partner countries]?" All respondents were asked all 14 questions, but some were asked the seven questions about the US first, and others were asked the seven questions about effects on trading partner countries first. Within each block of seven questions, the order of the seven dimensions of potential impact also was randomized.

As illustrated in Figure 2.3, the perceived impact of trade on other countries is seen as most positive for the availability of jobs. When it comes to the perceived effects on the US, it is least positive for jobs. This means that if one were to judge trade strictly in terms of its impact on jobs, one would favor it if one cared only about jobs overseas, and oppose it if one cared only about jobs at home. This pattern is indicative of the zero-sum way of thinking about trade; in this line of thought, trade merely takes a set number of jobs in the world and reallocates them from one country to another. Indeed, perceptions of effects on jobs is the one and only dimension of trade in which people's perceptions of how it affects the US is *negatively* correlated with how it is perceived to affect trading partner countries; the more one believes it helps jobs overseas, the more one believes it hurts the US.

For five of the seven dimensions of effects—stock prices, national security, product quality, job availability, and working conditions, people perceived trade to be significantly more beneficial to trading partner countries than to the US. The two exceptions were the environment and the cost of consumer goods, for which the US is perceived to benefit slightly more than trading partner countries. Overall, Americans see trade as a much better deal for our trading partner countries than it is for the US.

There are important differences in the extent to which Americans perceive their country to benefit from trade relative to other countries. However, what is interesting about the indicators in Figure 2.3 is that for six out of the seven pairs, perceptions of effects on one's own country are *positively* correlated with perceptions of effects on trading partner counties. If you think trade does good things for America via its effects on the cost of consumer goods or its impact on working conditions, then you are also very likely to think it is a positive force for trading partner countries. When it comes to all dimensions of trade's impact except one, people tend to be either for it or against it across the board, seeing it as having either all good or all bad consequences whether they were being asked about effects on their own country or on trading partner countries.

For job availability, the one exception, perceptions of trade's effects in the US and overseas are negatively correlated, indicating that the more a person thinks trade improves the availability of jobs overseas, the more they are likely to say that it hurts American jobs, and vice versa. So while zero-sum perceptions are evident when it comes to trade's effects on jobs, the other dimensions of trade's impact were not viewed through this zero-sum lens. People could form attitudes toward trade in whole or in part based on how they think trade affects their home country or based on how it affects other countries. But the way in which Americans are generally asked about their views on trade—questions addressing whether it is good or bad for *their* country—presumes that people only take into account its effects on their own country. This is clearly not the case. Using indexes comprised of all of the perceived effects on the US and a separate index comprised of all of the perceived effects on trading partner countries, perceived effects on other countries predict trade preferences above and beyond its perceived domestic effects.[34] However, consistent with a greater emphasis on trade's domestic effects, Americans' trade preferences are three times more strongly related to trade's perceived effects on the US compared to its perceived effects on trading partner countries.

It is virtually certain that most Americans do not think through all of these various dimensions of impact before forming a policy preference. Instead, people may like or dislike trade for other reasons and then infer that it must have good/bad effects on all aspects of life as a result. If one posited a rational, bottom-up decision-making process in which detailed judgments about individual dimensions of trade's impact were first synthesized in order to form an overall preference, then it seems unlikely that *all* dimensions of trade's impact on the US and other countries would just happen to be all positive or all negative. Instead, these assessments may flow from the top down, that is, from a gut feeling about trade's benefits and drawbacks, to inferences about individual dimensions of its impact. With data of this kind one cannot be certain either way. However, given that asking about these specific dimensions of trade's impact generated far more "don't know" answers than asking about support for international trade, my best guess would be that people's general attitudes toward trade precede their assessments of how trade affects each of these specific aspects of their nation and of trading partner nations. In other words, people are likely to be inferring these more specific kinds of positive and negative consequences—effects on the environment, on product quality, and so on—from how they feel about trade in general. Overall, people either think trade is a good thing or a bad thing, and they show little evidence of nuanced views that acknowledge that it may, for example, be good for prices in the US, but bad for working conditions overseas, or good for consumer prices, but bad for manufacturing jobs. This assessment is also consistent with the strong intercorrelations among questions asking about trade in general, specific trade agreements, the WTO and so forth.

Americans' Understanding of Trade

This chapter provided a first take on the ways in which people express and explain their views on trade. Although opinions on trade may not be economically well-informed, they are at least internally consistent for most citizens. There is a logic to their beliefs, even if it is not the same logic that economists would offer. There is a strong consensus among trade opponents about why trade is harmful, and this is because it takes away jobs from their fellow Americans. For average Americans, opposing trade is less of an expression of personal economic fear than a concern about one's fellow Americans, often coupled with the sense that foreigners are benefitting more than Americans from international trade.

Economic theories may provide useful guidance when decisions are made by political elites and policymakers, but they are unlikely to serve as the basis for decision-making on the part of the average citizen. Most Americans at best partially understand the economic consequences of protectionism, and few are familiar with the classical case for free trade.[35]

When viewed from an economic perspective, trade is extremely complex. It is often difficult for experts, let alone for ordinary Americans, to feel they have a firm grasp on how trade policies affect the outcomes they care about. Nonetheless, trade can be supported or opposed without reference to its economic impact on one's self or family, and even without knowledge of how it affects people in different occupations and industries. Protectionist attitudes in the US are driven largely by symbolic beliefs. As noted by previous scholars, "a primary driver of the beliefs someone forms about globalization . . . is how strongly they attach their social identity to the United States."[36] The strength of one's ingroup identity—in this case, one's national identity—plays an important role in how people view trade.

3

Partisan Trends in Mass Opinion on Trade

What originally enticed me to study attitudes toward trade and globalization was the fact that these issue positions did not appear to fall cleanly along party lines. Partisanship is such a strong force in shaping mass opinion in the US that most issue positions are very predictable, and they seldom change. Partisan reinforcement also gives them a resiliency that makes them frankly boring for people who like to study when and why people change their minds.

If trade were like most political issues in the US, then partisanship would be its strongest predictor. Political elites would cue their followers on what their trade positions should be, and their positions would neatly line up along party lines. At least for the last 20 years, however, it has not been clear where the two parties stand on trade. Depending upon how one chooses to identify a political party's position, one comes up with different answers. Is it what elites say when they are candidates for office? What they do once they become elected officials? What the public perceives their positions to be? Traditionally, parties on the right have taken more free trade stances than those on the left.[1] But in the US, party cues surrounding trade are far more complicated than they are for most political issues. As explored at length in this chapter, the two major US political parties have given their followers ambiguous cues on this issue. Elites in the two major parties have changed positions on the value of free trade over time, with an elite pro-trade

FIGURE 3.1. Republicans and Democrats on Trade, Then and Now

consensus giving way to another elite consensus, but in opposition to trade by 2016, as the cartoon in Figure 3.1 points out. The cues given by political leaders have been nothing if not confusing and contradictory. Partisanship has not been a consistent predictor of who supports or opposes trade in the US. For this reason, forming opinions on this issue is not as simple as turning to elite leadership for cues.

Trade has at times been a high-profile issue in America's political past.[2] But because it has rarely been a salient political issue in the post–World War period, Americans' impressions of where the two parties stand on this issue are understandably muted. In recent decades, the majority of Republican *elected officials* have leaned in a more pro-trade, free market direction, whereas the majority of Democratic elected officials leaned toward greater protectionism. Nonetheless, congressional votes regarding trade agreements have seldom been strictly along party lines.[3]

If, instead, one judged political parties by what their candidates said while running for office, then both parties would be viewed as protectionist. On the campaign trail, Democratic candidates that rely on organized labor for support often vocally oppose free trade. At the same time, few Republican candidates have showcased free trade support as part of their campaigns, thus making it unclear to observers what the partisan difference is.[4]

Once elected to office, most elites have appeared more open to international commerce than they were while campaigning. In fact, up until the financial crisis in 2008, many observers pointed to a bipartisan "Washington consensus" on a set of free-market economic policies that one would categorize as largely pro-trade. Although the exact meaning of this term has varied from user to user, and the Washington consensus has been declared dead many times since then, it suggested a baseline level of agreement among political elites about the need to promote international trade.[5]

Confusing messages about partisanship and trade have been further conveyed to the public by presidents in office. In 1993, Democratic president Bill Clinton signed NAFTA into law after Republican George H. W. Bush started the process of ratification. But more Republicans than Democrats supported the bill in both the House and the Senate. Years later, Democratic president Barack Obama signed KORUS, a trade agreement with South Korea. He also championed the Trans-Pacific Partnership (TPP) during his second term in office. In 2016, the Republican candidate, Donald Trump, was virulently anti-trade, and the Democratic candidate, Hillary Clinton, also worked hard to distance herself from virtually all trade agreements (especially NAFTA) as a presidential candidate. Republican Donald Trump withdrew the US from NAFTA and withdrew the US from the Trans-Pacific Partnership (TPP), calling it "a rape of our country." But then Trump later passed the United States Mexico Canada Agreement (USMCA), a trade agreement that to most Americans looked a whole lot like NAFTA.[6]

The political parties' official national platforms increasingly make their positions on free trade even more confusing. For example, in 1972, the Democratic national platform flatly stated, "In a prosperous economy, foreign trade has benefits for virtually everyone. . . . The Democratic party proposes no retreat from this commitment." The Republican platform, on the other hand, was more tepid in advocating "general expansion of trade" and an "open world market," but attention was focused instead on how to facilitate readjustment for the hardships faced by displaced workers. By the 1980s, trade was firmly entrenched in party platform language as a "challenge of economic competition," and references to "fair" trade became increasingly common in the platforms of both Democrats and Republicans. My more general point is that for most of recent history, even if a person were to carefully read both parties' platforms (something that virtually everyone agrees does *not* occur), it would be unclear from their language which was the more pro- or anti-trade party.

Over time, the Republican platforms have become more focused on issues such as the balance of trade, the trade deficit, and especially the notion of "trade through strength."[7] By 2012, the Republican party platform speaks of "reclaiming this country's traditional position of dominance in international trade."[8] In other words, trade is now more about "winning" and being able to dominate other countries. Both parties continue to emphasize "fair trade," but as discussed in the chapters that follow, they fundamentally disagree about what this idea means.

Trends in Mass Opinion on Trade

Given the muddled partisan cues characterizing this issue, it is unclear what to expect when looking at partisan trends over time in the mass public. Few sources of data have asked consistently-worded questions over time. But by piecing together both cross-sectional and panel data from multiple sources, a fairly consistent picture emerges of how mass opinion has evolved over time on trade, globalization and whether China is an economic opportunity or a threat.

WHEN DID REPUBLICANS AND DEMOCRATS DIVERGE ON TRADE?

As noted in Chapter 2, differently-worded questions about trade and globalization may produce different mean levels of support, but people's answers to these questions are so strongly correlated with one another that it would be difficult to argue that they tap anything other than one underlying pro-trade or anti-trade sentiment. Certain question wordings may make it sound slightly more palatable than others, and certain trade agreements may have somewhat more positive associations due to cues from relevant politicians or groups. But for the most part, people think trade is generally a good or a bad idea; they do not have highly nuanced views or detailed information about specific trade agreements that leads them to favor one agreement but oppose another. All survey questions have their peculiarities that can bump opinions up or down to a small extent, but these differences appear to matter little to tapping underlying trade preferences.

To begin, Figure 3.2 illustrates attitudes toward globalization of the economy. From the 1990s through 2005, it was difficult to distinguish the trade preferences of Republicans and Democrats in the mass public. By 2008, however, Democrats had become the party more likely to see a globalized economy as good for the US. The pattern of greater Democratic support persisted for almost ten years thereafter. This same timing is shown in Figure A3.1 in the online appendix where attitudes toward free trade agreements diverge by party beginning around 2008, and remain more highly favored

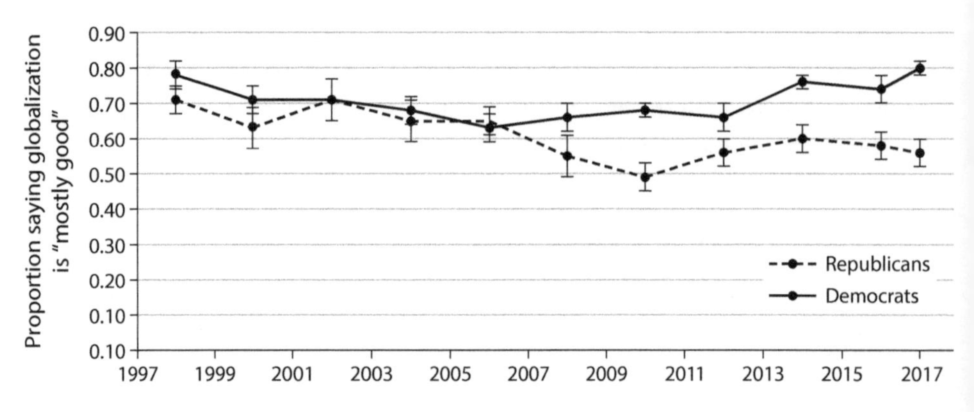

FIGURE 3.2. Support for Globalization, by Party, 1998–2017
Source: Chicago Council on Global Affairs Surveys.
Note: Estimates represent the proportion of Republicans/Democrats who said globalization was "mostly good" in response to a question asking, "Do you believe that globalization, especially the increasing connections of our economy with others around the world, is mostly good or mostly bad for the United States?"

by Democrats through 2016. Although its trend starts much later, Figure A3.2 likewise confirms that by 2012, free trade was a Democrat position more than a Republican one.

These three trends all suggest similar timing for the shift in partisan views on trade. Sometime between 2008 and 2010, the parties began to diverge in attitudes toward free trade agreements. Democrats did not change their views so much as Republicans became less supportive of free trade agreements, thus increasing the gap between partisan groups. As further confirmed in Figure 3.3, Democrats and Republicans were indistinguishable on trade until after 2008. But by 2010, Democrats became the party holding more favorable views of trade's impact on the economy, and the parties maintained this distinction up through 2016.

It is worth noting that this pattern of Republicans expressing more anti-trade and anti-globalization opinions than Democrats clearly predated Donald Trump, so he cannot rightly be either credited or blamed for such a shift. Sometime during the late 2000s, but long before Trump took office, Democrats became the party more favorably disposed toward trade and globalization.

Although the surveys associated with different trends end at different years, it is worth noting that the data in Figure 3.3 extend past Trump's election in 2016. There is a surprising change immediately after the 2016 election. After Trump takes office, Republican trade preferences become

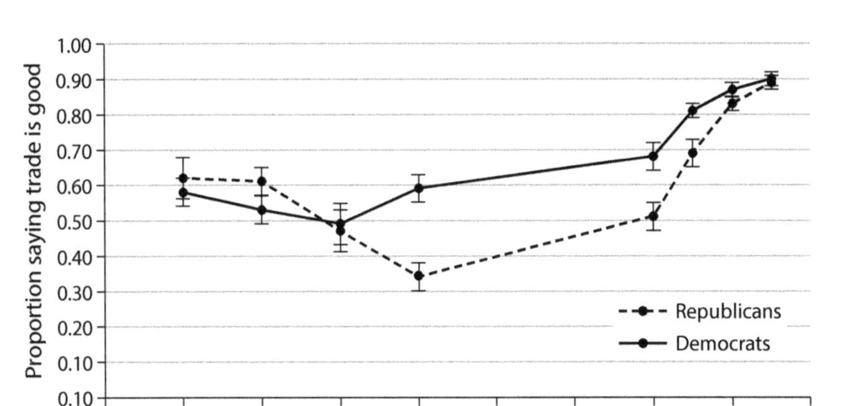

FIGURE 3.3. Perceptions of Whether Trade Is Good for the US Economy, by Party, 2004–2019
Source: Chicago Council on Global Affairs Surveys.
Note: Estimates refer to the proportion of Republicans/Democrats who said trade was good for the US economy in response to a question asking, "Overall, do you think international trade is good or bad for the United States economy?"

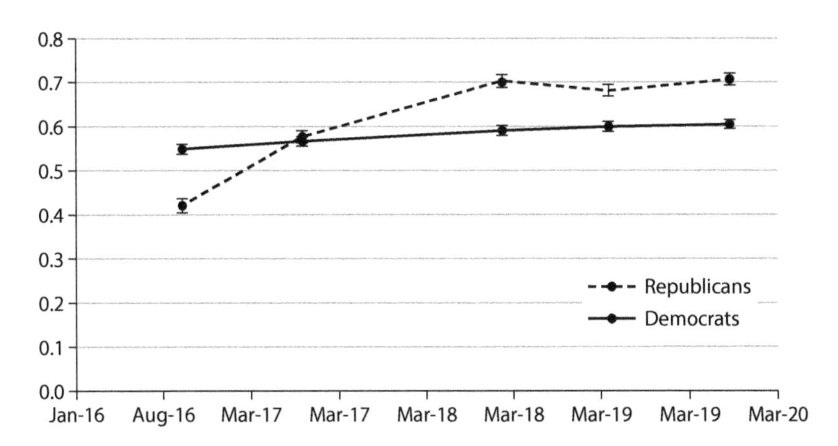

FIGURE 3.4. Support for Trade by Party, October 2016–March 2020
Source: ISCAP Panel Surveys 2016–2020 (Amerispeak/NORC).
Note: Trade preferences are measured on a 5-point scale rescaled to range from 0 to 1, with high scores representing favoring trade. Respondents were asked, "Do you favor or oppose the federal government in Washington negotiating more free trade agreements?"

more positive. By 2019, in Figure 3.3 there is once again no difference between Republicans and Democrats in their levels of support for trade. This same pattern is also evident in Figure 3.4, where panel data show that immediately after Trump's election, Republicans became increasingly positive toward trade. In fact, by late 2018, Republicans were significantly *more* supportive of trade than

Democrats. Because the increase in support among Republicans is significantly steeper than for Democrats, they quickly caught up to previous levels of Democratic support.

Why would electing a president who campaigned on a virulently anti-trade agenda result in a surge in mass support for international trade, especially among his co-partisans? One possibility is that Trump's trade war with China convinced Americans of both parties to reconsider their opposition to trade. However, this explanation seems unlikely for multiple reasons. For one, the timing is off; the surge in support for trade was already in evidence in 2017, yet the trade war did not get under way until midway through 2018 when Trump began to use tariffs and other barriers against China. Even as late as June 2019, only 22 percent of Republicans reported any awareness that the amount of international trade had decreased in the past year. A more impressive 44 percent of Democrats were aware of a trade slowdown, making it more likely to be an explanation for the increased support for trade among Democrats than for the increasing support among Republicans.

The explanation for this opinion change, which I explore at length in the remaining chapters of this book, is that Trump promised his fellow Republicans a completely different kind of trade policy, one that would be especially desirable to Republicans in particular. Trade under Trump was supposed to be a policy that essentially allowed America to have the upper hand and to use trade policy as a means to dominate other countries, thus allowing America to "win," as Trump put it. Of course, there were no new trade agreements by 2017 so people had to be responding more to rhetoric than reality. The USMCA was signed in 2018, though not in effect until 2020. Nonetheless, it seems likely that Trump's hardball negotiations with Canada and Mexico may have given Republicans the impression that trade under Trump would be nothing like trade under Obama or previous presidents.

As detailed at length in Chapter 4, trade as a means to dominance is a far more appealing idea to Republicans than trade as cooperation. Democrats who increasingly viewed trade as good for the economy could have been pushing back against Trump's strong anti-trade rhetoric or reacting to the fallout from the trade war. But Republicans are likely to have had something different in mind—the idea that trade would be wholly different once strongman Trump was in office. These explanations may well play a role in the increased support for international trade that came later on in Trump's administration. But as I describe next, there is also a simpler, more straightforward, explanation at least for the immediate surge in Republican support.

Effects of the Party-in-Power on Trade Support

As with many other policy issues, trade preferences are susceptible to what I call "party-in-power" effects. It is well known and widely documented, for example, that the economy as perceived by co-partisans becomes instantaneously rosier when a president from one's own party is elected and one from the opposite party is ousted. This effect has been observed and documented extensively for a very long time. Some observers suggest that partisan rationalization of perceptions of the economy has been exacerbated in recent years, perhaps by partisan news that reinforces party-consistent perceptions of the economy.[9] Less surprisingly, people's levels of trust in government are also susceptible to party-in-power effects. Trust in a co-partisan president is predictably high, and trust in government is predictably low when one's own party is out of the White House.[10]

Likewise, support for international trade appears to vacillate based on which party holds the White House. When there is a change in the party in power, co-partisans of the party that has just gained power almost immediately increase in their support for trade. In many ways, the 2016 election was a particularly difficult test of the party-in-power thesis because the Republican candidate campaigned on a strongly anti-trade platform. One would not logically predict that Trump's followers should become more pro-trade immediately after he was elected. Nonetheless, as shown in Figure 3.4, we see precisely this pattern: from pre- to post-election, Democratic support for trade was unchanged, while Republican support (defined as those who identified as Republican before the election) surged once Trump was elected.

Based solely on evidence from before and after Trump's election, it would be premature to jump to the conclusion that patterns of partisanship in trade support are driven by changes in the party holding the White House. If trade is, indeed, a party-in-power issue, this should not be limited to Trump's presidency. Democratic partisans who take control of the White House away from Republicans should also increase in their support for trade. Further, an election that does not create a change in the party in power should not differentially affect partisans from either party.[11]

The 2008 and 2012 elections provide opportunities to test both of these additional predictions. Figure 3.5 shows levels of trade support from before to after both the 2008 and 2012 presidential elections. The pre-election data in these analyses were gathered immediately before the presidential elections, and the post-election data were gathered one to two years into the new administration, asking the same questions of the same panelists. An

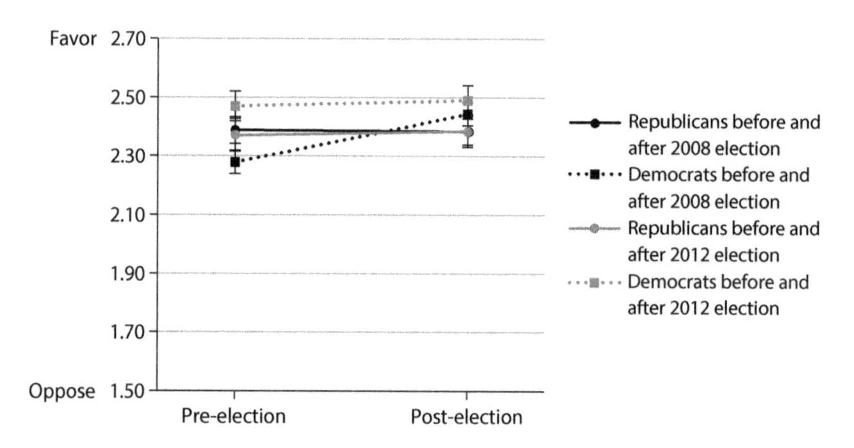

FIGURE 3.5. Effects of a Change in the Party-in-Power on Trade Preferences, 2008 and 2012 Presidential Elections

Source: National Annenberg Election Survey Panel Study 2008 (Knowledge Networks), ISCAP Panel Surveys, 2012 (GfK Ltd.).

Note: Trade preferences are measured on a 1 to 4 scale. The interaction between change over time pre- to post-election and Republican versus Democratic identification was significant in 2008 when a change in the party in party occurred, but not in 2012. Respondents were asked, "Do you favor or oppose the federal government in Washington negotiating more free trade agreements like NAFTA?" High scores indicate favoring.

individual's partisanship was determined by how he or she identified pre-election, to prevent the possibility of shifting identifications based on the election outcome.

The two black lines in Figure 3.5 illustrate the pre- to post-2008 election change in Republican and Democratic attitudes toward trade. As would be expected if trade is a party-in-power policy, when Obama won the election, Democrats increased significantly in their support for trade as shown by the broken black line representing Democratic opinions. Republican attitudes remained flat, as illustrated by the solid black line.[12] This finding is consistent with the boost in trade support experienced by Republicans in 2016, as illustrated in Figure 3.4.[13]

In 2012, when Obama won a second term, there was no change in the party in power, so one would not expect a change in trade attitudes based on partisanship. Indeed, as illustrated by the grey lines in Figure 3.5, Democrats sustained their more positive attitudes toward trade, and Republicans persisted in their pre-existing views. Without a change in the party holding the White House, levels of support for trade did not change differentially by party.[14]

Based on evidence from just three elections, it is difficult to know for sure that party-in-power effects are the explanation for these findings. However, it is worth noting that Obama's active efforts to champion the Trans-Pacific Partnership (TPP) did not occur until his second term, the period when Democrats' views on trade did *not* change, whereas they did change immediately after his election. This suggests that opinion leadership was not responsible for the increased support for trade among Democrats.[15] Moreover, in the 2016 election, the evidence is convincing precisely because one would not have expected Republicans to change their views so quickly after such a trade-bashing campaign.

These results naturally lead to the question of *why* trade support is subject to party-in-power effects. It is understandable that co-partisans of the president are motivated to see the economy through rose-colored glasses. And it is likewise logical that they should trust government more when a like-minded partisan is in power. But why favor trade policies more? Perhaps this occurs because the president is perceived to have the power to control trade policies. Without needing to know any of the details, trade agreements may automatically be perceived as more trustworthy and beneficial once one's own party is in office.

What Brings about Party-in-Power Effects?

Given that there is plenty of evidence that party-in-power effects influence vacillating levels of trust in government, as well as perceptions of the economy, it is worth considering whether party-in-power effects on trade preferences are merely downstream, secondary consequences of changes in perceptions of the economy and/or trust in government that occur when the party in the White House changes. If one simply does not trust the government until one's own co-partisan is in power, how can one trust it to administer trade policies? Even an identical trade policy could be supported less when the other party is in charge, regardless of the policy's origins or advocates. The political scientist Marc Hetherington has suggested that as government trust has declined, Americans have also lost faith in the delivery system for many progressive policies. Support for redistributive programs such as welfare and food stamps, as well as race-related programs, are thus all victims of declining trust in government. Putting healthcare in the hands of the national government is similarly opposed by many who do not trust the federal bureaucracy. But perhaps his argument is overly narrow. People may oppose all kinds of policies and programs administered by the federal government, not just social welfare policies, when trust in government is low. Likewise, the surge in trust in government when one's own party takes power could bolster support for policies such as trade.

In addition, we know that the public is more likely to favor trade when the economy is perceived to be strong. Thus, patterns of increasing support among co-partisans could be downstream consequences of the fact that the public engages in widespread partisan rationalization of the economy. Once their own party is in power, people also view the economy in far rosier terms, and thus may oppose trade less as a result.

To examine the role that changes in perceptions of the economy and changes in trust in government play in altering trade attitudes when a new party enters the White House, I used the panel data following the same individuals from pre- to post-election to examine whether individual-level change over time in attitudes toward trade among co-partisans of the incoming party-in-power disappear once I take into account these same individuals' changed perceptions of the economy after their candidate is elected.

When the party in power changed, whether in 2008 from Republican to Democrat, or in 2016 from Democrat to Republican, economic perceptions became much more favorable among in-party partisans. Nonetheless, party-in-power effects were still evident even after taking into account the improvements in people's attitudes toward trade that occur due to changes in their perceptions of the economy, as illustrated in Tables A3.2 and A3.5. In other words, the trade issue itself promotes a party-in-power effect; it is not simply an extension of the partisan rationalization of economic conditions.

So while trade support increases for the party in power, in part due to rationalized economic perceptions, this is obviously not the whole story. What about simultaneously taking into account the increased trust in government felt by in-party partisans? Could that predictable change in government trust, either on its own or in combination with more favorable economic perceptions, account for party-in-power effects for trade? The analyses shown in Table A3.3 in the online appendix suggest that as with improved economic perceptions, trade support increases to some extent as a result of individuals' increased trust in a government run by their own party. But above and beyond what would be expected based on individuals' improved economic perceptions and increased trust in government, partisans of the in-party still increase disproportionately in their support for trade.[16] Feeling as if one's ingroup is in control of the federal government is reassuring, but these effects cannot be fully accounted for by predictable changes in economic perceptions and trust in government.

The relationship between people's attitudes toward NAFTA and their attitudes toward the United States-Mexico-Canada-Agreement (USMCA) serves as another excellent illustration of the party-in-power effect. In 2016, Trump campaigned against NAFTA, but he later supported his own trade agreement, the USMCA, colloquially known as the "New NAFTA." In 2018, only 27 percent of Americans thought the USMCA was better than NAFTA. The remaining 73 percent either did not know enough to say or thought it was the same as or worse than NAFTA. Nonetheless, among those with opinions, Republicans were overwhelmingly more favorable toward the USMCA than toward NAFTA. As the cartoon in Figure 3.6 suggests, despite limited knowledge of specifics, Republicans assumed that a Trump trade agreement had to be a better trade agreement, one that would put America first.

Research on trust in government tells us that opinion change that is induced by a change in the party in power may be asymmetric. In general, the party-in-power effect is greater for Republicans than for Democrats.[17] This is believed to be because Republicans are inherently more suspicious of government. A central tenet of conservatism has been the idea of limited government involvement. Thus when Republicans are out of power, the policies administered by the federal government are inherently even more suspect. For Democrats, the same effect occurs, but at a smaller magnitude since liberals tend to be more trusting of government. The analyses of party in power effects for 2008 and 2016 involve two different scales for trade support, making direct statistical comparisons of the size of effects impossible. Nonetheless, consistent with the argument above, the magnitude of the 2016 effect appears to be far more impressive. If one looks at the percentage of Republicans opposing versus favoring trade, the 2016 post-election shift marked a double-digit increase in those percentages, whereas the 2008 effect among Democrats was far more modest.

Due to the paucity of panel data over time, it is unclear how many different political issues are susceptible to party-in-power effects, and/or asymmetries of this kind, but my guess is that there are more than we know of currently. It is always possible that the effects observed in these three elections could be attributed to idiosyncratic characteristics of these specific candidates and elections; only more data across more elections will allow greater confidence in this finding. However, I suspect that in an increasingly

FIGURE 3.6. USMCA: The Best Trade Deal in the World

polarized two-party political system, many policy issues may be subject to party-in-power effects.

Most importantly, party-in-power effects undermine political accountability for negative effects from import competition. If the public votes to oust a candidate of one party because of adverse effects from trade, but then immediately embraces trade to a greater degree simply because a new party is now in power, this hardly seems like the kind of reward-punishment process that would produce accountability for trade's negative effects.

Whatever Happened to Presidential Opinion Leadership?

Thus far, the pattern of opinions toward trade that I have described does not appear consistent with traditional theories of elite opinion leadership. Influential theories in public opinion research suggest that mass opinion typically flows from the top down, with political elites signaling members of the public as to where they should stand.[18] As a result of the levels of mass attention they command, presidents are thought to be the most prominent and successful of cue givers. Indeed, "going public" was at one point heralded as an extremely effective means by which presidents championed their pet issues among the mass public and thus pressured other elites to support their policies.[19] Whether presidents retain a powerful role in mass opinion leadership is subject to debate.[20] Some suggest that when presidents go public with their views, they simply energize their existing supporters, rather than change the tide of opinion.[21]

Regardless, it is widely agreed that successful opinion leadership depends on the clarity of cues given by presidents. With respect to trade, President Trump clearly stood out for his very strong anti-trade rhetoric. For opinion leadership to be effective, elite cues must be clear and unambiguous. Trump's bombastic language and the sheer frequency with which he talked about trade's devastating effects on the US certainly qualified. President Trump also accused other countries of trade violations at higher rates than Presidents George W. Bush and Barack Obama. The clarity of President Trump's views would seem to be a strong foundation for opinion leadership; it would be difficult not to know where he stood.

In addition, issues that require knowledge or expertise are more likely to facilitate cue-taking than issues that do not.[22,23] Low levels of information about complex issues leave people more vulnerable to opinion leadership.[24] Opinion leadership is further enhanced by loyalty to the cue-giver. Despite low average levels of popularity, Trump's levels of presidential approval did not vary over time, regardless of unfolding events.[25] His loyalists did not waver in their support. In an increasingly polarized country, this is perhaps not so surprising. More importantly, this loyalty suggested a strong potential for co-partisan opinion leadership.[26]

So did Trump lead mass opinion on trade? Panel analyses of Trump's co-partisans and even his most ardent supporters have generated no evidence of opinion leadership to date.[27] My co-author Elizabeth Martin and I looked long and hard for such evidence by evaluating change over time in a panel capable of identifying even very subtle changes in individuals' opinions. We first looked for evidence that Republicans were led by Trump, then looked at Trump voters, and then at his strongest and most loyal fans.[28] We further considered that we might have missed specific subgroups where some opinion leadership occurred. Perhaps the president led opinion among those who were paying close attention to politics, or among those who were attentive, but not so firm in their opinions as to be unpersuadable. We found nothing to counter our conclusions regarding a stark failure of presidential opinion leadership with respect to trade.[29]

We next considered the possibility that Trump's hardline stance might at least show up in the context of attitudes toward China, if not in attitudes toward trade policies per se. As the single country that most personifies the trade threat, a country that was repeatedly attacked in Trump's rhetoric, it seemed likely that his supporters would report greater threat from China as a result. Using a panel study that repeatedly asked about the extent to which China was a threat to US jobs or an opportunity for economic cooperation, we looked for evidence that either Republicans, Trump voters, or Trump enthusiasts were led in an anti-China direction over time.

Although Republicans are consistently more anti-China than are Democrats, as illustrated in Figure A3.3 in the online appendix, neither the aggregate pattern, nor the individual-level panel analyses focused on Trump's most loyal supporters, demonstrate any evidence of opinion leadership on China. Whatever threat Trump's followers felt from China before he was elected has persisted, but there is no evidence that the president has changed mass opinion on either of these issues.[30] Despite having many, if not most, of the characteristics predicting success at leading the opinions of his co-partisans, President Trump shifted mass opinion in a pro-trade direction during his presidency.

The only evidence potentially consistent with a role for Trump in these shifts comes from the 2016 campaign period, long before Trump was elected. Although Republicans were already the anti-trade party in the mass public by then, between January and October of 2016, they declined more in their support for international trade than Democrats, consistent with Trump's campaign pitch at the time. This accelerated decline in support was evident in the far right of Figure A3.1 in the online appendix.

With a large field of Republican primary candidates to potentially follow, opinion leadership by a single candidate seems unlikely when so many different voices could potentially lead. On the other hand, Trump was the first recent presidential candidate from a major party to challenge the wisdom of US involvement in international trade. To have a Republican presidential candidate blast trade as Trump did during his campaign was something new for Republicans, a signal that could have been effective in exacerbating the decline in Republican support that was already in progress while Democrats held the White House.

While presidents may have more access than candidates to a bully pulpit, Trump's views while he was still a primary candidate could have encouraged anti-trade sentiment among his followers. He received an unusually large amount of coverage relative to other Republican primary candidates. But if so, one would expect to see a disproportionate decline in support for trade among his supporters. This was not the case. Trump did not lead his followers in an anti-trade direction during this period. We compared panel data from

January 2016 to October 2016 to see if those who supported Trump in January were more likely than those supporting other Republican candidates to move in an anti-trade direction. The results of this analysis, shown in Table A3.8 in the online appendix, suggest that while Republicans as a whole became more anti-trade during this short period of time, Trump supporters were no more likely to shift their views than other Republicans. In short, there is little evidence that Trump led public opinion on this issue during the primaries, the general election campaign, or while president.

As I discuss further in Chapter 11, the truly impressive change in 2016 was not in people's opinions on trade, but the shift in people's *perceptions* of where the two parties stood on this issue. Although Republicans in the mass public became somewhat more anti-trade in their policy opinions between 2012 and 2016, far greater change occurred in where they perceived the Republican and Democratic parties to stand on this issue. Trump's statements were a dramatic departure from the muffled, ambivalent stands that Republican partisans had learned to expect from their elites. By the time of the 2016 election, Trump had moved people's perceptions of the Republican party's position clearly into the anti-trade camp. Thus Trump may have exacerbated what many had failed to acknowledge before 2016: that Democrats rather than Republicans in the mass public were by then the party of free trade.

Trade Turned Upside Down

Mass opinion in American politics is known for changing only at a glacial pace. It happens slowly and gradually, if at all. This background makes it all the more astonishing what has happened to trade since Trump's election in 2016. In only three years' time, opinions on international trade have changed drastically. It is not just that people moving in a pro-trade or anti-trade direction continued to do so. Instead, Republicans' opinions flipped virtually 180 degrees. For example, in 2016, 42 percent of Republicans opposed international trade, 23 percent favored it, and the rest were neither in favor nor opposed. By 2020, only 7 percent of those exact same Republicans said they were opposed to trade, and 62 percent were in favor. A change of this magnitude in only three years is striking and virtually unheard of.

Because these were panelists, it is possible to examine the characteristics that predicted changing in this more positive direction on trade. Overwhelmingly, it was Republicans who changed their minds, and the more highly they rated Trump in 2016, the more likely they were to change in the pro-trade direction between 2016 and 2020. Another major predictor of becoming increasingly pro-trade is believing that competition is a powerful positive force in society. Those who see competition, the creation of winners and losers, as a benevolent force embraced Trump's new version of trade. Changing in the pro-trade direction is further predicted by being high in social dominance orientation, that is, believing that some groups should rightfully dominate other groups in society. These were precisely the same people who were against trade in 2016.

This portrait of newfound trade enthusiasm suggests that something rather fundamental has transpired. The version of trade that Republicans believed they were getting from Trump was completely different from how they thought of trade before. Instead of being taken advantage of by international trade, trade became a means to dominate other countries in a competitive international arena. That explains its newfound popularity among those who believe in competition and particularly those who believe in the appropriateness of dominating others. What was viewed previously by Republicans as a zero-sum game that we were losing, was replaced in their minds by trade as a means to dominance.[31] These results suggest that Republicans are not rallying behind trade as cooperation so much as a competitive vision of trade that allows them to use it against rival countries like China. Trump promised not only to fight trade wars; he also claimed that "winning" trade wars would be easy.

Trade Turned Inside Out

What has happened since 2016 is not simply a matter of members of the two parties flipping their respective positions on trade. The pattern of underlying attitudes supporting these preferences has also been turned inside out. In other words, the individual characteristics undergirding trade support in 2016 no longer apply as of 2020. Figure 3.7 shows some major predictors of trade support in 2016, shortly before Trump was elected, and then these same predictors again in 2020. Notably the signs of these predictors have flipped in direction, not just in the degree to which they predict supporting international trade. As shown on the far right side, in 2016, being a Democrat predicted supporting international trade, and being a Republican predicted opposing it. But by 2020, Democratic party identification said virtually nothing about one's views on trade. Social dominance negatively predicts support for international trade in 2016. This is consistent with the idea that America should rightfully dominate other countries because we are simply better, and more deserving than others, and we do not feel we

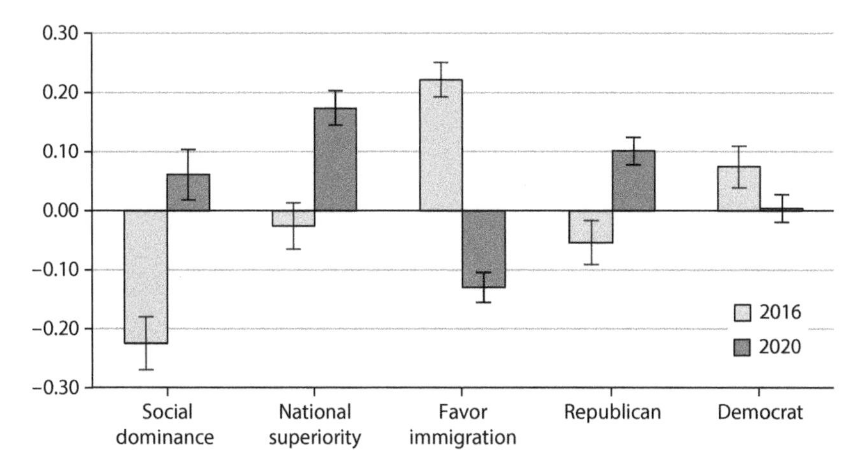

FIGURE 3.7. Major Correlates of Support for International Trade, 2016 and 2020
Source: ISCAP Panel Surveys 2016–2020 (Amerispeak/NORC).
Note: Columns show the size of the OLS regression coefficients predicting support for trade without other controls in cross-sectional analyses.

are winning this competition as we would be if the playing field were level. But surprisingly, by 2020, those high in social dominance are significantly *more* positively predisposed toward Trump's new-better-different version of trade. Finally, although my own and others' previous studies have consistently found that a sense of national superiority is a negative predictor of support for international trade in the US,[32] by 2020, those high in national superiority are significantly more pro-trade. So long as trade is seen as a competition that we are "winning," it is a good thing.

Trump's other signature campaign issue, restricting immigration, also completely flips in its relationship with trade support from 2016 to 2020. In 2016, favoring immigration and favoring trade went hand in hand, thus making Trump's anti-immigration and anti-trade positions seemingly quite consistent in opposing foreign products as well as foreign people. Both advocated turning inward and away from the rest of the world. By 2020, however, opposing immigration is significantly associated with favoring trade. In fact, every single predictor becomes significant in the opposite direction! The patterns in Figure 3.7 only make much sense if trade has shifted from being seen by Republicans as a competition that we were losing, to being viewed as a means of successfully dominating our international rivals.

To further confirm that I had the correct interpretation, I looked at respondents' perceptions of US standing in the eyes of the rest of the

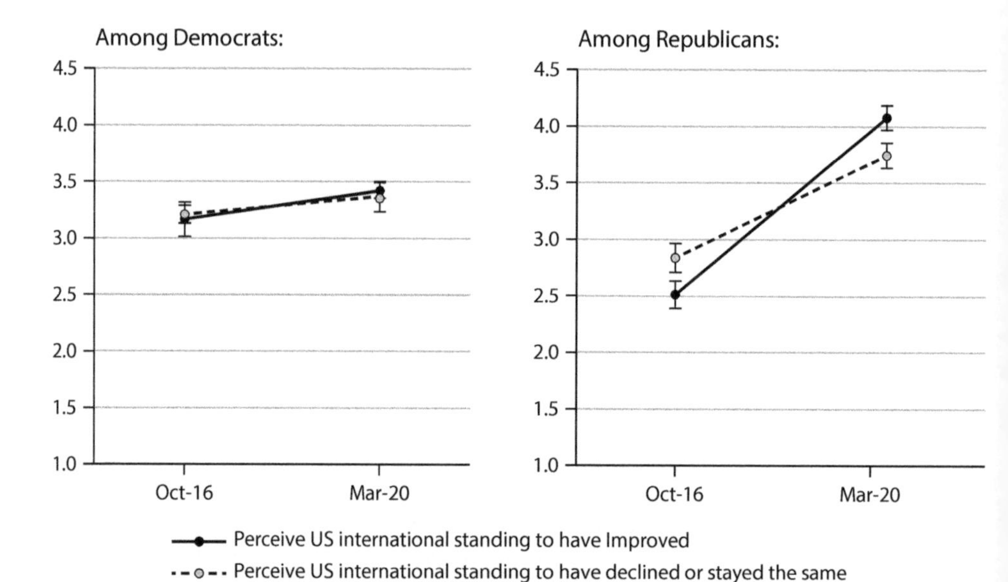

FIGURE 3.8. Over-Time Increases in Individual Support for Trade by Change in the Perceived Standing of the US in the World, by Party, 2016–2020

Note: In an analysis of change over time in Trade Support, Republican identification had its expected large impact ($F = 178.52$, $p < .001$), as did increases in Perceived US Standing ($F = 17.60$, $p < 001$). Consistent with the hypothesis that Republicans increased their support for trade because they became convinced that they were now dominating internationally, the interaction between Party and Change in US Standing was also significant ($F = 18.79$, $p < .001$).

world, and whether they thought it was better, worse, or about the same.[33] Of course, Republicans would be more likely that Democrats to say that the country's international status had been improving during the Trump presidency. But party loyalties aside, if my interpretation is correct, those Republicans who perceived greater improvement in US standing since 2016 should be disproportionately likely to have become more pro-trade. Using panelists interviewed in both 2016 and 2020, I looked at whether individual Republicans and Democrats who perceived the country's international standing to have improved from 2016 to 2020 were also more likely to change their trade preferences in a positive direction. As shown in Figure 3.8, this was indeed the case. The perceived standing of the country made no difference whatsoever to change over time in Democrats' trade preferences. But among Republicans, those who thought America was now more positively regarded internationally increased in their support for trade more than 1.7 times the amount of the increase among their fellow Republicans who did not think the US had become more respected in the world. This pattern is consistent with the trade-as-dominance interpretation.

Partisanship and Mass Opinion toward Trade

American attitudes toward trade are unusual in their lack of a consistent relationship with the major political parties. Even within as short a span as the last 20 years, the relationship between partisanship and trade has gone through two major transitions. From the 1990s through roughly 2008, Republicans and Democrats in the mass public had largely indistinguishable views on trade. After Barack Obama's election through 2016, Democrats in the mass public were consistently more favorable toward trade and globalization than were Republicans. Once Trump was elected, his followers suddenly changed their views on trade, to an extent that is rarely seen in the typically slow evolution of public opinion on policy issues.

The obvious next question is what happens in 2021, given that Democrats have taken back the White House? Based on this evidence as well as the chapters that follow, I doubt that Republican enthusiasm for trade will outlast Trump's presidency for three key reasons. First, Republicans will no longer be buoyed by their temporarily high levels of trust in government, nor by rationalized perceptions of the economy. The party-in-power effect will evaporate. When Republicans revert to baseline, it will be to much lower levels of trust in government than Democrats.

In addition, Republicans are now the less-educated political party, a characteristic that was not true twenty years ago. As discussed in Chapter 1, education is by far the strongest and most reliable predictor of support for trade, and education no longer favors Republican support since Democrats are now the better educated party. Xenophobia and negative attitudes toward racial outgroups characterize Republicans more than Democrats, as well as the less-educated more than the well educated.

Finally, it is also the case that President Trump's vision of international trade is unique in its insistence that trade is a means to dominance, a way of asserting superiority over other countries and ultimately "winning" trade wars. When trade is viewed as a competition, other countries become little more than obstacles to US success. As I describe further in the chapters that follow, this conception of trade-as-dominance appealed to Republicans in 2016 when they felt a loss of national and international status. By 2020, with their party in power, they perceived America as having a much higher status in the world. This perception was undoubtedly reassuring, but evidence suggests that it was simply untrue. America's status in the eyes of the rest of the world had declined substantially by 2020, and wishful thinking on the part of Republicans could not change this.[34] Trump's successor will have to deal with this reality.

4

How Much Is One American Worth?

Given that international trade has consequences for both the home country and for trading partner countries, for both "us" and for "them," it would be surprising if trade preferences were not driven at least in part by an individual's tendency to think in terms of ingroups and outgroups. Humans have a strong, automatic tendency to divide the world into groups of insiders and outsiders, although this tendency varies by people as well as by contexts. Trade provides yet another context in which group identities and allegiances are made salient.

Competition heightens people's tendencies to favor ingroups over outgroups.[1] When benefits to one group are perceived to go hand in hand with losses to another, ingroup favoritism intensifies.[2] Thus viewing trade as a form of international competition is likely to do the same. Trade is frequently said to be a policy that creates winners and losers when it comes to jobs. However, as noted in Chapter 1, when economists refer to trade as a practice that creates winners and losers, they are typically referring to winners and losers *within their own country*, not to an international competition.

But even if a person understands the winners and losers of trade to be people who are in different lines of work within the US, trade still poses a moral dilemma. A policy that creates "losers" of any kind is inherently a policy that harms people. Very few government policies are openly acknowledged to hurt some people in order to help a larger number of people.[3] This kind of logic is not an easy sell with the mass public. What's more, because the harm that trade causes is concentrated on a relative few, and the benefits of trade are more diffuse and difficult to observe, those who are hurt by trade tend to be more visible to the public than the many who are helped.

Scholars, as well as frequent viewers of *The Good Place*, may recognize this dilemma as similar to a trolley problem in moral philosophy. In this thought experiment, people are asked to decide between taking an action that will divert a trolley onto a different track so that it kills only one person, or to let it continue on its present course and kill five people instead. Although no one dies in the case of trade, trade clearly harms some individuals in order to generate collective benefits. A utilitarian response—diverting the trolley's course so that it harms only one person—serves the greater good by saving more lives. But it also violates moral rules about doing harm to others.

Studies of the trolley problem make it clear that people find it uncomfortable choosing actions that will hurt others, even though doing nothing may hurt more people. For example, women and those high in empathy are less likely to flip the switch and divert the train because they are more averse to doing harm to others.[4,5,6] To express support for a trade policy could seem to some like taking action to flip the switch in the trolley problem. It requires a willingness to harm some people for purposes of benefiting a larger number of people. Studies involving variations of the trolley problem show that people are even less likely to make the utilitarian choice if the many people who would be saved by flipping the switch are outgroup members, and/or the one who would be saved by doing nothing is an ingroup member.[7] Not all lives are valued equally.

When the public at large thinks about winners and losers due to trade, instead of workers within the US, they are more likely to think of it as a competitive sporting event involving the US versus a trading partner country. Further, because many Americans think of trade as a zero-sum game,[8] it seems obvious to many that if our trading partners are gaining due to trade, our own country must be losing. Although economists have tried to dispel this idea for a long time, it seems to be an intuitive understanding that ordinary people hold about trade. For example, in a recent book entitled *The Betrayal of the American Dream*, the authors advocate precisely this competitive view of international trade.[9] As they recount, a global hedge fund investor reported that

> his firm's investment committee often discusses the question of who wins and who loses in today's economy. . . . His point [the CEO explained] was that if the transformation of the world economy lifts four people in China and India out of poverty and into the middle class, and meanwhile means one American drops out of the middle class, that's not such a bad trade.[10]

Indeed, this represents a net gain of three good jobs. But, as the authors relaying this story continue, "The only problem is that no one told working Americans they were going to forfeit their future so that people in China, India, Brazil and other developing countries could become part of a global middle class"[11] There is a net gain in the collective well-being of humanity in this example, yet this is deemed undesirable because it does not produce an outcome clearly in the best interests of Americans. When trade is viewed as a competition with winners and losers, this changes the way in which people evaluate trade policies, particularly if people see their own country as on the losing end of this competition.[12]

In Chapter 2 I described how, as of 2013, roughly 50 percent of Americans perceived trade to be good for creating jobs in trading partner countries, but bad for American jobs. Interestingly, this pattern of "good for them, bad for us" was not true for other perceived impacts of trade; when it comes to the impact on the environment, the treatment of labor, consumer costs, and so forth people's perceptions of impact on the United States are, if anything, positively related to their perceived impact on trading partners. The impact of trade on jobs is an exception, but it is an extremely important exception since employment is the most salient reason for opposing trade, as shown in Chapter 2.

Jobs are a concrete entity, and they are conceived of as zero-sum in a way that trade's impact on other facets of well-being is not. When trade is seen as a form of competition over a finite and desirable resource—in this case, good jobs—then forming opinions toward trade raises a whole host of other considerations. In the case of international trade, this means valuing Americans more than people in trading partner countries.

Surveys have found trade opposition to be related to personality characteristics such as authoritarianism, that is, believing in the desirability of obedience to authority at the expense of personal freedom.[13] Trade opposition is also related to ethnocentrism, that is, the tendency to view racial and ethnic outgroups as inferior to one's own group,[14] and to a sense of national superiority.[15] What all three of these concepts share is the tendency to think in black and white, right versus wrong, us versus them terms. It is worth noting that from an economic perspective there is no obvious reason why a measure of how domestic Blacks, whites, and Hispanics feel about one another should have anything to do with their preferences for international trade. However, to the extent that ethnocentrism taps a more general tendency to favor the ingroup over the outgroup, to think of the world in us versus them terms, then it makes sense that those high in ethnocentrism should extend their outgroup animosity to people of other countries.

The fact that nationalistic sentiments are related to trade preferences is also consistent with the idea that ingroup favoritism matters. Nationalism has been operationalized in many different ways, but when tapped as a belief that American citizens are more deserving than citizens of other countries (as opposed to a sense of patriotism or pride in one's country or government), it also serves as an indicator of perceived ingroup superiority. A number of surveys have found nationalism predictive of anti-trade attitudes.[16] Moreover, to the extent that authoritarianism is closely related to ingroup-outgroup modes of thinking,[17] the significant relationship between authoritarianism and preferences for trade protectionism is also consistent with opposition due to ingroup favoritism. Unfortunately, the observational nature of most of this evidence has made it difficult to know whether people rationalize their perceptions of trade's impact based on their pre-existing views, or whether perceptions of trade's impact drive their policy views.

Some experimental evidence lends further confidence to the idea that ingroup favoritism affects trade support. For example, in one study, American respondents were told about a policy that would potentially ease trade restrictions. The company that would be positively affected by this policy was given either a culturally familiar name, "Gordon & Roberts" which was widely believed to be British, or an ambiguously foreign-sounding name, "Tuntyakore & Zideying," believed by most to be African or Asian.[18] The company's name affected people's trade preferences among prejudiced respondents. They were more likely to report protectionist views when assigned to the condition with the culturally foreign-sounding company name.

While these results are consistent with the theory that ingroup favoritism drives trade preferences, they leave open the possibility that manipulating the perceived nationality of the company reduced support for trade liberalization for other reasons. As discussed in Chapter 5, Americans are clearly more positive about trade with some countries than with others, and many factors could account for this—perceived military threat, past inter-country relations, and government ideology—to name just a few possibilities.

In another study seeking to establish that non-economic considerations influence trade attitudes,[19] "Perceived cultural threat" was primed by preceding a question about trade with questions about social and cultural threat. Although cultural threat did not have a direct effect on trade preferences, there was some evidence that it affected those with low levels of education, a core group opposed to international trade.

The principle uniting these closely-related psychological constructs (prejudice, ethnocentrism, nationalism, and authoritarianism) is the general tendency to see the world in ingroup versus outgroup, us versus them, categories. This pervasive human tendency is known to affect many political and social attitudes.[20] Some have dubbed nationalism "that potentially most destructive form of in-group bias."[21] But precisely why and under what circumstances ingroup-outgroup dynamics should affect trade preferences is not clear. After all, trade involves *products* that cross national borders, not people. Do consumers really care whether their melon was grown in California as opposed to someplace in Asia, where melons are part of their native agriculture? I will return to this question of individual consumer behavior later in the book. But suffice it to say that nationality is an important social identity for most Americans.[22] Given that even minimal, meaningless forms of social identity can provoke ingroup favoritism,[23] it should not be surprising if national identity does the same.

By systematically changing people's perceptions of how a specific trade policy will affect jobs within their own nation as well as in trading partner countries, the study I describe in this chapter makes it possible to observe the causal impact of these perceptions on support for international trade. What has been well established at this point is that trade policy attitudes are largely "sociotropic"; that is, people's policy attitudes are more strongly related to their perceptions of how trade affects the nation as a whole than how it affects their own financial situations.[24] For public opinion scholars, this pattern is not particularly surprising since policy attitudes are usually much easier for people to connect to collective, rather than individual, outcomes. In other words, I might simply have lost my job due to a reorganization at the plant where I worked or some other local event rather than due to a change in government policies. But if thousands of others like me have also lost their jobs, it is more plausible to assume that these job losses are a result of a policy change that has affected all of us.[25]

To examine the causal impact of people's perceptions of the impact of trade policies on the nation as a whole, a study executed by Eunji Kim and I embedded two experiments in a representative national survey. By systematically altering the impact a trade policy is said to have on job gains/losses in the US, and in other countries, we were able to evaluate the consequences for trade support of perceptions of trade's impact on both the home country as well as on trading partner countries.

Favoring the National Ingroup

When people view trade as a zero-sum competition for a finite number of jobs, ingroup favoritism should matter to people's trade attitudes. Further, if a trade agreement is perceived to produce job gains in one country at another country's expense, ingroup—or in this case, in-country—favoritism seems sure to play a role. To evaluate how such perceptions affect trade preferences, I randomly assigned a representative national probability sample of Americans to evaluate one of two trade policies. Respondents either read about an agreement in which the US would gain jobs while the Trading Partner loses jobs, or one in which the US would lose jobs while the Trading Partner gains them. Across conditions, I also varied precisely how many jobs were gained or lost.[26] The key difference was whether the jobs would go to citizens *within their own country* or to those *in the trading partner country.*

To alter perceptions of job gains and losses so that they were easily understood, the US and trading partner countries were described as gaining/losing jobs using round whole numbers:[27]

> For each [1/10/100/1000] [person/people in the U.S.] who lose(s) a job and can no longer provide for their family, [1/10/100/1000] [person/people] in a country that we trade with will gain [a] new job[s] and now be able to provide for their family.
>
> Would you be likely to support this trade policy or oppose this trade policy? Are you strongly supportive of/opposed to this new trade policy or somewhat supportive of/opposed to this new trade policy?

These questions were used to create a 4-point scale indicating the strength of support for this trade policy. In order to ensure that people understood these scenarios as intended, at the very end of the study, respondents were asked how many jobs the US would gain or lose from the policy and how many the trading partner countries would gain or lose. Answers to these questions confirmed that the descriptions of the trade agreements were understood as intended.[28] After reporting levels of support for the specific trade policy, a final question asked respondents what kinds of thoughts they had while evaluating the trade policy. Answers to this open-ended question were used to add further insight into the thought processes involved in evaluating trade policies. Respondents were free to describe what went through their minds in deciding whether or not the policy described should be supported or opposed.

It will surprise no one that Americans randomly assigned to the policy in which the US gains jobs while the trading partner loses them are more favorable, than those assigned to the policy in which US loses jobs while the trading partner countries gain them. In quantitative terms, the mean level of support more than doubled from the former (US gains) to the latter (Trading Partner gains) description.[29] Jobs for the ingroup country clearly mattered more than jobs for the outgroup countries.

Two additional predictions further illuminated the role of ingroup favoritism. First, if my thesis that ingroup favoritism matters is what is driving this pattern of findings, then the tendency to favor the in-country over trading partner countries should increase with people's perceived level of national superiority. In a survey that occurred three months prior to the survey-experiment, these same respondents were asked a standard three-item scale assessing national superiority, that is, the extent to which they believe their country is superior to other countries. If ingroup favoritism is the driving force behind trade opposition, then those who see their nation as better than other nations should have especially strong tendencies to favor the policy that benefits the ingroup.

This was, indeed, the case. For those assigned to the description in which the agreement benefited strictly US jobs, support rose steadily with higher levels of national superiority, as shown in Figure 4.1. For those in the condition in which the trading partner gained jobs, national superiority mattered little to their level of support for the agreement.[30] People with low levels of national superiority viewed the two experimental conditions as equally attractive. But for people with high levels of national superiority, the difference in levels of support for an agreement that benefits the home country is roughly *seven times larger* than when it benefits trading partner countries. This result confirmed the significant role of perceived national superiority in exacerbating ingroup favoritism with respect to trade preferences.

Overwhelmingly the most common reason offered for opposing trade in people's open-ended comments was, as one respondent emphatically put it, "AMERICA FIRST!!!" As another respondent commented, "I thought of

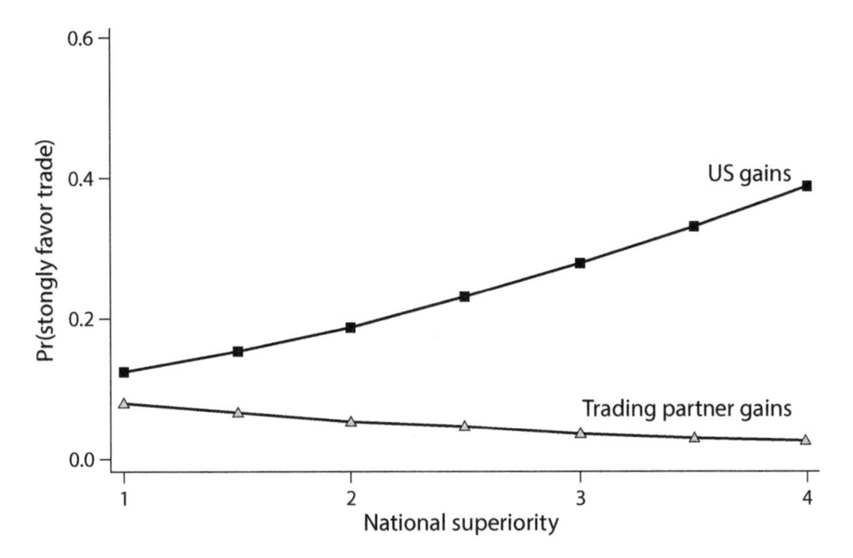

FIGURE 4.1. Change in the Probability of Strongly Favoring Trade, by Levels of Perceived National Superiority, by Experimental Condition
Source: US Trade Survey-Experiment, 2013–2014 (GfK Ltd.).
Note: The two lines with the square and triangle markers respectively represent the predicted probabilities for strongly favoring trade when interacting experimental manipulation of (1) US Gains/Trading Partner Loses and (2) Trading Partner Gains/US Loses with National Superiority. Estimates are based on Long and Freese's (2014) SPOST13 module for plotting interactions in ordered logit. The interaction grows progressively larger at higher levels of national superiority. See Mutz and Kim (2017) for details.

the U.S.A. and their loss. I could care less about the other country." Others were even more strident in their opposition to consideration of foreigners:

> *OH NO!!! The American people are getting crapped on again. We lose more and more every day, because OUR government thinks they should help everyone else in the world before they help the Americans!!! Somehow along the way we became the world saviors and they never ask US if we wanted to give our jobs and money away. If politicians want to help all of those other people so much, they should MOVE THERE and give all of their money away.*
>
> *The U.S. should worry about people in this country NOT other countries. That is why we have become a F*** up country.*

But what about those respondents who were not vehemently anti-foreigner, those who favored the ingroup without an obvious sense of national superiority? Their open-ended responses suggested that their preferences were driven by straightforward identification as American, devoid of necessarily feeling Americans are more deserving:

> *Hard situation. But I live in this country so I would choose a person from this country.*
>
> *I . . . saw in my mind's eye the foreign people that would not be working, but perhaps they will be able to get another job. Since I'm an American, I favor Americans working.*
>
> *I thought about the 1000 people who would lose their jobs. I would feel really bad for them, but I live in the United States and the United States has to take care of the United States first.*

Some respondents took great pains to indicate they were not indifferent to foreigners, but that the "natural" and appropriate priority was to put the ingroup first. As one respondent voiced this sentiment, "Although I sympathize with all people, I was thinking we need to take care of our own first, because that is most natural." Interestingly, in contrast to expressions of obvious sexism or racism, favoring people strictly because they are fellow citizens appears to be highly socially acceptable; indeed, some respondents argued that it was unpatriotic to do anything but favor their national ingroup.[31]

The design of this study made it possible to see whether there were any limitations to the precedence Americans' gave the ingroup with respect to trade. Within the experiment, the number of jobs gained and lost by each country was varied over seven different levels in order to see whether there was some number of jobs gained overseas that might make a trade agreement seem worthwhile, even without benefitting the home country. For example, for those in an experimental condition in which 1000 people in the trading partner country gained jobs, and only one American lost his or her job, surely respondents would perceive some merit in the large number of jobs gained overseas, despite the fact that they did not go to ingroup members. And surely it makes little sense to support an agreement that will result in 1000 people in a trading partner country losing jobs, if only one American gains a job as a result. In short, the full experimental design allowed me to quantify the extent to which people are ethnocentric in valuing job gains and losses, weighing them more heavily when they benefit the ingroup than the outgroup.[32]

As shown in Figure 4.2, different conditions within the experiment were assigned to different magnitudes of job gain/loss for the US and for the trading partner country. The number before the slash on the x-axis in Figure 4.2 indicates the number of *Trading Partner jobs* gained or lost, and the number

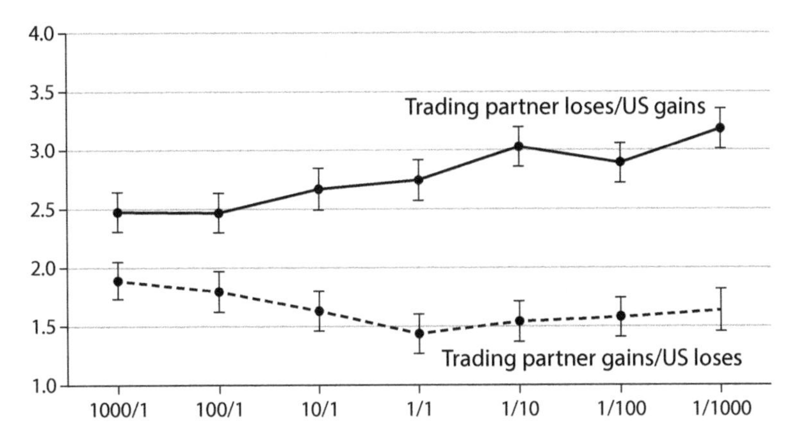

FIGURE 4.2. Support for Trade Policies When Varying How Many Jobs Are Gained/Lost by US and Trading Partners

Source: US Trade Survey-Experiment, 2013–2014 (GfK Ltd.)

Note: After reading a description of the trade policy, respondents were asked whether they would be likely to support or oppose it, and subsequently how strongly they would support/oppose the policy. Responses are on a 1 to 4 scale on which high scores mean greater support.

following the slash indicates the number of *American jobs* gained or lost in the specific trade agreement. The broken line on left side of Figure 4.2 essentially quantifies how many foreigners must benefit for a trade policy to offset the cost of one job loss at home.

On the right side, we see that as the number of total jobs gained by the US increases, so does average support for the trade policy as shown by the solid black line. But as shown by the broken line on the left, when one American loses a job, even the scenario in which 1 American loses a job and 1000 people in trading partner countries gain jobs produces low levels of support. Even with a net gain of 999 jobs, only 22 percent of Americans favored the policy, while over 78 percent opposed it.

These reactions raise the question of whether there is any level of gain to other countries that would prompt the average American to favor a trade policy that did not directly benefit the US. In fact, what is most notable about the two lines in Figure 4.2 is that they never cross or even come very close to one another on the far left. Even when 1,000 trading partner jobs are gained for only one job loss in the US, levels of support for trade do not equalize. It is, of course, possible that the lines would cross if the descriptions went to greater extremes so that one American job loss corresponded to 100,000 jobs gained elsewhere. However, as numbers get larger and less comprehensible to the average person, people generally demonstrate greater indifference to magnitude. Even though the extreme job gains or losses are 1000 times the level at the center of Figure 4.2, opinions never change even 1 point on a 4-point scale. These patterns suggest that there may be no extent of gain to trading partner countries that would justify even one American job loss in the minds of most Americans.

A few respondents nonetheless espoused less parochial thinking. As one respondent suggested, "All lives [are] equal, so while it is hard to think about the one person losing their job, you can't ignore the fact that 100 others will gain jobs." Others expressly negated the logic of ingroup favoritism and suggested more universalistic values:

> *[It's a] numbers game. Have to consciously suppress tribalism.*
> *People shouldn't be favored just because of where they live.*

Still others acknowledged helping the developing world as a positive externality. For example, one respondent indicated thinking about ". . . how much good we could do if we created 10 jobs for each 1 job here. It could help tons of the developing world." As another suggested, "I first thought of jobs gained by poor foreigners. Then I thought about jobs lost by Americans. They have more to gain than we have to lose from that trade-off, on a basic human level."

Overall, both the central role of nationalism and people's razor-sharp focus on ingroup gains in this experiment lend support to the idea that differences in levels of trade support are in part a function of variations in ethnocentric valuation, that is, the extent to which people in the ingroup are valued more than those in the outgroup. Because nations serve as highly salient group memberships, trade agreements trigger ingroup/outgroup dynamics that favor the national ingroup. And since people reliably favor ingroups over outgroups in allocating resources,[33] citizens who see their own and other nations as in competition for finite resources largely react as they do with other ingroups and outgroups, that is, with greater favoritism toward the ingroup.

Outgroup Indifference

In contrast to economists' focus on personal self-interest, or the emphasis on collective national interest documented above, psychologists often assume that social motivations trump self-interested ones. For example, when faced with social dilemmas, people often cooperate even when they have no self-interested incentive to do so.[34] Evolutionary psychology emphasizes the importance of cooperation with others as a survival skill. People generally want to alleviate others' suffering, and unemployment could certainly qualify as such; however, when those others are outgroup members, people may not be as motivated to do so.[35] Based on this logic, one would expect cooperation with outgroup members to be less common, although research suggests that people do at times include others, even those outside their ingroup, in their "scope of moral concern."[36] This perspective raises the possibility that people may take into account the effects of trade policies on those in other countries, *all else being equal.*

Of course, in the experimental comparison described above, all else was not equal. Within a single trade policy, one country's gain was coupled with another country's loss. But what if the extent of job gains to Americans were held constant, and only the gains versus losses to the trading partner country varied? This comparison would tell us about the extent to which effects on other countries are taken into account in evaluating trade agreements. So long as Americans are gaining jobs, one might assume that the competitive element would recede in the decision-making process, and benefits for trading partner countries would become just more icing on the cake of a mutually beneficial trade agreement.

While this may seem like a rational expectation, there are reasons for caution. For one thing, previous studies of decision making suggest that some "individuals or groups are perceived as outside the boundary in which moral values, rules, and considerations of fairness apply."[37] This is the definition of what is known as "moral exclusion." Moral inclusion refers to the polar opposite of ethnocentrism, that is, to incorporating all of humanity as part of one's ingroup.[38] In contrast, moral exclusion suggests that at least some people simply do not count. They are deemed undeserving or for other reasons outside the scope of one's moral concern. To the extent that effects on trading partner countries are deemed irrelevant to attitudes toward trade policies, citizens can be said to engage in moral exclusion. When trade does not produce winners and losers and instead benefits all to varying degrees, moral exclusion suggests that people will be indifferent to the positive effects on others in evaluating the desirability of a policy. Instead they will rely exclusively on how much their own country benefits. Comparing reactions to a trade scenario in which both countries gain, to levels of support for a policy in which the home country gains the same amount, but the trading partner loses jobs, allows us to quantify the extent of moral exclusion.

This first comparison produced a somewhat startling null result. Even when the United States consistently benefits from a trade agreement and

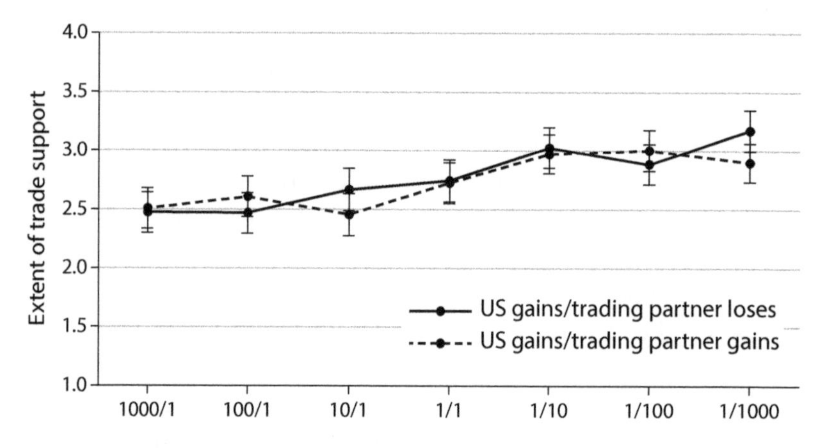

FIGURE 4.3. Effects of Trading Partner Gains/Losses on Support for Trade Policy, Holding US Gains Constant

Source: US Trade Survey-Experiment, 2013–2014 (GfK Ltd.)

Note: No significant differences were found between groups in which the Trading Partner lost versus gained jobs. However, there was a significant interaction between the Magnitude of job gains/losses and Experimental condition ($F = 15.13$, $p < .001$).

gains jobs, it appears to make no difference whatsoever how it affects the trading partner. The mean level of support for the policy that was "win-win" was identical to support for the policy that benefited the US and harmed jobs in the trading partner country. Although support increased to some degree as a greater number of American jobs were created, the lines shown in Figure 4.3 are statistically indistinguishable. Regardless of how much the US is benefitting, respondents were on the whole unmoved by the extent of any positive or negative effects on trading partner countries. This is a textbook example of indifference to outgroup members. On average, it simply did not matter to this representative sample of Americans what the effects of a trade policy were for their trading partners.

The Desire to Dominate

Beyond benign neglect, another well-documented intergroup dynamic centers on consideration of the *relative* gains acquired by the ingroup compared to an outgroup.[39] In this case, people may reject even mutually beneficial policies that do not benefit their home country *more than* the trading partner country. For those considering relative gains, even a "win-win" trade scenario in which both countries gain jobs is not enough reason to support a trade policy. Instead, trade is seen as valuable only to the extent that it gives one's own country the upper hand. In other words, what is important is who "wins" by scoring more advantages from a trade deal than the other country. Thus, the desire to compete and win—not to tie or participate in "friendlies" as they are known in soccer parlance—drives citizens to evaluate trade agreements differently.

A person's goal in this case is not just to reap benefits for the home country so much as to gain a greater advantage over the trading partner country. In other words, one wants the home country to dominate other countries to a greater degree. In some situations, intergroup competition even prompts people to *disadvantage* their own ingroup in order to maximize their advantage. This tendency has been dubbed "Vladimir's Choice," by Sidanius and colleagues,[40] based on an Eastern European folk tale in which a peasant is told by God that he can be granted any wish he wants under the condition that whatever he is given, his neighbor Ivan will be given twice over. Vladimir cleverly decides to request that God take out one of his eyes. As irrational as this choice may seem from the perspective of self-interest, it accomplishes the end that Vladimir sought: to ensure that he was better off than his neighbor, who would lose both eyes. A surprisingly consistent line of research[41] shows that some people make choices in line with this logic "even when doing so clearly *minimizes* absolute ingroup gains."[42]

Vladimir's choice is unlikely to characterize the majority of Americans, but the likelihood of exhibiting preferences based on this logic is known to increase with higher levels of perceived intergroup competition and with higher levels of social dominance orientation, that is, the tendency to value hierarchy over equality.[43] Because inter-country competition is frequently referenced in the context of international trade, I expected to see this pattern of ingroup favoritism primarily among those who view trade in more competitive, zero-sum terms.

The first wave of this survey, three months before the survey-experiment, included questions that allowed me to identify the 50 percent of Americans who reported both that trade hurt the availability of jobs in the US and that it increased employment opportunities in trading partner countries. In addition, the survey included pre-experiment measures of social dominance orientation. As Sidanius and colleagues suggest,[44] "The greater one's desire to maintain and establish group-based social hierarchy, the more likely one should be to endorse the relative advantage of dominant groups over subordinate groups."[45] Americans high in social dominance orientation and/or those already prone to see trade in competitive terms based on jobs gains and losses should be more likely to oppose trade, even when the U.S. benefits, if they perceive that the trading partner country *also* benefits, thereby canceling out their *relative* advantage.

To examine whether relative advantage is being considered, I compared the same two experimental conditions, one in which the US gains jobs while the Trading Partner loses jobs, and one in which the US gains jobs *and* the Trading Partner also gains jobs, but this time focusing on subgroups most likely to feel threatened if they are not "winning" the trade competition by gaining a relative advantage. This is most likely to occur among those who view trade's impact on jobs in competitive, zero-sum terms, and among those high in social dominance orientation, that is, those who believe some groups should rightly dominate others. In discussions of trade, tremendous concern is often expressed about who is getting the "better" deal, a fundamentally different question from whether each is getting a good deal or a fair deal. But if one's goal is to dominate another country, then a win-win trade agreement is not necessarily a selling point. Why settle for a tie rather than a win?

Thus far my findings have suggested benign neglect; that is, Americans put themselves first over other countries, and they appear not to care much about how trading partner countries are affected by trade policies. But the results in Figure 4.4 paint a much bleaker picture. When examining those groups known to be most susceptible to the pull of competition, that is, those high in social dominance orientation, and those who perceive trade to have zero-sum consequences, a trade policy is significantly *less* attractive when both the US and its trading partners benefit. For those high in social dominance, a trade policy is significantly *more* attractive when trading partner countries are hurt rather than helped, holding US job benefits constant. As shown in the left panel of Figure 4.4, *Social Dominance Orientation* interacts with whether the trading partner country also gains. Consistent with the desire to maintain group hierarchy, those with high levels of social dominance respond to the *relative* advantage of the US over others rather than to how much the ingroup gains.

Likewise, on the right-hand side of Figure 4.4, there is a similar interaction based on whether the respondent perceived trade's impact on jobs to be zero-sum in the pre-experiment survey. For the 50 percent of Americans who believe that when trade helps jobs in one country, it must hurt jobs in another, the trade policy described as helping the US and hurting trading partner countries is significantly more attractive than the policy that helps both the US and trading partner countries. Far from worrying about the exploitation of other countries through trade, many Americans support

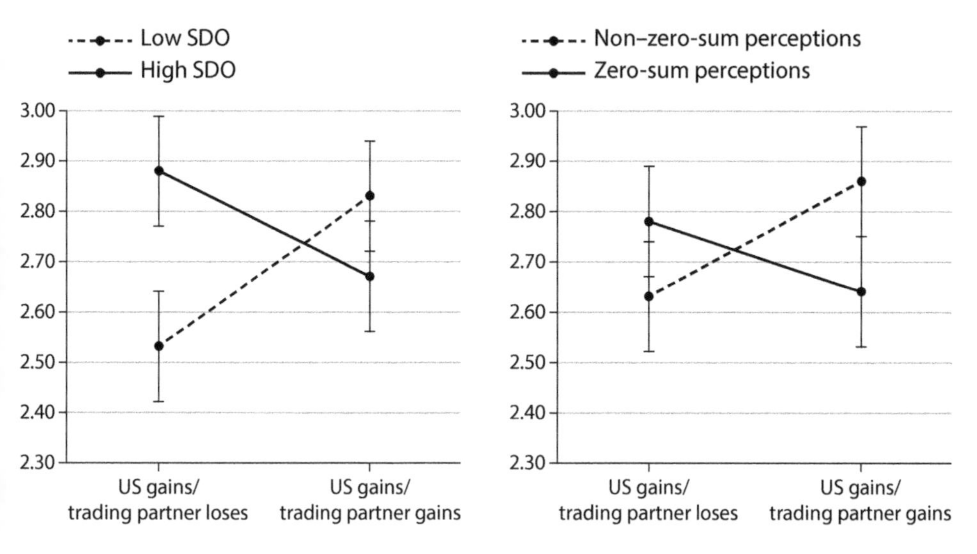

FIGURE 4.4. Preference for Relative Gains Among Those High in Social Dominance and Those Perceiving Trade as Zero-Sum

Source: US Trade Survey-Experiment, 2013–2014 (GfK Ltd.)

Note: The left panel shows a statistically significant interaction between Social Dominance Orientation and whether the trading partner country gains. ($F = 17.84$, $p < .001$). For those who are high in Social Dominance Orientation, trade is less attractive when the trading partner country also benefits. The right panel shows a similar interaction ($F = 9.17$, $p < .01$), in which respondents who perceive trade as zero-sum in the pre-experiment survey support trade more when the trading partner loses. See Mutz and Kim (2017), Appendix C, Table 2, for full model results.

trade *more* when it increases the relative advantage America has over its trading partner countries.

It is natural to wonder whether the two interactions shown in Figure 4.4 are basically the same phenomenon involving the same people. The weak negative correlation between social dominance and zero-sum perceptions of trade suggests this is not the case.[46] Both groups—those high in social dominance and those who perceive trade as zero-sum—tend to be conservative, white, and Republican. But zero-sum perceptions are more likely to be held by older people, the well-educated, and those with high incomes. In contrast, poorly educated men are higher in social dominance.

To see whether both groups add independently to ingroup favoritism, I combined these two analyses to evaluate the size of their respective contributions when considered simultaneously. The results confirmed that these are not redundant effects.[47] Both interactions retain their significant negative impact on trade preferences indicating that they are more likely to oppose trade if it does not explicitly advantage their country relative to trading partner countries. But those high in social dominance are especially strongly opposed to trade if it benefits the outgroup as well as the ingroup, with a much larger difference in support among those low versus high in social dominance than among those who do or do not perceive trade to be zero-sum.

To see if respondents' open-ended explanations for their choices were consistent with my own narrative, I had coders categorize the open-ended comments given by respondents into two groups: 1) those offering justifications for favoring the ingroup (e.g., "We should care about our people first, not another country's people") and/or comments denigrating the outgroup (e.g., "Frankly the rest of the world is uncivilized. Jobs matter more to us than to them."); and 2) those suggesting justifications for favoring the outgroup and/or denigrating the ingroup (e.g., "100 people with jobs is better for the world than one American. At the end of the day, humanity, not nationality, is what matters.").

The types of comments that people offered varied considerably by experimental condition. Reactions of any kind were more likely when people were randomly assigned to the scenario in which the US Loses and the Trading Partner gains. This scenario set people off. This experimental condition also produced significantly more comments arguing that the national ingroup was more worthy relative to the outgroup. In contrast, the scenario in which both countries gained from trade produced the highest percentage of respondents who volunteered outgroup-favoring comments, and the fewest ingroup-favoring comments. In short, when trade was framed as a competition, it prompted significantly more evidence of threat, coupled with outgroup vilification and bolstering of the ingroup's value.

The findings from these survey experiments demonstrate the allure of the America First agenda. Although these data were gathered in 2013—long before Donald Trump's ascendance—putting American interests above those of all other nationalities was already a prominent theme and a popular reason for opposing trade policies. Even when a trade policy obviously benefitted employment elsewhere, most would not support it unless it benefitted the US in particular. Further, when gains to the US were held constant, the extent to which a trade policy helped or hurt trading partner countries was not taken into consideration. This overall pattern conceals the fact that some Americans are significantly *more* likely to support a trade agreement that benefits both the US and other countries, whereas others are significantly *less* likely to do so. In particular, those who see as appropriate hierarchies in which some groups dominate others are also more likely to demand that trade agreements benefit the US more than they benefit other countries.

Partisan Patterns of Trade Support

These experimental results also shed further light on how party identification is related to trade preferences in the United States. As illustrated in Figure 4.5, both of our experimental comparisons produced significant interactions with partisanship. Republicans and Democrats reacted quite differently to the experimental trade scenarios. As shown at the top of Figure 4.5, Republicans demonstrated significantly stronger evidence of ingroup favoritism than Democrats. Both groups favor the agreement in which the US gains and the trading partner countries lose over the reverse. But the difference in their responses to the two conditions is far greater among Republicans than Democrats. Putting the ingroup first is clearly more motivating to Republicans. When holding the net gain in jobs due to trade constant, Republicans are more favorable toward the agreement that benefits Americans only, and less favorable toward the policy that benefits only trading partner countries.

The right side of Figure 4.5 illustrates the extent of outgroup indifference by partisanship. Recall that within the population as a whole, there is no difference between levels of support for a trade agreement that benefits both the US and trading partner countries, and one that benefits strictly the United States. But across political parties, the pattern of preferences is clearly different. In the comparison between *U.S. Gains/Trading Partner Loses* and *U.S. Gains/Trading Partner Gains* conditions, Democrats are more supportive of the latter, win-win scenario than the agreement in which the US gains jobs but the trading partner does not. Republicans, on the other hand, go beyond sheer indifference to how the trading partner fares. As shown in Figure 4.5, Republicans are *more* supportive of a trade agreement in which the US gains jobs and the Trading Partner countries lose them. In other words, Republicans care about dominating; they prefer an agreement that gives them a leg up on their trading partner—a relative advantage—more than they care about absolute gains. Given that the relationship between party identification and trade support depends not only on whether a given partisan generally favors trade and expects his or her country to benefit from it, but also on whether he or she believes their country will gain a relative advantage, it is no wonder that findings are inconsistent with respect to the direction of partisanship's influence; it depends who people think is winning this "competition." These experimental results also lend additional support to the interpretation of partisan trends discussed in Chapter 3. Trade-as-dominance is favored by Republicans, whereas trade-as-cooperation and trade-as-aid are favored more by Democrats.

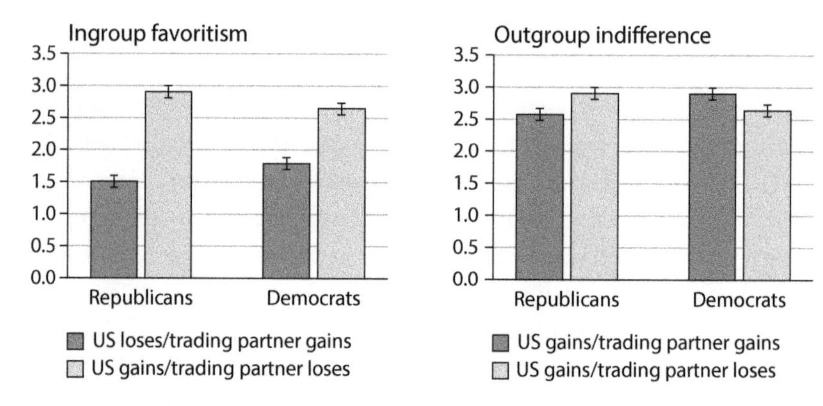

FIGURE 4.5. Ingroup Favoritism and Outgroup Indifference by Partisanship
Source: US Trade Survey-Experiment, 2013–2014 (GfK Ltd.).
Ingroup Favoritism:
Note: In addition to the large and significant main effect of experimental condition ($F = 572.21$, $p < .001$), the interaction between experimental condition and partisanship was also significant ($F = 33.42$, $p < .001$).
Outgroup Indifference:
Note: The experimental treatment had no main effect on levels of support for the trade policy, but the treatment interacted with partisanship ($F = 37.86$, $p < .001$).

These partisan differences also parallel how men and women differ in their trade views, as illustrated in Figures A4.2 and A4.3 in the online appendix. Men produce basically the same pattern of results as Republicans, demonstrating greater ingroup favoritism than women, and favoring relative advantage over the win-win trade scenario. In contrast to observational findings, women favor international trade as much as men do, so long as they perceive the agreement to benefit both countries. But when a trade agreement is instead seen as a competition involving winners and losers, women find it significantly less attractive than men. Surveys often suggest that women are more opposed to trade than men are, but that is only the case when trade is seen as a competition.[48]

Implications for Real-World Trade Support

These experimental results have revealed how people are likely to react to a policy given explicit knowledge about its effects on jobs. Since the same representative sample used in these experiments was also interviewed three months in advance of being presented with these randomly-assigned trade agreements, we also know what Americans, as of 2013, were likely to say about the extent to which trade helped and hurt jobs in their own country and trading partner countries. In the pre-experiment survey, respondents could say that trade helped, hurt, or had no effect on employment in the US. They were asked the same question about its effects on trading partner countries. The percentage of Americans perceiving trade to be a "win-win" scenario was a mere 11 percent. Roughly 7 percent viewed it as hurting employment in *both* the US and trading partner countries, which again leaves one wondering how they explain the fact that any nation would want to take part. The proportion that viewed it as exploitative of trading partner countries (helping the US, but hurting *others*) was under 1 percent.

In stark contrast to these tiny percentages, fully 50 percent of the national sample said that international trade *helped* trading partner countries and *hurt* the US.[49] Indeed, as mentioned in Chapter 2, these two perceptions were *negatively* correlated; the more a person perceived trade to be a negative influence on job availability within the US, the more he or she perceived it to benefit jobs in trading partner countries. Given that most Americans at that time believed trade hurt the US and benefitted trading partner countries, the effects of ingroup favoritism on trade preferences observed in this experiment are likely to be common. Further, given that half of Americans viewed trade through the lens of intergroup competition long before any experimental treatment, still more may oppose trade even if they perceive it as benefitting the US, if only because it does not increase their *relative* advantage over other countries.

Consistent with the scenarios we described to respondents, the versions in which the agreement was said to result in American job gains were, indeed, perceived to produce more job gains for Americans, as indicated by the experiment's manipulation checks. But interestingly, those US gains were perceived to be significantly greater when subjects were told that the other country *lost jobs* relative to when the other country also gained jobs. In other words, in the real world, sociotropic perceptions of gain and loss for the in-country are also shaped by how trade is perceived to affect its trading partner countries. Ironically, the seemingly ideal "gain-gain" scenario is likely to make people feel as if their home country has gained fewer jobs. Perhaps most obviously, these experimental results confirm that perceptions of how trade affects the home country as a whole do, indeed, have a large and important causal impact on trade preferences. By systematically manipulating perceptions of a trade policy's effects on the US, we confirmed that sociotropic perceptions influence support for trade policies.

Some have suggested that the judgment suggested by these results is overly harsh. Americans could simply view it as their duty to support policies that favor the ingroup. Some see such a duty even when they judge the consequences of favoring the home country to be less desirable.[50] Normative political theorists have argued that citizens may reasonably be said to have special duties to their co-nationals; however, discriminating against out-country members in situations that are mutually beneficial is not considered an acceptable form of partiality toward compatriots, nor is exploiting an outgroup.[51]

National groups are often large, amorphous, impersonal, and diverse, all characteristics that reduce people's willingness to consider themselves members of a mutual ingroup.[52] In a country as diverse as the US, people often demonstrate very little enthusiasm for helping other compatriots unless they can personally select *which* particular members benefit, as is the case with charitable giving or volunteering.[53] But one must wonder, if Americans oppose trade policies out of a sense of duty to care for their compatriots whom they perceive to be hurt by trade, then why is there so little evidence of a sense of duty when it comes to helping compatriots in need via social welfare policies?[54] Instead, Americans with high levels of national attachment tend to oppose social welfare and to favor more restrictive definitions of who should count as an American.[55] A sense of duty to the nation tends to characterize racially homogeneous more than heterogeneous societies.[56]

Unlike most forms of ingroup favoritism, favoring the national ingroup is viewed as socially acceptable and even socially desirable in contemporary America. In informal conversations, I have noticed that some of my neighbors tend to equate opposition to trade deals with supporting the home country's troops in times of war, just as Kevin Watje did in Chapter 1. Of course, any decent American should do so! Whereas relatively few people proudly announce that they are racist or sexist, feeling that one's own nation is superior to others does not have the same negative, socially undesirable cast. In the case of trade policy opinions, the consequences of linking love of country to trade opposition is to "naturalize" this form of ingroup favoritism in the same way that other ingroup biases were made to seem inevitable and natural in the past. While it may be more defensible to favor the people in one's own country than it is to favor people of a particular race or gender, as more and more serious problems require international cooperation, this too may change.

In addition to in-country favoritism, these results also illustrated *out-country indifference*. Levels of support for trade are, on average, identical whether the trading partner country benefits or not. However, this aggregate pattern conceals two contravening patterns that underlie trade opinions. While some Americans genuinely care about the nature of trade's effects on trading partner countries and demonstrate cooperation that benefits the *out-country,* others are significantly *more* supportive of policies that hurt the out-country, holding constant the benefits to the US. In this latter case, they are basing their views on the gains the US receives relative to other countries. They favor agreements only so long as the US "wins" this competition. In other words, what appears to be out-country indifference is more accurately described as a heterogeneous combination of relative gains considerations among some citizens, and cooperation favoring the out-country in others. When framed in terms of the standard theories of international relations, one would say that economists are liberal institutionalists who view the world in terms of the gains that can be obtained from mutual cooperation.[57] The mass public's understanding of trade, on the other hand, tends more toward a competitive, zero-sum, realist framework.

In considering the usefulness of theories of ingroup favoritism for purposes of understanding trade preferences, it is worth pondering where people's norms come from about when and under what conditions it is morally appropriate to favor the ingroup. Should Americans—or the citizens of any nation for that matter—weigh the consequences for all people's lives equally? An answer to this question is beyond the scope of this chapter, but it is worth taking stock of where norms for *favoring* the ingroup come from as well as from where norms *against* favoring the ingroup emanate. There is normative pressure to favor ingroup members, but there is also normative pressure to treat people fairly and equally, that is, a social norm of non-discrimination. Experimental research suggests that social norms encouraging ingroup favoritism come from ingroup members themselves; following these norms makes a person better accepted by the ingroup.[58] But norms that prohibit discrimination based on people's social categories tend to come from supraordinate, external entities outside the intergroup framework. In the international context, human rights organizations, institutions of higher learning,[59] and international organizations[60] have all promoted the norm of equal treatment.

In shaping views of trade, the ideology of fairness thus constrains forces that promote ingroup favoritism.[61] In this respect, it is somewhat surprising that when fairness comes up, the main concern being voiced is overwhelmingly that *American workers* are not getting their fair share of the benefits of trade. The "fair trade" movement was borne of concerns that *workers in developing countries* were not being paid adequate wages or being given adequate working conditions. So while norms of fairness may be alive and well, along with norms promoting ingroup favoritism, the way in which these norms affect judgments about trade depends entirely on which group one believes to be benefitting more or less than the other.

5

Trade with Whom?

Why do Americans favor trade agreements with some countries more than others? Given the lack of nuance in trade opinions noted in Chapter 2, combined with people's low levels of information, how are average citizens differentiating between the desirability of trading with one country versus another? Americans are far more positive toward trading with Canada, for example, than trading with Mexico. While this fact may seem unsurprising, how exactly do we explain it?

Traditional economic rationales for these differences would require that members of the public know about the gains and/or losses they would personally expect from a specific trade relationship. Supposing people's opinions are instead sociotropic, that is, based on their perceptions of the impact these agreements would have on the country as a whole, it would still be quite difficult for them to base their opinions on expected economic gains or losses. They would need simultaneously to consider jobs lost due to import competition, jobs gained due to larger export markets, changes in the costs of consumer goods, the cost of potential interruptions to the supply chain, potential retaliation from other countries in the form of new tariffs, and so forth. It is extremely difficult to assess how one's immediate community or the nation as a whole is influenced by trade with one country versus another.

Despite the obvious difficulty of forming these assessments on an economic basis, it is clear that Americans' opinions vary a great deal based on which trading partner is involved. For example, when the Pew Research Global Attitudes Project asked Americans in 2014 about their support for increasing trade with various countries, a full 80 percent of Americans thought it would be a good or a very good idea to increase trade with the European Union. Only 58 percent thought increasing trade with China was a good or very good idea. "Trade with whom?" is clearly a relevant consideration.

Predicting Actual Trade Flows

Classic economic theory claims that the dissimilarity of preferences, technologies, and the talents of workers across countries is the reason that international trade makes sense.[1] From an economic standpoint, the volume of trade should be greater if countries' economies are more different from one another. In actual practice, however, this is not how it works.

Economists have a standard model for predicting the extent of actual trade flows between countries. Known as the "gravity model,"[2] by analogy to Newton's law of gravitation, the model is a very simple equation suggesting that the amount of trade between any two countries will be a function of two characteristics of the countries. First, trade flows will be proportional to the size of their economies, as measured by gross domestic product (GDP). Second, trade flows will be inversely proportional to the geographic distance between the two countries. The negative impact of distance on trade flows is intended to take into account trade costs that increase with distance, such as transportation.

Later versions of this model attempted to incorporate other characteristics of countries that appear to increase trade flows, such as whether or not the countries share a border, have a common language, a common currency, or similar legal systems. Shorter distances between countries, common borders, and common languages all have positive effects on the extent of trade, purportedly because they lower the costs of doing business internationally.

In actual practice, factors beyond spatial distance appear to matter in predicting trade flows between countries. Most importantly, the extent of similarity between countries appears to matter a great deal. For example, democracies cooperate more with one another than with non-democratic governments.[3] Democracies are more likely to trade with other democracies,[4] but there is also more trade between countries with cultural and language similarities.[5] Language similarities may play an especially important role for practical reasons; people make deals with others whom they can understand easily.[6] Further, cultural commonality may make it easier and more efficient for people with the same language to trust and communicate with each other. Beyond similarities in type of government, culture, and language, countries with similar per capita incomes are more likely to engage in trade with one another.[7] Americans tend to think of trade as involving large, economically powerful countries trading with poor, less developed countries. But in reality, developed countries trade more with other developed countries, and less developed countries are more likely to trade with other less developed countries.

For a few dimensions of similarity, the fact that trade flows are inversely proportional to distance makes good economic sense. For example, if transportation costs negatively affect the efficiency of trade,[8] or if the costs of creating new contacts overseas increases with distance,[9] then it becomes difficult to disentangle economic and psychological reasons for favoring trade with some countries but not others.

The gravity model has been somewhat successful in explaining trade flows. But in the contemporary economy, distance only makes sense as a negative economic influence on trade for certain kinds of goods, and even less so for services. As transportation and communication technologies have improved over time, it has become less clear precisely what distance represents in this equation.

Whatever its appropriate interpretation may be, if one views these factors as costs in the monetary sense, then the gravity model merely predicts economic rationality in trade flows. Although the model successfully predicts trade flows to some extent, it seems safe to say that average Americans are unlikely to be formally or implicitly drawing on the gravity model or calculating costs and benefits. Given that roughly two-thirds of Americans do not own passports and have never left the country,[10] their direct personal experience with the larger international world is limited, and their abstract economic knowledge of these countries is more limited still. Nonetheless, they know they favor trade with some countries more than with others. How? Some guidance is provided by studies of international business and consumer attitudes. Ultimately, however, basic human psychology provides the most probable explanation.

Human beings think differently about places and people that are near and far. When the mass public thinks about distant countries, it invokes many of the same considerations that appear to successfully augment the gravity model. For example, the thought processes surrounding near and distant objects involve different sensory systems and representational systems[11] and possibly even different parts of the brain.[12] Because different forms of distance—social distance, temporal distance, and spatial distance—are tightly linked in the human brain,[13] altering one dimension of distance–such as how far away something is—changes the other dimensions of distance as well. It is no accident that psychologists use the spatial distance between people as an implicit measure of emotional closeness; we naturally expect people with mutually positive feelings to be physically closer to one another.

Forming abstract mental images of distant people and countries involves the ability to mentally construe things that one cannot directly observe. Because human brains have a tendency to link physical distance to psychological distance, proximity is tied to the perceived similarity between countries and to greater perceptions of trustworthiness. In the gravity model, distance is supposed to represent the actual monetary costs of doing business internationally. However, in practice, just as actual distance and psychological distance are difficult to disentangle, so are psychological and economic costs. For example, doing business across languages may have real costs associated with translation, but it also makes people in the other country seem more psychologically distant and less trustworthy when they do not speak the same language.

Psychic Closeness in International Business

According to research on international business, when companies first begin the process of "internationalization," that is, of engaging in overseas commerce, they tend to do so in countries that seem "psychically" close to their own.[14] The concept of psychic distance is meant to account for factors beyond physical distance and economic barriers, and it has been defined as "factors preventing or disturbing the flow of information between potential or actual suppliers and customers."[15] Theoretically, it is supposed to represent the perceived reduction of uncertainty; in actual practice, it is rooted in similarities between countries. Psychic distance and cultural distance are used as synonyms to refer to similar levels of economic development, similar education levels, and a shared language. Firms tend to follow a predictable process when internationalizing, starting with the most culturally similar markets, then over time entering more psychically distant markets. Precisely why this is the usual pattern is less clear, although it may have psychological as well as economic underpinnings; similar countries may just seem easier to work with, but they may also require fewer accommodations, thus saving the business money.

The "psychic paradox" refers to the fact that while psychic distance predicts where firms may venture internationally, it does not take not take into account the performance of firms in new markets. Failure rates can be higher when perceived similarities lead companies to underestimate differences in how business is done in various countries. Superficial similarities do not necessarily increase the probability of success: "The similarity perceived to exist when entering psychically close countries does not necessarily reduce the level of uncertainty faced, nor make it easier to learn about the country. . . . Whereas the implicit assumption of the model is that similarity is easier, our results show that similarity may hide unexpected and unforeseen barriers to successful entry and performance."[16]

Ethnocentric Consumer Preferences

Although actual trade flows are not necessarily indicative of mass public opinion, consumer preferences come closer to helping us understand public attitudes toward foreign countries. Country-of-origin research directly assesses the attitudes of members of the public toward products from one country versus another. These views are not the same as people's attitudes toward trade with the country per se, but these preferences shed light on why the public favors trade with some countries more than others. First and foremost, country-of-origin studies have shown that consumers evaluate products made in their own countries systematically more favorably than products made elsewhere.[17] Moreover, country-of-origin studies demonstrate a strong preference for products made in culturally similar countries.[18] American consumers with a strong sense of national superiority are especially likely to favor products from countries perceived to be similar to their own.[19] Subjective barriers such as lack of trust in the country of origin account for limited foreign purchases more than objective barriers.[20]

These appear to be expressive, symbolic choices more than decisions rooted in economics. For example, in 2003, when the US and France disagreed over whether to invade Iraq, there were calls to boycott French products in the US. Even the US House of Representatives cafeteria temporarily renamed its french fries and french toast, "freedom fries" and "freedom toast."[21] An analysis of supermarket products during this period demonstrated that sales decreased for products with French-sounding names—for example, Tresemmé shampoo, Raison D'Être beer, and other French-sounding products—even though these were American-made products.[22] Apparently neither members of Congress nor consumers are particularly adept at identifying foreign products: after all, french fries come from Belgium, not France. Nonetheless, consumer avoidance of foreign-sounding products is well documented.[23] When current events make international adversaries salient, sales go down even though the product itself remains the same. This same tendency also accounts for conservative reluctance to drink lattes, an Italian beverage, even though the additional milk in these beverages is a boon to the US dairy industry.[24]

The Psychology of Similarity

Similarity is a highly plausible shortcut for forming opinions on potential trading partners. It works not only for individuals trading sandwiches, but also for countries trading goods and services. In interpersonal relations, perceived similarity is important psychologically because it serves as the basis for judgments about whether another person can be trusted. People form these judgments quickly and easily based on intuition, whereas utility-maximizing judgments involve slow and deliberate processes,[25] thus making them less plausible among the mass public. At times, the psychological benefits of a similar trade partner and the economic benefits of a similar partner converge, thus making it difficult establish which consideration is driving preferences. However, what we know about the mass public's economic knowledge favors the idea that similarity is what matters.

If the same principle applies to reasoning about potential trade partners, people will likewise prefer trading with countries they perceive to be more similar, perhaps even more than with trading partner countries that maximize the home country's monetary gains. For example, in a study asking how warm or cold Americans felt toward specific foreign countries, Americans' liking of the other country predicted actual trade flows beyond what could be explained by standard economic models.[26] The effect appears to be substantial; a one standard deviation increase in warmth toward a country was associated with a 20 to 31 percent larger US trade volume with that country. How warm Americans feel toward specific foreign countries is, in turn, influenced by levels of religious and ethnic similarity, the extent to which the country is perceived to be democratic, enjoy a similar per capita income, and have a common language. Physical distance and genetic distance are also negatively related to holding warm feelings toward a country, consistent with the idea that distance, dissimilarity, and distrust all go hand in hand.

Outside the context of international trade, decisions about with whom to cooperate are known to be heavily influenced by similarity. People generally comply with the requests of those they like and trust,[27] and they tend to like and trust those who are similar.[28] Similarity has extremely reliable effects, especially when we are deciding whether to trust strangers. Without information, people use similarity as a substitute on which to base their judgments.[29] Even when the particular dimension of similarity is incidental and devoid of meaningful content, its effects are still pervasive. For example, similarity in nonverbal cues (i.e., posture, mood, and verbal style) increases compliance with requests.[30] Similarity is a shortcut that facilitates quick decisions, even when the dimension of similarity is entirely superficial.[31]

Few studies have focused specifically on the role of similarity in mass trade preferences, with the exception of whether the country is also a democracy. In one experiment based on a convenience sample of Americans, people were 9 percent more likely to support a trade agreement with a democratic government compared to a non-democracy.[32] More generally, evidence supports the claim that similarity leads to greater trust. Less trust between two countries' populations leads to less trade between them[33] as well as less inward foreign direct investment,[34] even after taking into account economic similarities between countries. Perhaps even more convincing, it is not the characteristics of the country being evaluated as a potential trading partner that matter, it is the *match* between the two countries that is important. Countries with religious and linguistic commonalities are more likely to want to trade with one another, and so are those with lesser genetic distance between their two populations. Even seemingly peripheral similarities matter, such as the frequency of specific traits in the population including hair color and height.

As disconcerting as it may be, it is clear from psychological research that "People trust people who look more like them."[35] Facial resemblance enhances trust. For example, when experimental subjects were motivated to choose trustworthy partners, and they had a choice between someone whose picture (unbeknownst to them) had been digitally morphed with their own photo, or instead was morphed with an unknown person, they were more likely to choose the facially similar photo. When the potential partner had a face that resembled the subject's own face, he or she trusted that person more in two-person sequential trust games, whereas control subjects with identical picture sets did not show the same preferences.[36]

While some commonalities may result in more trade between similar countries due to lower transaction costs, for other factors it is difficult to make an economic argument. Why should religious similarities matter to whether two countries engage in economic transactions with one another? And why should blonde countries prefer trading with other blonde countries? A simpler, more straightforward interpretation of these findings is that people want to trade with those whom they trust, and they tend to trust those who are similar, regardless of whether those others are individuals or countries, and regardless of whether the similar characteristics have anything to do with their likelihood of economic success. In other words, as outlined in Chapter 1, people use the same shortcuts in deciding whom to trust in interpersonal settings as they do in international ones.

Social trust, that is, the generalized sense that other people are typically trustworthy, also predicts support for international trade. Two studies thus far have suggested that high levels of social trust and support for international trade are related, but results often make it difficult to tell whether social trust plays a causal role in encouraging favorable attitudes toward trade.[37,38]

Does Perceived Similarity Drive Country-Specific Trade Attitudes?

Are people systematically more favorable toward trade with countries perceived to be similar to their own? Studies of actual trade flows, international business practices, consumer preferences, and human psychology all point in this general direction. While Americans have been asked about their attitudes toward trade with a series of specific countries before, it is not as easy as it sounds to infer from those preferences what they are using as the basis for their decisions. The problem with asking about country after country individually and comparing people's responses is that although we can show that they are more favorable toward trading with one country than another, many country characteristics are so highly correlated with one another that the results are difficult to interpret. For example, China could be viewed as a less desirable trading partner than Canada because it is not a democracy, or perhaps because it is seen as a military threat to the United States.

In addition, the direction of influence is not always clear. Does income similarity with another country lead to greater trade, or does greater trade lead to greater income similarity? Reverse causation would happen only very slowly over time, but it is still plausible. The histories of US relationships with countries likewise makes it difficult to sort out what accounts for the greater or lesser favorability. Specific countries inevitably come with a lot of baggage.

These problems make this research question ripe for an experimental study that can disentangle specific country characteristics as well as establish the direction of causation. Toward that end, a representative national sample of 2,500 Americans was interviewed online in the summer of 2015. After answering a preliminary series of questions involving their general support for international trade, respondents were told:

> Next we're going to describe a specific country for you. After we describe it, we'd like for you to tell us whether or not you think the United States should consider being involved in a trade agreement with this country. Please read each part of the country description carefully because you may be asked to recall this information later.

The next screen that people saw described a single country including five different characteristics of the country, each of which was randomly assigned across all respondents. All of the information was presented at the same time on a single screen, but the order in which the characteristics were described was randomized, so as not to emphasize one country characteristic any more than another. No specific country was mentioned in order to avoid the complications that could come from naming individual countries.

To examine the impact of similarity to the US, three of these randomly-assigned characteristics described the country as either 1) a well-established democracy or not a democracy; 2) similar or dissimilar to the US with respect to its cultural values and language; and 3) a country with a very high or very low standard of living in terms of the health and well-being of its citizens. Respondents were then asked three largely redundant questions about their support for a trade agreement with the country described, including 1) whether they think the US should consider negotiating a trade agreement with this country; 2) whether they personally favor or oppose participating in a trade agreement with this country; and 3) whether they would oppose or support this trade policy assuming US trade negotiators had agreed on the specifics of a trade policy that included this country.[39] Because people were randomly assigned to varying descriptions, we would expect no differences in their trade preferences if similarity to the US is unimportant.

To ensure that the experimental treatments were actually read and understood by the respondents, at the very end of the survey-experiment, after asking about support for trade with this specific country, respondents were asked about the characteristics that varied by experimental conditions. Subjects in the non-democracy condition were far more likely to say that the country they were asked about was not a democracy. Likewise, those assigned to conditions saying the country was culturally similar indicated the country they evaluated was significantly more like the US than in the dissimilar condition. And those told that the potential trading partner had a high standard of living in terms of citizen health and well-being likewise perceived it to be more similar to the American standard of living.

The Role of Similarity

How much did country similarity matter to people's desire to trade with this country? Figure 5.1 illustrates three tests of whether country similarity influences Americans' willingness to engage in trade with another country.[40] As shown in Figure 5.1, all three dimensions of similarity made significant differences in how respondents evaluated the trade policy. The size of the effects from similarity in government type, culture, and standard of living were indistinguishable, but each type of similarity had an independent additive impact on willingness trade. Each dimension of similarity contributed roughly an additional 7 percent on the scale of eagerness to trade, so a country that was similar to the US on all three dimensions was evaluated 21 percent more favorably as a trade partner than one with no dimensions of obvious similarity.

To facilitate a more in-depth understanding of these findings, an open-ended question was asked of all respondents at the end of the study, after their support for trading with the country had been assessed: "As you were thinking about this potential trading partner, what kinds of thoughts went through your mind?" Respondents were also asked to guess what particular country was being described based on the description.

What kinds of thoughts went through the respondents' minds as they were thinking about the potential trading partner country we had described? A large number of people used the open-ended comment to simply reiterate that they favored or opposed the trade agreement or trade more generally, typically emphasizing the same arguments described in Chapter 2. Those who opposed trade mentioned jobs lost due to trade, as well as the need to help ourselves before assisting others, that is, to put America first. Those who favored trade mentioned a wide variety of arguments, including the idea that trade is good for the economy and good for our relationships with other countries. Many simply speculated as to what country was being described to them, suggesting options ranging from China, to Iraq to Belize and Canada. These open-ended comments were used to obtain a better sense of the underlying reasoning behind their varying levels of support, and how similarity to their own country affected their preferences.

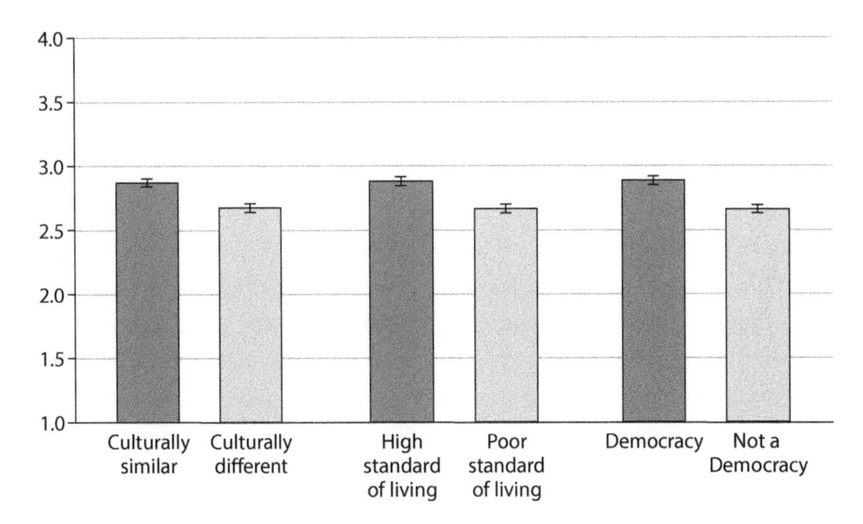

FIGURE 5.1. Favorability Toward Trade Agreement Based on Experimental Manipulation of Similarity of Country Characteristics
Source: Trade with Whom Survey-Experiment 2015 (YouGov).
Note: All three sets of paired means are significantly different from one another ($p < .01$). Support for trading with the country is based on an index ranging from 1 to 4 with higher scores indicating greater support/favorability.

An analysis of the open-ended comments across all experimental conditions revealed that the most commonly used word was "trust." A large percentage of respondents reflected on either why they felt the country could (not) be trusted or was (not) trustworthy or used closely related terms such as honest/honesty or reputation. Those opposed to trading with the country mentioned risk, or being careful or cautious in dealing the country because they might not be fair to the US or have worthy morals. But whether they were for or against trading with the country, they consistently commented on whether the country could or could not be trusted.

Very different culture and it made me cautious.
I'm not sure if trading with this country would be a trustworthy decision.
Are they worthy?
They can be trustworthy.
Are they honest and do they have integrity?
Not a safe thing to do.
Is this government trustworthy?
Do you jump in bed with anyone?
I do not trust other countries and feel it puts USA at risk.

Unreliable.
Be careful.
Hope they keep their word.
Nervous.
Need to get to know them.

We know from Figure 5.1 that respondents were systematically more favorable toward trading with other well-established democracies, even when that was just one of many different characteristics of potential similarity or difference. Respondents' open-ended comments indicated that this logic was patently obvious to them; if they were exposed to the treatment describing the other country as a well-established democracy, many commented on the fact that it was good or important to trade with a country that was stable: "We shouldn't enter an environment as unpredictable as this in my opinion." It is unclear whether the type of stability desired was economic or political, but predictability clearly mattered.

Those told it was not a democratic country often mentioned that they did not like countries with communists or dictators:

We should try to trade with democratic countries as much as possible.
It is not a democracy so their citizens have no say or influence regarding their government.
Is it a dictatorship? Because "not a democracy" tends to be code for "dictatorship." Which is something I oppose.
Government controlled; suppressed people.
NOT A COUNTRY I WOULD LIKE.
Is it communist? Is it a totalitarian government?
Trade with non-democratic countries is problematic.
Monarchy taking from poor to live rich lifestyle.
Communist or ruled by a king/queen.

It is unclear from these statements whether people favored trade only with democracies as an official foreign policy stance, or because they just didn't trust non-democracies. But far from being rational utility maximizers, responses suggested that they wanted to *like* their trading partners, and this alone made non-democracies harder to stomach as potential trade partners.

Respondents were also systematically more favorable toward trading with a country that was similar in its standard of living to the US. Although a few respondents commented on the potential for trade with a poor country to be a good thing because it could improve the other country's standard of living, most saw a country with a lower standard of living as a negative in a trade partner, in part because they believed that poor countries would make inferior products:

The standard of the products were most likely poor & a health risk, bad standard.
Poor people make poor products.

Others saw trading with a less well-off country as problematic because they perceived trade to be zero-sum, so if it helped the poor country, it must, therefore, hurt the US:

If other country is poor, will be bad for us because it will help them at our expense.
Since their country is poorer it may [turn] out to be another NAFTA-like disaster.

For others, a poor country seemed to imply bad leadership and corruption such that the workers in the poor country would be taken advantage of by trade:

Help the people improve their standard of living, but depending on the government, that might not work.
Because they are poor, they are being taken advantage of.
They have a poor economy and poor standard of living, I worry that trade would include some kind of sweat shop work.
Treats citizens poorly, prioritizes military strength over standard of living—China on steroids?

Many comments also made it clear that respondents were more favorable toward trading with countries whose populations were described as culturally similar to Americans. Many explicitly mentioned the importance of having a shared language:

Need to be able to communicate with language.
Language difference.
They need to speak English if we have to deal with them.
Can we break the language barriers?

Religion, morals and values also came up often:

I don't think we should trade with any country that doesn't believe in our values or speak English.
If they were like minded in views, morals and work ethic.

We should be careful as Americans to not compromise our values by trading with such a country.
Many English-speaking countries don't agree with our way of life 'Saudi Arabia.'
Do they have a good lifestyle; freedom; family values.
Was this a Christian country?
If Islamic then do not trade.
Do they have Christian morals?
If it's an Islamic country I would have a problem.
What is their main religion?
They speak the same language and have a relatable culture.
Their moral views.
How well do we really know this country's political values?

If my daughter were going to marry, I can imagine such thoughts running through my mind: How well did she really know her prospective life partner's values and morals? And did the prospective partner respect my daughter's way of life? But a country is not a person, so I was somewhat surprised to learn that what was running through people's minds was more akin to drawing inferences about profiles on a dating website than evaluating potential economic policies.

The most frequent inference from dissimilarity cues was generalized suspicion:

The devil is in the details.
Be careful of the terms given in the agreement.
We need to be sure we are not taken advantage of.
I hope they are nice honest people!
Always verify everything before agreements.

Among those who received cues suggesting that the country was similar in one or more dimensions to the US, the comments instead suggested that the other country would probably be fair and honest in their dealings if they were like Americans.

And just as prospective online daters worry about whether the person they like will like them back, Americans in this study who received cultural dissimilarity cues worried about whether the other country would like America:

It sounds like a culture that probably doesn't care for us.
Do they harbor terrorist groups?

Afraid that this might be ISIS.
What is their opinion of our country?
How do they feel about us?
Them trying to change American way of life.

Can Similarity Threaten?

All three dimensions of similarity produced positive effects suggesting that greater similarity leads to more favorable opinions toward a potential trade partner. These findings mirror extensive psychological research on the effects of similarity on interpersonal liking.[41] People like similar others more than dissimilar others, and they prefer to trade with similar countries as well. But to suggest that all psychological research is in line with this theory would be misleading.

The function of similarity in interpersonal relations is clear; it enhances trust and liking. But when people reason about international relations, it is not clear whether they generalize habits and modes of thought from the world of interpersonal relations or from intergroup contexts. In studies of intergroup relations, similarity is not something that always leads to greater trust and smoother relations; in fact, often quite the opposite. Intergroup similarity can exacerbate intergroup tensions, particularly under competitive conditions. In other words, it is plausible that too much similarity could make a trading partner less attractive and more of a competitor.

Sports radio in Philadelphia makes this kind of logic abundantly clear. Eagles fans did not want to see quarterback Nick Foles traded to another team in the same division because then he would become an immediate Eagles competitor. When another team has an equally good record as your own team, you will be especially reluctant to do anything that might help them out. Similarity combined with competition intensifies conflict and could lead to precisely the opposite of cooperation.

Social identity theory, a prominent model for analyzing intergroup relations, predicts that greater similarity between groups will drive people to see their own group as threatened under competitive conditions. This sense of threat leads people to differentiate their ingroup from the outgroup, or in this case, the out-country. High levels of similarity and competition conspire to instigate a desire for group distinctiveness and superiority.[42] This kind of reaction obviously does not bode well for international cooperation.

In the context of trade, this suggests that Americans could view a highly similar country as threatening, particularly if it is similar in all of the military might and economic power that characterizes the US. So perhaps a country assumed to be economically or militarily stronger than the US would be regarded systematically *less* favorably as a trading partner.

Among international relations scholars, such reasoning has been cast as a strategic decision based on security considerations. People should be more likely to oppose trade with countries that are similar to the home country because a country that is stronger than the home country economically or militarily will be perceived as a potential security threat.[43] The logic behind this is assumed to be that people believe trade will boost the trading partner country's economy, thus allowing them to divert resources to a stronger military. An adversary with a stronger military is obviously undesirable. So too, would be an adversarial country with a stronger economy than the home country, especially if those extra resources are assumed to go toward a military build-up.

Although this thought process may be plausible when trading with avowed adversaries, it requires that an ordinary American make several key connections. First, it requires that they believe trade will strengthen the trading partner's economy to a greater degree than it will help the American economy, thus resulting in a strategic economic advantage for the trading partner. This is plausible for some Americans, though definitely not all. Second, it requires them to believe that a strong economy in the trading partner country will lead to a bigger, better-funded military in that country that will be used against American interests. Beyond a handful of obvious countries, it is unclear if ordinary Americans have a clear sense of which countries are America's allies versus adversaries. I suspect that most countries in the world are perceived to be in that grey area somewhere in between.

Two of the five experimental treatments embedded in the representative survey were included as tests of whether similarity or even superiority can, indeed, be threatening. As part of this five-factor experimental design, one of the variations in country descriptions stated that the potential trading partner had a national economy that was considered either weaker or stronger than the US economy. If people do fear benefitting economic powerhouses like China by trading with them, then an experimental treatment indicating that another country is challenging America's economic dominance should cause them to be less enthusiastic about trading with them. Even more to the point on potential security concerns, a second treatment attempted to directly trigger military threat by stating that, "In terms of military strength, this country is considered [more powerful / less powerful] than the U.S. military."[44]

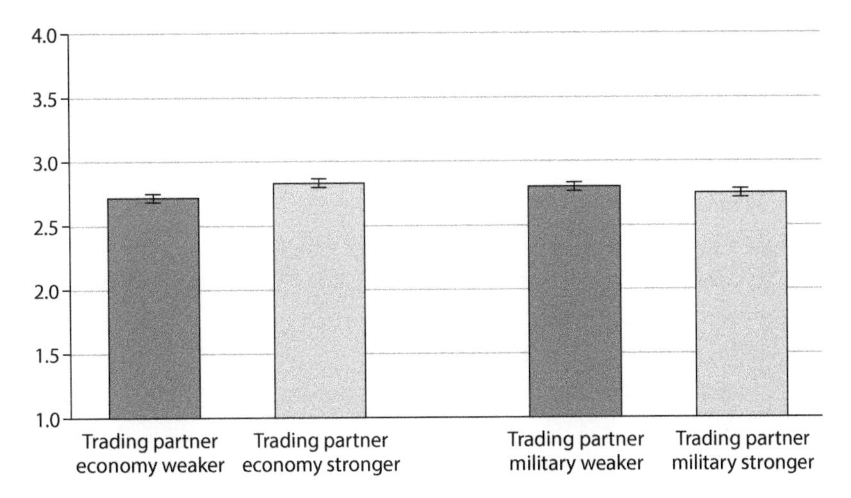

FIGURE 5.2. Favorability Toward Trade Agreement Based on Dissimilarity/Potential Threat from Trading Partner Country
Source: Trade with Whom Survey-Experiment 2015 (YouGov).
Note: The means for the economy are significantly different from one another. However, the means for military strength are only marginally different ($p < .10$). Support for trading with the country is based on an index ranging from 1 to 4 with higher scores indicating greater support/favorability.

My assumption was that Americans would feel threatened by countries described as more powerful on one or more of these dimensions and would be less likely to trade with them as a result. But I was clearly wrong. As illustrated in Figure 5.2, when a potential trading partner was described as economically or militarily stronger than the US, this did not discourage enthusiasm for trading with them. In fact, rather than eschew trade with countries that are economically stronger, Americans were *more* likely to say they wanted to trade with such a country than with one that was weaker than the US economically. Surprisingly, they wanted to trade with the *more* economically successful country to a significantly greater extent than with the *less* economically successful country. This pattern of results offers little support for a generalized fear of trading partners who might grow economically more dominant.

Comments on what they were thinking about as they decided whether they favored the trade agreement suggested two possible explanations for this pattern of results. Some gave reasons for not wanting to trade with an economically weaker country, while others provided reasons for wanting to trade with a more economically powerful one. When respondents volunteered that weaker economies were less desirable trade partners, it was often because they viewed this as the United States "helping" another country rather than as a mutually beneficial trade agreement:

Why aren't they helping themselves. They have a stronger economy and military. They don't need our help.
Here's another country the US will wind up supporting.
If this country is so weak, why would the United States support them?
More leeches.
We always have to bail someone out.
We owe so much money to other countries we don't need to take on more debt.
I THINK THAT WE SHOULD TAKE CARE OF OURSELVES AND LEAVE OTHERS TO DO THE SAME.
We would be giving them lots of money to 'trade' with us falsely inflating their economy and making them more dependent on us for future handouts.
They would be getting more out of a trade deal than we would.

Some explanations for preferring trade with another strong economy cast the fact that the country was well off as a sign that they were stable and trustworthy:

They have a somewhat stable economy.
Strong economy means a stable nation.
WEAK, ECONOMY NOT STABLE
How their economy can affect political stability.

Even more common was the assumption that a potential trading partner with a strong economy would mean the US would benefit *more* economically from the agreement, or that a trading partner with a weak economy would mean the US would benefit *less* economically from the agreement:

Since their economy is better it might be a better financial choice for trading. maybe cheaper since they are better off than the US.
Since they have a strong economy, I think they would be good trade partners.
I thought that they probably wouldn't be a very good trading partner if their economy was weaker than America's.
They have a strong economy so we can make money selling them stuff.

If their economy was strong enough to purchase enough goods and services to make a trade agreement valuable.
Stronger economy means they have a lot of money to invest.
Their good economy could help boost ours.

Peace, Military Threat, or Military Assistance?

Those evaluating a country described as militarily stronger as opposed to one that was militarily weaker than the US demonstrated no net difference in either direction in support for the trade agreement. Interestingly, many assumed that the militarily strong country being described was China, but they were still no more or less opposed to trading with them. Open-ended comments referencing the country's military strength suggested that there were two countervailing logics at work, and they may have combined to cancel one another out in their effects on overall support for trade.

By far the most common explanation for preferring trade with a militarily strong trade partner was the desire to keep the peace. Many respondents saw trade as likely to promote peaceful relations between trading partners, which they deemed especially important if they were trading with another country that had a strong military. Their support for trading with a militarily powerful country was intended to avert a potential threat. As respondents remarked,

Better to have them as an ally than an enemy.
Keep your enemies close.
That we need the agreement so their citizens won't want to harm us.
It's good for the United States to have good relationships.
Reach out, Good gestures have better outcomes.
Keep potential enemies tied to us economically.
Trade to reduce potential conflict.
Cooperation in the future.
We need to have them in our back pocket so they don't invade us.
Better to be allied with a country with good economy and superior military strength.
Security wise it's good to trade with a country with a stronger military then risk conflict.
Keep your enemies close—being connected by trade might be a good influence on them.
It may become an ally.
Keep them closer.

The idea that trade promotes peaceful relations is well established in the international relations literature, though I had no idea it was so widely believed by ordinary Americans. But if, as I have suggested, people think of these relationships by analogy to interpersonal ones, then it makes perfect sense that people would intuit this without having to read academic journals. There is a very high probability that people who trade sandwiches at lunch are also friends; trade demonstrates more than simply that one desires a different kind of sandwich. It is evidence of a partnership, a relationship of the sort that could make countries allies.

Many respondents explicitly mentioned the advantage of having a trade partner who was militarily strong. Although the description itself did not state whether the country was an ally or an adversary, many simply assumed that a trading partner would become an ally:

Security wise it's good to trade with a country with a stronger military than risk conflict.
I was thinking this would be a great trading partner having a strong military is an added bonus.
Strong military could be called upon to help in world crises.
We want allies with an excellent military.
Probably a good idea to be on good terms with a country that has a larger military.
It is better to be friends than enemies since they have a stronger military and economy.
Because keeps things peaceful, avoids war.
Better to be allied with a country with good economics and superior military strength.
If their military is stronger we should probably be friends with them.
Military ally.
The Citizens of the country, and the economy, sound nice. Other factors don't, such as weak Military.

Only one respondent out of a representative 2,500 people reasoned that trading with another country could improve the other country's economy and thus further strengthen the extent of its military, producing a greater potential threat to American military supremacy:

If they have too much money, they can increase military and dominate us. They have different values already and could be a threat. They are already more powerful.

Nonetheless, quite a few respondents mentioned that a country with a stronger military seemed threatening. Even if they did not see this as a reason not to trade with them, they still reacted negatively to the idea of a country with a stronger military:

Their military is much more than us and if something went bad would they attack us especially because we're losing our military strength.
They could end up fighting the US since they have a bigger military.
Potential for military strife.
What would happen if we became enemies with this country? With them having a larger military?
Don't like that they have a stronger military.
I was worried about their superior military strength.
Military strength, not a democracy and a weak economy are red flags.
They have a powerful military that could mean trouble later on and we should stay out of there.
Possibility of Military adventurism on the part of the partner Country.
Don't like that they have a stronger military, glad they're a democracy.
Them taking over the US.
They will bomb us.
Would take over America.
Will they try to overthrow our government.
If something went bad would they attack us.

Despite these obvious fears, superior military strength was neither a benefit nor a hindrance to trade in its net effects on mass preferences. Instead, it was the only country characteristic without any impact on trade support.

Liking Some Countries and Their People More than Others

After indicating their support or opposition to a trade agreement with this country, respondents were also asked how warm or cold they felt toward the country described, and how warm or cold they felt toward the people of this country, with these two questions in a randomized order. As is generally the case, people felt consistently warmer toward the people of the country than toward the country as a whole. However, because attitudes toward the people and the country are strongly correlated, it is difficult to disentangle their consequences statistically. However, it is notable that the similarity cues had a greater influence on people's feelings toward the foreign *country* described to them than toward the *people* of that country. Since they were primarily given characteristics of the country, rather than the country's people, this makes perfect sense. But in contrast, their trade preferences were equally if not more strongly related to their feelings toward the *people* of the foreign country.

Overall, these findings lend support to the idea that attitudes toward international relations and interpersonal relations are not so distinct as they might seem. That said, people's attitudes toward trade were not reducible to their positive or negative feelings toward the foreign country and its people. In fact, even when taking into account their general attitudes toward trade (measured long before the specific country was described) as well as their cold/warm feelings toward the country described, as well as toward its people, the experimental treatments still had significant independent effects on trade attitudes. This was not due to interactions among the five country characteristics that were described. In fact, out of the many potential interactions among five different experimental treatments, only one mattered at all. People were especially negative toward a country that spent a great deal on their military while neglecting the health and well-being of their citizens, thus producing an interaction between military strength and standard of living.

The influence of perceived country similarity appears to be both consistent and strong. Seeing countries similar to our own as good trade partners apparently goes beyond merely feeling more positively or negatively toward them. In response to the question asking what they were thinking about, many respondents simply commented on what was alike about our countries as if these provided obvious reasons to be partners:

> *That they sound an awful lot like us. Almost sounds like a perfect world.*
> *That they have much in common with the USA.*
> *They're a lot like us, so why not trade with them?*
> *Similar traits of the country compared to US.*
> *The people sounded like us.*
> *That they were like us in many ways.*
> *Similarity to US.*
> *Very close to the USA.*
> *It would seem that we could benefit each other because we are so similar.*

Just as potential life partners who have a lot in common are assumed to make better mates, so too are potential trading partners. What we know less about is how many different country characteristics matter to these judgments.

Trading with Whom: Beliefs versus Reality?

Thus far I have explored how country similarity influences preferences for trading with one country versus another by describing countries stripped of the baggage of their actual identities. This does not address the question of which countries most Americans have in mind when they think about our trade partners. To examine people's assumptions about our major trading partners, a representative national probability survey conducted in 2017 asked respondents to name America's top three trading partner countries to the best of their ability. Their responses were later coded to indicate how many were accurate mentions of Canada, Mexico or China, our top three trading partners, as well as other countries.

Only 22 percent of Americans could name all three major trading partners. Another 34 percent was able to name two of the three countries. As shown in Figure 5.3, China was by far the most often mentioned trading partner, with 85 percent of respondents naming it, followed by 52 percent who mentioned Mexico, and 33 percent who mentioned Canada. Japan was mentioned by 27 percent of respondents, but after that the percentage of people naming any one specific country dropped off quickly. Their suggestions of other countries were, quite literally, all over the map.

Does knowing who our trading partners are make any difference to one's support for trade? Education is known to be by far the strongest and most consistent predictor of trade support, and one would expect people with higher levels of education to be more accurate in their knowledge. But beyond education, does accurate knowledge of this sort matter? To answer this question, I estimated a model including education, income, gender, age, party identification and the accuracy of people's knowledge about US trading partners. As shown in Figure 5.4, accuracy did, indeed, elevate levels of trade support beyond what could be predicted based on these other characteristics. Perhaps most surprising, the size of its impact was quite large, rivaling the impact of educational level, a well-known engine of support for trade. Those more knowledgeable about the identity of our trading partners are more supportive of it. The difference between someone who cannot name any US trading partners as opposed to someone who can name all three is a 10 percent higher level of support

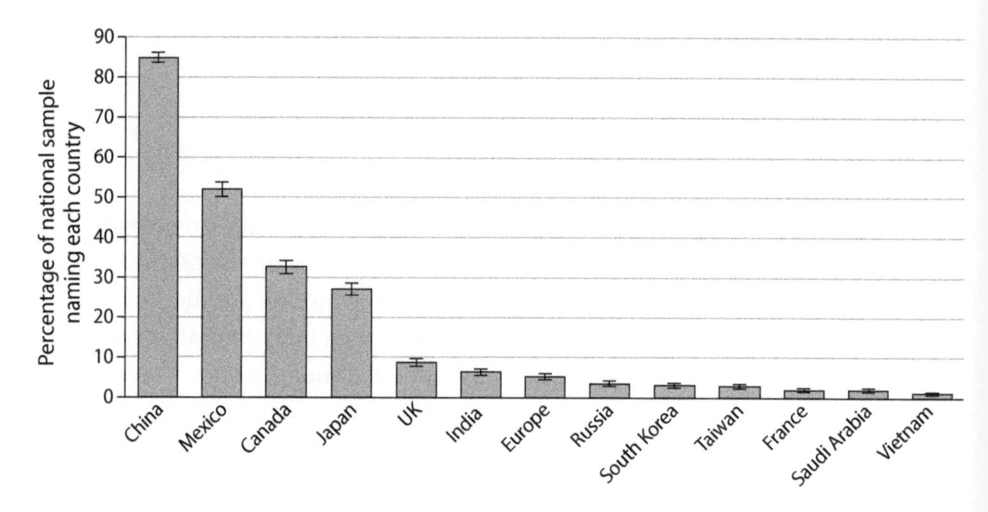

FIGURE 5.3. American Perceptions of Top Trading Partners
Source: ISCAP Panel Survey 2017 (Amerispeak/NORC).
Note: Bars represent the percentage of respondents naming a specific country or, in some cases, a collection of countries. Respondents were asked to name the three countries the US trades with the most. These countries represent the top 13 countries named in order of frequency. All other countries were named by less than 1 percent of the sample.

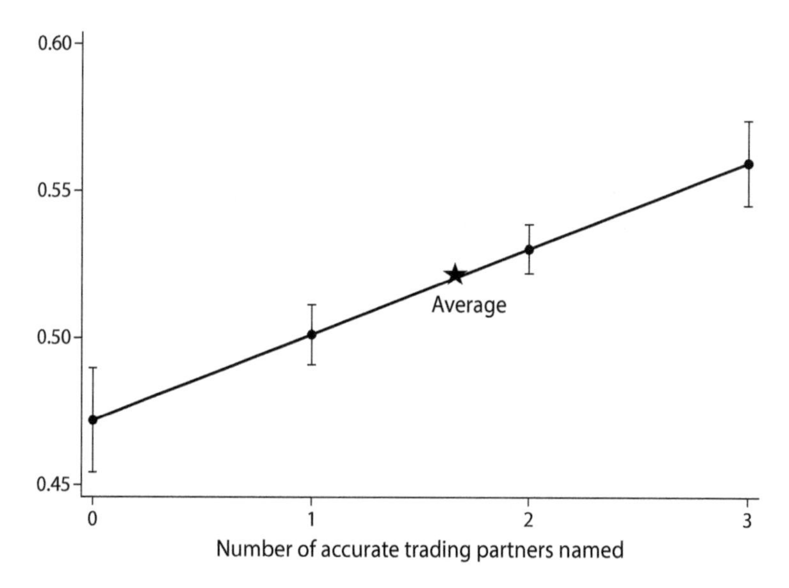

FIGURE 5.4. Relationship Between Accurate Knowledge of Trading Partners and Support for International Trade
Source: ISCAP Panel Survey 2017 (Amerispeak/NORC).
Note: Vertical axis illustrates support for international trade on a 0 to 1 scale, controlling for political party, age, education, income, and gender. Error bars represent 95 percent confidence intervals.

for trade among those most knowledgeable of trading partner countries, all else being equal.

Forgetting Canada

Accuracy of trading partner knowledge represents a type of political knowledge that goes beyond level of formal education. The average American could correctly name only 1.7 countries. Whether that seems high or low depends on one's initial expectations. However, the theory I have proposed suggests that the specific kinds of errors people make is relevant to their trade views, above and beyond their level of accuracy. If similarity drives trade attitudes, then forgetting that Canada is a major US trading partner could have serious consequences for trade preferences. Canada is notably third in frequency among the countries mentioned, even though up until 2015 it was America's #1 trading partner. Nowadays it comes in at #2 in actual trade volume (after China), but as #3 in terms of trading countries that come to mind in the mass public.

The reason that forgetting Canada should matter is that Americans perceive Canadians to be very similar to themselves, more so than the citizens of any other country. So strong is the impulse to think of Canadians as "one of us" that a 2018 *Reader's Digest* article advised Americans that one of the top ten statements to avoid saying in front of a Canadian is "Canada is the 51st state."[45]

If my theory is correct, forgetting Canada should have deleterious effects on people's level of overall support for international trade, above and beyond the extent of their accuracy. If one forgets about Canada, a close neighbor and strong ally, this should make our trading partners seem generally more foreign. And indeed, this is the case. Adding a variable representing "forgetting Canada" to the model described above (which already includes accuracy) lowers support for international trade by 4 percent.

In contrast, forgetting China, the most dissimilar of our top three trading partners, raises predicted trade support by 5 percent. The much greater popular attention directed toward trade with China, a more dissimilar country, relative to trade with Canada, a more similar one, has probably had deleterious consequences for how Americans think about international trade. In everyday language, dissimilarity and foreignness are essentially synonyms. In the context of trade, the dissimilarities of trading partner countries make international trade itself seem more "foreign," that is, more psychically distant and more difficult to trust.

Trading with Ourselves?

At the beginning of this chapter, I noted that from an economic perspective, the dissimilarity of preferences, technologies, and the talents of workers across countries is the reason that international trade makes sense. Nonetheless, both actual trade flows and public preferences about with whom the US should trade are rooted in perceived similarities. Just as people are more favorable toward similar others in their interpersonal relations, they are also more favorable toward trading with countries similar to their own country in the context of international trade. When faced with a large complex international economic system and the potentially quite difficult choice of deciding whether to engage in trade with one country versus another, people form views in part by reducing the problem to one they face every day: whom to trust. In deciding which countries are more trustworthy, Americans are likely to favor fellow democracies, countries that are similarly well developed economically, culturally similar, and countries that maintain a high standard of living for their citizens. The only exception that I have identified thus far is military dominance by another country. The military strength of another country provides both reasons to want a trading relationship with that country and, due to potential threat, a reason not to, thus producing no net effect on trade preferences.

There is little evidence that Americans want to abstain from trading with other countries because they fear trade will boost the trading partner country's economy, thus funneling greater resources toward their military, and subsequently threatening the US. On the one hand, people dislike the idea of a militarily stronger partner. On the other hand, many suggested that it would be a beneficial thing for the US to have an ally with a strong military. Those who favored trading with militarily strong countries also did so because they believed that it would reduce the probability of conflict. Indeed, the idea that trade can lead to greater peace between countries has more adherents in the general population than one might expect. Because those who trade things with one another naturally appear to be friendly with one another, this understanding appears to be an easier, more accessible argument in favor of trade than complex economic arguments. It essentially mirrors the way people understand and assess interpersonal relationships.

I have suggested that the American public is quite capable of distinguishing its support for trade with one country versus another even without economic knowledge. My theory explaining how they do this does not require economic knowledge or insight into how one is personally affected by trade. Perhaps most importantly, this theory points to the fact that considerations beyond either individual or collective economic gains and losses shape trade preferences between trading partner countries.

I have no direct evidence that the same principle of similarity operates in other countries with other populations. However, given this theory's roots in basic human psychology and the tendency to trust similar others, it would not be surprising if populations outside the US made judgments on the same basis. There is good reason to believe that humans retain evolved mechanisms that helped our ancestors defend against threats, largely by making us "hypervigilant against unfamiliar stimuli, including unfamiliar individuals."[46] In other words, people are motivated to avoid dissimilar others. These reactions are typically outside of our conscious awareness, which makes them all that much more difficult to overcome. Behavioral tendencies to avoid dissimilarity may have served us well when exposure to foreign peoples and products potentially brought us into contact with new diseases and pathogens. But today their lingering effects continue to influence contemporary policy preferences, especially on issues involving foreigners and foreignness.

Similarity is such a powerful heuristic for whom to trust that people in our study automatically drew inferences about similarity on one dimension and applied it to another, even though they were given information to the contrary. For example, as illustrated in Figure A5.1 in the online appendix, my manipulation checks show that the experimental treatments meant to induce perceived cultural similarity with the other country did so, but they also influenced perceptions of the standard of living and the type of government. Likewise, the standard of living treatment induced greater perceptions of cultural similarity and economic strength. People infer that likes go with likes, so when one dimension of similarity is known, it also influences other dimensions to a lesser degree, even when people have been given information to the contrary.

Comments about race, a very obvious dimension of similarity and dissimilarity, are notably absent from respondents' comments in this chapter. Although similarity in culture and values might be interpreted by some as racial similarity, there was no direct acknowledgement of group differences other than references to religious groups. Although one respondent did refer to "shithole" countries, this was long before Donald Trump made his well-known comment linking his opposition to immigration specifically to dark-skinned countries such as Haiti or Africa, as opposed to what he viewed as desirable immigrants from Norway.[47] I suspect that mentioning racial differences or racial similarity as reasons not to trade or to trade with a specific country may be too socially undesirable to show up in volunteered responses to a national survey.

Nonetheless, it would be surprising if race were not a salient dimension of country similarity given its general salience in American society. Trade opposition in both survey and experimental studies is driven in part by prejudice and ethnocentrism.[48] For this reason, I address this question at length in Chapter 6.

Large-scale systems that require people to be interdependent with dissimilar others are not an easy sell. Some of the most optimistic findings in this chapter demonstrate that even in the face of perceiving an economic or military threat from other countries, many see trading as preferable to not trading for the simple reason that it will help to make us allies rather than enemies.

However, for trade to realize its full potential, countries with differing characteristics need to trade with one another. The preference of rich countries for trading with similarly rich countries hampers the ability of trade to improve the economies of poorer countries and limits the benefits of trade for wealthy countries. Even if public opinion is just one of many factors influencing trade policy, it constrains the behavior of political actors. Moreover, political elites are human beings first, and they are likely to judge other countries as trustworthy or not for some of the very same reasons that members of the public view them as such.

Overall, the basis for people's decisions appears quite simple: the more dimensions of perceived similarity between the US and the country described, the greater respondents' support for trading with that country. At times, considerations tied to similarity may converge with economic rationality, but I see little evidence of this in the views of the mass public. Similarity induces trust for reasons that predate national economies, let alone the complex international economy.

6

How Racial Attitudes Affect Support for International Trade

Until recently, studies of trade preferences have not considered race or racism as potentially important factors. Because trade is thought to be primarily an economic issue, not a social issue, race has been considered relevant only due to the economic disadvantages that characterize many racial minority groups in the United States.[1] Interestingly, race is not even included among the many demographic control variables in most individual-level analyses of trade preferences, let alone the focus of inquiry. In one of our early studies of trade preferences, Ed Mansfield and I noticed that even after controlling for partisanship, education, income, and a whole host of other predictors, being a minority still predicted being more supportive of international trade.[2] In fact, during the roughly ten-year period described in Chapter 3, when trade was perceived to be predominantly foreign aid, minorities were consistently more supportive of trade than whites, even after taking their partisanship into account.[3] We found it surprising that no one had noticed this.

When conducting additional studies, I started looking for differences by race. Surprisingly, I found white versus minority group variation in virtually every study I conducted. Although these were not pre-registered hypotheses by any means, these findings were both consistent and logical once I had come to view trade in ingroup-outgroup terms. Minority status in America means that people are part of a subordinate group; this changes the way they think about the winners and losers of trade. Belief in the benefits of competition is systematically lower among minorities relative to whites. The dominant groups in a society are essentially its "winners," so perhaps it is not surprising that subordinate groups are less likely to buy into competition as a fair way to allocate resources. Whites are also higher in social dominance orientation, suggesting that they believe some groups deserve to be treated better than others. These differences hold the potential to alter minority perspectives on trade relative to majority whites.

This chapter first draws on previous work to outline some potential reasons why white and minority trade preferences may differ. Next, I use the experimental studies already described in Chapters 4 and 5 to examine what difference it makes to preferences on international trade if a person is part of the dominant majority racial group or if instead he or she identifies with a subordinate racial group. After examining white and minority attitudes toward trade in the context of these two representative national survey experiments, I turn to other sources to better understand levels of minority support for trade despite these groups' economic and educational disadvantages.

Why Might Race or Racial Attitudes Influence Trade Preferences?

Racial and ethnic minorities should be more protectionist than whites based on theories that emphasize material self-interest. In the United States, trade disproportionately benefits high-skill labor and harms low-skill labor; thus one would expect that lower-skilled people should hold less favorable opinions than higher-skilled people.[4] Among minority groups in the US, African-Americans and Hispanics tend to be lower skilled than whites, and should therefore be more protectionist if they are basing views on their individual or collective pocketbooks.

Some suggest that skill level is not as important to trade preferences as volatility in employment.[5] But here again, African-Americans and Hispanics face greater risks from job volatility than whites, giving them yet another basis for greater opposition to trade. African-Americans and Hispanics are simply more economically vulnerable than whites; they experience higher rates of unemployment, live in areas with higher unemployment rates, and have lower incomes on average, all factors that should generate protectionist sentiment based on theories emphasizing material self-interest.[6,7] The only survey analysis of trade preferences by race to date combines minorities and women into a single category, obscuring a direct comparison of whites to minorities.[8]

Economic considerations notwithstanding, both survey and experimental studies have suggested that trade opposition is facilitated by racial prejudice and ethnocentrism, and that whites are generally higher on such measures.[9] Even though ethnocentrism questions tap domestic racial attitudes, not attitudes toward foreigners, assessments of people's racial ingroup relative to racial outgroups strongly predicts opposition to trade.[10] The tendency to evaluate outgroups more negatively than ingroups is a characteristic of high-status majority groups relative to lower-status minority groups, but not the reverse. In fact, psychologists have found that only dominant groups in a society demonstrate consistent ingroup bias and outgroup prejudice.[11]

In the US, whites are viewed by both Blacks and Hispanics as a higher-status group than their own group. This results from objective differences in power, status, and wealth.[12] For example, Blacks offer similar evaluations of Blacks and whites, whereas whites assess themselves far more positively than Blacks.[13] Other kinds of preferences illustrate this same pattern, in that minority group members are generally more accepting of both minority and majority group members than majority group members are of minorities. For example, 62 percent of white Americans report that they would accept a Black person marrying into their family, and over 70 percent would do so if the person was Asian or Hispanic. However, 83 percent of Blacks would accept a white, an Asian, or a Hispanic marrying into their family.[14] Residential preferences demonstrate a similar pattern. Whites' willingness to move into a neighborhood is inversely related to the density of Black residents, whereas Blacks prefer integrated neighborhoods that incorporate both ingroup and outgroup members.[15] In short, the extent of aversion to dissimilar others is not symmetric among majority whites and minorities.

In addition to racial prejudice, still another reason that minorities may respond to trade differently emerges from the ingroup/outgroup framework presented in Chapter 4. To put "America First," as Donald Trump's slogan admonished, is to appeal to home country ingroup favoritism. But favoritism toward the American ingroup is quantitatively different among minorities and whites. Members of a nation's dominant group often feel more ownership of the nation than lower-status groups.[16] Given that both whites and minorities see whites as more quintessentially American, it is not surprising that these same characteristics predict a stronger sense of national superiority. As the African-American poet Langston Hughes put it, "America never was America to me."[17] In other words, the land of opportunity that white Americans take pride in is not the same America known to minorities. It should not be surprising that they do not hold America in as high of a regard as whites do. African-Americans report lower levels of national pride as well as less perceived national superiority.[18,19] This same pattern of less national attachment and national superiority among minority groups occurs both in the US and in other countries.[20]

Taken together, this evidence suggests that if psychological considerations dominate, particularly whites' greater aversion to difference, greater prejudice, and higher levels of national superiority, then members of the dominant white racial group should be more reactive than minorities to the similarity of the trading partner and to whether trade policies result in dominance for their national ingroup. Because minorities exhibit less ethnocentrism than whites, this should lead to more supportive trade preferences, all else being equal. Of course, there are many other things that could influence trade support that are not equal between whites and minorities in the US, thus complicating interpretations of racial differences in trade support. For this reason, experiments are ideal for understanding what difference racial identification makes because we can at least hold constant many characteristics of what people are judging.

Racial Differences in the Impact of Country Similarity

To directly address whether similarity to the home country matters more for majority whites than for minorities, I turned to the representative national survey–experimental design described in Chapter 5. The goal in this experiment was to disentangle the cluster of characteristics associated with any given country by randomly assigning characteristics that were either similar to, or different from, the US in a description of a potential trading partner. Results suggested that similar country characteristics consistently raised the likelihood that a person would support trading with that particular country. But do these results differ by majority and minority racial status? For purposes of the studies in this chapter, I define minorities using the federal government's definition of under-represented minorities, that is, African-Americans, American Indians / Alaska Natives, Latinos, and those who identify with two or more groups.[21]

Each of the three dimensions of similarity manipulated in the experimental treatments—cultural and language similarity, similarity in standard of living, and similarity in democratic governance—positively influenced

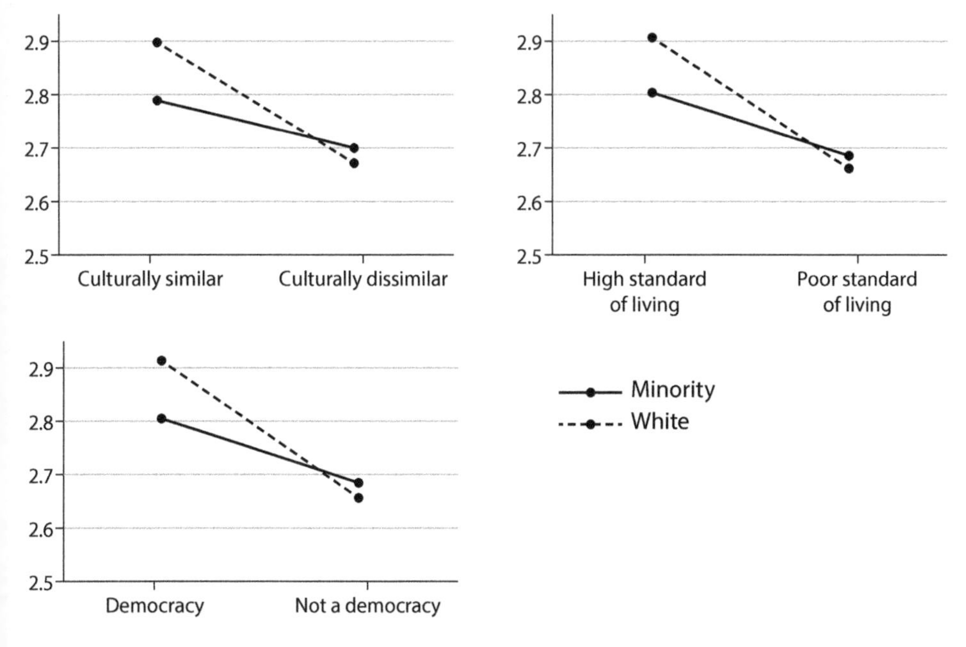

FIGURE 6.1. Racial Differences in the Effects of Country Similarity on Support for Trade Agreements

Source: Trade with Whom Survey-Experiment 2015 (YouGov).

Note: All three interactions shown above are statistically significant, $p < .01$.

support for a trade agreement with that country. But consistent with the idea that dominant and subordinate groups may weigh this evidence differently, similarity affected whites and minorities to different extents. As illustrated in Figure 6.1, results were identical for each of the three different types of similarity, with significant interactions between minority/majority group membership and each dimension of similarity.

When the country with whom the US is considering a trade agreement was described as culturally dissimilar, minorities were slightly more supportive than whites; but when it was culturally similar, whites were much more supportive of the trade agreement than minorities. Likewise, when the potential trade partner was described as similar in terms of having a high standard of living, whites were more supportive of the agreement than minorities. But when the partner had a low standard of living, minorities were slightly more supportive. Finally, minorities and whites were roughly equally willing to forge a trade agreement with a country that was not a democracy. But whites were significantly more supportive than minorities if the trading partner country was a democracy.

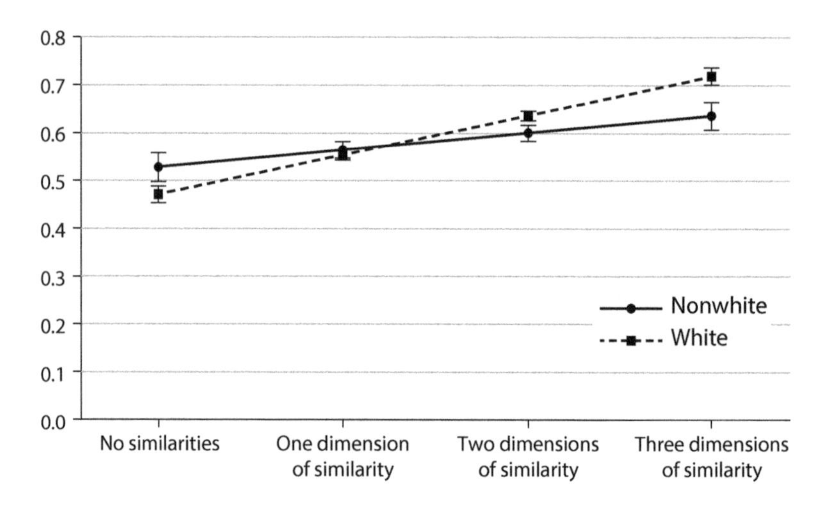

FIGURE 6.2. Effects of Country Similarity on Support for Trade Agreement, by Race of Respondent
Source: Trade with Whom Survey-Experiment 2015 (YouGov).
Note: The interaction between Race and Number of Dimensions of Similarity is statistically significant ($F = 4.55$, $p < 0.001$). Trade support is shown here on a 0-1 scale.

These results make it clear that whites will not always be less supportive of trade than minorities. In fact, whites are consistently *more* supportive of trade than minorities when the country is highly similar to the US. Similarity to the US is simply a more important consideration to whites when considering a potential trading partner than it is to minorities. Countries that are less like the US are less likely to be perceived by whites as trustworthy and reliable trading partners.

Each dimension of similarity manipulated in this factorial experiment added incrementally to the impact of the others to increase trade support. In other words, they each produced roughly the same magnitude of effect, without interactions, and each additional dimension of similarity added further to the country's attractiveness as a trade partner. It does not seem to matter if the type of similarity is cultural, style of government, or standard of living—all work to increase trade support. Most importantly for purposes of this chapter, they all increase support more among whites and minorities.

Since each dimension of similarity affects trade support to roughly the same extent, I illustrate effects of the total number of dimensions of similarity to which a person happened to be randomly assigned in Figure 6.2, broken down by whether people were whites or minorities. Although both groups increase in support for trade as the trading partner country is increasingly described in ways that are similar to the US, the impact of similarity is about 2.5 times as great for whites as for non-whites. When all three manipulated descriptors of the country suggest that it is not similar to the US, minorities are more likely to support trade. When only one aspect of the country described is similar to the US, then racial minorities and majority whites support a trade agreement to roughly the same extent. But as the similarities between the US and the potential trading partner increase, whites exhibit steadily greater support. Because supporting trade is facilitated by trusting the other country, and similarity breeds trust, more similarities mean more support, and particularly so if one is part of the dominant white majority in the US.

The size of these effects is considerable. Among minorities, each additional dimension of similarity raises support for trade by around 4 percentage points. But among white Americans, each additional dimension of similarity raises trade support by around 9 percentage points. This means that going from a country without any specified similar characteristics to one with three similar characteristics raises support for trade among whites by over 25 percentage points. This is a substantial impact.

It is an especially impressive effect size, given that we know that these characteristics are inferred to be correlated in people's minds. As detailed in Chapter 5, when given one dimension of similarity/dissimilarity, people sometimes erroneously infer other types of similarity or dissimilarity, even when the information they were given directly contradicts this. This pattern suggests that in the absence of contradictory information, what little people do know about a potential trading partner can lead them to be much more or less supportive, based on degrees of similarity. In the real world, one known dimension of similarity often leads to assumptions about others—a democracy, for example, is widely assumed to have a higher standard of living—thus the total impact of even one dimension of known similarity is likely to be far greater in the real world than what we estimate here where people were always told either that the country was like the US or not like the US on each dimension.

How Dominant and Subordinate Groups Reason Differently about Trade

Thus far I have shown that whites in the US are more influenced by the extent of similarity between their own country and potential trading partner countries when deciding whether we should have trade relations with them.

This pattern occurs because whites are more likely to distrust countries that are different from the US in various ways. But similarities aside, do outgroup members reason differently about what makes a trade agreement desirable? Minorities in America are simultaneously part of the American ingroup, but also a minority outgroup within that ingroup. This raises the possibility that even if American minorities do not identify with outgroups from other countries, their experience with minority outgroup status may generate less prejudice toward foreign people and products.[22] As a result of their differing positions in society, whites and minorities may reason differently about trade, even when the consequences of that trade agreement are identical.

As the societally-dominant group, whites are less likely to be concerned about equality than are minorities.[23] But it remains unclear whether this general tendency crosses over into the realm of how a person views interactions with another country. If we hold constant the positive and negative effects of a given trade agreement, will minority and majority racial groups still differ in their support for it? Or is the basis for more positive views among minorities rooted in different assumptions about who gains or loses from such an agreement?

Using the representative national survey experiment initially described in Chapter 4, I answer this question by examining how minorities and majority whites respond when I randomly assign them to different versions of a trade agreement that varies in its consequences for the home country and trading partner countries. My suspicion was that the pattern of results observed in Chapter 4 was less likely to characterize minorities than majority group members. Ethnocentric valuation of human lives—when some people's well-being is given a higher priority than others'—is especially likely to characterize those in positions of dominance in society. For this reason, I expected minorities to be more egalitarian when evaluating the desirability of trade for the home country and trading partner countries.

Using job gains and losses as the primary currency of what is gained and lost due to trade, both whites and minorities were assigned to a description of a trade agreement varying how many jobs the home country versus the trading partner gains and loses from the agreement. The initial results in Chapter 4 demonstrated what one might expect: people value in-country job gains far more than jobs for foreigners. The question I ask here is whether that tendency is stronger for majority group members than for minorities. In other words, setting partisan preferences aside, is the "America First" philosophy, the idea that our compatriots are more deserving than foreigners, inherently more appealing when people feel themselves to be more a part of the dominant national ingroup?

The answer is yes. As shown in Figure 6.3, both whites and minorities express greater support for the agreement in which the US gains jobs and the trading partner countries lose jobs, relative to the agreement that results in the same number of jobs gained and lost, but puts the burden instead on the US. This result should come as no surprise. But as also shown on the left-hand side of Figure 6.3, the gap between bars, representing the extent of ingroup favoritism, is significantly greater for whites than for minorities. Because people are randomly assigned to these descriptions, any differences within racial groups result from how whites and minorities reason differently about trade scenarios in which the US dominates and Americans are the primary beneficiaries versus when the trading partner countries are the ones who benefit.

Minorities are more supportive of trade than whites only when the home country loses and the trading partner countries gain jobs. Indeed, at the time of this study, a majority of people in the US thought precisely that trade benefitted trading partner countries at the expense of U.S. jobs.[24] Under these conditions, it is not surprising to find that minorities hold higher levels of support for international trade than whites. If it were the other way around, with gains assumed to be concentrated in the US and losses overseas, then whites would be more supportive. Ethnocentric valuation is in evidence across the board, but it is stronger among majority whites than among minorities.

This same survey experiment also makes it possible to examine racial differences in people's consideration of trade's impact on trading partner countries. To what extent do the trade preferences of whites and minorities take foreigners into consideration, that is, incorporating all of humanity into the ingroup?[25] Logically, one would expect that the "win-win" scenario, in which both the US and its trading partner countries benefit, to be the most widely supported policy. After all, what's not to like when everybody wins? But if people are equally supportive of an agreement that is win-win versus one that is win-lose, that suggests that the gains to others are irrelevant; only in-country gains matter. This was the case for the population of the US as a whole in Chapter 4. But does the extent of moral exclusion vary by majority/minority status?

The results on the right-hand side of Figure 6.3 suggest that minorities are more likely to take into consideration the effects on trading partner countries. They are more likely to support the "win-win" trade agreement than one where only the home country gains. But whites are, on average, *more* supportive of an agreement when the home country gains and the trading partner country loses jobs. Minorities and whites obviously differ in

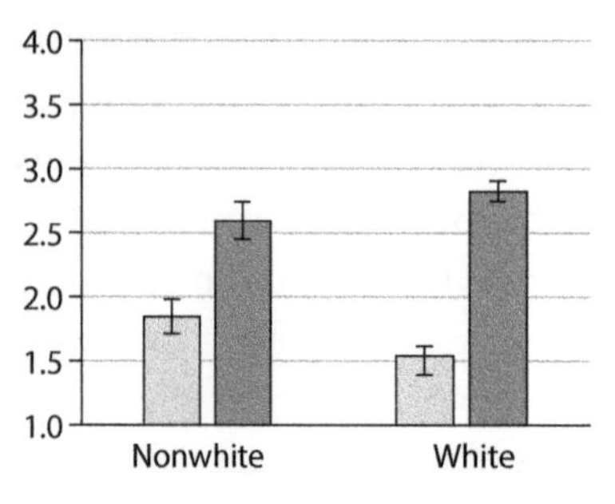

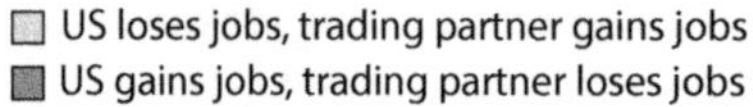

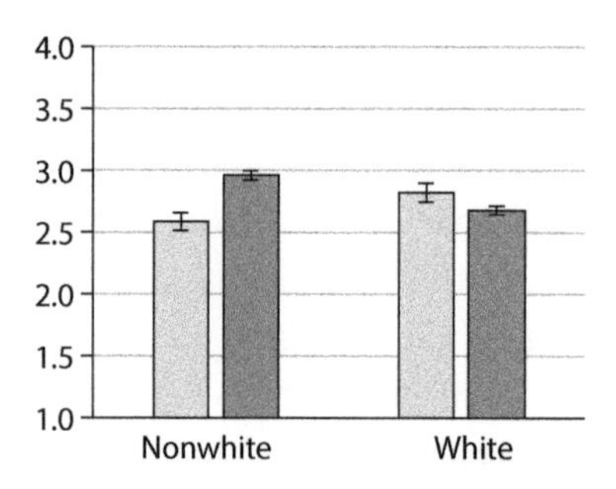

US gains jobs, trading partner loses jobs
US gains jobs, trading partner gains jobs

FIGURE 6.3. Support for Trade Agreements by Whether US or Trading Partner Country Gains/Loses Jobs, by Race of Respondent
Source: US Trade Survey-Experiment, 2013–2014 (GfK Ltd.).
Note: The dependent variable represents extent of Support for Trade on a 1 to 4 scale where high scores indicate greater support. On the left, the interaction between Race of respondent and whether jobs were gained versus lost by the US or the Trading Partner was statistically significant ($F = 21.54$, $p < .001$), as was the overall preference for job gains within one's own nation (main effect of condition: $F = 308.16$, $p < .001$). On the right, the interaction between Race of respondent and whether the Trading partner also gained jobs was statistically significant ($F = 18.72$, $p < .001$). An index of trade support assessed months earlier was used as a covariate in these analyses. The representative national sample included 1138 whites and 348 non-whites.

their reasoning about trade. Dominant groups are most supportive when the agreement furthers a dominant position. Minorities are, in contrast, significantly more supportive than whites of the policy in which everyone benefits.

The findings in Figure 6.3 suggest that being a part of a dominant or subordinate group conditions the way in which one evaluates the same trade agreement. Minorities perceive trade most positively when it benefits both the home country and trading partner countries. They appear to take into consideration effects on "others" when forming their views. Whites, on the other hand, are most supportive of a policy when it benefits the home country, but harms the trading partner country. Even though a trade agreement between two countries is not supposed to be a competition with winners and losers, whites' preferences reflect a desire to "win" and maintain dominance in the international hierarchy.

The same pattern of results shown for whites and non-whites was also true for men and women, as shown in Chapter 4. Like whites, men tend to have more ethnocentric patterns of trade support than women do. Although women are frequently said to favor trade less than men, this experiment demonstrated that this is really only true when trade is viewed as an arrangement in which the US dominates other countries, gaining things at others' expense. As subordinate groups, women and minorities are both less likely to favor a policy that creates winners and losers, even when their home country is the supposed winner.

These findings suggest that dominant groups expect to dominate; what is thought of as a "fair" trade agreement to a dominant group is one that gives them a greater relative advantage over the foreign outgroup. This is obviously a very high standard for a trade policy, and one that should make other nations reluctant to engage in agreements with the US.

In the lead up to the 2016 election, Trump encouraged Americans to view themselves as having been taken advantage of by trade with other countries. Thus they felt entitled to get more from a trade agreement than their trading partners would. Notably, this is not "fairness" by most traditional definitions; instead, it is based on the assumption that America has been taken advantage of in the past, and thus deserves to have an opportunity to even the score. It goes beyond the "myopic and self-indulgent pursuit of 'what's in it for us' economic policies"[26] to the pursuit of retribution, based on the assumption that foreigners have made past gains at US expense.

A Racial Basis to Favoring Trade Partners

The results in Chapter 5 establish that people's assumptions about with whom the US trades most vary a great deal, from the UK and Europe to African countries, to Bangladesh, Peru, and Brazil. But do these assumptions influence their overall attitudes toward trade along racial lines? Are those Americans who assume we trade more with light-skinned countries more supportive of trade if they are light-skinned themselves? The 2017 survey described in Chapter 5 asked respondents to name America's top three trading partner countries to the best of their ability. I later asked college students to code the countries that respondents had mentioned according to whether their impression was that the country was primarily a dark-skinned country or a light-skinned country.[27] To the extent that general trade preferences are driven by people's assumptions about the country's main trade partners, and trade preferences are tied to racial similarity, white Americans who name more dark-skinned countries would be predicted to be more opposed to trade. Given that two out of our three top trading partners are, indeed, racially different from the US (China and Mexico, but not Canada), some proportion of dark-skinned country mentions is to be expected due to a desire to name trading partners accurately, so I took this into account in modeling whether the dominant race of a country made a difference to respondents of majority/minority races. To the extent that racial similarity matters, then whites who assume that the US trades largely with dark-skinned countries will be more opposed to trade than those who assume that it trades more with light-skinned countries. The same should not be true of minorities.

The results of this analysis are shown in Table A6.1 in the online appendix. They suggest that as the proportion of dark-skinned countries that were mentioned rose, white respondents exhibited increasing hostility toward trade, whereas minorities did not.[28] For example, a white person who believed the top US trading partner countries were all dark-skinned had levels of trade support that were 10 percent lower than those assuming they were light-skinned.

These results do not necessarily indicate that mistaken perceptions of the countries with whom the US trades drive opposition to foreign commerce. Given the observational nature of this evidence, it could be that those who oppose trade simply named what they see as less desirable trading partners to reinforce their point that trade is not a good thing. But it could be the case that whites who presume we trade primarily with dark-skinned countries are less favorable as a result. The fact that this relationship is important strictly for white Americans but not for minorities lends support to this interpretation. So do the findings in Chapter 5 indicating that forgetting Canada as one of our primary trading partners lowers trade support, whereas forgetting China makes people more positive toward trade. But because dark-skinned countries may differ from the US in other ways, this observational evidence is suggestive at best.

Race, Trade, and Product Preferences

Additional survey data allowed yet another examination of my hypothesis that minorities and majority whites evaluate trade in ways that reflect their own experiences as dominant/subordinate groups in society. In 2008, a survey by *Fortune* magazine asked a nationally representative sample of Americans, “Here are some places which export many products to the US. For each one, please tell me whether you are more likely to purchase a product manufactured in this area, less likely, or doesn’t it matter to you in

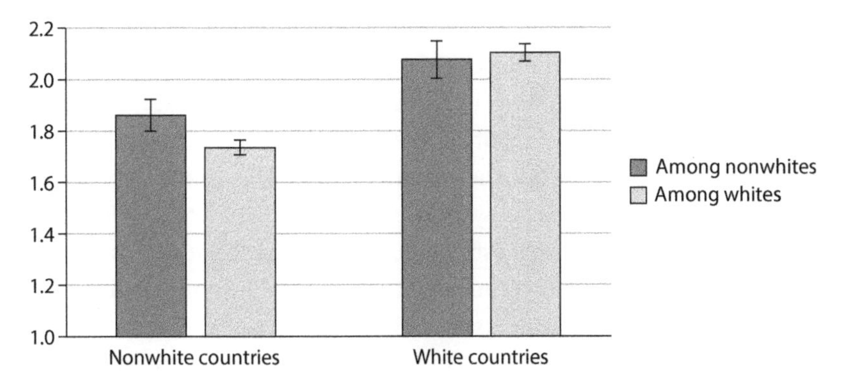

FIGURE 6.4. Favorability Toward Purchasing Imports from Trading Countries Based on Dominant Skin Color in Trading Partner Country, by Race of US Respondent
Source: Fortune magazine 2008 (Abt SRBI, Inc.)
Note: The interaction between Race of respondent and the dominant Race of trading partner countries is significant ($F = 12.77$, $p < .001$), as is the main effect of race of country ($F = 94.70$, $p < .001$). Sample sizes included 815 whites and 177 Blacks and Hispanics. Age and Education served as covariates in this analysis given their well-known relationship with general support for international trade.

your purchase decision?" Responses were coded on a three-point scale. The order in which the countries were asked about was randomized, and the list included five countries and one continent with predominately non-white populations (India, China, Mexico, Japan, South Korea, and Africa) and three countries/continents with predominately light-skinned populations (Western Europe, Eastern Europe, and Canada). For each respondent, I constructed a measure of his or her desire to buy products made in light-skinned and dark-skinned countries based on the respondent's average level of support for each of these two subsets of countries.

People are frequently unaware of where a product is made, and thus their actual behavior may not reflect the attitudes they express in a survey. But it almost certainly reflects their *attitudes* toward buying exports from said country. If my theory is correct, to the extent that the race of the target country influences an individual's purchase decision, it should have a more pronounced effect on majority white Americans than on minorities. Although buying products made in another country is not the same thing as favoring trade relations with them, my theory implies that people should have greater trust in products as well as countries with people who seem similar.

As shown on the right side of Figure 6.4, both whites and non-whites in the US express greater enthusiasm for buying imports from light-skinned countries/continents, such as Europe and Great Britain. [29] This pattern could reflect attributes of the specific dark-skinned and light-skinned countries that were named, or the generally higher status of whites. However, as shown on the left side of Figure 6.4, when evaluating the desirability of imports from non-white countries/continents, such as China, Japan, and Africa, minorities are significantly more enthusiastic than whites.[30] The pattern in Figure 6.4 clearly suggests a racial component to attitudes toward products made in different countries. Respondents' own racial identities influence their views of products made in light-skinned and dark-skinned countries. Products made in dark-skinned countries were more favored by minorities than by whites, and products made in light-skinned countries were equally favored by both.

Implications for Minority Opinions toward Trade

Given that the US will become a majority minority nation in the near future, it is worth considering what these results suggest about whether minorities will be likely to support or oppose international trade in the coming years. The trade preferences that minorities express can be expected to reflect multiple considerations, including a trading partner country's similarities and differences from the US, and whether trade is perceived to be a policy for mutual benefit or for exploitation of the trading partner. Minorities are more likely to favor trade if it is framed as cooperation rather than exploitation.

Instead of conceiving of trade preferences as a function of individuals assessing their personal financial interests, this evidence suggests that trade preferences are informed by people's collective identities, not just as Americans, but also as members of racial and ethnic groups. The extent to which foreignness affects people's judgments about the trustworthiness of others is different for subordinate and dominant groups. Although they are also Americans, minorities are known to be deemed more "foreign" by parts of mainstream white culture in the US. President Trump, for example, told a group of four minority congresswomen that they should "go back" to the countries they came from.[31] To the extent that the American identity is still tied to being white, minorities are unlikely to view trade from the perspective of an American ingroup versus foreign outgroups.

Despite minorities' disadvantaged economic status, during the ten years leading up to 2016, these groups consistently expressed greater support for free trade than whites, even after controlling for the usual demographic suspects. In Figures A6.1 and A6.2 in the online appendix, I summarize some of this evidence drawing on questions about international trade in general, opinions of specific trade agreements, and attitudes toward globalization and outsourcing.[32] The size of the racial gap in trade preferences grew in magnitude during this period, steadily increasing in size from 2007 to 2016.[33] The difference in opinions by race is generally small, relative to say, the gap between how whites and minorities view affirmative action or social welfare policies. But the number of minorities in many survey samples is also small, making it surprising that racial differences are consistently identifiable during this period.

In addition, the extent to which party identification accounts for racial differences in trade preferences steadily increased. In 2007 it accounted for only 6 percent of the gap; in 2013, this became 12 percent; by 2016, partisanship accounted for a whopping 38 percent of the racial gap in trade preferences.[34] Over time, the gap in trade support between whites and minorities has become closely aligned with differences in party identification. Nonwhites are more likely to be Democrats, and, as described in Chapter 3, Democrats became the more pro-trade of the two American political parties as of the early 2000s.[35]

As the US minority population grows larger and more internally diverse, it is natural to wonder if all or only some groups react as I have outlined in this chapter. Because nationally representative surveys tend to have small numbers of distinct minority groups, I cannot easily answer that question. However, in one unusually large survey, there were enough minorities so that they could be broken down by specific races and ethnicities while still maintaining adequate numbers of people per group. Results suggested that Hispanics/Latinos were most favorable toward trade, and African-Americans less favorable, though not as unfavorable toward trade as Whites. A fourth catchall group of "Others," including those of mixed races, fell in between Hispanics and Blacks.[36]

Hispanics' especially positive views on trade may reflect an ongoing identification with other countries as well as identification as a non-dominant race in the US. For example, it would make sense for a Mexican-American to favor a trade agreement between the US and Mexico if he or she believed it would help Mexican jobs as well as US jobs. Affective ties to other countries should logically make it harder to adopt a "screw the trading partner" attitude toward trade policies and promote greater support for agreements perceived to be mutually beneficial "win-win" policies.

During the period that the "trade-as-aid" perspective dominated the American public's thinking about trade, minorities were quite supportive, just as the experimental findings suggest they should be. But since Trump's election, trade has been increasingly portrayed by the president as a means of dominating other countries. Republican support for trade has soared as a result. But what has this shift meant for minority support for trade?

Since the 2016 election, the effects of party have swamped race. Republicans became increasingly pro-trade just as soon as Trump took office, and this surge in support has continued thus far. Both white and minority Republicans show similar trajectories. Non-white Democrats did not change their levels of support for trade; in fact, they persisted with the same level of support as before. But the increased support among Republicans was enough to make non-whites less supportive of trade than whites by 2020, despite the lack of any change in non-whites' views on trade. White Democrats also increased their trade support to a small extent around 2018 when Trump's trade war was heavily featured in the news.

Implications of Racial Differences in Evaluating Trade

Collectively, these results have several noteworthy implications. First, they reinforce previous findings suggesting that non-material factors can influence trade attitudes. If under-represented minorities were motivated primarily by economic considerations, these results would look quite different. Because country similarity matters less to minorities than to whites, just as it matters less to minorities that their neighborhood look like them, they are open to trading with even highly dissimilar countries. More surprisingly, even when the so-called winners and losers from a given trade agreement are known, minorities reason differently and are more likely to value the gains of trading partners than are whites.

A second implication of these findings is related to the rising proportion of Americans who are minorities. Minorities tend to hold more favorable views of trade than whites when it is framed as a form of cooperation for mutual benefit. But they hold more negative views of trade framed as a competition with winners and losers. Which framing of trade is likely to persist?

My guess is that Trump's repackaging of trade as a policy of international dominance is unlikely to survive the Trump presidency for multiple reasons. Once Republicans are no longer in power, they are likely to sour on trade once again, in part due to the party-in-power effect documented in Chapter 3. Once they are out of office, Republicans are likely to default to even lower levels of trust in government than Democrats had. This negative change could be quite pronounced and mimic the decline in Republican support for trade during the Obama administration. The rising proportion of minority Americans is probably a more natural constituency in support of international trade than Republicans have been. However, political leaders who talk about trade as cooperation will gain more ground with minorities than those who promote it as a competition among great powers, regardless of who they claim is "winning."

Once racial minorities are a majority, is it possible that they will also prefer competition and dominance to equality in trade relationships? This seems doubtful. Even though minorities will constitute a numerical majority, they are unlikely to achieve economic and social dominance in that same time period. When whites are a smaller proportion of the population, they are still likely to be more economically well off than racial minorities. Because minorities will still experience non-dominant status in American society, they will still be likely to take the impact on outgroup members into account more than whites.

A third implication is tied to how whites and minorities view social welfare programs. In the US, negative views of trade stem overwhelmingly from concerns that open foreign commerce contributes to job losses. Trade advocates have long assumed that if the social safety net in the US were only stronger, then job displacement would be viewed less negatively, and trade would receive more widespread support. I demonstrate in Chapter 7 that stronger safety nets do indeed predict more pro-trade views in both the US and Canada. But the problem with pursuing better safety nets as a means to bolster trade support is that at least before 2016, the people most unhappy with trade were the same people most opposed to social welfare programs. Minority support for safety nets comports nicely with the tendency to support free trade. But whites are more likely to oppose strengthening the social safety net, in part because it is perceived to benefit those who are not similar to them. Even though it is supposedly white men who are most upset about the loss of manufacturing jobs, if white Americans view policies such as Trade Adjustment Assistance (TAA) as yet another undesirable government handout, this approach can do little to offset the negative effects of trade on these groups. In a rapidly shifting global economy, the US will inevitably be at a severe disadvantage if it cannot help its workforce respond effectively to change.

7

Is This Inevitable?

A CROSS-NATIONAL COMPARISON

Nations serve as highly salient group memberships. Is it therefore inevitable that attitudes toward international trade must be rooted in ingroup-outgroup biases? The results from Chapter 4 imply that this could be the case. To the extent that human tendencies toward tribalism are simply extended to nation-states, trade agreements might seem doomed to be viewed as competitions in which each country seeks to take advantage of the other.

At the same time, just as there are individual differences in this tendency, there are vast differences from country to country in the extent to which one country's gains from trade are seen as another country's losses. Differences in absolute levels of support for trade may occur across countries for a whole host of reasons, including the relative size of nations, their historical dependence on trade, their locations, and their access to natural resources. For my purposes, I am less interested in the myriad influences on a country's average level of trade support than I am in whether people in different countries respond the same way that Americans do by increasing or decreasing their support for trade due to the same kinds of ingroup-outgroup considerations.

Competitiveness in the US and Canada

In Chapter 4, I showed how differences in attitudes toward trade in the US were related to differences in how people feel about competition and dominance. For example, Republicans and Democrats have different reactions to the same experimentally-specified trade agreements, just as differences between men and women result in differences in levels of support for identical agreements. I attributed this to the fact that both men and Republicans are likely to see greater value in competition. Republicans and men are also more likely to view trade as competition. The desire to "win" and to dominate the outgroup thus becomes the goal of trade rather than reaping mutual benefits.

Likewise, cross-national differences in attitudes toward free trade should be related to how people in different nations feel about competition. Certainly, people care more about their home team than the other team. That much is likely to be universal. But competitiveness *increases* the extent to which people favor their ingroups over outgroups. This suggests that perhaps the extent of ingroup favoritism evident in American trade preferences is not universal.

America is a highly competitive culture. Its enthusiasm for competition is unmatched by any other industrialized country in the world.[1] As mentioned in Chapter 1, it is the country most favorable toward competition of any country studied by the World Values Surveys. Canadians are less positively predisposed toward competition. To examine whether a less competitive national culture might respond differently to the same ingroup and outgroup considerations, I conducted the same large-scale survey experiment described at length in Chapter 4, but this time using a representative sample of English-speaking and French-speaking Canadians. My goal was to evaluate the role of ingroup and outgroup considerations experimentally in these two countries in order to better understand what it is about the American response to trade that is unique.

I chose Canada as the basis for a cross-national comparison for several reasons. In both the US and Canada, trade policies are viewed mainly in terms of their potential effects on job availability.[2] Jobs thus lend a common currency for evaluating how much a country gains or loses. Both countries are also high-skill, wealthy democracies.

Key differences between these two countries are equally useful for these purposes. Most importantly, Canadians are significantly less enthusiastic about the benefits of competition. Comparisons of US and Canadian culture suggest that Americans emphasize individualism and achievement, whereas Canadians are more collectivist in their value orientations.[3] Canadians have been characterized as self-deprecators, who can tolerate losing, whereas Americans are "descended from winners."[4] For this reason, the effects of ingroup favoritism on trade support should be weaker in Canada than in the US, even when forming attitudes toward identical trade policies and even when they start from differing initial levels of support. Competitive attitudes discourage consideration of the other country, and encourage differential valuation of the home country's well-being relative to the trading partner country's well-being. In other words, competition should intensify ingroup favoritism and encourage outgroup indifference.

Canadians are known to be more supportive of trade than Americans, as is true in my national surveys as well. But by using identical experiments in the US and Canada, and holding constant the costs and/or benefits of specific trade agreements to the home country and to trading partner countries, I can easily observe differences in how much people take the home country and trading partner country gains and losses into account, independent of their pre-existing preferences.

In the survey-experiment on American trade preferences described in Chapter 4, results suggested that when Americans decided whether to support a trade agreement, it was not simply based on how many total jobs were created by the agreement. Instead, I observed three distinct patterns of ingroup-outgroup bias. First, Americans were more likely to favor an agreement that benefitted Americans than one that provided the same total benefits to trading partner countries; that is, they consistently demonstrated ingroup favoritism. Since Canadians are less competitive, one would expect less evidence of ingroup favoritism among these citizens. Competitiveness is known to increase ingroup favoritism.[5]

Outgroup indifference is the second form of intergroup bias examined in Chapter 4; when Americans' level of support for a policy was driven entirely by how much it benefitted Americans, without regard for how trading partner countries were affected. Indeed, in the American case, a trade policy that also benefitted the availability of jobs in trading partner countries was viewed no more favorably on average than one that did not. As with ingroup favoritism, competition is known to influence the extent to which people take others into account; in other words, it circumscribes the extent of moral inclusion versus exclusion. People's moral circles—the boundaries distinguishing those deemed deserving of moral consideration from those not deserving—contract when they feel threatened by competition.[6] Competitive contexts constrict people's scope of moral concern and increase the extent to which others are deemed outside the boundaries of those whose well-being "counts." Competition should lead to greater devaluation of the effects of trade on those in other countries, even when both countries are benefitting from a trade agreement. In the context of trade, this would manifest itself in exclusive attention to a policy's effects on the home country and lack of consideration given to any effects on trading partner countries. In other words, competition should encourage people to be indifferent to how the outgroup is affected.

A third form of intergroup bias that was evident in Chapter 4 involved Americans who demonstrated a desire to forego trade's benefits for their own country unless they could benefit *more than* their trading partner countries. If they could not "win" and dominate the other country by getting a relatively *better* deal than the others were, then they were willing to sacrifice the job gains that a trade agreement would bring. This emphasis on relative gains has been noted in past studies of American opinions on trade,[7] but it is unclear whether favoring strictly a policy that guarantees that the home country gain more than the trading partner is universally attractive or peculiarly desirable for highly competitive countries like the US. By comparing how Canadians reacted to these identical agreements, my co-author, Amber Hye-Yon Lee and I shed light on the extent to which these patterns of preferences are unique or common in inter-country relations.

My Country First? The Role of Ingroup Favoritism

In his inaugural address, Trump celebrated "the right of all nations to put their own interests first."[8] On trade policy, in particular, he denounced "the ravages of other countries, making our products, stealing our companies, and destroying our jobs." Trump referred to trade deals as the "raping" of the United States by other countries, benefitting trading partner countries while exploiting Americans.[9] His perspective glorified the idea of favoring one's fellow Americans over the citizens of other countries. The "America First" argument encouraged Americans to value the well-being of distant others less than those closer to home.

In my studies of both the US and Canada, many citizens in both countries responded with virtually indistinguishable pleas to "Put Canada/America first!" But such exclamations are not an accurate means of assessing the extent to which ingroup favoritism influences their levels of trade support. Toward that end I looked at differences in people's levels of support for trade when the same number of jobs were gained and lost in total, and only *who* gained or lost them, the home country or the trading partner country, was altered.

As illustrated in Figure 7.1, in the two representative national survey experiments, both Americans and Canadians exhibited clear ingroup favoritism in that they favored a trade policy to a greater extent when it benefitted

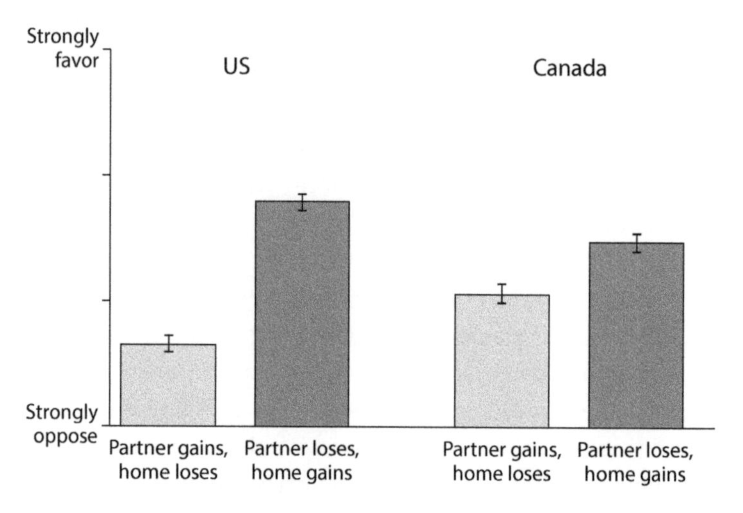

FIGURE 7.1. Ingroup Favoritism: Trade Support by Country and Who Wins versus Loses

Source: US Trade Survey-Experiment, 2013–2014 and Canadian Trade Survey-Experiment 2015.

Note: The results of the analysis confirming a significant interaction between *Who wins vs. loses* and *Country* are presented in Table A7.1 ($p < .001$).

the home country instead of trading partner countries. However, the extent of ingroup favoritism—as illustrated by the differences between the two experimental conditions—is significantly greater for Americans than for Canadians.[10] When the trading partner gains and the home country loses jobs, Canadians are more supportive than Americans of the same policy. When the home country gains and the trading partner loses jobs, Americans are significantly more supportive of the policy than Canadians. Ingroup favoritism is evident across both countries, but it is a much stronger force among Americans, the more highly competitive country.

In the detailed analyses shown in Table A7.1 in the online appendix, it is also worth noting that once the US-Canadian difference in the extent of ingroup favoritism is taken into account, there are no remaining differences in mean levels of support for trade in the US and Canada. This suggests that the source of difference identified here is a fairly important one.

In Chapter 4, I noted that ingroup favoritism is greater among Americans who are high in social dominance orientation, that is, those who believe that some groups should rightfully dominate others. Do differences in social dominance between the two countries likewise explain differences in the extent of ingroup favoritism between Americans and Canadians? Using the same SDO scale asked of representative samples in both countries, I found

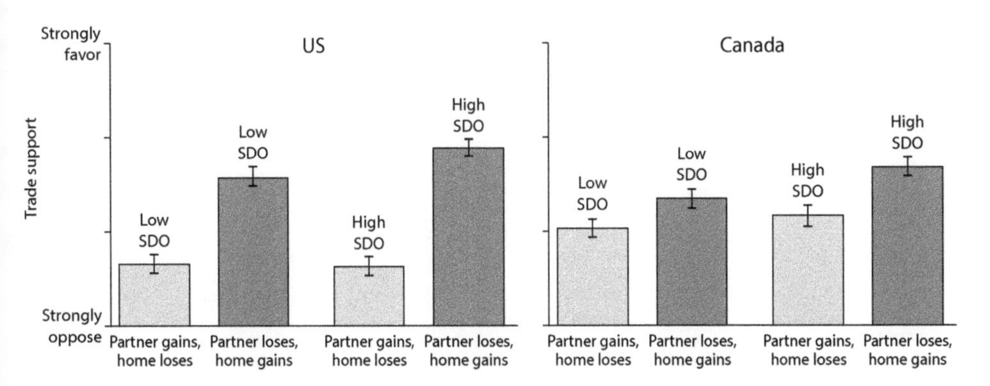

FIGURE 7.2. High Social Dominance Encourages Ingroup Favoritism, Especially in the US
Source: US Trade Survey-Experiment, 2013–2014 and Canadian Trade Survey-Experiment 2015.
Note: The pooled sample produces a significant interaction between *Who wins vs. loses* and *Social dominance orientation* ($p < .001$), as well as between *Country* and *Who wins vs. loses* ($p < .001$). See Table A7.2.

that Canadians have significantly lower levels of social dominance than Americans.[11] This is consistent with evidence that ingroup favoritism plays less of a role in Canadian trade preferences.

In Figure 7.2, I show levels of trade support in identical experimental conditions for those low and high in social dominance, dividing the sample at their pooled US-Canadian median. The difference in the height of the light and dark columns represents the extent of ingroup favoritism in each comparison. Two findings jump out in Figure 7.2. First, there is consistently greater ingroup favoritism among those high in social dominance in both the US and Canada. If a person believes in hierarchy, they also believe that *their* group should get more and end up on top.

The second pattern evident in Figure 7.2 is that even when holding SDO constant, that is, comparing strictly within low and high SDO groups, Americans consistently demonstrate a greater extent of ingroup favoritism than Canadians. Americans are not only higher in SDO overall, a characteristic that encourages ingroup favoritism, they are also more likely to demonstrate ingroup favoritism *within* identically-defined low and high SDO groups.

One final comparison further illustrates differences in the extent of ingroup favoritism in the US and Canada. Using a pre-experiment measure of whether respondents in the US and Canada already viewed the effects of trade on jobs in competitive, zero-sum terms, Figure 7.3 demonstrates how viewing trade as an inherently competitive enterprise influences the extent of ingroup favoritism in response to experimental treatments. Again, comparing the difference in height of the dark and light columns, Figure 7.3

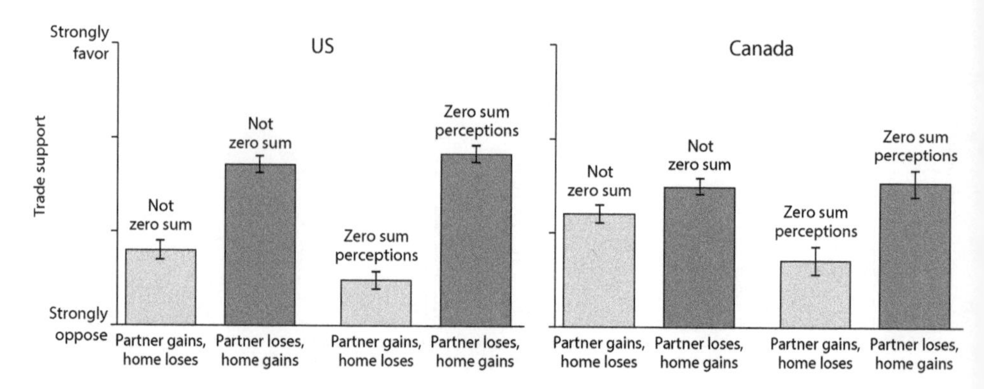

FIGURE 7.3. Zero-Sum Perceptions Encourage Ingroup Favoritism, Especially in the US
Note: The pooled sample produces a significant interaction between *Who wins vs. loses* and *Zero-sum perceptions* ($p < .001$), as well as between *Country* and *Who wins vs. loses* ($p < .001$). See Table A7.3.

shows that those who view trade as zero-sum demonstrate far more ingroup favoritism in response to experimental treatments across both countries. Even though the exact consequences of these trade agreements is specified identically for respondents, those who already viewed trade as a zero-sum endeavor exhibited far more ingroup favoritism than those who did not.

The second key finding in Figure 7.3 is that the size of these ingroup favoritism effects is consistently muted for Canadians. Even among identically-defined subgroups, Canadians responded much less strongly to treatments indicating who would win or lose from a given trade agreement. Ingroup favoritism is evident in both countries, but even when examining subgroups that are most prone to it, that is, those who start out believing trade is zero-sum with respect to jobs, and those high in SDO, Canadians appear less reactive to competitive impulses.

The findings in Figures 7.1, 7.2, and 7.3 all suggest that Americans are more prone to ingroup favoritism than are Canadians. Aside from making some of us want to move to Canada, what implications can be drawn from these findings? A national culture that emphasizes competition is much less fertile ground for viewing trade as a form of cooperation.

Outgroup Indifference or Moral Inclusion?

Trade preferences are clearly influenced by the perceived effects of trade on the well-being of the home country.[12] But how much do the consequences of trade for trading partner countries factor into people's support for trade? Under some circumstances, people care about the well-being of outsiders and include them in their scope of moral concern.[13] One would think that a "win-win" trade agreement that benefits both countries would elicit the greatest support from all nations. After all, the "fair trade" movement emerged from a concern that workers in other countries were being taken advantage of by international trade. What could be better than a trade agreement that clearly benefits everyone?

Ironically, when Americans talk about "fairness" in the context of trade today, it comes up more often in the context of questioning whether there is a level playing field in a competition among nations.[14] As the US Chamber of Commerce admonished, "No one wants to go into a basketball game down by a dozen points from the tip-off."[15] The implication here is that American businesses have been disadvantaged in the past and therefore "fairness" would require *better,* rather than equal, treatment.

If my expectation regarding the significance of competitiveness is correct, then the extent to which effects on "others" are considered should vary by country depending upon the value placed on competition and winning. To examine whether the less competitive Canadians were more likely to take into account effects on trading partners, I compared mean levels of trade support between the two experimental conditions in which the home country gains jobs from trade in both, but in one condition the trading partner loses jobs, while in the second condition the trading partner also gains jobs, along with the home country. If there are no differences in levels of support for a trade policy that benefits the home country but costs the trading partner, versus a "win-win" policy in which *both* countries gain jobs, then citizens are ignoring the well-being of those in the other country and excluding them from their scope of moral concern.

Figure 7.4 illustrates how for Americans, the only thing that mattered was the extent of job gains for Americans. They were equally supportive of the trade policy regardless of how it affected the trading partner countries. Canadians, in contrast, were more supportive of a policy in which *both* Canadians and their trading partners gained jobs.[16] Americans were indifferent to whether the trade policy helped or hurt jobs in the trading partner country so long as it benefitted the US, whereas Canadians were more supportive of mutual gains.

Of course, as shown in Chapter 4, it is possible that this aggregate American "indifference" to how trading partners are affected masks subgroups who are more favorable when the trading partner also benefits, and those who are less favorable when the trading partner benefits. To examine this possibility, I next break these findings down by the subgroups most likely to demonstrate such patterns.

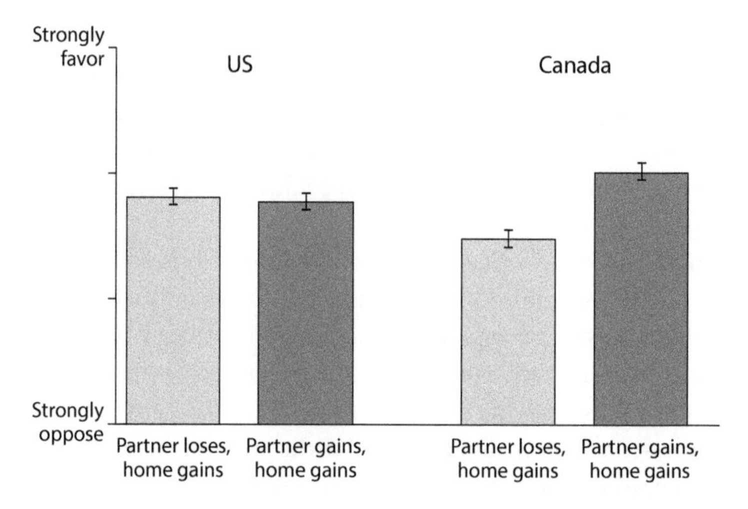

FIGURE 7.4. Outgroup Indifference: Trade Support by Country and Whether Trading Partners Also Win
Source: US Trade Survey-Experiment, 2013–2014 and Canadian Trade Survey-Experiment 2015.
Note: The results of the analysis confirm a significant interaction between *Whether trading partner also wins* and *Country* ($p < .001$). See Table A7.4.

"Winning" at Trade

In the classic minimal group psychological experiment illustrating the desire for group dominance, when people are given a choice of taking their ingroup's maximum benefit, which also provides the same benefit to the outgroup, as opposed to an option in which the ingroup benefits less than the maximum, but benefits *more than* the outgroup, they typically choose the latter. As the authors of this classic study note, "It is the winning that seems more important to them."[17] Sacrificing ingroup benefits in order to maximize the difference in the amounts the two groups receive is a competitive act just as in the choice Vladimir makes in Chapter 4. Likewise, in a series of experiments focused on neglect of the interests of outsiders, researchers found that people place high value on doing not just well, but doing *better than* others.[18]

Although the studies in this chapter were done long before Trump was elected president, he spoke directly to Americans' competitive instincts when he announced for office:

> Our country is in serious trouble. We don't have victories anymore. We used to have victories, but we don't have them. When was the last time

anybody saw us beating, let's say, China in a trade deal? They kill us. I beat China all the time. All the time."[19]

As seen through this lens, what is important in trade agreements is not cooperation for mutual benefit, nor fairness, but taking advantage of another country. Trump described trade as an exercise in dominance, an opportunity to win a competition. As he promised, "We will have so much winning if I get elected, that you may get bored with winning."[20]

Figure 7.5 examines separately those Americans and Canadians who are most likely to care about winning, those high in social dominance orientation. On the right-hand side of Figure 7.5, it is clear that even high SDO Canadians prefer the win-win policy more than the one in which they win and their trading partners lose jobs. This is also true for Americans low in SDO. But high SDO Americans, in contrast, are more keen on the policy in which Americans win and their trading partners lose. One would assume that the win-win trade deal would be most popular across the board since there is no downside to having one's trading partner benefit as well. But Americans who are high in social dominance are significantly *less* likely to support a win-win trade agreement than one that provides Americans with a relative advantage by helping Americans while hurting foreigners. Americans' most competitive instincts are in evidence in their desire to "win" by gaining more than the other country.

The same American hyper-competitiveness is evident when evaluating trade support among Americans and Canadians who view trade through a zero-sum framework. As shown in Figure 7.6, among Canadians, the win-win agreement is consistently more strongly supported, regardless of whether the Canadians started with a zero-sum frame. Among Americans, in contrast, those approaching trade with zero-sum assumptions are less likely to favor the win-win agreement.

Zero-sum perceptions lower support for trade in the US relative to Canada in two ways. First, Americans are roughly twice as likely as Canadians to believe that trade benefits the availability of jobs in foreign countries at the expense of the home country. Second, zero-sum thinking alters how Canadians and Americans react to identical trade agreements, making Americans less likely to support even a mutually beneficial policy.

Overall, these results are highly consistent with the argument that valuing competition and viewing trade as competitive increases the role of ingroup favoritism, that is, assigning greater value to co-nationals' well-being than

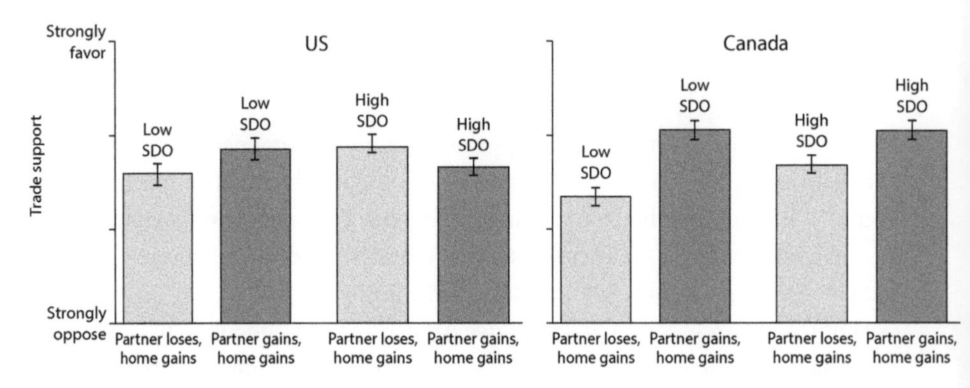

FIGURE 7.5. High Social Dominance Orientation Encourages Outgroup Indifference in the US, but not in Canada

Source: US Trade Survey-Experiment, 2013–2014 and Canadian Trade Survey-Experiment 2015.

Note: The pooled sample produces a significant interaction between *Whether trading partner also wins and social dominance orientation* ($p < .001$) as well as C*ountry* and *Whether trading partner also wins* ($p < .001$). See Table A7.5.

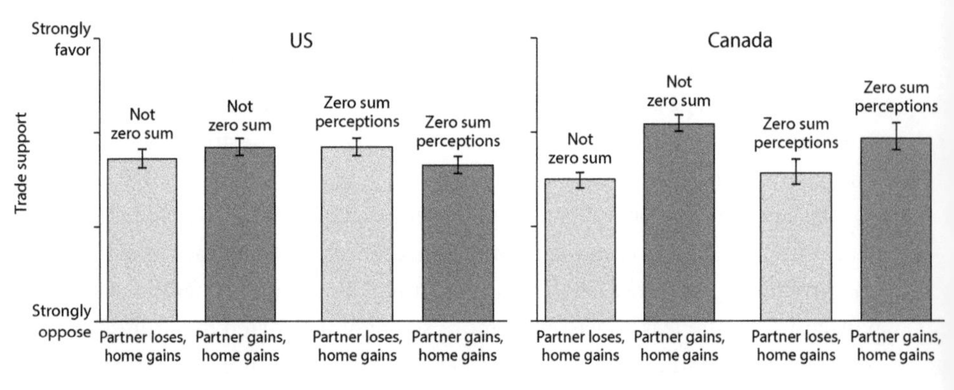

FIGURE 7.6. Zero-Sum Perceptions Encourage Desire for Greater Relative Gains in the US, but not in Canada.

Source: US Trade Survey-Experiment, 2013–2014 and Canadian Trade Survey-Experiment 2015.

Note: The pooled sample produces a significant interaction between *whether trading partner also wins* and *zero-sum perceptions* ($p < .001$) as well as between country and *whether trading partner also wins* ($p < .001$). See Table A7.6.

to how outsiders are affected. Among Americans, competition also encourages outgroup indifference, that is, neglecting how the outgroup is affected. Finally, Americans also have more negative attitudes toward policies that benefit those outside of their national ingroup, even when the size of the benefit to their own country is the same.

The Inevitability of Ingroup Bias

These findings indirectly speak to concerns about whether international trade is doomed to be a policy involving countries jockeying to get the best of their supposed opponents. If tendencies toward ingroup favoritism simply represent human nature, then the experimental treatments should induce roughly the same differences across experimental conditions in Canada and the US, regardless of these populations' initial levels of support for trade. While Canadians show evidence of ingroup favoritism in these results just as Americans do, the ingroup biases that are ratcheted up by competition are much stronger in the American sample than in the Canadian one. This suggests that the magnitude of effects found in the US is not inevitable. Under conditions in which people are less likely to view trade as a zero-sum game, or less concerned about dominating the other, support for trade agreements is higher.

Should we expect the observations in these experiments to be reflected in real-world trade support in Canada and the US? On the one hand, the samples of respondents are highly representative and closely mirror their respective national populations, so the generalizability of the samples is high.[21] On the other hand, we purposely described trade policies as if there were *known* consequences for the home country and trading partner countries. We do not know which of these scenarios most Americans or Canadians assume when they formed opinions about, say, NAFTA, the TPP, or the USMCA. Nonetheless, our results are useful for understanding the theoretical basis underlying trade preferences and how linking trade to competition as opposed to cooperation may adversely affect levels of support.

Is it realistic to think that in the real world, people form trade attitudes based on their impressions of job losses and gains in the home country and in trading partner countries? Survey data suggest that people do hold such impressions. Moreover, our experimental findings confirm that these perceptions have consequences for trade preferences. When forming attitudes toward trade, citizens think about how their own country will be affected as well as how they believe trading partner countries will be affected. As noted in Chapter 1, trade is in this sense doubly sociotropic; its collective effects on both the home country and on other countries are relevant. Further, competitiveness alters the extent to which these factors influence trade preferences. Trade preferences in the US are a function of trade's perceived impact on the home country and on trading partner countries, moderated by the extent to which trade itself is perceived to be a form of competition as opposed to cooperation and whether an individual believes that competition is a beneficial force.

When a trading partner was described as gaining a large number of jobs in our study, many respondents who offered open-ended comments claimed the agreement was therefore "unfair." However, if trade is considered in moral terms, "it seems important to contemplate how to assign and compare the values of a new job to someone who would otherwise be stuck in dire poverty and a lost job for someone with at least some version of a safety net."[22] The limitations of the American safety net are well-known, but they may still be better than what people envision for workers in trading partner countries.

How Much Is One American/Canadian Worth?

I have thus far ignored the variations in experimental treatments produced by the *magnitude* of home country and trading partner country gains and losses. Because they cancel one another out in the aggregate, it was simpler to describe results in terms of who gains or loses jobs. Although an economist might expect these numbers to influence levels of trade support, I did not necessarily expect this because trade seemed to be viewed by the public in largely symbolic rather than instrumental terms. Studies of price elasticity, that is, the extent to which demand for a product goes down as its cost increases, demonstrate that public goods are highly inelastic relative to private consumer goods.[23] For example, small increases in the cost of a consumer good reduce the proportion of people willing pay for it. But the willingness of people to pay more for a public good such as the environment is far less sensitive to the price tag attached. Even the exact same good framed as a public versus a private good will generate less elasticity in willingness to pay as a public good across a broad range of costs.[24]

On the one hand, trade is often framed in terms of the personal benefit of jobs to individuals. On the other hand, if these jobs are not viewed as individual goods so much as collective goods, then they may well follow the pattern described for public goods. For example, in an experimental study varying how many outgroup and ingroup lives were lost in hypothetical war under competitive and non-competitive contexts, the researchers found that even when very large numbers of enemy civilian lives were at stake, the magnitude of loss mattered little.[25] People are just not very sensitive to the magnitude of gains and losses.

Using the data on varying levels of job gain and loss in the experimental scenarios, Figure 7.7 quantifies roughly how many foreigners must benefit

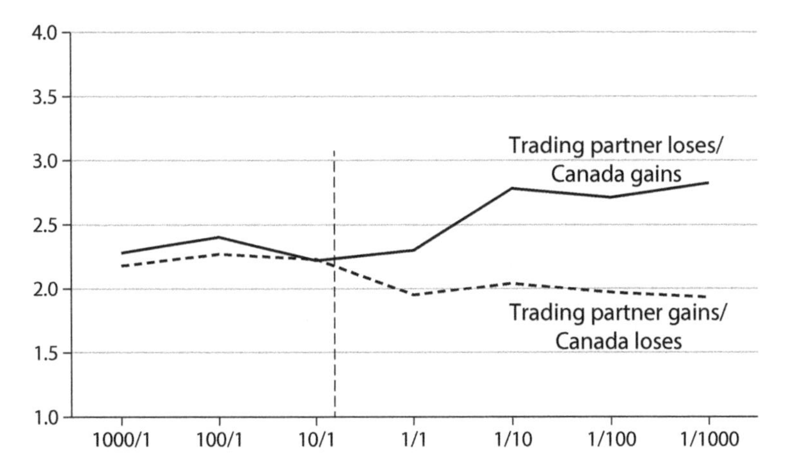

FIGURE 7.7. How Much Is One Canadian Job Worth According to Canadians?
Source: Canadian Trade Survey-Experiment 2015.
Note: The y-axis represents support for a trade agreement between the home country and foreign country. The Canadian lines are not significantly different from one another to the left of the dashed vertical line.

for a trade policy to offset the cost of one home country job loss in Canada. As shown by the grey vertical line in the top panel of Figure 7.7, the answer to the question of how much one Canadian job is worth to Canadians is that roughly 10 jobs gained by foreigners offsets the cost of one Canadian job loss in the minds of Canadians. Levels of public support for the trade policy become roughly equal at that point. Recall that Figure 4.2 shows the same result for this survey-experiment in the US. For Americans, the two lines never cross or even come close to one another. Even when 1,000 jobs were gained in the trading partner country for one job loss in the US, levels of support for trade did not equalize. Americans clearly demonstrate far more extreme ingroup favoritism than Canadians when considering trade agreements.

There will inevitably be those who point to other, largely economic, differences between the US and Canada as the reason that they react differently from Americans to whether the home country and trading partner countries gain or lose jobs. For example, one obvious difference is the greater strength of the social welfare system in Canada. If one has a stronger safety net, then there is good reason not to fear job loss to the same extent that Americans might. I asked both the American and Canadian samples about the perceived strength of their safety nets in the pre-experiment survey, and Canadians did, indeed, rate their welfare system as stronger than Americans rated their own. Nonetheless, the perceived strength of their respective social welfare systems did not alter their reactions to these treatments in which respondents were randomly assigned across conditions.

National Superiority: The Strength of Ingroup Identity

In one sense economists already have acknowledged the role of ingroup favoritism and outgroup negativity in trade preferences. Many years ago, two studies used survey data from the International Social Survey Program (ISSP) to demonstrate that a sense of national superiority encouraged more protectionist views across a large sample of countries.[26] Using a single question that asked respondents how much they agreed or disagreed with the statement that their country "should limit the import of foreign products in order to protect its national economy" they found that protectionism was strongly correlated with a sense of national superiority across their sample of countries. Those with strong national identities are assumed to hold more ingroup pride and outgroup prejudice, although this is not always the case. Some dimensions of national pride promote negative views of outgroups, while others do not.[27] The ISSP protectionism question was less than ideal for testing this relationship because many people (and most economists) do not believe the basic premise of the question, that is, that limiting imports protects the national economy. Nonetheless, these early analyses confirmed that non-economic factors, and particularly the strength of national ingroup identity, was negatively related to support for trade.

Many political theorists would find a negative relationship between strong national identity and support for global engagement somewhat troubling.[28] Shouldn't citizens be able to feel a sense of pride in their country without succumbing to negative outgroup attitudes and economic protectionism? These results could have been a function of the ISSP question wording that aligns caring about the home country's economy with being protectionist, thus encouraging those with strong positive feelings about their country to endorse protectionism. Regardless, my US-Canadian evidence suggests that if this pattern of results was truly universal at that time, it is no longer.

In the American and Canadian survey-experiments discussed above, the pre-experimental part of the study simply surveyed respondents, both Americans and Canadians asking the same series of questions about their trade preferences as well as about their sense of national superiority and other characteristics. Since these questions were asked before the experimental portion of the study, they could be analyzed as observational data in order to provide a direct comparison of the relationship between national superiority and trade support in the US and Canada. In addition to asking about national superiority in a way that avoided the loaded question wording of the ISSP, these surveys included a highly reliable multi-item index of trade support, along with a reliable multi-item measure of national superiority, the chauvinistic sense that one's own country is better than others'.

When predicting trade support based on national superiority as well as a whole host of other predictors, the results were not what previous research would have predicted. As shown in Table A7.7 in the online appendix, among Americans in 2013, national superiority negatively predicted support for trade just as one would expect. But in the Canadian survey, national superiority *positively* predicted support for trade; the more a respondent thought Canada was the best country, the more they supported free trade agreements.

My first reaction, after thoroughly rechecking my data coding, was to assume that this reversal must be a function of some other variable in the multivariate equation that was skewing these relationships. But as it turned out, even the bivariate relationships between trade support and national superiority confirmed this same pattern. Americans who thought their country was superior to other countries reacted as one would expect from a strong ingroup identity; they were less likely to support international trade. In Canada, by contrast, a sense of national superiority and support for international trade went hand in hand.

Rather than pretend that I predicted this finding, I will offer a well-considered post-hoc interpretation based on Canadian history and previous scholarship. Canadian national identity is somewhat unique. Unlike the United States, Canada has officially defined itself as a multicultural nation. Canada is the only country in which multiculturalism is officially enshrined as part its constitution, by virtue of the 1988 Canadian Multiculturalism Act.[29] While many fear that multiculturalism leads to less solidarity among citizens of a nation,[30] in Canada's case, it appears to have led to a stronger and more diverse sense of shared national identification.[31]

Indeed, the clearest precedent for the unusual pattern I observe with national superiority here is in studies of Canadian attitudes toward immigration.[32] As scholars have noted, "In many countries, native-born citizens with a strong sense of national identity or national pride tend to be more distrusting of immigrants and minorities, who are seen as a threat to their cherished national identity."[33] In contrast, Canada is striking in its "high level of mutual identification among immigrants and native-born Canadians.

Canadians view immigrants and demographic diversity as the strength of Canadian national identity."[34] Others have noted that Canada is the only Western country where strength of national identity is correlated positively rather than negatively with pro-immigration attitudes.[35] In the US, a strong sense of national superiority goes hand in hand with anti-immigrant views. But not in Canada.

Upon observing this pattern in others' research on immigration and in my own evidence of support for international trade, I viewed this as an impressive accomplishment if it was indeed due to the official Canadian commitment to diversity. To be able to change a relationship from a negative one to a positive one seems like quite a feat, and one with tremendous potential benefits for the country. In the American case, as seen in Chapter 3, these two opinions only go together among those who believe trade policy is a means of dominating other countries.

Nonetheless, it is worth noting that the positive relationship between trade support and national superiority in Canada could be interpreted in more than one way. Most optimistically, it could be that by establishing an official multicultural policy, Canadians redefined their national identity in a more inclusive way, one that circumvents the typically strong forces of intergroup bias. On the other hand, it could be that by publicly aligning the Canadian government with multiculturalism, Canadians simply encouraged those who did not approve of multiculturalism in the direction of more negative attitudes toward Canada. If diversity and inclusion are what the government stands for, and you are a Canadian who disagrees with these goals, this change will encourage a positive relationship between national superiority and support for trade, but at the expense of positive feelings toward the nation.

Both Canadians and Americans demonstrate links between their support for the free flow of people in the form of immigration and support for the free flow of goods in the form of international trade. These issues are obviously not the same thing, but they share common roots in how natives feel about those from other countries. By defining their national identity as a global, multicultural one, Canada may have evaded the negative attitudes toward globalization that have been seen in the US. My interviews with Canadians included the exact same kinds of complaints that Americans had, often in identical language: Canada First! But it is also true that Canada remains "one of the few industrialized countries where anti-globalization has not (yet) become a major political force."[36] Even when its economy was flagging in the 1980s and 1990s, Canada did not withdraw from the world and instead signed still more trade agreements. I will leave it to economists to determine whether these choices ultimately helped the Canadian economy thrive in the long term. But the desire to withdraw is an especially powerful force to resist when times are bad.

A sense of solidarity and shared identity with immigrants and minorities is a far cry from a good economic reason to support trade. Nonetheless, if, as I have suggested, people form attitudes about trading with other countries more or less the same way that they form attitudes toward trading with another individual, then this is not as surprising. The impact of national identity on trade preferences depends on the content of national identity. A national identity that incorporates norms of openness and tolerance of difference is not only compatible with support for international trade, it appears to actively encourage it.[37]

Canada is not immune to ingroup favoritism as my survey-experimental findings have demonstrated. But the extent to which Canadians make decisions that systematically favor the home country over other countries is consistently less than in the US. Further, they show no evidence of outgroup indifference; in the experiment, they consistently valued job gains for other countries as well as for their own country. Moreover, Canadians showed little desire to use trade as a means of dominating other countries and of "winning" a more powerful position in the world.

Intergroup Bias and Trade Attitudes

I began this chapter by asking whether the patterns of ingroup and outgroup biases first observed in Chapter 4 were something "natural" that one should routinely expect to influence trade attitudes. My answer is yes and no. Yes, intergroup biases will play a role, but they probably play a far more important role in the highly competitive United States than elsewhere. Few countries are accustomed to as much global dominance as the US has enjoyed. Competition plays a powerful role in most societies,[38] but there is variation in the confidence people have in the laudatory effects of competition.[39] Americans simply expect to be on top. Their pride in their country's political power is correlated with positive attitudes toward trade.[40] More so than in other countries, Americans tend to believe in competition and individual achievement, so outcomes in which one country dominates another seem more acceptable, perhaps even appropriate. Competition always produces winners and losers,[41] but people and societies differ in the extent to which they see the harm that losers experience as justifiable harm. To be harmed by competition is not the same thing as being wronged by competition.[42]

The perceived desirability of competition plays an important role in conditioning attitudes toward trade. In evaluating trade agreements, there will be greater ingroup favoritism in more competition-oriented countries such as the United States, as well as among citizens high in social dominance, and among those who see trade as a zero-sum policy. All of these characteristics produce the predicted reactions to experimentally-manipulated trade policies. Competition, particularly among those comfortable with unequal outcomes, exacerbates ingroup favoritism and promotes indifference toward how the outgroup is treated.

Differences between the US and Canada were large and consistent. Canadians were more likely to support policies that benefitted both the home country and trading partner countries, whereas Americans were more likely to favor agreements in which strictly the home country benefitted or to disregard effects on the trading partner country altogether. For citizens who value winning, even when the home country does gain, negative reactions are still likely if the home country is not gaining *more than* the trading partner. A tie game is not a win. Far from viewing trade as a cooperative venture with mutual benefits, for those in a competitive mindset, trade is more like a sports competition in which one must win, lose, or refuse to play the game at all.

A full explanation for why Americans are so much more enthusiastic about competition than Canadians is beyond the scope of this study. Competition is unlikely to be the whole story. On the one hand, differences in trade support by country usually disappeared once I took into account differences in characteristics tied to competitiveness. On the other hand, several cross-country differences may account for the fact that Americans are far more enthusiastic about competition, winning, and domination than are Canadians. The US is larger and more geopolitically dominant than Canada. The US is less dependent on trade than Canada. To the extent that American and Canadian character reflects these national differences, it makes sense that Canadians are not swaggering bullies insisting that a "fair" trade agreement be one in which they win and others lose.

The original rationale for trade was simple and unconnected to notions of competition. It was something that individuals could relate to in their everyday lives. Adam Smith's logic was that people can produce more things of value if they specialize in producing specific things, rather than trying to do everything themselves. They can then trade what they produce themselves for the other things they need. Based on this simple logic, trade is good for everyone because all will have access to more if we do not try to do it all ourselves.

In contrast to Smith's idea, Ricardo's comparative advantage framework stresses that different countries and their populations have different capacities to produce certain products. As a result, the effects of trade on different groups of people will differ. As consumers, all people should benefit under either logic, but as workers there will be winners and losers. It is perhaps no coincidence that the term "comparative advantage" is often confused with "competitive advantage" in everyday parlance. When trading partner countries are cast as competitive outgroups, this increases the role that ingroup favoritism and outgroup neglect play in the formation of trade attitudes. While we would be naive to suggest that the public has either Smith or Ricardo in mind, it is clear that once trade is viewed in terms of winners and losers, people evaluate it differently from when it is viewed as cooperative.

Few would argue with the claim that trade has helped the world economy.[43,44] Collectively, people have benefitted and levels of worldwide inequality have dropped as a result. But when the culture within a country encourages favoring co-nationals in a supposed competition against citizens of other countries, these benefits may not be persuasive. By focusing strictly on self-interested economic motives, research on political economy seldom confronts this issue.

After indicating their support or opposition to a given trade policy, respondents in both countries were asked to comment on what they were thinking with respect to the trade policy they had evaluated. Their responses focused heavily on two themes: the issue of fairness and desert. Interestingly, there was no consensus on what counted as "fair trade" because people had different ideas about who deserved these jobs. To most respondents, the term "fair trade" connoted a concern for whether what one's country received and/or sacrificed in a deal made it a "fair" trade.

For some, particularly those who envisioned less developed countries as the recipients of these jobs, the policy was deemed unfair because it did not benefit the trading partner country *enough*: "God wants us to love all people, not just ones of our own nationality. All people worldwide deserve the opportunity to provide for their families the best they can." Fairness for these respondents required moral inclusion: "I just thought, why is anybody from any country any more deserving of a job than another." Indeed, some saw the trading partners as *more* deserving due to their neediness: "I thought

FIGURE 7.8. American Exceptionalism: We're Number 1!

of the third world countries whose children do not have enough food to eat or clean water to drink. They deserve better."

For those who valued competition, it was perfectly fair that Americans gained and others lost because, as one respondent put it, "The American people deserve more." As another suggested, "I think the people born in this country deserve the right to make a living and no other country should gain by someone else here losing their job." Some clearly indicated that the people in trading partner countries were not in need, stating, "The other countries can support their own, they do not need our jobs and employers in the USA. Need to remember we deserve the jobs and need an income to support our families."

The comparison of results between the US and Canada makes it clear that it is not inevitable or "natural" that citizens ignore the well-being of outgroup members. It is even possible to redefine a nation's identity in more inclusive ways that do not foment outgroup resentment and the tension between ingroup pride and consideration of others.[45] This raises the question of how

Americans came to see themselves as more worthy and deserving of these livelihoods than citizens of other countries. The data in these studies were collected well before President Trump was elected, so we cannot attribute this to his campaign slogans or opinion leadership. The notion that America is unique and special in some regard was encapsulated long ago in the notion of American exceptionalism.[46] However, the meaning of American exceptionalism has perhaps gone awry, transmogrified into the idea that America's past somehow grants it a right to dominance and superiority. If there is no number of livelihoods that could be gained elsewhere that would be worth the loss of even one American job, then Americans are indeed full of themselves. Trump's regime repeatedly emphasized the importance of dominance and being Number #1 at virtually everything, as noted ironically in the cartoon in Figure 7.8. Even when the honor is dubious, winning is everything.

These findings also demonstrate how theories of intergroup competition are applicable to understanding international relationships. Nations are abstract, distant entities that do not elicit the same levels of empathy or cooperation as do other human beings. Nonetheless, people reason about the relationships between countries in ways that resemble interpersonal relationships. Thus theories and evidence from studies of small group interactions may prove extremely useful for understanding the dynamics of public opinion toward trade.

8

Media Coverage of Trade

THE VIVIDNESS OF LOSERS

Media coverage plays an especially important role in how people think about political issues that are complex and distant. Trade seems to fit this bill very well. Few of us can imagine the millions of interactions that constitute the international trade system, not to mention their downstream consequences for companies or for individual human beings. All of this makes the "pictures in our heads" about the consequences of trade all the more important, and media a likely source of these images.

Once scholars learned that sociotropic perceptions of trade's impact on the country as a whole influenced people's trade preferences, the natural next question was where such perceptions came from. Given that no individual experiences the national impact of trade, mass media were the most obvious source of collective-level national perceptions. Studies of media effects are consistent with this expectation given that media more easily change people's views about the state of collectives than about their own personal opinions and beliefs.[1]

In addition to understanding the origins of sociotropic perceptions, media coverage of trade has been of interest as a potential explanation for why mass opinion and elite opinion have diverged to such an unusual extent. Normally, mass opinion is assumed to follow elite opinion, particularly with respect to highly complex issues like trade. When faced with "hard" issues,[2] that is, issues that require more technical knowledge, the public is assumed to rely on what elites say rather than what they actually do. But because elites are often ambivalent about trade, media coverage of trade's benefits and drawbacks may play a more important role.

Media also are of interest as a potential source of change in mass opinion. Particularly since the 2016 election of Donald Trump, changing opinions toward trade have been a focus of speculation. Double-digit changes in public opinion of any kind are unusual, so the fact that public opinion on whether trade is good for the country has changed by over 20 percentage points since 2016 is noteworthy.

In this chapter I review what is known about the positive versus negative tone of media coverage of trade and its consequences. I then present evidence linking the tone of people's media exposure to perceptions of trade's collective national impact, that is, to sociotropic judgments about trade. Third, I address the impact of the style of media coverage of trade. I suggest that the ways in which trade stories are framed may matter even more than their frequency and tone. In the subsequent chapter, I examine the role of media coverage in influencing public understanding of job loss. Since job loss is *the* major concern of the American public when it comes to trade, the attributions of responsibility that are made for job loss by the popular press are critical to understanding American attitudes toward trade.

The Tone of Trade Coverage

Media coverage of the economy is known to include multiple types of distortion.[3] A conservative news organization may portray economic news in ways that compliment a Republican administration, whereas a liberal news outlet may paint a Democratic presidency in a more positive light.[4] Aside from partisan bias in some sources, the most widely-documented distortion is a tendency to over-emphasize negative economic news when the economy falters, relative to positive coverage when the economy is growing.[5] Media also produce more economic coverage in general during times of economic downturn.[6] However, less is known about effects of the tone of media coverage on people's retrospective perceptions of the economy.[7]

Media coverage of international trade has received even less attention, although trade's abstract nature and distance from many people's everyday lives make media a likely source of public perceptions. What we do know suggests that trade coverage and economic coverage have many parallel characteristics. Coverage of trade is far less extensive than economic coverage more generally, but both appear to be biased in favor of negative news.

The most comprehensive examination to date of trade coverage confirms this negative emphasis in television news coverage as well as in campaign-related communications from politicians.[8] Both kinds of communications are often driven by the regular release of macroeconomic government statistics such as unemployment, GDP, and the like. News about international trade is often driven by the release of statistics pertaining to the trade deficit. Since the Commerce Department releases this statistic on a monthly basis, the trade balance is a common news peg for stories involving trade. Leaving aside the issue of whether this statistic is meaningful as an indicator of the country's economic health, coverage of the trade deficit suffers from the same kind of unevenness as the economy more generally. Increases in the deficit are covered far more extensively than decreases, thus potentially creating the impression that trade is always causing problems.[9] In most respects, this is unsurprising because it reflects the public statements of political elites. Even though the so-called Washington consensus had until recently been pro trade for many decades, the *public* statements of elites have not been consistently pro trade.[10] Because of candidates' fears of public backlash, and the widespread belief that the public is generally more negative about trade than elites, trade tends to have few advocates at election time.

Boosterism in Media Coverage of Trade

When thinking about effects that flow from the tone of trade coverage, people usually have in mind whether or not trade is cast as beneficial as opposed to harmful to the US in a news story. Is it basically a good thing or a bad thing? However, a more subtle form of biased coverage may also be important in a global economy. A boosterish domestic news media may serve as a "veiled and indirect means of supporting their national industries."[11] In other words, the media in any given nation may be predisposed to make negative assumptions about foreign companies while it makes positive assumptions about domestic ones.

Boosterism is a well-established tradition in American news media, but it has typically been studied in the context of local news that offers coverage that boosts local businesses and esprit de corps.[12] It is not unusual for local news sources to proclaim their communities the best places to live, work and raise a family, without any concern for the truth value of such statements. Today, such bias is especially evident when foreign and domestic companies experience similar problems, and the foreign companies are treated more harshly by the home country's media coverage. One study of media coverage of automobile recalls in Chinese newspapers showed that recalls of foreign cars received systematically more coverage than recalls of domestic cars. This pattern was especially strong in government-controlled Chinese newspapers relative to nonofficial Chinese newspapers.[13]

Of course, one might argue that this backdoor effort at protectionism depends upon government control of the media, so its applicability in the privately-owned, profit-driven US media is questionable. But even here in the US, there is reason for concern about a pro-America bias potentially tilting the playing field in favor of American businesses. To the extent that media audiences prefer positive news about domestic companies and/or negative news about foreign companies, commercial pressures would also promote US boosterism. The desire for larger audiences in a competitive media environment could have similar effects on coverage. For example, one study found that newspapers in the US and Canada were more likely to give coverage to international disputes filed by other countries against the US or Canada, as opposed to those filed by the US against other firms.[14] Because people in the home country are likely to feel defensive about such accusations, this kind of news may negatively affect the home country's perceptions of the fairness of international agreements. When *they* are out to get *us,* it is natural for people to rally around the home team.

To the extent that it feels more negative and threatening to be accused of wrongdoing than to accuse others of it, one could argue that this pattern fits the more general bias in favor of greater coverage of negative news. But it may have more to do with the same kind of home country favoritism that was documented in Chinese newspapers. American journalists have long acknowledged the widespread practice of local and national self-promotion by means of boosterism in news.[15] It seems "natural" to want to promote the home country's economy. In contrast, the idea that all companies or products or all people's well-being should be treated equally, regardless of whether they are American or foreign, is not intuitive to journalists serving American audiences. In fact, I suspect many see their roles as explicitly bound up with American interests.

For example, the American news media often describe in highly approving terms those who go out of their way to buy American-made products over foreign imports. As a 2011 *New York Times* article began, "Anders Lewendal, a general contractor who managed to survive the housing collapse, has hit upon a plan that he thinks will revive the construction industry and help lead the nation out of the economic wilderness: build houses using only American-made materials."[16] The article goes on to laud the contractor for his efforts, even though obtaining such products turns out to be time-consuming and a lot more expensive. Contrary to what this article suggests, the value of buying American is not something that all Americans agree on. Nonetheless, it is treated by the media as if this is a consensus view, largely because few, if any, political elites are willing to voice views to the contrary.[17] Surely all good Americans want to support their country.

In another story, fashion designer Nanette Lepore is lauded as "a cheerleader for New York City's garment district. Most of her contemporary women's clothing line, which sells at stores like Saks Fifth Avenue and Bloomingdale's, is made locally." The article goes on to discuss the unfortunate demise of American clothing manufacturers who make affordable items, as well as the greater perceived quality of American-made clothing relative to clothing made overseas. Those fashion designers who try to "keep it local" are the heroes of the story, whereas Americans who are unwilling to pay more for their clothing (or homes) by buying American-made products are explicitly linked to the mistreatment of workers: "Even when consumers are confronted with the human costs of cheap production, like the factory collapse in Bangladesh that killed more than 1,000 garment workers, garment makers say, they show little inclination to pay more for clothes."[18]

Note that coverage of this kind says nothing directly about international trade. In fact, the word "trade" is never even mentioned. Nonetheless, the implications are straightforward: We would all be better people—and particularly better Americans—if we would simply pony up and pay higher prices in order to "Buy American." Interestingly, in the article headlining houses that are "All-American, Floor to Roof," the contractor advocating American-made homes opines, "I don't see any politics to it at all. . . . It's about jobs." To him, as to many observers, it is simply common sense to advocate buying American. Indeed, I seriously doubt that anyone accused the *New York Times* of any form of bias for articles such as these. They would have been highly unlikely to be noticed because boosterism promoting the "home team" is so common and widely accepted as to go unnoticed.

Buy American campaigns, like tariffs, are designed to dissuade people from buying imported products. They go as far back as the founding of the country itself, when George Washington boasted of wearing "homespun" clothing to his inauguration, conveniently made by his slaves.[19] I see nothing wrong with citizens using their pocketbooks to promote causes they believe in. What concerns me about buying American is that people are

FIGURE 8.1. Domestic Tariffs Made in America

being misled about what exactly they are promoting. The frequently stated and always implied promise is that buying American-made products will create more jobs in the US. At one level, this argument seems logical, but promoting protectionism within the US makes it a lot more difficult to sell things to the world's consumers who live overseas.

As the cartoon in Figure 8.1 humorously suggests, some US farmers found out during the trade war with China that tariffs did not help them economically. Tariffs invited retaliation from trading partner countries who likewise shunned American-made products, reducing exports and the many American jobs that are supported by export markets. Nonetheless, in 2018, the *National Interest* proposed that the US government facilitate a new "buy American wave":

> Going forward, the US government should fund and maintain an online database where consumers can seek information about domestic content on a plethora of different brands for many different types of goods. . . . Believers in pure free trade may be aghast at the idea of helping consumers figure out when to buy American based on pure patriotism or (shudder to say it) economic nationalism. . . . Allowing individual consumers

> to invoke patriotism to buy American is not only a longstanding government practice (since the government-sanctioned "Made in America" label has been around for decades). It is also nothing to be ashamed of. . . . [20]

There are important differences between a manufacturer who chooses to label a product MADE IN AMERICA, and having the US government spend public funds advocating that people buy American-made products. The latter policy suggests that without an appeal to ingroup favoritism, such purchases would not otherwise happen. In other words, it is not the product itself driving the purchase, it is the national identity linked to the product. These days, due to complex supply chains, even products widely viewed as American-made include parts from elsewhere, and products viewed as foreign in origin include materials and components made in the US. The high level of entanglement in the global economy means that buying American may well hurt those one assumes are being helped. In short, people cannot reasonably assume that buying American will reduce the trade deficit or contribute to more US jobs.

Most importantly, Buy American campaigns often fan the flames of racism and nativism. The historian Dana Frank suggests that it is no coincidence that the timing of such movements in the US coincides with a rise in foreigner-bashing.[21] The Buy American campaign of the 1930s occurred when the publisher William Randolph Hearst used his newspapers to promote the claim that the US faced a "Yellow Peril," a threat from both Japanese products and people. Xenophobia was also a part of the Buy American movement in the late '70s and early '80s, when Americans and union workers in particular became threatened by Japanese cars, the so-called demons in the parking lot.[22] The idea that "America First" can be separated from putting "Elsewhere Last" sounds plausible. But ultimately putting American well-being above that of others means discriminating against foreigners:

> People who might think they can separate out some sort of progressive version of "Buy American" will ultimately be unable to escape it sliding into "Hire American" or "America First," and the notion that the United States shouldn't be concerned with the struggles of working people in other countries.[23]

To summarize, press boosterism surrounding American companies and American jobs has not been well documented or widely acknowledged because it is seemingly uncontroversial. Laudatory articles on buying

American to support American workers is just one manifestation of this tendency. As one expatriate journalist admonished other journalists back in the 1980s, "Vanity, thy name is mindless USA boosterism."[24] Reasonable people can obviously disagree about whether boosterism is appropriate in American media or not. But given that it is not a consensus view, it seems incumbent upon journalists to be aware of this tendency and present more than one side to these controversies.

Does Media Coverage Influence Sociotropic Perceptions?

Aside from trying to promote American businesses more generally, does media coverage inform people's ideas on how trade affects the nation? Between 2004 and 2010, Ed Mansfield and I conducted two systematic content analyses of the tone of news coverage of trade using laborious human coding to capture the extent to which stories suggested that trade was good or bad for the nation.[25] Based on our findings, two things were clear about coverage of trade during the first decade of the twenty-first century. First, there was relatively little of it. Despite the ongoing expansion of globalization during this period, trade was not a frequent news topic. Second, the coverage that existed during this time period was overwhelmingly negative. It centered on problems caused by trade, especially job displacement through factory closings. Because both of these content analyses were executed in conjunction with national surveys that tapped respondents' media consumption, we used them to examine whether variations in the media individuals consume relates to variations in their sociotropic perceptions.

Assessing the impact of mass media consumption on perceptions of how trade has affected the nation is difficult for many of the same reasons that it is difficult to study media effects more generally. One can look for associations between the content of media that a person consumes and their perceptions of trade, but one cannot easily interpret the results. A person's political leanings may drive their choice of news source as well as their views on trade. Moreover, reverse causation is potentially a concern; people may read a particular newspaper because its political views are already similar to their own views.

However, when it comes to media coverage of trade, many of the usual concerns are less problematic. For example, how likely is it that a person would self-select a news source because of its views on trade? Given that trade is such a small proportion of the news, this seems unlikely indeed. If liberals tend to read a more liberal newspaper or watch more liberal news programs, and those same readers also have more favorable views of a liberal candidate (who is also covered more favorably by the news source), then the most likely explanation is that people are self-selecting into like-minded sources of news. However, precisely because trade attitudes do not fall neatly along liberal/conservative or Democrat/Republican lines, it would be more difficult for people to self-select into a news source that shared their views on trade, especially before Trump raised the profile of this issue. There are some exceptions; for example, a newspaper known to be pro-business such as the *Wall Street Journal* might cover trade differently from another source. But the usual bases for questioning causal relationships—self-selection based on political views, or spuriously-related media content and public attitudes—are at least somewhat less problematic with trade.

To create individual-level measures of how each person's media diet portrayed trade, the nineteen most frequently read newspapers in our nationally representative survey were analyzed, as well as transcripts of their major sources of television news, including ABC, CBS, NBC, the *Lehrer News Hour*, *Fox News*, CNN, and MSNBC.[26] For each source, we compiled all of the articles and stories involving international trade that were written or reported during the first six months of 2004, just prior to when the national survey sample was collected. A random sample of ten qualifying articles from each newspaper or television news source was used to characterize the general tone of each source on trade.[27] Each article was coded as having either a pro-trade tone, an anti-trade tone, or neither. These data were aggregated up to the level of a single score per newspaper or television news program by taking the mean across all stories. News sources with positive means had a predominantly pro-trade slant, those with negative means were more anti-trade, and those with means close to zero were either neutral or balanced in their coverage of the issue. Most sources were either negative or neutral in overall tone. Finally, we matched to each respondent the mean media tone for each person's most frequently read newspaper and most frequently viewed source of television news.[28]

To our knowledge, there have been no previous studies directly linking consumption of trade news to perceptions of trade's effects on the nation as whole. However, some studies of media's effects on sociotropic perceptions of the economy as a whole are similar in design and suggest some additional sources to take into account when examining this relationship. First, people could generalize sociotropic perceptions from their own personal experiences. In addition to indicators of unemployment, we also included variables derived from respondents' industries and occupations. Average occupational wage was included along with whether the industry of employment was export-oriented or import-competing. To be comprehensive in taking into account other possibilities, we included a subjective measure of how people thought trade had influenced them personally, however accurate or inaccurate such an assessment might be. Union membership was included since those in unionized positions were likely to have additional sources informing their members about trade.

Even after controlling for a whole host of economic characteristics, subjective perceptions of how much trade affects the respondent and so forth, both the extent of pro-trade versus anti-trade slant in the respondents' newspapers and in their television consumption significantly predicted their perception of how trade affected the nation as a whole. The full results of this analysis are included in Table A8.1 in the online appendix. We specify a variety of different models that do not change the predictive strength of newspaper or television coverage. On average we find that newspaper coverage is a stronger predictor of sociotropic perceptions than television coverage, perhaps because there is more coverage of trade in newspapers. In both cases the effects are modest, but they are impressively robust predictors in a model in which even education—traditionally the most stalwart predictor of trade preferences—no longer predicts people's ideas about whether trade is good or bad for the country. Sociotropic perceptions are also positively related to how people think trade affects their own personal finances, and negatively related to union membership, as one might expect.

These results were suggestive, but they have the obvious limitation of being cross-sectional analyses. People may self-select into news sources they find more agreeable, although this is less likely with a single, low-profile issue. To see whether or not this relationship held up when examined in the context of change over time in media coverage of trade, we next used a panel study, from before to after the Great Recession from 2007–2009, in order to ascertain whether or not changes in media coverage during this period might help to account for changes in people's sociotropic perceptions of trade. During this time period, perceptions of trade's impact on the nation as a whole became significantly more negative.[29] This is obviously illogical since the recession did not result from trade-related economic turmoil. The public was well aware of that fact. For example, in January 2008, before the downturn was officially declared a recession, a representative sample of Americans was asked, "If the nation falls into a recession, who or what do you think should get most of the blame: President Bush, or the Democrats in Congress, or the Republicans in Congress, or mortgage lenders who made risky loans, or borrowers who are defaulting on their loans, or the Federal Reserve Board, or the weakening of the dollar, or the trade deficit, or is there someone or something else that should get the most blame?" Trade or the trade deficit was named as a target of blame by under 5 percent of respondents.

When a downturn is perceived as overwhelmingly a function of other factors, why reduce support for trade? Studies conducted after the recession similarly indicated that Americans blamed government institutions that did not do enough to regulate banks and financial institutions. The fact that trade support nonetheless declined during the recession poses the question of why economic downturns negatively affect public attitudes toward trade, even when the decline is not seen as having anything to do with trade.

In addition to examining predictors of change in sociotropic perceptions over time, this analysis allowed us to be more inclusive in terms of the media content we tracked. Our analysis of media coverage during this two-year period is consistent with the poll findings reported above, in that we find very little coverage of international trade; instead, coverage was focused heavily on the domestic economy. The most concrete and visible consequence of the recession was the huge surge in unemployment, which received large amounts of coverage. For this reason, we incorporated unemployment coverage into our content analyses for this study. Given that ordinary Americans tend to understand the economy in terms of concrete phenomena that are easily grasped,[30] and given that trade in the US is framed by the media and understood by the public mainly as about jobs, a more inclusive definition of relevant news seemed appropriate.

As in the previous study, in both the pre- and post-recession waves of survey data collection, we incorporated measures of personal experience as well as media exposure as sources of sociotropic trade perceptions. Perceptions of the economy can be rationalizations of pre-existing partisanship, particularly in cross-sectional analyses.[31] However, in this case our approach explains *change over time* within the same individual in perceptions of trade's effects on the nation as a whole. Because partisanship is stable, it cannot account for changing perceptions of trade's impact on the nation. However, between the first and second wave of our panel, from 2007 to 2009, the party of the presidency changed from Republican to Democrat. Thus, to take into account party-in-power effects, the likely decrease in trade support among Republicans and increase among Democrats, we included in our analyses an interaction between survey wave and party, indicating whether, media coverage aside, Republicans were more likely than Democrats to turn against trade during this period.

The results of our analyses are included in Table A8.2 in the online appendix. As one would expect, unemployment news increased substantially from pre- to post-recession. While measures of individual media exposure were very stable,[32] what changed a great deal was the extent to which those news sources carried news about unemployment. Ninety-three percent of respondents in our study experienced an increase in economic coverage in their news sources, and 7 percent experienced no change. On average, respondents saw 0.2 stories per day in 2007 as opposed to 1.9 stories per day in 2009, a significant increase.[33]

More to the purpose of our study, those who experienced increased exposure to unemployment news during this time period were the same people who changed their minds in a more negative direction about trade's impact on the nation. Our analyses suggest that the more of an increase from 2007 to 2009 in a given person's number of stories on unemployment per day, the more likely that person was to change their views in the direction of saying that trade was bad for the country as a whole. Regardless of what else we took into account, the effect of change in coverage remained very stable, providing strong support for the idea that changes in exposure to unemployment news alter perceptions about how trade influences the nation as a whole. Change in *personal unemployment* was also a significant predictor of beliefs about trade's impact on the nation as a whole. Increased unemployment, however, accounted for only 5 percent of the decline in sociotropic trade attitudes, and other factors were far more influential.

More to the point, even when we take into account subjectively-assessed changes in how people felt they were influenced by trade, changes in individuals' news diets continued to predict changes in sociotropic perceptions of trade's impact. Given that unemployment levels were rising radically during this period, media served as a useful conduit conveying such information even to those who were not personally experiencing unemployment.

Across both cross-sectional and panel models, media coverage appeared to play an important role in shaping the public's sociotropic perceptions of trade's impact. Consistent with previous studies of both the power and limitations of media effects, news coverage is especially potent in influencing people's perceptions of how others in the nation at large are being affected.[34]

Our results also suggest an important caveat about studying trade news. In discussing the tone of media coverage of trade, it may be unwise to limit the media content to news that is about trade per se. Unemployment is so closely linked to trade fears in the US that even coverage that never mentions trade at all may turn the public against trade. Even when people themselves said they did not blame international trade for job loss, implicitly they did. I return to this puzzle in Chapter 10. How can people say they do not blame trade for job losses in the nation, yet seemingly do so when unemployment increases? Collective economic distress usually takes a toll on trade support, even when it is not linked to trade. So economic coverage more generally—not simply coverage of trade—must be taken into account in understanding changes in Americans' willingness to support trade.

Visualizing Trade's Impact: The Role of the Media

As Walter Lippmann once put it, "The only feeling that anyone can have about an event he does not experience is the feeling aroused by his mental image of that event."[35] When forming policy opinions, it matters a great deal which people are envisioned to be affected by a given policy. For example, in a comparative study of social welfare attitudes, despite large historical differences in levels of social welfare support, Danes and Americans showed indistinguishable levels of support for social welfare policies when the welfare recipients described appeared equally deserving. The difference in American and Scandinavian attitudes toward social welfare policies are driven less by ideology or culture than by the assumptions people carry around in their heads about how deserving welfare recipients are likely to be.[36]

This naturally raises the question of who Americans visualize as the winners and losers when thinking about job losses or job gains due to trade. What kind of mental images come to mind? Since most people are not, in their own view, directly impacted by trade, it matters a great deal what kinds of things come to mind when they envision trade's consequences. While thinking about the mental imagery associated with trade, I tried a Google image search to see what kind of not-so random images would come up if I simply googled "job loss," and then compared them to the images that came up when I searched for "job gain." Although individual searches varied, for job loss what I saw was lots of sad white men holding pink slips or boxes of office supplies indicating that they had been sacked. For job gains, what I saw was entirely different—mainly statistics, graphs and charts showing collective trends over time. Job loss was consistently illustrated at the level of an individual who had lost a job, whereas job gains were illustrated with abstract, thematic statistical representations.

It occurred to me that even if an American journalist wanted to do an upbeat story on a sympathetic person who had gained a job due to trade, this would be difficult to pull off. It is easy to identify an individual person who has lost his job due to a factory closing or the outsourcing of jobs to another country. Although we know theoretically that the export markets created by liberalizing trade allow American businesses to expand through exports and hire more people, how could one identify the worker who gained his job due to trade? The link between job gains and trade would be indirect at best. The lack of concrete examples of trade winners in the US news suggests that Americans may have trouble visualizing trade winners.

In Chapter 4, I described how trade is in many ways a moral dilemma, much like the classic trolley problem. In order to encourage economic growth and more jobs overall, one must choose to sacrifice the well-being of a smaller group who will end up losing their jobs and need to find new ones, just as flipping the switch in the trolley problem saves lives overall, but sacrifices an individual in order to make that possible. It may be the best utilitarian choice to make, but it feels morally wrong to many, especially in a country with a relatively weak safety net such as the US.

Consistent with Lippmann's emphasis on mental imagery, experimental studies of the trolley problem suggest that visual imagery makes utilitarian choices less likely.[37] For example, evidence suggests that people who are better at visual as opposed to verbal tasks are less likely to make utilitarian choices; in other words, they are less willing to flip the switch to alter the outcome. In a second study, the people making choices were randomly assigned to experience interference that was either visual or verbal. Those assigned to receive visual interference made more utilitarian judgments than those receiving verbal interference. In other words, if they were distracted from forming (often unpleasant) mental imagery, they were more likely to make the utilitarian choice that saved more people.

There is a stronger tendency to visualize harmful effects relative to beneficial ones. In other words, when people mentally visualize the harm that will occur as a result of their action—flipping the trolley switch and sacrificing the one person—then they are significantly less likely to make that choice as a result. Even though flipping the switch saves a larger number of people, they are less likely to visualize the positive imagery associated with saving lives.[38]

I suspect that visual imagery regarding trade losers and trade winners may result in a similar bias toward visualizing negative consequences more than positive ones. The experiment described in Chapters 4 and 7 involved a trade agreement enumerating a specific number of job gains and losses for the US and for the trading partner country. Given that people were randomly assigned to conditions that included trade winners as well as trade losers, there should theoretically be an equal chance that they would visualize winners and losers. Recall that whether the winners/losers were Americans or citizens of a trading partner country was also randomly determined, as was the number of winners/losers.

But were they equally likely to visualize trade winners and losers? In order to examine the idea that mental images of losers should be more vivid in people's minds, after respondents reported their level of support for this trade agreement, they were asked two follow-up questions. The first was an open-ended question: "While you were thinking about the question about trade policy, what first came to mind? Did you picture the people that were mentioned in your mind's eye? Which ones? Please take a minute to describe your thoughts." Note that the question does not specify which people they should describe, and each policy description included both winners and losers, with one winner or loser in each scenario compared to multiple winners/losers on the other side.[39]

Based on the trolley studies, I expected that people would be more likely to report picturing those who were hurt by trade in their mind's eye than those who were helped. As with responses to any open-ended question, a fair number of people simply reiterated their opinion on the policy. Indeed, the single most common response involved affirming that Americans need jobs or that jobs should go to Americans first.

But among those who did report what was in their minds' eye as they answered, most of them visualized the person or people who were losing jobs, even though they had been told about both trade winners and losers:

I thought of the people that were out of a job for months, especially the new grads and seniors.
Parents losing their jobs and little ones going hungry.
Homeless people.
I wish to NOT see anyone hungry or in poverty.
The person who would lose their job and be unable to support their families
Closing a factory.
A lot of people going hungry. I pictured poor people needing jobs.
I imagined the people that would be negatively affected more so than the single person who would be positively affected.

The first thing that came to mind was the people in our country who are suffering because of a job lost.

Yes, people. The providers of their families. I feel empathy for bread winners.

Thought about the folks losing their jobs. Wouldn't want to be in their shoes.

I pictured the people here who would be jobless.

I pictured the people that would automatically lose their jobs and having been a direct cause of that would make me feel too guilty.

I pictured the people who would not be able to feed and shelter their family.

Overall, trade losers came to mind more often than trade winners. Even when the trade winners were Americans, and the losers were overseas, negative images of trade losers still came to mind:

I thought of the people in third world countries that would be worse off.

Although my first thought was of the person here in the U.S., my thoughts quickly switched to all those losing their jobs.

Pictured people in other countries as poorer than in US.

People at poverty levels in other countries are much worse than those in America.

I thought about people who live in impoverished areas who are already underpaid by US companies who hire them in the first place.

This pattern of negative mental imagery has important implications for media coverage in that it suggests that even if news media gave equal amounts of attention to trade winners and trade losers—as was the case in this experiment—people would visualize the losers more than the winners. Thus trade coverage has a double disadvantage when it comes to suggesting beneficial effects from trade. First, it tends to be covered mainly when it causes problems of some kind, and not when it produces beneficial consequences. Second, even when both positive and negative consequences are featured, what grabs people's attention is typically the imagery surrounding its negative consequences. This was the case regardless of how many winners or losers there were.

A final set of closed-ended questions in the same representative national survey-experiment allowed me to statistically test whether trade winners or trade losers were more vivid in people's minds in this representative sample of respondents. Each person was asked two questions in a randomized order

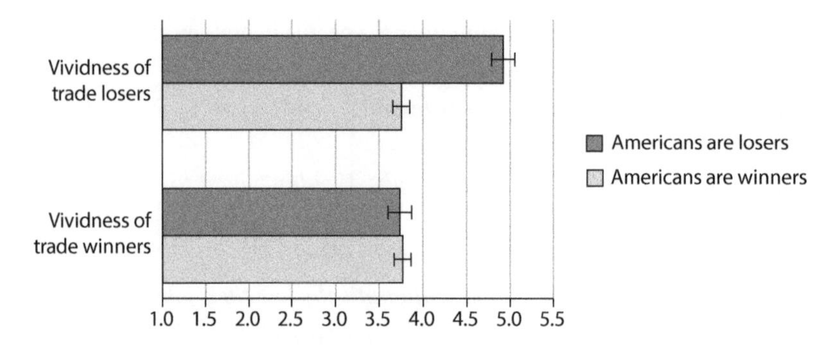

FIGURE 8.2. Vividness of Trade Winners and Losers, by Whether the US Gains/Loses Jobs
Source: US Trade Survey-Experiment, 2013–2014 (GfK Ltd.).
Note: Bars represent means on 7-point scales. The means for trade winners and trade losers are significantly different in the sample as a whole ($t = 9.02$, $p < .001$). The interaction between the vividness of winners versus losers and whether the US is the winner or loser is also significant ($F = 177.11$, $p < .001$).

with wording tailored to their experimental condition. One question was about the trade losers mentioned in their scenario, and another was about the trade winners in their randomly assigned trade policy: "How vivid in your mind [was the person who gained/lost a job/were the people who gained/lost jobs] [in the United States / in the country that we trade with]? Respondents answered both questions on a seven-point scale from "not at all vivid" to "extremely vivid."

As illustrated in Figure 8.2, the answers to these questions largely confirmed my impression from the open-ended responses. The vividness of trade losers was systematically higher than the vividness of trade winners by a large margin. Winners were not very vivid to people, regardless of where they were from. Trade losers are what drew people's attention. However, respondents did not find the trade losers in trading partner countries as vivid in their minds as the American losers. In fact, as illustrated in Figure 8.2, the overall pattern of greater vividness for losers was driven exclusively by the greater vividness of losers in the versions of the trade policy in which the US was the loser and the trading partner was the winner. Negative outcomes that were close to home were far more vivid than positive outcomes that were close to home. Negative outcomes for those overseas were no more or less vivid than positive outcomes in the eyes of these Americans respondents.

A great number of respondents implied in their open-ended responses that the choice of whether to support the trade agreement was, indeed, a moral dilemma for them, even when more jobs were gained within the US.

The mere idea of a trade-off of any kind was often deemed morally repugnant and rejected out of hand, even with a net gain in the total number of people employed. Even in the US, a country unusually enthusiastic about competition, some saw policies that created winners and losers as inherently problematic. Many simply rejected the idea that *anyone anywhere* should have to suffer a job loss in order to produce broader job gains:

> *What a tough choice to make! Sacrifice one job for many others to lose their jobs! I pictured 1000 people from another country left without financial support and stability.*
>
> *One person's gain should not reflect on another person's loss.*
>
> *I know it's selfish, but I worry more about American jobs than poverty around the world.*
>
> *I thought that though trade is important, how in the world could I possibly say "Sure let's make an American lose a job." Come on man. . . . or am I reading this incorrectly?*
>
> *I'm all for us getting new jobs, but why does anyone have to lose a job?*
>
> *My thought was why would we enter into a treaty that would make someone lose a job anywhere? That is why I wouldn't support it.*
>
> *Why should another country benefit when our own loses a job?*
>
> *I do not want to cause more stress or harm to anyone, especially those less fortunate than us.*
>
> *It is very unfortunate that the US, and probably the world, has taken the "US vs THEM" mentality and will do whatever it takes for us to thrive despite how it affects others.*
>
> *Do not want to learn people will lose jobs.*
>
> *The US citizens need employment opportunities, but for anyone, even one person, to lose a job is disturbing.*
>
> *I would never encourage the success of one person if it meant the downfall of another.*
>
> *I don't want anyone to lose their jobs but there must be a way so no one loses.*
>
> *I did consider the people who would benefit; however, at the expense of taking away a job from an American family it isn't worth the trade off whatever the ROI would be.*
>
> *Although it would be unfortunate that 10 people could lose their employment because one person obtained employment in our country, I believe we need to take care of citizens of our country.*

Even among trade's strongest advocates, it is widely acknowledged that trade liberalization results in labor market churn, that is, movement among workers within a labor market from one job to another as the market adjusts to a new distribution of jobs. To many American citizens, this consequence is simply unacceptable, almost as a general principle.

In some ways it is not surprising that ordinary Americans have little or no mental imagery that is salient in their minds with respect to who the winners are in international trade. Despite the fact that economists are far more enamored with the benefits of trade than most citizens, economists have done a poor job of documenting those who benefit and how lives are changed for the good by international trade.[40] How many millions of people have escaped extreme poverty through jobs directly or indirectly created by trade? Although concerns about inequality within the US have received huge amounts of attention, the enormous reduction of global inequality due to trade has received relatively less attention.[41] As David Autor, a co-author of one of the most widely cited papers on the "China Shock" argues, the costs and virtues of trade in the US pale in comparison with the basic humanitarian benefits that people in other places have experienced as a result of trade: "The gains to the people who benefited are so enormous—they were destitute, and now they were brought into the global middle class. . . . The fact that there are adverse consequences in the United States should be taken seriously, but it doesn't tilt the balance."[42] We have no way to compare the value of a new job to someone who would otherwise be in dire poverty to a lost job for an American. The metric the public was using in their open-ended comments appeared to be that the only "fair" trade deal was one in which an equal number of jobs were gained in both places.

Even when presented with trade agreements in which the trading partner gained jobs, many respondents envisioned these new jobs to have a negative impact on these people:

Poor people in the non-Chinese far eastern countries. I see them currently living in bad conditions—little or no housing, wearing rags for clothes, poor hygiene.

I saw people in a third world working for pennies a day.

The 100 people are in a 3rd world country; need assistance and will be paid poorly.

First to mind was the policy to allow China most favored nation status under President Clinton. This policy has led to inferior and even some dangerous imports from a nation that allows near slave labor conditions for their people. It has also resulted in an imbalance of import/export ratio. Other Asian nations also allow extremely poor working conditions such as long hours, low wages, and unsafe buildings.

A little girl making a shirt in Bangladesh.

I pictured 100 women and children in a hot dirty factory setting versus the one American i.e., my son-in-law who could better support his family with a decent wage and afford to buy quality American products (thereby supporting more American families) instead of only being able to afford cheaper China junk from Walmart.

THE ONE VERSUS THE MANY

In contrast to having difficulty visualizing trade winners, respondents had no difficulty conjuring mental images of trade losers. Indeed, case studies in news reports are full of them. They are often, but not always, sturdy-looking white men in jobs requiring manual labor.

In the US media, the dominant frame in media coverage of unemployment is an individual person's job loss.[43] Highlighting a single individual might logically seem unlikely to generate public reactions given that it is just one person who has lost one job. But as suggested by the quote frequently attributed to Stalin, "One death is a tragedy; one million is a statistic." Individual victims evoke sympathy and a sense of moral responsibility in ways that collectives do not.[44] These studies attribute their highly consistent findings to the stronger emotional reactions evoked by the identified victims, especially in cases involving victims experiencing loss.[45] More emotionally engaging portrayals create greater sympathy for victims and facilitate effects on policy attitudes.[46] Individuals are essentially affect-rich and highly vivid targets, whereas statistical collectives are affect-poor and less vivid in the mental images they facilitate.

In the experiment on trade winners and losers, I did not provide respondents with personal details about those experiencing job losses or gains, so there were no individuals identified by name or other characteristics. Nonetheless, many generated their own mental images of trade winners and losers. Because the study describes one loser (or winner) who is an American/foreigner and a collective of other winners (or losers) who are Americans/foreigners, it is possible to examine whether the greater vividness of individuals versus collectives applies even when the individuals are not described to audiences. Given that all characteristics were randomly assigned—who gained/lost jobs and whether the winner/loser was described as a single individual or as a multiple—I compare the vividness of the depersonalized single individual to a collective of losers/winners. Based on the general theory, when the policy was described as one in which 1 person would lose [gain] a job for every 100 who gained [lost] jobs, the individual, rather than the collective, should be more vivid, all else being equal, that is, regardless of whether the individual was the loser or the winner.

As shown in Figure 8.3, this expected pattern did not arise in the vividness of people's mental imagery, perhaps due to the lack of personalized identification of the single individuals. In this case, collectives were used as a means of giving respondents a sense of the quantity of people helped or hurt by the policy rather than as human interest devices. In direct contrast to expectations, when one compares the vividness of a single foreigner in the mind's eye with the vividness of a whole collective of foreigners, the collective is more vivid than the individual. When forming mental images of distant winners and losers in trading partner countries, the more abstract mass collective of foreigners produced greater vividness than the individual foreigner. This finding brings to mind the emotional impact for many Americans of viewing mass poverty in an underdeveloped country. Even though the focus is on an undifferentiated collective rather than on individual people, the sheer scale of negative images can be jarring and highly vivid. While unexpected, this pattern is consistent with psychological theories suggesting that distant targets are more influential when considered in abstract, collective terms, whereas psychologically and physically closer targets are more influential when they are concrete.[47] Most studies of individuals versus collectives contrast coverage of individual exemplars relative to collectives that are equally distal (e.g., one American who suffers job loss relative to a collective of Americans experiencing the same), and the individuals typically demonstrate greater influence. But collectives may work best when encouraging moral consideration of people who are far away.

To summarize, it is easy for most Americans to imagine a single American who has lost a job due to trade, and this is likely to be a highly vivid mental image. It is more difficult for people to visualize one who has gained a job due to trade. And it is easier for Americans to imagine an undifferentiated collective of foreigners than to imagine an individual foreign person. Some of this ease probably comes from what we are accustomed to seeing in the media: mostly Americans, and few foreigners who are featured as detailed, identified individual victims. Thus, the finding of greater vividness for individual victims makes sense, but it may not travel well and generalize to how Americans think about foreigners. Targets that are physically close are

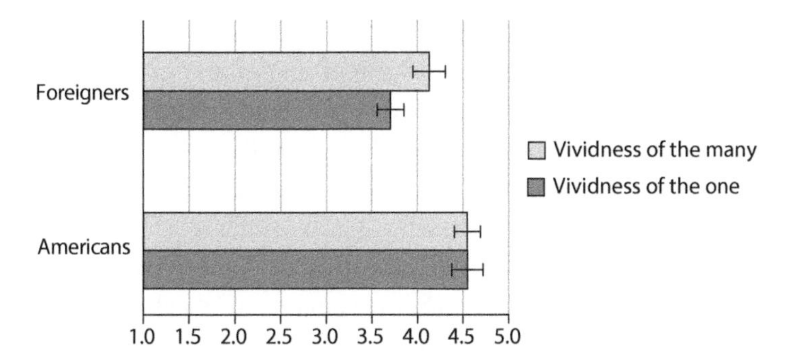

FIGURE 8.3. The Vividness of Individual versus Collective Trade Winners/Losers, by Whether the Winners/Losers Are Americans or Foreigners
Source: US Trade Survey-Experiment, 2013–2014 (GfK Ltd.).
Note: Bars represent the mean level of vividness attributed to the single winner/loser or the collective winners/losers. Results based on an analysis of variance with One versus Many as a within-subject factor, Whether the US Wins or Loses as a between-subject factor and whether the Judgment target is American vs. a foreigner. Results produced a main effect of One versus Many ($F = 8.40$, $p < .004$), as well as an interaction between One vs. Many and whether the Judgment target is American vs. foreign ($F = 147.73$, $p < .001$).

generally easier to see as concrete individuals, and they are easier to empathize with. In the open-ended responses, one person nicely articulated the difference between having distant individual foreigners lose jobs as opposed to more proximate individuals:

> *I feel like someone in my family could be affected or someone close to me. It is easy to accept someone losing their job if you do not know them, but hard when the shoe is on the other foot.*

In a sense this respondent is channeling Adam Smith in *The Theory of Moral Sentiments*, who noted the importance of distance in people's capacity for empathy or lack thereof:

> If he was to lose his little finger to-morrow, he would not sleep tonight; but, provided he never saw them, he would snore with the most profound security over the ruin of a hundred million of his brethren. The destruction of that immense multitude seems plainly an object less interesting to him than this paltry misfortune of his own. To prevent, therefore, this paltry misfortune to himself would a man of humanity be willing to sacrifice the lives of a hundred million of his brethren, provided he had never seen them?

When presented with a trade policy that involved both job losses and job gains due to trade, people paid more attention to those hurt by trade than those helped by it. Overall, these findings highlight the difficulties that trade faces with respect to the images provided by media as well as those people generate in their own minds. First, there is little good news about trade in the American media. Trade makes headlines mainly when it creates problems. Second, the good news about job creation tends to be embedded in statistical portrayals rather than in human interest stories about sympathetic Americans. Further, given that trade does indeed displace some people from their jobs, people are likely to visualize the harm to trade losers far more than the benefits to trade winners.

THE NEW VICTIMS OF TRADE: EMPATHY BITES BACK

Overall, the American media paint a highly negative portrait of trade in the American mind. Moreover, trade's victims play an outsized role in shaping public reactions to trade policy. There is, however, a twist to this story that emerged in the midst of President Trump's new tariffs and trade wars. During Trump's trade war, coverage of trade still included the formulaic story of a single individual losing a job at a factory. But it also included highly sympathetic coverage of those who were victims of *lack of trade* by virtue of the trade war, such as farmers who cannot export their crops, or small business people whose supply chains have been interrupted by new tariffs.

Take, for example, a *Washington Post* feature article about a farmer in South Dakota who fell into debt and committed suicide as a result of desperation over his family's finances:

> American agriculture was booming when Chris joined the business. Global demand stoked high commodity prices, with corn nearly $5 a bushel and soybeans more than $13 a bushel. This was before Trump started his trade wars with China, Mexico and Canada. Before rain gauges in Sioux Falls registered 39.2 inches of rain in 2018, the wettest year on record. Before a freak spring blizzard claimed the lives of three dozen of Chris's lambs and calves. Before the roads flooded and hemmed in nearly $100,000 worth of corn and soybeans he had been holding onto since last fall, hoping better prices would return.[48]

Although the article is careful to attribute Chris's financial troubles to bad weather as well as to trade wars, he is clearly portrayed as a victim of the trade war. Likewise, in a *New York Times* article entitled, "How Trump's

Tariffs Can Hit the Little Guy," a journalist describes another victim of lack of trade:

> Shane Cusick started his small business, Pello, in 2014 with the goal of making lightweight bikes for children. His experience over the past year is a case study in how a trade war can disrupt a fledgling enterprise.
>
> The company designs its bikes in the United States but imports them from China because domestic factories are not equipped to churn out tiny bike frames en masse.
>
> "I love American-made products," Mr. Cusick said. "There's no other choice. It has to be done over there."[49]

The article goes on to explain that because the bikes are assembled in China, and tariffs keep being raised, Cusick can no longer afford to sell the bikes at an affordable price to US consumers.

Although newfangled trade victims such as these were a frequent focus of coverage during the Trump administration, there was also some pro-trade coverage that did not feature specific victims suggesting that perhaps trade in general is not as bad as it had been cracked up to be. In one example that appeared on the business pages of the *New York Times,* the economist Greg Mankiw attempted to explain in everyday parlance why Trump's extreme concern over bilateral trade deficits was foolish:

> To understand what's wrong with that inference, consider some of the many bilateral trade deficits that I run. Whenever my family goes out to dinner, the restaurateur gets some money, and we get a meal. In economics parlance, the Mankiw family runs a trade deficit with that restaurant. But that doesn't make us losers. After all, we leave with full stomachs.
>
> To be sure, I would be happy to have balanced trade. I would be delighted if every time my family went out to dinner, the restaurateur bought one of my books. But it would be harebrained for me to expect that or to boycott restaurants that had no interest in adding to their collection of economics textbooks.

Beyond dismissing bilateral trade deficits, Mankiw goes on to explain why concerns about the *global* trade deficit may also be misplaced:

> Whether a [global] trade deficit represents a problem depends on whether our spending is prudent or profligate. When a family takes out

> a loan to buy a car, it runs a trade deficit, but that need not be a reason for concern, as long as it can afford the car in the long run.
>
> On the other hand, if a family runs a trade deficit by persistently living beyond its means, that's a problem because debts eventually come due. But in this case, the trouble comes not from disreputable trading partners but from poor financial planning. If you eat at expensive restaurants too often, blame yourself, not the restaurateur.[50]

Clearly some recent journalism beyond the op-ed pages has countered the "trade causes problems" trope.

Although I have not quantified this shift, sympathetic coverage of losers due to trade and losers due to lack of trade appears to have been stimulated by having an avowedly anti-trade president in office. Donald Trump's candidacy in 2016 made trade a partisan political issue, with a clear divide between the two major party candidates. When an issue becomes one on which the main political parties disagree, the mainstream press often responds with greater efforts to balance coverage. The tracking of coverage that I provided in Figure 1.1 indirectly bears that out. Although "trade as competition" remains the dominant theme in news coverage throughout, there are notably more mentions of trade linked to cooperation after the 2016 election than at any time going back to the turn of the last century.

This newer form of trade coverage may serve dual purposes for reporters. First, it extends the news media's emphasis on the downtrodden and those who are suffering from whatever is happening at the time, whether it be burgeoning international trade or a trade war. The highly personalized "little guy" (with an occasional female victim) remains the most common frame for trade coverage. In both versions of trade victimhood, trade is emasculating in that it takes away the male breadwinner's capacity to support his family or, in other cases, the female worker's independence.

Anecdotally, the few accounts that I have seen featuring female victims of trade are notably less angry in tone. For example, in the story of Shannon Mulcahy, "a woman who escaped domestic violence by becoming a steelworker at the Rexnord bearing plant in Indianapolis," she is clearly conflicted about the Mexican workers who will be paid less to do her job. As the journalist describes, "Working at the factory gave her financial independence, a sense of identity and a chance to master one of the most dangerous, complicated and highly-paid jobs in the plant." But when Shannon's factory moves to McAllen, Texas, and Monterrey, Mexico, it is the new Mexican factory that serves as the focus for the story rather than the one on the American side of the border. One of Shannon's Mexican replacements is quoted as saying, "My friend tells me that the reason a lot of people don't like us is because we're taking their jobs." After observing the Mexican workers' considerably lower standard of living while training them, Shannon does not begrudge them their good fortune, and replies, "I'm not mad at you. . . . I'm happy that you get the opportunity to make some money. I was blessed for a while. I hate to see it go. Now it's your turn to be blessed."[51] This type of coverage remains sympathetic to trade victims, but without demonizing foreigners. The same news story is also explicitly critical of Shannon for continuing to buy products made in China, implying that her consumer behavior is hypocritical. A recurrent theme here and elsewhere is that consumerism is the real underlying problem and that if Americans could just stop buying inexpensive things from China, and buy American instead, our job problems would be solved. This is obviously a simplistic view, but it is at least a more nuanced portrayal than was common in the news five years before.

The mixed messages that are now common in coverage of international trade may also serve a purpose for journalists who want to ensure balance in their coverage. When an issue moves from being within the realm of elite consensus to being a matter of elite disagreement, media coverage generally also changes, but not due to journalistic bias.[52] Instead this occurs because most media coverage results from reporting on what political elites have said or done. When elites speak out with differing points of view, and the media cover those statements, this naturally changes the tone of coverage that is produced.[53]

When the Washington consensus among elites was essentially pro-trade, most politicians saw it as more politically astute to lay low on this issue so as not to attract potential voter opposition. At election time the candidates of both parties often sounded anti-trade in their public statements. But given that elites are united in publicly attacking trade, journalists sticking to their usual newsgathering practices need not cover "both sides" of this issue when elites are not on opposing sides. Although there are exceptions—such as when presidents are "going public"[54] to promote congressional support for trade deals—few elites who supported free trade dared call public attention to that fact.

The strong protectionist stance taken by Donald Trump in 2016 was unusual for any major party candidate in recent history. Although Hillary Clinton could hardly be considered pro-trade in her public statements, the Democrat party had taken over the pro-trade position by 2016. Overwhelmingly, both Democrats and Republicans saw Trump as more opposed to trade than Clinton, and this made trade more of a partisan issue than in the recent past. To provide balanced coverage, journalists included coverage of job losers due to trade, while also emphasizing trade losers who suffer from a deficit of trade rather than a surfeit of it.

It is easy for economists writing about trade to bemoan journalistic and public misunderstanding of the complex dilemmas surrounding international trade. The tone of these comments can seem dismissive, suggesting that they expect people to be more on top of international economics. As a scholar of mass opinion who is accustomed to finding low levels of knowledge among the public, I am less surprised than amazed that so many people support trade given all of the dismal associations they have with it. Media coverage provides a largely one-sided story in this regard, although it is probably more balanced in its treatment of this topic now than it was before Trump took office.

The gut-wrenching narratives of victims of trade do not make it easy for elites or anyone else to publicly espouse support for free trade. Whether the coverage illustrating the harm done by trade wars and tariffs will help change that fact remains to be seen. Interestingly, none of the 2020 presidential candidates presented themselves as advocates for international trade.[55] At most they advocated "fair"' trade, a term that serves to suggest that most trade is unfair to someone, although typically it is unclear whom. This amorphous term serves to incorporate both those who oppose trade because they feel the US has been taken advantage of by other countries—that is, Trump's theme, as well as those who oppose trade because they think it allows the US to exploit poorer countries—a more common concern among liberals. Although many of the Democratic primary candidates were thought to hold different views privately, there was little to no willingness to advocate in favor of free trade.

9

Attributing Responsibility for Job Loss

Beyond the tone of trade-related news, and its effects on how people visualize trade winners and losers, media may also play a role in influencing trade attitudes by virtue of how news sources attribute responsibility for unemployment in America. During the 2016 election, job loss due to trade was a major focus of public attention in the United States. The "left behind manufacturing worker" became such a frequent trope in political journalism that journalists themselves began parodying their own coverage of "Real America":[1]

> In the shadow of the old flag factory, Craig Slabornik sits whittling away on a rusty nail, his only hobby since the plant shut down. He is an American like millions of Americans, and he has no regrets about pulling the lever for Donald Trump in November—twice, in fact, which Craig says is just more evidence of the voter fraud plaguing the country.[2]

Other journalists complained that interviews with people in small town diners had "become a cliché, a traffic jam, a theatrical genre"[3] with media "blinded by its obsession with rural white Trump voters," especially unemployed coal miners and manufacturing workers.[4]

The high salience of unemployment was unexpected in 2016 for several reasons. First, the timing was off. Following precipitous and severe job losses beginning in the late 1990s and ending in 2010, manufacturing employment in the United States *increased* from 2010 to 2016.[5] Thus 2016 was an odd time for this issue to surface. One could argue that a backlash had been brewing for some time, but for it to explode during the prosperity of unusually low unemployment was puzzling. Mass opinion tends to respond to short-term concerns more than it registers long-term perspectives.[6]

In addition, based on traditional partisan alliances, one would have expected trade-related job loss to be a focus of Democratic rather than Republican attention. As recently as 2012, free trade was an official part of the Republican presidential platform. Nonetheless, the 2016 Republican presidential candidate's strong anti-trade stance was predicated on the widely accepted idea that American manufacturing workers had taken the brunt of the negative consequences from open markets.

Manufacturing job loss was also a surprising focus of media attention because the conventional wisdom among economists is that most manufacturing job loss is due primarily to automation rather than import competition. Contrary to political rhetoric on the left and right, economists suggest that most of the manufacturing jobs lost in the US—roughly 85 percent—have been lost due to increased automation rather than job displacement due to trade.[7] Estimates vary, but they are comparable in suggesting that job loss due to automation is more threatening than offshoring.[8,9] Even so, the impact on individual local communities is often devastating because the new jobs that offset the loss of manufacturing employment are seldom in the same location, nor are they the same jobs. Even when net employment across the country does not suffer at all, many communities and individuals do.

Since long before the late H. Ross Perot described the "giant sucking sound of jobs leaving the country," trade has been viewed as detrimental to domestic employment in America.[10] My question in this chapter is whether media coverage may have played a role in encouraging attributions of responsibility for job loss to trade as opposed to automation. The attributions of causal responsibility that people make for social problems are known to have consequences for their policy attitudes.[11] For example, if poverty is attributed to laziness, people will be less likely to favor social welfare policies; if poverty is instead attributed to bad luck or discrimination, people will be more likely to favor social welfare programs.[12]

But what difference does it make if one believes job loss to be caused by trade as opposed to automation? Causal attributions for job loss are likely to matter for several reasons. Most obviously, it matters because seeing

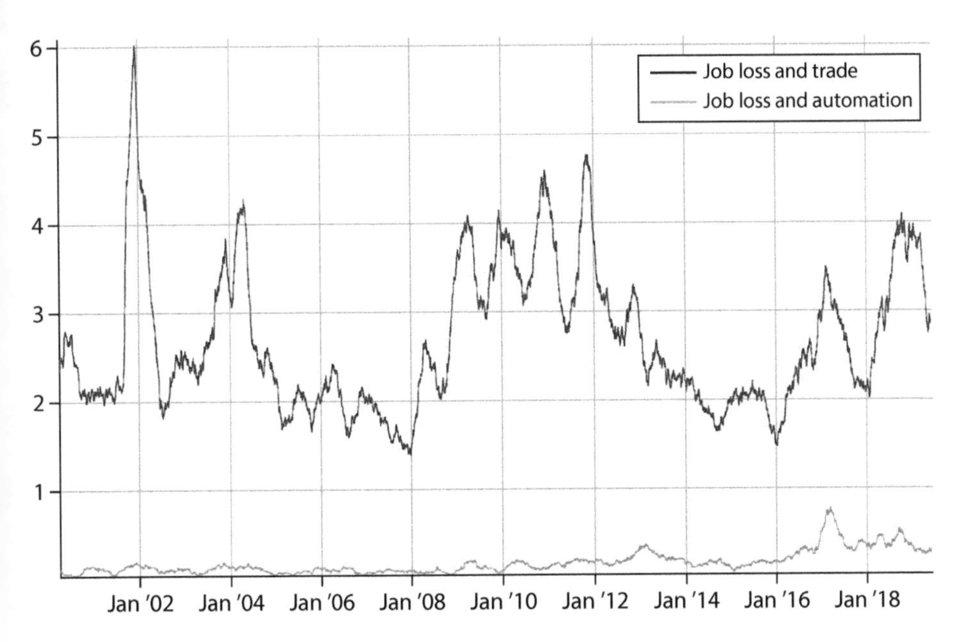

FIGURE 9.1. Newspaper Articles Linking Job Loss to Trade versus Automation
Note: Vertical axis represents counts of articles per day as a 7-day moving average. Solid black line represents job loss linked to trade; grey line represents job loss linked to technology/automation.

international trade as the culprit in this narrative should reduce public support for trade. According to public discourse in the news, job loss in America is more closely linked to trade than to automation. In Figure 9.1, I use a massive data base of major US newspapers to plot both the average number of articles per day mentioning job loss in conjunction with trade, and the average number mentioning job loss in conjunction with automation.[13] Although one might quibble as to whether all important synonyms for automation or trade have been accounted for, the evidence overwhelmingly suggests that job loss is more frequently mentioned in close proximity to trade than to automation. Articles mentioning job loss in conjunction with automation hover near zero from 2000 through 2012, and then gradually increase over time, but they never reach even one-eighth of the prevalence of those mentioning job loss linked to trade. Articles mentioning trade in conjunction with job loss remain high throughout, reaching a peak in 2002. Interestingly, since 2016 such mentions have increased, perhaps as a result of the 2016 election campaign. Americans clearly encounter trade in relation to job loss far more than they encounter automation or technology as a source of job loss.

I suspect that repeatedly linking job loss to trade as opposed to linking it to automation has important consequences for mass opinion. Although job loss is a painful event, regardless of cause, there is something psychologically different about losing one's job to technological advances as opposed to losing one's job due to another human being. In reality, of course, there is no zero-sum, one-to-one swap of a job from one American to one foreigner. But that is the kind of mental imagery associated with trade. The idea that jobs that are rightfully "ours" are being sent overseas rings of injustice to say the least. As a result, I expected job loss due to trade to be a more emotionally-charged issue for Americans than job loss due to automation.

Another reason that attribution of responsibility to trade as opposed to automation is likely to make a difference is because perceived intent is known to play an important role in attribution;[14] in fact, intent sometimes matters more than outcomes. People in other countries who "take American jobs" are more likely to be viewed as humans with intent than are robots who take jobs as a result of automation. When a person argues that "foreigners are stealing our jobs," this is an assertion of a purposeful, malicious act on the part of foreigners. Robots do not have intent and thus are less likely to be viewed in the same way.

Another reason these two kinds of attributions are likely to have different consequences is because foreigners are easily seen as members of an outgroup. As Rose (2010) notes, "We don't think twice about trade between different states. Indeed, federal law prohibits anything that creates barriers to interstate trade. Should we think twice about trade between countries?" Americans do not have the same aversion to interstate trade that they do to international trade.[15] Attributing American job loss to international trade may produce a sense of outgroup threat that automation does not. What social identity theory,[16] group position theory[17] and most theories of intergroup conflict all share is a prediction that when a dominant ingroup's power is threatened, ingroup members respond either by reasserting the superiority of their own status, and/or by derogating the outgroup.[18]

When it comes to job loss, foreigners are easy targets for blame and scapegoating. For example, in a study of climate-change policy attitudes, Americans who were told that the excessive energy use by Americans was driving climate change were more likely to attribute climate change to factors outside of human control in order to deflect blame from Americans.[19] When blame cannot be externally attributed, people predictably become defensive as a means of maintaining a positive ingroup identity. Thus blaming trade for domestic job loss should also result in more negative views of foreigners relative to citizens of one's own country.[20]

This same combination of intent and outgroup status that can be attributed to foreigners cannot be attributed to robots. And while robots may certainly threaten one's livelihood, they are mere machines that are unlikely to suffer from outgroup derogation in any case. For these reasons, attributions of responsibility for job loss to trade are far more potentially pernicious and influential than attributions of job loss to automation. Job loss due to trade allows citizens to personify the enemy-as-foreigner in a way that automation does not.

To find out if these expectations were correct, I designed a survey experiment involving a representative national sample of just over 1000 white Americans.[21] Each person was randomly assigned to one of three experimental conditions and asked to read a single news story. The news stories were identical in describing a manufacturing worker who had lost his job.[22] The experimental conditions varied only one thing: the attribution of responsibility for his job loss was either not mentioned, attributed to trade with China, or attributed to automation.

Even though the trade loser was just one single individual described in the news story, past research suggests that these exemplars can nonetheless have a large impact on policy attitudes. The story used in the experiment was based on a front page article from the *New York Times*.[23] Like many news stories about job loss, it featured a man who had recently lost his manufacturing job:

> When Michael Morrison took a job at the steel mill in the center of Granite City, Ill., in 1999, he assumed his future was ironclad. He was 38, a father with three young children.
>
> "I felt like I had finally gotten into a place that was so reliable I could retire there," he said.
>
> Although it had changed hands, the mill had been there since the end of the 19th century. For those willing to sweat, the mill was a reliable means of supporting a family.
>
> Mr. Morrison began by shoveling slag out of the furnaces, working his way up to crane driver. From inside a cockpit tucked in the rafters of the building, he manned the controls, guiding a 350-ton ladle that spilled molten iron.
>
> It was a difficult job requiring perpetual focus and he was paid accordingly.

Only one part of the article varied across the three experimental conditions. In the control condition, readers learned simply that his job was eliminated, but they were not told why:

> Now his job has been eliminated.

In the trade-related job loss condition, they were told that his job was eliminated due to Chinese trade competition:

> Now his job has been eliminated due to trade with China. Chinese workers now man the same machine that Mr. Morrison once operated. As the company website describes, "Of the 74 machines that were operating in the factory, 63 are now operating in China."

In the automation-related job loss condition, Mr. Morrison was replaced by a robot:

> Now his job has been eliminated due to automation. Robots now man the same machine that Mr. Morrison once operated. As the company website describes, "Of the 74 machines that were operating in the factory, 63 now run on their own with no human intervention."

All versions of the article ended identically as follows:

> Mr. Morrison has not been able to find other work, and he has no idea how he will pay for his children's college educations. "When they don't need me anymore," he said, "I'm nothing."

Since the man loses his job across all conditions, the negative tone of the story and the extent of job loss remain constant.[24]

After reading the article, respondents were asked to assess their emotional reactions to the story. They rated the extent to which reading the article made them sad, angry, resentful, and irritated. I combined these responses into a single indicator of overall negative emotions.[25] Emotionally-charged attributions of responsibility are particularly potent.[26] Moreover, the personification of the enemy was expected to anger people more than automation-related job loss.

I executed this same basic experiment twice, once using a convenience sample of people recruited from Amazon's Mechanical Turk, including only the two treatment conditions, and then a second time using a representative national sample made possible by Time-sharing Experiments for the Social Sciences (TESS). The main difference was that the larger representative study also included a control condition in which people were not told why the man lost his job one way or the other. The results of these two studies were highly consistent, so I will relegate the pilot study's findings to the online appendix,[27] and focus here on the representative national results.

Were people's emotional reactions to the story different based on whether this one man's job loss was attributed to trade versus automation? Or is it simply job loss alone that makes this an emotional issue? As shown in Figure 9.2, attribution of responsibility to trade produced far more negative emotions than attributing job loss to automation. The extent of negative emotions was 11 percent lower when job loss was attributed to automation as opposed to trade. In short, job loss due to trade made people angry in a way that job loss due to automation did not. If one compares the control condition to each of these treatment groups separately, it is the trade attribution article that demonstrates significantly more negative emotions; the attribution of responsibility to automation does not have a symmetric positive effect.[28]

Did this stronger negative reaction translate into greater opposition to trade? To answer this question, I asked a series of questions—whether people thought that government should try to encourage or discourage international trade, whether the respondent believed that economic globalization was good or bad for the United States, whether they favored or opposed the federal government in Washington negotiating more free trade agreements, and whether the increasing amount of trade between the U.S. and other countries has helped or hurt the United States economy. As shown in Figure 9.2, I found that support for trade was 6 percent higher when this one man's job loss was attributed to automation as opposed to trade.[29] By deflecting blame away from trade by attributing his job loss to automation rather than to trade, exposure to this story made international trade significantly more palatable.

In this case, it was the automation condition that produced the significant deviation from the control group baseline.[30] Not surprisingly, people's default explanation for job loss appears to be that trade is responsible, so by providing information counter to those expectations, the automation treatment increased support for trade. Relative to the control condition, explicitly attributing this man's job loss to automation raised people's support for trade by 5 percent. Whether this seems like a lot or a little impact is a matter of perspective. But it is worth noting that other experimental treatments—for example, those suggesting that trade leads to lower prices for consumers—have not produced a significant positive impact on trade attitudes.[31]

The political implications of media coverage that blames automation versus trade become even more apparent in the findings pertaining to people's

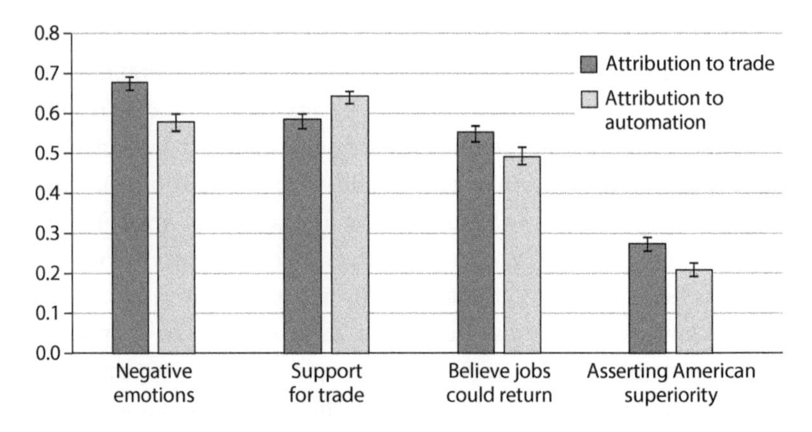

FIGURE 9.2. Effects of Attribution of Job Loss to Trade versus Automation
Source: Attributing the Causes of Job Loss, (TESS, Amerispeak/NORC).
Note: Means are all statistically significant from one another, $p < .001$, $p < .001$, $p < .01$, $p < .01$, respectively.

beliefs about whether manufacturing jobs can return to the US. Respondents were asked to agree or disagree with a statement asserting, "The manufacturing jobs that have left the US will come back if we put taxes or tariffs on foreign goods coming into the US." As shown in Figure 9.2, those assigned to the trade attribution condition were 6 percent more likely to believe that manufacturing jobs could be brought back with the right government policies. Apparently, if robots take your job, it is not coming back. But if international trade is responsible, people are more likely to believe that the right government policies could bring them back.

Job loss is understandably threatening to Americans, so attributing responsibility to foreigners could also increase negative feelings toward these groups when job loss is attributed to trade. In 1982, two Chrysler autoworkers killed Chinese-American Vincent Chin based on their resentment over unemployment in the auto industry, which they blamed on Japanese imports. Although such events are uncommon, and Chin's assailants obviously got his ethnicity wrong, this event is indicative of the strength of underlying resentments that may fester due to trade.

At the same time, when measuring the expression of negative attitudes toward ethnic groups, respondents may be reluctant to state explicitly negative views of outgroups because it is deemed social inappropriate. Thus, instead of asking respondents in my study direct questions about how they felt about Chinese people, I asked them to evaluate a series of statements that might (or might not) be considered acceptable in a social situation.

These statements derogated Chinese or Asians in general using common stereotypes. I did not ask people directly whether they personally agreed or disagreed with these statements; instead, I asked them how appropriate or inappropriate it was for someone to make such a statement:

> Now we are going to show you a list of statements and we would like you to tell us which ones you would consider polite and appropriate for someone to say at a party among people he or she does not know, and which ones would seem rude and inappropriate. We are not asking if you personally agree with these statements, just whether they are polite conversation or not. Just imagine someone made one of these statements. Would you regard it as definitely not appropriate to say, definitely appropriate to say, or something in between?

The list of five statements included derogatory comments about Chinese people such as "Asians are bad drivers" as well as assertions of American superiority such as "Americans are far more innovative than the Chinese."[32] These items were used to create an index of the Acceptability of Asserting American Superiority to the Chinese, with all variables coded so that high scores indicated greater American superiority relative to the Chinese.[33] Based on how threat is known to affect ingroup/outgroup attitudes, I expected that these negative stereotypes would be deemed more socially acceptable if respondents had been recently reminded by the newspaper article of manufacturing job loss due to trade with China. If a person views China as threatening, then such statements will seem more deserved than derogatory. Indeed, as shown in Figure 9.2, assertions of American superiority to the Chinese were 6 percent higher when the person had read an article attributing the man's job loss to trade rather than to automation.[34] There was significantly more animosity after reading the story attributing the man's job loss to trade relative to the control condition.

All comparisons of attitudes between the trade versus automation attribution conditions differed from one another, even though the article was about only one person's job loss. Because the control condition respondents were not given any explanation for the job loss of the man in the article, this allowed me to assess their default reactions and interpretation. Given that even the control condition involved job loss, it is clear that these negative emotions are not simply a response to a man losing a job. In other words, it is not the negativity of job loss per se to which people are reacting. It is job loss due to trade in particular that makes people angry in a way that job loss due to automation does not.

Compared to the control condition, attributing one man's job loss to automation also produced significantly more support for international trade relative to the control condition. Attributing job loss to trade had no impact, but this is due to the fact that people already associated job loss strongly with trade, even in the control condition, where this was not stated to be the cause.

Attributing responsibility for job loss to a foreign threat also increased the extent to which Americans felt a need to assert their own superiority over other nationalities, in this case, the Chinese. Reading the version of the story that attributes the man's job loss to trade increased the extent to which people thought it was acceptable to claim American superiority to the Chinese by 4 percent relative to the control condition. Reading the story attributing responsibility for job loss to automation decreased the extent to which people felt it was appropriate to claim American superiority relative to the control condition. Overall, these results suggest that media coverage emphasizing trade-induced job loss may affect public attitudes toward trade as well as anger directed toward foreigners.

I also examined whether these effects varied by education, the characteristic most closely tied to holding a strong national identity, as well as to levels of trade support. As shown in Table A9.3 in the online appendix, education altered the impact of attributions significantly in all four analyses. But most importantly, and consistent with my hypotheses about why trade and nationalistic opinions are closely related, the effects of attribution cues on the perceived acceptability of claiming American superiority were much greater for those without a college education. As shown in Figure 9.3, the largest effects were among those with the strongest attachment to American national identity. This finding lends further support to the idea that increasingly nationalistic attitudes can be a response to perceived threat to the national ingroup such as the threat perceived to be posed by trade. In other words, nationalistic beliefs are not only a potential cause of protectionist views, increased nationalism is also a result of a perceived international threat. For those who feel America is threatened by international competition, trade-related fears produce stronger assertions of American superiority. Simply changing the attribution for a single man's job loss from trade to automation produced a 9 percent difference in levels of American superiority. Among the less-educated in particular, an attribution of job loss to automation reduced the extent to which China-bashing seemed appropriate and decreased the acceptability of asserting American superiority.

Education levels conditioned other reactions as well. For example, among those without a college education, that is, those who were more likely to

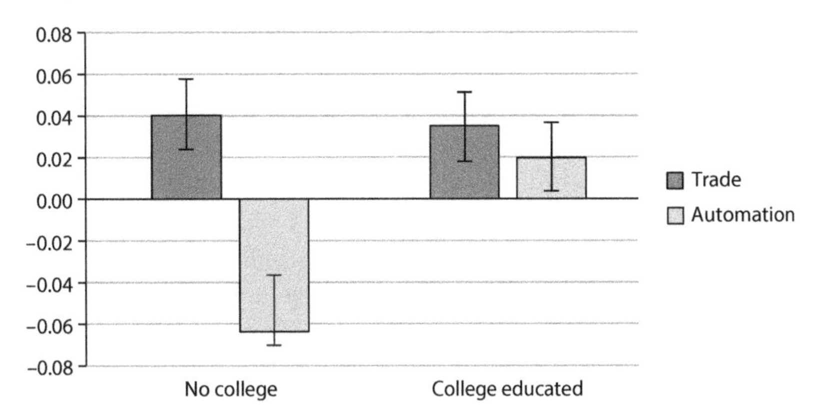

FIGURE 9.3. The Perceived Acceptability of American Superiority, by Education and Attribution of Job Loss to Trade versus Automation
Source: Attributing the Causes of Job Loss, (TESS, Amerispeak/NORC).
Note: Means are adjusted so that the control condition mean is represented by zero on the y axis, and deviations from the control condition due to attributions are shown for trade-related attribution and automation-related attributions. See Chapter 9 Appendix for details.

believe that job loss was due to trade to begin with, the largest impact was from attribution of responsibility to automation, which increased trade support by 6 percent. Among those with a college education, those who were more likely to attribute job loss to automation than their less-educated counterparts, the largest impact was from the story attributing responsibility to trade. In each case, a single story that highlighted the attribution of responsibility that was less prominent in their minds produced a significant change in levels of support for trade.

The same pattern occurred for believing that manufacturing jobs can be brought back. Those without a college education were more influenced relative to the control condition by the automation cue, and those with a college education were more influenced relative to baseline by the trade attribution. These effects are substantial. For example, a single story attributing job loss to trade boosted beliefs among the college educated that policies could bring manufacturing jobs back by 8 percent.

Of course, the size of the effects documented here reflects a short exposure to a single news story. While it is clear that this type of news story is common, it is impossible to assess the persistence of the observed effects over time. At the same time, the fact that a single short news story had such an impact is somewhat surprising. The article says nothing about job loss as a larger-scale phenomenon or about whether the attribution for this one man's job loss is representative of others who have lost jobs. The story appears to have simply prompted people to think about possible alternative reasons for job loss, but not to have completely altered their base-rate judgments about how likely various causes of unemployment might be. I can only speculate as to the longer-term, cumulative impact of attributions of responsibility that are prevalent over time. But given the overwhelming dominance of linkages between job loss and trade in news coverage, and the relatively minor attention given to job loss tied to automation, it is hardly surprisingly that Americans are ambivalent about trade.

According to one recent study, even manufacturing workers themselves are often confused about why their jobs have disappeared. Case reports in the news like the one used in this experiment make the attribution of responsibility for a person's job loss very straightforward. But in the real world, workers may not actually know why their job has been eliminated. Based on evidence that displaced workers are more likely to erroneously file petitions for Trade Adjustment Assistance in areas that have been affected by automation, one recent study argues that many workers displaced by automation believe themselves to have been victims of trade.[35] Of course, it is also possible that virtually everyone—regardless of their job situation—over-attributes job loss to trade as opposed to automation. The salience of trade as an issue is far greater than that of automation, as illustrated in Figure 9.1. Although recent years have seen increased news attention to automation as a cause of job loss, it still receives nowhere near the emphasis that trade does. Moreover, it is not clear that automation can be called an "issue" at all.[36] By this, I mean that few Americans truly question whether we should go back to having human pin setters in bowling alleys. Automation tends to be seen as progress and is seldom questioned. It is simply not as controversial an issue as trade.

Media coverage emphasizing trade as the major source of job loss as opposed to automation has had important consequences for American public opinion. Job loss due to trade produces far more negative emotional reactions than job loss due to automation. These angry reactions to trade are not simply about job loss, although job loss is obviously an enormously negative event for any individual. What makes people far more upset is the idea that other people are benefiting from their own bad fortune. When those other people are foreigners, it is especially upsetting. Casting foreigners as the villains in this narrative has consequences that go beyond potentially misperceiving the main source of job loss; it encourages and seemingly justifies ethnocentrism.

One might ask why these seemingly subtle differences in a single article successfully increase levels of trade support when far more involved argumentation often does not. When people try to increase Americans' support for international trade, they typically turn to economic arguments, suggesting, for example, that trade is more efficient or that the prices consumers pay will decline as a result of international trade. To understand such arguments requires complex economic understanding. Attributions of responsibility, on the other hand, are a common component of everyday reasoning. In the absence of information, people still automatically assign responsibility for events spontaneously,[37] even when these are entirely random, chance events.[38] These attributions, in turn, have powerful effects on attitudes and behavior.

While attributions of responsibility are prominent in everyday thinking, they are not likely to prompt counter-arguments to the same extent that persuasive arguments do. It is relatively easy for a person confronted with the argument that trade saves them money to counter that this is not what is most important to them, or that they do not believe this to be the case. On the other hand, when an article in a story says that a single individual lost his job due to trade or due to automation, it seems unlikely that they will doubt this claim. Believing this claim does not, on its face, ask them to change their views about trade. Nonetheless, by prompting them to think about a sympathetically portrayed job loss as caused by automation versus trade, it can have significant downstream effects.

The alignment of nationalism, xenophobia, and trade opposition functions as a mutually reinforcing worldview. Often nationalism is portrayed as a *cause* of support for isolationist policies such as trade opposition. People who believe their country is superior to other countries are less likely to want to do business with those countries. But nationalism and trade opposition are even closer bedfellows because being threatened by trade produces an increased need to assert national superiority. When people attribute job loss to foreigners taking their jobs, the psychological response to this threat is to bolster attitudes toward their national ingroup while actively denigrating the outgroup. Thus nationalism, ethnocentrism, and trade opposition go hand in hand in a way that nationalism and job loss due to automation do not.

More recently, automation seems to be receiving increasing attention in the news as a source of job loss, a development that is evident in Figure 9.1

beginning in 2017. This is potentially important since coverage emphasizing attributions of responsibility to automation rather than trade is likely to have consequences. Surprisingly, such coverage matters even when the stories are simply illustrative examples and not factual claims about the total number of people displaced by trade versus automation. The size of these effects is substantial. When journalists make choices about whom to feature when discussing manufacturing job loss, this choice is not without consequence.

10

The Impact of Trade on Elections

There are two strikingly different narratives about the relevance of mass opinion on international trade to electoral behavior. The original, perhaps more widely accepted view within political science circles, is that trade matters very little or not at all to most election outcomes. More recently, however, in the wake of increasing amounts of international trade and particularly the decision of Congress in 2000 to extend status of "permanent normal trade relations" to China, economists have challenged this general conclusion. Drawing on economic studies of voting, some have argued that trade now has a substantial impact on presidential vote choice. This chapter explores the evidence behind these arguments in greater depth. Does the American public hold presidents or congressional representatives accountable for the effects of international trade, whether they are positive or negative? Based on what is known about voting behavior more generally, is trade an issue that should be expected to influence vote choice?

Although trade has long been a controversial issue in the US, when I started this project in 2014, most election scholars found the idea that trade was relevant to electoral politics preposterous for some pretty good reasons. For one, trade was not a salient political issue. Globalization was increasing apace, to be sure, but with the exception of some third party candidates such as Ross Perot, it was not something candidates for office talked much about.[1] Moreover, because candidates often fear electoral punishment for openly supporting international trade, the differences between candidates' positions on trade were seldom clear. While the idea that economic conditions could influence voting was well-regarded and widely established, scholars did not suggest that trade could impact voting beyond any effects it might have on general economic conditions.

Now that has changed. In this chapter I provide an overview of previous studies as well as my own evidence weighing in on whether trade influences voting behavior. Many previous studies have been suggestive, but also problematic because they are long on economic data in the aggregate, and short on mechanisms that can plausibly explain the relationships that they find. In addition, they rely heavily on the reward-punishment theory of economic voting, an idea that is increasingly popular among political economists just as it is experiencing diminishing credibility among political scientists.

Many of the aggregate-level analyses used to study economic voting combine huge amounts of data across multiple elections, arguing that elections hold political leaders accountable for the real world effects of trade. These studies often do not consider the dynamics of which party is in power or how the candidates have positioned themselves on trade issues. In this chapter I offer my own interpretation of how and when trade is likely to matter to elections, drawing on panel studies of the Great Recession and Donald Trump's election to office in 2016.

Although political scientists' initial reticence to consider trade an election issue makes sense, trade has at least one characteristic that recommends it as an issue that might change votes. Most voting in the US is along predictable party lines, but unlike most political issues in a highly polarized country, views on trade do not map reliably onto partisan identities. Because trade views are not part of the usual package of issue opinions that one party is for and the other against, when the issue becomes salient, these views could be especially important to causing defections from people's usual partisan voting behavior.

How Scholars Study the Electoral Effects of Trade

Two types of studies provide evidence on the electoral effects of trade. Both endeavor to answer the same basic question: Does trade affect voting behavior? Beyond this, they are distinct in their approach as well as in their assumptions. One model relies primarily on survey-based measures of public attitudes toward trade to evaluate whether positions on this issue influence voting behavior.[2] Survey-based studies also attempt to account for past voting behavior at the individual level, political party identification, attitudes toward other issues, and perceptions of the economy more generally.

Often they are based on cross-sectional evidence from a single election, and at other times they draw on panel data connecting voting behavior across multiple elections.

The second type of study follows the political economy model. Studies of this kind rely on government data from geographic collectives such as congressional districts or commuter zones to measure how much a geographic unit has been affected by trade. Indicators of some form of economic impact are matched to the aggregate number of votes for candidates of each party within each geographic unit. These studies are typically limited to economic variables, meaning that they do not incorporate non-economic reasons that a geographic area might support one party over the other. However, because government data on economic characteristics and voting behavior do not use the same geographic units, mapping one onto the other can be challenging. Researchers compare variation across geographic units as well as change over time within those units in the extent of import penetration in order to explain changes in voting behavior, with the assumption that those changes are what is causing people to vote differently.

A central advantage of individual-level studies is that individual people are the actual units of analysis that make voting decisions. If voting decisions are affected by trade, the mechanism that produces that outcome is most likely to be found within the individual. As noted in Chapter 2, most Americans are employed in trade-neutral lines of work, so aggregate-level studies assuming that people's views are rooted in their personal experience only make predictions for those personally affected. For elected officials to be held accountable for trade's impact, the only alternative is that people have accurate knowledge of how their communities have been affected by trade.

In contrast, survey-based studies do not assume accurate knowledge. They instead ask how people perceive their communities or the nation to have been affected by trade. Surveys have their own strengths and limitations. Many are static, cross-sectional snapshots that make causal interpretations quite difficult. On the other hand, these studies are usually able to account for a broader range of potentially spurious causes of these relationships because they are not limited to aggregated economic data.

Thus far, most evidence affirming a relationship between trade and electoral behavior comes from studies of population aggregates such as counties or commuter zones, that is, from the political economy model described above. Aggregate economic circumstances or changes in circumstances are shown to relate to aggregate patterns of voting, with the assumption that these variations are causally related either due to economic self-interest among individuals in the affected communities, or due to voting based on perceived community-level interests with respect to trade. Importantly, these studies do not demonstrate that people perceive trade to be hurting them or their communities, nor do they assess people's attitudes toward international trade at all. And as with many observational analyses, it is difficult to make strong causal arguments because so many other characteristics also vary across communities. In addition, interpretations of these relationships are subject to the ecological fallacy whereby individual-level mechanisms of influence are mistakenly inferred from aggregate-level evidence. As is frequently observed, communities don't vote; people do.[3]

In contrast to economic studies, survey-based studies have not often found evidence linking voting behavior to trade preferences. For example, a large-scale study of the 2006 midterm congressional elections suggested that the issue was too low in salience to influence voting. Voters did not know the candidates' stands and thus could not have voted on this basis, nor were they more or less likely to support the incumbent based on their trade preferences.[4] Even among those groups most likely to be affected by trade policy, the issue was not particularly salient. In two additional studies examining the relationship between trade preferences and vote choice in the 2016 election, neither found evidence that this issue mattered, despite its high salience in 2016.[5] In one exception to the lack of survey-based findings, survey data from the 1996 election suggested that those with high levels of job insecurity were more likely to support Ross Perot, a third party candidate whose central election issue was opposition to NAFTA.[6] Because major party presidential candidates seldom highlight disagreements about trade during elections, it is less likely that the public perceives differences between the major party candidates on this issue.

When relationships have been found in aggregate-level economic studies, the usual mechanism proposed is voting based on personal economic self-interest. Those who lose jobs or experience depressed wages due to import competition are assumed to react at the ballot box and hold political leadership accountable. But this mechanism seemingly contradicts the common pattern found in studies of economic voting and electoral behavior, where perceptions of national-level impact matter a great deal more than how a policy affects an individual and his or her family. Concern about the local community has been posited as an alternative explanation for influence in both economic and political science studies of the impact of trade; if one's community has been hurt by trade, then people should turn against it and vote accordingly. But here again, survey evidence suggests that what matters to policy attitudes is not how an individual perceives himself or herself to have been affected by trade, nor how the local community is perceived to have been affected. Instead, perceived national-level impact is far more closely tied to policy opinions on trade. I illustrate this familiar pattern in Table A10.1 in the online appendix. When the perceived impact of trade on one's own family, on one's local community and on the nation as a whole are simultaneously used to predict trade policy preferences, trade's perceived national impact blows the other predictors out of the water. It predicts trade policy preferences more than three times as much as trade's perceived impact on one's local community; the perceived impact on one's family barely predicts at all. At all three levels, family, community, and nation, these are subjectively-assessed perceptions, yet people do not connect personal or local impact with trade policy preferences the same way they do national impact. This pattern makes it seem unlikely that trade's personal or community-level impact affects voting more than trade's perceived consequences for the nation.

Four Theories Linking Trade to Electoral Behavior

Even scholars who agree that trade is electorally consequential disagree on the direction in which people are likely to react. To date, four different theories have been proposed, suggesting either 1) that negative effects from trade favor candidates of the Democratic party; 2) that negative effects from trade favor candidates of the Republican party; 3) that negative effects from trade favor whichever candidate is perceived to be more opposed to trade, or 4) that negative effects of trade in a local area result in more votes against the *incumbent* party, whichever party that might be.

These four theories obviously cannot all be correct. To sort through the evidence on which they are based, I review work supporting each of these conclusions as well as the mechanisms proposed to underlie them. Because these studies tend to be based solely on economic data, I then highlight how political psychology can contribute to a better understanding of these relationships.

Negative Consequences of Trade Favor Democrats. One theory suggests that the economic hardships caused by trade exposure lead to more Democratic voting because Democrats are known to be more favorable toward social welfare programs. For example, based on a study of congressional elections from 1992 to 2010, trade exposure in the local area is argued to favor the election of a greater number of Democratic representatives.[7] The suggested mechanism is that the economic assistance provided by redistributive social policies makes Democratic leadership seem like a better bet when people are experiencing financial stress due to higher levels of import exposure. Beyond the US, a panel study of support for political parties in the Netherlands also suggests that those whose incomes declined during the recession increasingly supported radical left parties, and voiced support for more redistributive economic policies.[8]

Negative Consequences of Trade Favor Republicans. A second theory predicts precisely the opposite, that is, that Republican candidates should benefit from import exposure. This theory is a common explanation for Trump's election in the US. Why should those negatively affected by trade pin their hopes on electing Republicans? According to theories of "status anxiety" or "cultural backlash," the shift from being an economically secure, post-materialist society to an economically insecure one triggers a backlash favoring rightwing populist leaders.[9] Local economic downturns due to import competition create a cultural backlash and increased resentment of outsiders. When people become economically insecure, they are hypothesized to take out their frustrations on outgroup members. Economic downturns and financial insecurity are argued to contribute to greater intolerance and more negativity toward outgroups, but—puzzlingly—not necessarily more negative attitudes toward trade.[10] Instead, the story is that economically insecure citizens support more nativist politicians because of their opposition to immigration, a reaction that ends up also favoring economically isolationist candidates since they tend to be the same people.[11]

Evidence in support of this argument has been drawn primarily from European countries, although scholars have suggested that the same theory also explains the rise of Donald Trump in the United States. In many respects, this theory is similar to the controversial "left behind" explanation for Trump's victory: Those left behind by globalization who never quite recovered from the recession embraced a strong populist leader.

However, applying this idea to the US case raises multiple questions. Before 2016, few would have labelled the Republican party as populist. Nonetheless, this same theory has been used to explain a link between local trade shocks from China and increased support for Republican candidates in American presidential elections before 2016.[12,13] A second complication is that at least in the US (but also in some European countries cited), economic growth was strong during this period, with declining levels of unemployment, and rising incomes, so fewer people were experiencing a decline in their personal financial well-being at the time. The work-around explanation for this apparent inconsistency is that because growth was overly concentrated in top earners, rising inequality contributed to a sense of *relative* decline, despite low unemployment and strong economic growth.[14] Thus inequality is said to contribute to "status anxiety"; even though people are no worse off financially than before, they feel like they are because they perceive others to be doing better than they are.

In most versions of this theory, economic insecurity rather than economic hardship is cast as the root cause of rising support for populist parties. Elaborations of this general idea suggest that economic and cultural developments have combined to produce status anxiety, which in turn leads to increasing support for populists.[15] In cross-sectional surveys, measures of subjective social status have been shown to be negatively related to support for the populist right as well as to holding anti-trade and anti-immigration views. But it is unclear what measures of subjective social status are tapping. What contributes to a subjective sense of low versus high social status? People may also feel more aggrieved when their party is out of power, thus producing lower status perceptions among out-party partisans.

I cannot speak to how well economic theories fit data from other countries, but I am skeptical about the economically-driven cultural backlash explanation in the American case. Political trends in Europe are so frequently linked to Trump's rise that they are often considered evidence of a single phenomenon. The cultural backlash argument includes rising popular opposition to immigration as a central feature. The problem with applying this theory to explain public opinion in the US is that none of the major surveys documenting public opinion trends over time shows rising opposition to immigration in the US. Instead, support for immigration has grown progressively more positive since the 1990s, a trend that has continued unabated during Trump's administration. For example, in 1994, only 31 percent of Americans endorsed the view that "immigrants strengthen the country because of their hard work and talents" as opposed to "burdening the country by taking jobs, housing and healthcare." By 2018, fully 65 percent endorsed this positive view—a 34 percentage point increase since 1994. Immigration attitudes have become more divided along partisan lines, but neither Republicans nor Democrats have become more opposed to immigration.[16] Surveys from The Pew Foundation and The Chicago Council on Global Affairs confirm this same pattern with slightly different questions.[17] As I discuss later in the chapter, the alignment between the views of the average American and the Republican nominee on immigration policies actually *decreased* from 2012 to 2016 due to Trump's very extreme positions on immigration. While the perceived position of the Republican nominee became more opposed to immigration, the public moved in the opposite direction.[18,19]

Yet another study implying that economic hardships brought on by trade may lead to support for more extreme, nativist politicians is the often-cited study of China shocks and voting by David Autor and his colleagues.[20] Their evidence demonstrates that trade-exposed local areas end up with more conservative Republican and more liberal Democratic members of congress based on members' congressional voting records. In other words, import penetration resulted in polarized elites rather than more Republicans or more Democrats, and this supposedly occurred due to changes in the voting patterns of the mass public, although this is not explicitly spelled out. In addition, this study finds that counties with greater trade exposure became more Republican-supportive in the 2000, 2008, and 2016 presidential elections, purportedly due to trade's negative impact on their counties.[21]

Negative Consequences of Trade Favor the Outparty. The third and most popular mechanism used to link trade to congressional and presidential voting is the same reward-punishment theory that is popular in studying the general impact of economic change on voting. If trade has had deleterious effects on job availability, wages, or other forms of economic well-being, candidates of the incumbent party are deemed responsible for this downturn, and thus people vote against candidates of the incumbent party, whichever that party happens to be at the time. According to this narrative, incumbent party candidates are blamed for trade's deleterious economic effects, regardless of these politicians' views on trade, and regardless of whether the economic decline was actually caused by trade or some other factor. In this case, the theory of retrospective economic voting and of trade's electoral impact become one and the same. This is not a theory about trade's impact per se, since anything that affects economic well-being is treated the same, even if it is due, for example, to a recession or a pandemic.

However, at least one study advancing this theory suggests that accountability is, indeed, trade-specific. Yotam Margalit suggests that between 1996 and 2004, voters punished incumbents specifically for job loss due to trade as opposed to job loss from other causes.[22] His study argues that voters were affected by job loss due to foreign competition differently from job loss due to domestic competition. It seems logical that people would respond differently if they knew how much job loss was due to foreign versus domestic competition. However, the level of citizen knowledge and competence implied by these findings would come as a surprise to scholars of American electoral behavior. According to this line of argument, not only do citizens hold incumbents accountable for the extent of job loss in their counties in the years preceding an election, they are able to differentiate job loss due to trade from job loss due to other phenomena. Further, the same study argues that if people in a geographic area receive more job retraining and income assistance, then they are less likely to hold the incumbent party responsible for job loss.[23]

As noted in the previous chapter, displaced workers often erroneously file petitions for Trade Adjustment Assistance (TAA) when they are ineligible because their jobs were actually displaced by automation.[24] This low level of citizen self-knowledge may seem surprising, but such determinations are not always straightforward. Moreover, evidence remains mixed on whether TAA encourages support for trade.[25]

Studies based on aggregated economic data and the reward-punishment theory vary a great deal in which of many potential economic indicators they suggest should be tied to voting. For example, one study of county-level data from six presidential elections from 1992 to 2012 used unemployment, change in unemployment, wages for low-wage tradable manufacturing, and wages for high-wage service employment, as well as average pay levels.[26] In this study, only employment *volatility* consistently predicted changes in aggregate levels of incumbent support, a finding the authors interpret as indicating that *prospective* job insecurity predicts anti-incumbent voting. In addition, counties with large percentages of high-skill, tradable services were more likely to increase their support for incumbents, while incumbent support decreased in areas with low-skill manufacturing employment. Sometimes it is a county's unemployment level or employment volatility that predicts change in incumbent vote shares, and in other cases it is argued to be change over time in these indicators.

Relationships between descriptive characteristics of counties and incumbent support are less clearly suggestive of a causal explanation than are relationships between changes over time, since over-time change is less likely to be confounded with other county characteristics. Based on national-level analyses going back to the 1936 election, Jensen, Quinn, and Weymouth conclude that there is "strong and consistent evidence that citizen exposure to trade influences US presidential elections."[27] However, this study does not claim people's attitudes toward trade changed at all, only that citizens responded to, or were fearful of, economic change, not of trade in particular.

In essence, the theoretical framework in their study reduces trade's potential effects on electoral behavior to a subspecies of retrospective economic voting, a well-studied phenomenon. If economic conditions get worse, voters are more likely to oust incumbents, whereas if economic conditions are improving, incumbent politicians are credited for the improvements and receive more votes. This means that people are reacting to general economic change, not to trade in particular. They may, as a result, punish or reward incumbents for things that have nothing whatsoever to do with trade. As economists have noted, "Trade is neither the only, nor even the most important source of shocks in labour markets."[28] If this is true, how are citizens differentiating job loss and employment volatility due to trade versus other factors? And since non-trade-related indicators of economic change are typically not included in these models, how do we know that people are reacting to trade-induced economic impacts as opposed to the economy more generally?

Negative Consequences of Trade Favor Candidates Known to Oppose Trade. A fourth potential explanation for why trade exposure favors particular candidates is based on issue agreement. The straightforward idea here is that those who oppose trade will, all else being equal, favor candidates known to oppose trade.[29] Those experiencing adverse effects from import competition assumed to be opposed to trade and thus more likely to vote for the Democrat, because Democratic elites in the past have been more likely to vote to limit import competition. Of course, this mechanism assumes that people did, in fact, perceive Democrats to be more anti-trade. Because candidates of both parties talk like protectionists at election time,[30] it can be difficult for the average voter to differentiate whether the Republican or Democrat is more anti-trade. And of course, this same theory implies that if the Republican candidate were perceived to be more opposed to trade—as was the case in the 2016 election—then trade shocks should favor Republicans.

To disentangle one argument from the other ideally requires elections in which the positions of the two parties switch. As I describe further in Chapter 11, 2016 comes close to providing just such an opportunity. If voters negatively affected by trade engage in issue-based voting, this should logically push them toward supporting whichever candidate appears to be more protectionist than the other. When the candidates' perceived stances on trade are similar, no relationship with voting should be expected.

The Plausibility of Causal Links between Trade's Impact and Voting Behavior

Across three of the four theories I have described, changes in public opinion on trade are posited to serve as the mechanism by which trade affects voting. In many economic studies, however, it is left unstated whether people are changing their attitudes toward trade and then voting on that basis, or simply reacting directly to a declining economy. When outcome measures are based on the behavior of political elites rather than that of voters, studies often assume as a mechanism that trade shocks affect individual attitudes toward international trade, thus increasing public demands for protectionist policies. This surge in protectionism, in turn, produces a greater number of protectionist elected officials.[31] But elites could easily respond to trade shocks regardless of whether the public takes note and pressures them to do so. These studies are thus not necessarily evidence of the public holding leaders accountable.[32]

Although aggregated demographic characteristics are often included in the kinds of models offered by political economists, education is typically not. Instead, education is treated as an indicator of skill level and how economically vulnerable an individual or area is to trade's impact.[33] As previously mentioned, for psychologists education level represents a whole host of characteristics that are not necessarily tied to economic well-being. These include racial attitudes, social dominance, isolationism, authoritarianism, social trust, openness to change, and other differences—many of which could potentially confound these purely economic interpretations.

Any compelling theory linking positive or negative effects of trade to voting behavior must take into account not only what is already known about economic voting, but also what is known about how voters make decisions. Students of American electoral behavior are likely to find some aspects of the above theories far-fetched based on what they know about the American voter. Some economic studies assume that average Americans can differentiate the negative effects of trade on their local economies from negative effects that stem from other sources. They assume people can distinguish job loss due to trade from job loss due to other factors such as automation. And they assume that people will react differently to downturns resulting from trade with China as opposed to trade with other countries. Further, homeowners in heavy manufacturing areas are assumed to know that trade could cause housing values to depreciate and, as a result, to oppose trade more than renters do.[34] In economic studies, people are also believed to react to information about agricultural subsidies based on how large they believe such subsidies to be in other countries. Scholars of electoral behavior may look askance at such claims because they are acutely aware of just how little information average voters possess.

While experimental studies make it plausible that people can react to information when it is directly supplied to them, the well-documented low levels of voter information belie the relevance of some theories to the real world. Few voters can accurately assess how much their commuter zone or congressional district has been affected by trade relative to its effects in preceding years or relative to its effects on other commuter zones or congressional districts. Nonetheless, these comparisons are assumed to change their highly ingrained, habitual voting habits. The beef that students of electoral behavior are likely to have with the political economy models is not that their statistics are incorrect or that their instrumental variables are not good enough. It is that the mechanism producing these aggregate-level observational relationships is either unclear and/or inconsistent with much of what is known about voting behavior.

In contrast, the strong appeal of the incumbency-oriented reward-punishment theory is precisely that it does not require that people know much more than that their pocketbooks aren't as full as they used to be, or that their immediate communities are experiencing economic decline as evidenced by store closings, boarded-up houses, homelessness, and so forth. Importantly, this theory does not require people to have opinions on trade, they do not need to follow the news closely, and they do not need to know candidates' positions on trade. All of this makes the mechanism underlying this theory far more plausible. The main drawback is that this theory has the least to do with trade. It suggests a means of accountability for economic decline in general, but not for trade in particular.

A theory with low information requirements is especially important when arguing that trade shocks are *changing* people's voting behavior. What we know from decades of research on voting behavior is that it is exceedingly difficult to get people to change their vote from one party to another. People tend to be Republicans or Democrats for life. Moreover, in US presidential elections, over 90 percent of partisans typically vote for the candidate of the same party as in the previous election. Despite Trump's unusual candidacy, this was true in 2016 as well. Those who supported major party candidates voted highly consistently from election to election. For example, 96 percent of Romney supporters chose Trump over Clinton, and over 90 percent of Obama supporters chose Clinton over Trump.[35] What's more, Americans' choices have become increasingly consistent with their initial party choice over time,[36] a trend that is exacerbated by mass polarization. So-called swing voters, which constitute around 5 to 10 percent of the electorate, sometimes change their votes. However, this same group tends to be especially poorly informed. In addition to being less knowledgeable about the economy, they would be less likely to know about differences between candidates on issues such as trade.

The End of Economic Voting?

The general reward-punishment theory linking economic change to voting behavior seems plausible enough that it has attracted the attention of researchers more or less continually for almost five decades now. What is particularly ironic about having the electoral effects of trade cast as a subspecies of the reward-punishment theory of economic voting is that this is occurring at precisely the same time that scholars of American political behavior are expressing serious doubts about the utility of the general economic reward-punishment theory.[37] In other words, while many economists are signaling the importance of retrospective voting based on import competition, some political scientists are heralding "the end of economic voting."[38] These two simultaneous trends are puzzling, especially since it seems more likely that people would vote on the basis of general economic decline or improvement than based specifically on how trade has affected their communities. The requirements of retrospective voting based on import competition seem frankly more demanding than the requirements for general economic voting.

It is worth considering why enthusiasm for the economic voting paradigm has waned. A review of the rise and fall of the powerful economic voting paradigm concludes that "economic voting does not function as envisioned by advocates of democratic accountability." What was treated for a long time as an "incontrovertible scientific fact" is really highly dependent upon context[39] and "only intermittently borne out by the facts."[40]

One would assume that a weak theory would become known as such fairly quickly. So it seems reasonable to ask why this paradigm has persisted for so long. The initial lack of supportive evidence was attributed to methodological problems:

> Looking back on more than 20 years of quite rigorous research, it appeared that social scientists by and large had come to believe that a

> relationship existed between economics and political attitudes/behavior and that the "true" relationship between economic conditions and public support could be demonstrated if we only looked hard enough. And looking hard enough meant using the right data and modeling and estimating the economy-mass opinion relationship in the "right" way rather than questioning the underlying assumptions that guided economic voting models.[41]

Today, political scientists regularly question this relationship.[42] Incumbents are not consistently punished for bad economic times or rewarded for good ones. So why should they be punished specifically for bad economic times brought on by import exposure, a far more difficult distinction for most Americans? I cannot provide an answer to this question, but the central problem is clear. We have aggregate-level economic studies suggesting that presidents (or in some cases, members of Congress) are held responsible for the local impact of import competition in their communities, as distinct from general changes in the economy. Yet we lack a compelling narrative to explain this relationship other than general economic voting.

There are many reasons that even the seemingly straightforward reward-punishment theory linking economics and voting works sporadically at best. One impediment is the public's generally low level of information about the economy. It is not that easy to understand economic indicators of various kinds; further, indicators are not always consistent with one another. In order to promote accountability for trade's impact, even this minimalist theory still requires agreeing on what constitutes the objective economy and perceiving it accurately.[43] Is it stock market performance? Unemployment?

Opinions vary on the extent to which real economic change is registered in public opinion. We know that variation in individual levels of attention and interest, combined with irregular media attention, produce perceptions of economic change that only partially reflect reality. Some analyses suggest that economic evaluations stem more from how media choose to present them than from actual objective change.[44]

One popular explanation for why macro-level evidence of economic voting and micro-level evidence do not tell the same story is the higher degree of "noise" in surveys, which supposedly cancels out when studying aggregates. But even when national economic perceptions are aggregated, they include systematic biases that lend little support to the idea that the reward-punishment theory works as proposed.[45]

Additional problems stem from individual motivations and predispositions. Economic perceptions are heavily influenced by whether one's own party is currently in power. Virtually overnight, when the party in power changes, *voilà*, so do partisans' perceptions of the economy.[46] Scholars disagree on the extent to which economic perceptions do, or do not, follow economic reality.[47] But importantly, these arguments are about the *extent* of partisan rationalization of the economy, not about whether it occurs. The size of rationalization effects is quite substantial and is realized very quickly after a presidential election that changes the party in power. Further, the extent of partisan differences in economic perceptions has increased significantly over the last twenty years, suggesting that "partisan economic perceptions have become increasingly decoupled from the actual state of the economy."[48]

Even when partisan predispositions do not overwhelm the signals produced by actual economic change, partisans may attribute responsibility for those same changes differently, based on their predispositions.[49] One can acknowledge that the economy is doing well, for example, but still not credit the president for this accomplishment. Voters engage in motivated reasoning about the state of the economy as well as about who is responsible for it.[50] All of these issues hinder economic accountability.

Economic voting involves translating subjective perceptions of economic change into changes in vote choice. This process is not as simple as it sounds. In fact, the process has so many individual causal links in the process that scholars of electoral behavior find it highly unlikely to occur even under the best of circumstances. The extent to which a bad economy leads to lower support for the party in power has been characterized as "intermittent, highly contingent, and substantively small."[51] It is no longer considered a "robust fact"; in fact, in concluding an *Annual Review of Political Science* review article, Anderson suggests, "It is not unreasonable to ask whether the research agenda on economics and elections has run its course."[52]

Mass media remain the most likely source of information on economic change at the national level. But notably, most political economy models depend on people's knowledge of, or sensitivity to, variation over time in *local* economic conditions. The role of local conditions in retrospective economic voting—the basis of evidence for most political economy models involving trade—has even less empirical support than does national-level economic accountability. The well-documented decline of local news makes it unlikely that people have accurate knowledge of local conditions.

Back when the major news sources portrayed roughly the same economic trends over time, holding the incumbent party accountable for national-level economic change seemed at least plausible. But the resurgence of partisan media in the United States has raised yet another problem. Rather than passively relay statistics on economic change to their audiences, partisan media may produce even greater variation in perceptions of economic change. Partisan media now serve as a source of systematic distortion in economic perceptions.[53] Thus growth in partisan media exposure has generated further skepticism about the public's ability to hold leadership accountable for economic change.

As the ability of the public to hold leaders accountable for general economic change has come under fire, this evidence indirectly also challenges the idea that political leaders are held accountable by voters for the negative effects of trade on their local communities' economies. If the public doesn't get it right on the economy at large, how can we expect them to know about the impact of trade in particular? In short, there are many reasons to doubt the reward-punishment theory as applied to trade's impact.

Trade as a Campaign Issue

Another possibility is that trade affects voting like most other issues, through the candidates' stated issue positions and campaign agenda. But how likely are people to know who stands where? Using two panel surveys covering the period from 2008 to 2016, I examined when and whether this seemed plausible. In each presidential election year, responses are from respondents in the October wave of a panel immediately preceding the November election. In other words, these data were collected when people were *most* likely to be tuned in to and knowledgeable about political issues, right before a presidential election. The top left of Figure 10.1 illustrates the percentage of Americans who placed themselves on a four-point agree-disagree scale in response to the question, "Do you favor or oppose the federal government in Washington negotiating more free trade agreements like NAFTA?" in representative national probability samples in both 2008 and 2012. Immediately after this question, respondents were asked, "Which presidential candidate's views are most like your own when it comes to trade agreements? You can pick more than one candidate if you like, or 'Don't know enough to say' if you don't feel you know enough about them yet." The names of all presidential candidates followed, so respondents could pick one or more or none at all.

Respondents were also asked, "Are there any presidential candidates whose views on trade agreements are UNACCEPTABLE to you? Again, you can pick more than one candidate if you like, or 'Don't know enough to say' if you don't feel you know enough about them yet." Given that these results are from immediately before the presidential election, respondents can be assumed to have all of the information they are likely to get before going to the polls.

The top panel of Figure 10.1 tells us that in 2008 and 2012, most respondents had no problem answering a question about whether they favored or opposed free trade agreements. In both years, well over 90 percent of people provided an opinion. However, when asked whether there were presidential candidates who shared their views, under 50 percent could select a candidate. If they were just not certain, it would be fairly simple for people to choose the candidate they already supported and simply assume that candidate was likely to share their views. But most did not. Even smaller percentages of people—around 20 to 30 percent in 2008 and 2012—could pick a candidate with whom they disagreed on trade. This result suggests that regardless of one's views on trade, this specific issue was unlikely to affect candidates' electoral prospects in 2008 or 2012 because voters had no sense of who stood where, or that there was a clear difference.

In order for trade to influence vote choice by means of issue agreement or disagreement, that is, voting for the candidate who shares or opposes one's view, people would, at a minimum, need to have an opinion on the issue and know of a candidate they agreed with or whose views they disagreed with. On the far right of Figure 10.1, I calculated the total percentage of people who could not identify either a candidate they agreed with *or* one they disagreed with on trade; in other words, people who had no basis for linking trade policy preferences to voting. The percentage of these "know nothings" on trade was just over 60 percent in 2008, but it declined to just under 50 percent by 2012, indicating that over the four-year period, the issue had at least become more salient.

In the bottom panel of Figure 10.1, I show results from a separate panel running from 2012 through 2016 using somewhat different survey questions toward the same general goal. In this case, the task faced by respondents was somewhat more difficult because they were asked to place themselves on a 7-point scale: "Some people think that the United States should have more trade agreements with other countries. Others believe that the U.S. should have fewer trade agreements. Of course, some other people have opinions

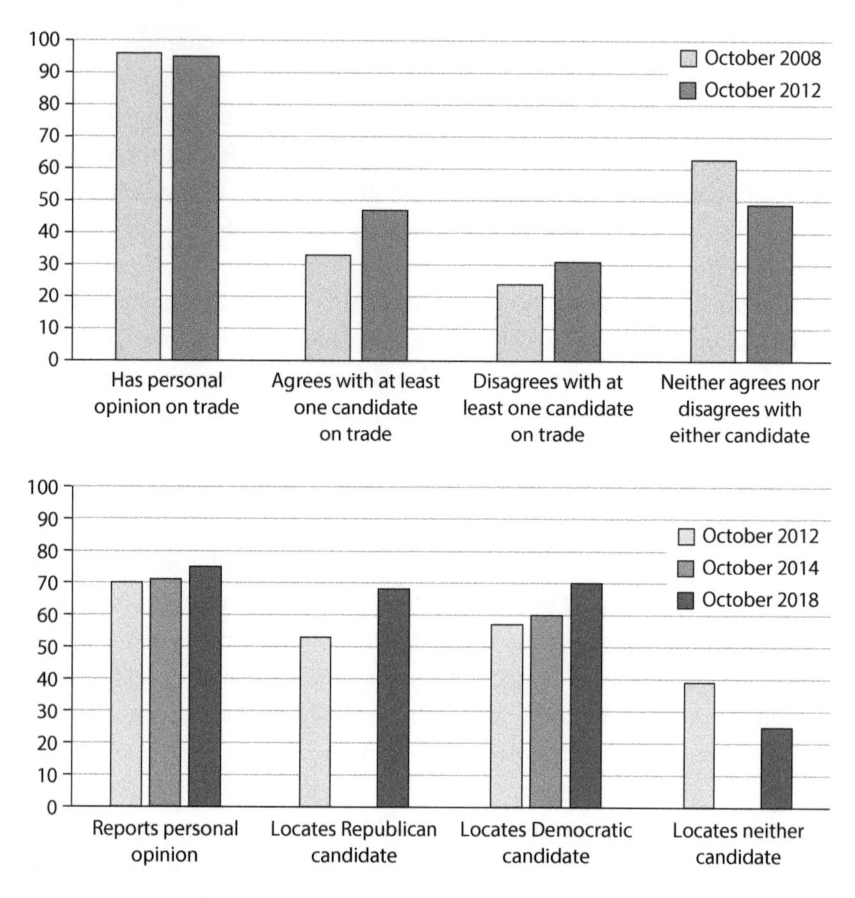

FIGURE 10.1. Percentage of Americans with Personal Opinions on Trade and Perceptions of the Major Party Candidates on Trade, 2008–2016

Source: National Annenberg Election Survey Panel Study 2008 (Knowledge Networks), ISCAP Panel Surveys, 2012–2016 (GfK Ltd.), ISCAP Panel Surveys 2016–2019 (Amerispeak/NORC).

Note: In the top panel, respondents answered on a scale that ranged from strongly oppose to strongly favor. They were then asked separately whether they agreed with any presidential candidate(s) on this issue and whether they disagreed with any presidential candidate(s) on this issue. In the bottom panel, respondents were asked to locate themselves and the two major party presidential candidates on a 7-point scale.

somewhere in between. Where would you place yourself on this scale, or haven't you thought much about this?" After placing themselves on this scale, they were asked two more questions in random order: "Where would you place [Democratic candidate/Republican candidate] on this same scale?"

As before, the results shown are from respondents interviewed in October preceding a major election. Despite the somewhat more difficult question, over 70 percent of respondents located themselves on this scale. The percentage who could do so increased somewhat from 2012 to 2016. Far fewer people could locate the Republican or Democratic candidates' positions on trade than had opinions themselves. Nonetheless, comparing knowledge of the candidates' positions on trade from 2012 to 2016 suggests a significant increase in knowledge of where the candidates stood on trade. As between 2008 and 2012, their assumed knowledge of candidate positions increased.

To be clear, I am not evaluating the *accuracy* of their perceptions on this scale, only whether they could make an assessment. The proportion of people who could identify the Democratic candidate's position rose by over 10 percentage points from 2012 to 2016, and the percentage who felt they knew the Democratic candidate's position also rose by over 10 percentage points. Overall, the number of people who could not place either candidate dropped from 39 percent in 2012 to around 25 percent in 2016, a substantial increase in awareness of issue positions. In short, it appears that the reason that trade has been unlikely to influence voters as a policy issue is not because they do not have opinions on the issue. The far bigger problem is that the candidates purposely obfuscate or do not advertise their views so that prospective voters do not understand where they stand on this issue.

"Trade shock" is a common term used by economists to refer to any net gain or loss due to trade. But it is not something one is likely to hear on the campaign trail or from those informally discussing politics within their local communities. Nonetheless, calling it a trade "shock" implies more than its bland definition suggests. First, a shock clearly does not sound like something desirable. Although it technically refers to positive or negative effects, research is primarily about trade's negative impact. Second, it contributes to the impression that trade's effects are far-reaching and obvious; one could not help but be aware of a "shock" if such a thing happened in one's community. In reality, the negative effects of trade are highly concentrated on a narrow segment of the population. That does not make it any less painful for those people who lose jobs, but it does make it harder for others to observe. Although whole communities can be destroyed, that is not the norm.

Third, the term "trade shock" also contributes to the impression that it is something exogenous that happens more or less randomly to some communities and not others, somewhat like lightning from the sky. More accurately we know that predictable pre-existing characteristics of communities make them more susceptible to negative effects from import competition. Large shocks tend to occur in places that are heavily populated by manufacturing as well as by less-educated people. These same characteristics make them susceptible to other kinds of change as well, thus complicating our ability to isolate the impact of trade in particular.

In order for trade to affect voting, consistent with the fourth theory I have described, voters need to have a sense of where the candidates stand on this issue, and the candidates need to differ in their views. In the 2008 presidential election, few Americans saw the major candidates as either for or against trade, although almost everyone had personal opinions on the issue. The Republican candidate was perceived to be somewhat more pro-NAFTA than the Democrat, but NAFTA supporters perceived support coming from both parties.[54]

In 2012, candidates Barack Obama and Mitt Romney were perceived to have completely indistinguishable, middle-of-the-road positions on trade in the eyes of the mass public, thus making it impossible for people to say one candidate was more for or against trade. By 2016, however, Trump was perceived to be by far the more anti-trade candidate, despite Hillary Clinton's efforts to distance herself from trade. Thus it seems unlikely that the American public perceived a difference between the major party candidates on this issue until the 2016 election. How is electoral accountability for the impact of trade possible when the candidates are perceived to be indistinguishable in their positions?

When comparing explanations based on political economy models with political scientists' expectations, there is a huge gap in their conceptions of voters. The problem for political scientists is understanding why these aggregate-level models produce relationships that seem implausible based on individual-level voting behavior. The problem for economists is what compelling narrative explains the mechanism underlying the relationships in their models. If people are not voting based on the impact of trade, and are instead simply reacting to general economic improvement or decline, then it is difficult to argue that voters are holding leaders accountable for the impact of trade per se. For this to be so, trade would need to be *the* major driver of economic change. In other words, import exposure would need to serve as a proxy for economic decline more generally. For better or worse, the two are not in lock step. Thus the question of accountability at the ballot box for trade-induced hardships or for the job-related anxiety produced by trade remains an open question.

Economic Decline versus the Economic Impact of Trade

The ideal situation in which to examine whether political leaders are likely to be held accountable for trade's impact independent of general economic change is one in which these two forces diverge. The Great Recession from 2007 to 2009 provides just such an opportunity. During the Great Recession in 2008, virtually everyone agreed that the economy took a serious nosedive. Partisans on both sides agreed that the state of the economy was terrible. According to polls at the time, over 90 percent of Americans said the economy had "gotten worse" in the past year.[55] Most importantly for these purposes, Americans also agreed that trade was not the cause of this decline. As reviewed in Chapter 8; trade or the trade deficit was named as a cause of the Great Recession by less than 5 percent of respondents.[56] The targets of blame for the recession did not involve trade, offshore outsourcing, or foreign competition. Thus, there was no ostensible reason for the American public to become more anti-trade or to punish leaders who favored trade in response to this economic decline.[57]

Nonetheless, support for trade declined dramatically. Identical survey questions asked of a national panel sample in 2007, before the recession had begun, and again in 2009, after it was declared over, showed an 18 percentage point decline in support for trade. Republicans declined even more, most likely due to a party-in-power effect once Obama was elected.

If people were capable of distinguishing the impact of trade from other reasons for economic hardship, then the Great Recession would not have changed attitudes toward trade. When a downturn is overwhelmingly perceived to be a result of causes *other than* trade, why should people reduce their support for trade? Perhaps even though people did not see trade as the cause of extensive unemployment during the Great Recession, they opposed trade more then because they perceived it as creating greater competition for jobs that could reduce people's chances of re-employment.[58] But data suggests that increasing unemployment had very modest effects on support for trade relative to the impact of perceptions of national economic decline.[59]

Overall, this pattern suggests that people are not skilled at differentiating the negative effects of trade from negative economic change that occurs for other reasons. Of course, if one thinks trade is good for the economy and the economy tanks, one would think that trade should be pursued more enthusiastically than ever due to the urgent need for economic improvement. If trade were believed to be bad for the US economy, then economic decline should cause people to become even more opposed to trade.

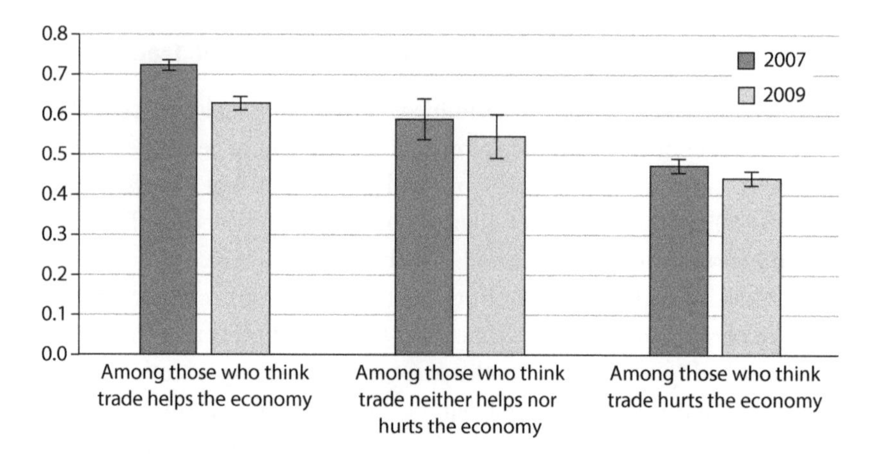

FIGURE 10.2. Change in Support for Trade Pre- to Post-Recession Based on 2007 Assessment of Whether Trade Helps or Hurts the Economy
Source: Mansfield-Mutz Survey 2007–2009 (GfK Ltd.).

On the contrary, as shown in Figure 10.2, *both* those who in 2007 thought trade was good for the economy *and* those who thought trade was bad for the economy declined in their support for trade from 2007 to 2009 to roughly the same degree. Once the economy declined, those people viewing trade as good for the economy might logically have been itching for more trade in order to stimulate the flagging national economy. But far from it, their support for trade dropped as well. In addition, after the Great Recession, these same people claimed that trade was no longer good for the economy.

This pattern is inconsistent with the idea that the public is capable of holding leadership accountable for trade-related job loss and economic decline. In this case, trade support declined despite the fact that trade was not responsible for the downturn. Unless one is willing to believe that political leaders are held responsible for trade-related economic downturns without having the downturn affect the public's attitudes toward trade, it is difficult to understand a mechanism specific to trade-related loss that would account for these changes.

Few dispute the relationship between economic downturns, rising unemployment, and declining support for trade. But a logical response would be polarization of trade support between those who believe it helps versus hurts the economy. Those who think trade is good for the economy should want to trade now more than ever, and those who think it is bad for the economy should favor it even less. But polarization is not what happened. Instead, everyone became more anti-trade. The effects of economic decline on trade support apparently do not have much to do with rational economic calculations.

Notably, all of these influences pale in comparison to the impact of *prospective* financial concern. Worry about the *future* increased, and this mattered a great deal to support for trade.[60] Moreover, the prospect of future economic loss appears to be what caused people to adopt more protectionist stances, even when they had not personally been affected in adverse ways.[61] Unfortunately, prospective concerns are not an accurate means of holding leaders accountable for the impact of their trade policies.

How Trade Impacts Elections

The work reviewed in this chapter makes it clear that we do not yet have a definitive answer to the question of whether and how trade enters into voters' candidate preferences. Evidence has been offered suggesting that people adversely affected by trade are more likely to support Democrats, that they are more likely to support Republicans, and that they are more likely to oppose the incumbent party, regardless of which party is currently in power, and regardless of their stance on trade. There is simply too little evidence over too few elections to date to determine which if any of these theories seems most plausible. Low information levels among voters lend greater plausibility to the anti-incumbent theory since it does not require that voters know the candidates' positions on trade or that they perceive a difference between how the two parties feel about trade.

The problem with the incumbency-oriented theory linking trade's impact to voting is that it does not offer the possibility of political accountability for the negative impact that trade can have on American livelihoods. When people vote out incumbents due to economic decline, they seldom have accurate information on who or what is responsible for that decline. If trade were the only influence on the economy, then trade-related accountability would be identical to retrospective economic voting. But given that trade is only one of many influences, and given that people do not distinguish economic downturns due to trade from economic downturns due to other phenomena, this mechanism holds little promise as a means of political accountability.

A fourth possibility, issue-based voting, only seems to have become plausible since 2016. By then, the American public had a sense of where both candidates stood on trade and also saw a clear distinction between them. In the next chapter, I examine in greater depth the role of trade in the 2016 presidential election. Americans' trade attitudes did not neatly divide along party lines in 2016, thus making trade a potential wedge issue that could draw former Obama voters into Trump's camp. Further, the abrupt change in public perceptions of where the Republican party stood on trade gave the issue newfound relevance to voters who might swing the election outcome.

11

The Role of Trade in the 2016 Election

Despite the surfeit of theories offered in the previous chapter, we still lack a compelling explanation for why people turn against trade during economic downturns, even when they do not see trade as the cause of that economic distress, and even when they perceive trade to be good for the economy. We likewise lack an explanation for why trade was elevated to the status of a high-profile campaign issue in 2016, during a period of steady economic improvement. In this chapter I offer a theory explaining how both of these phenomena may come about, even within a relatively inattentive mass public.

Turning Inward as a Response to Threat

Recessions, like many other negative events, heighten people's feelings of lack of control.[1] Economic downturns produce generalized fear, regardless of whether a given individual is personally suffering. A variety of phrases have been used to describe this psychological state and people's usual reactions. Some call it "turning inward" or "hunkering down." The desire is to take shelter from harm by staying put and not venturing far from home. This reaction helps people to feel more psychologically protected, however vague one's sense of the threat might be.[2]

In the context of trade, the term "protectionism" technically implies protection from foreign competition. But protection from dangers of all kinds is an especially appealing idea when people feel they threatened and cannot control the negative events around them. If one feels threatened, it will not seem like a good time to risk involvement in things beyond one's immediate reach or control. As one *Wall Street Journal* article put it, "Worried Americans Look Inward."[3]

Psychology teaches us that negative stimuli automatically cause aversive reactions; we instinctively pull away when something turns out to be painfully hot to the touch. Moreover, a wide range of negative events—from economic downturns to terrorist acts to natural disasters—can make people more cautious. When people realize that times are hard, they may become fearful about their future well-being even if they have not yet personally suffered. For example, one study of a natural disaster in Thailand showed that individual financial damage or loss of life within the family did not affect levels of risk aversion among those specific people. Instead, a desire to hunker down and avoid risk stemmed from merely living in an environment where bad things had happened to others.[4] Likewise, macroeconomic shocks can affect financial risk-taking independent of how an individual person has been affected.[5] As one recent study concluded, "Risk aversion increases even among those who did not experience any loss . . . [because] investors were emotionally affected by a stock market crash even if they were not financially affected by it."[6] When bad things happen, one need not be personally affected in order to experience a feeling of threat.[7]

One of my favorite demonstrations of this phenomenon comes from a study randomly assigning students to watch (or not) a fictional horror movie before tapping their levels of financial risk aversion.[8] Financial risk aversion rose in response to a fictional horror movie even though there was no logical connection between them. This same pattern has been noted in studies of terrorist attacks.[9] Fear is particularly promising as an explanation for foreign trade aversion in response to a domestic economic crisis because it allows that cause and effect need not be logically related. As reviewed in Chapter 10, Americans did not believe that trade was responsible for the Great Recession. Nonetheless, they became more likely to think that they could be future victims of all kind of things.[10] Widespread anxiety—enough to affect aggregate levels of support for trade—is only likely when something is so highly publicized that it arouses anxiety in large numbers of people simultaneously. The Great Recession qualified as just such an event.

Protectionism as a response to fear suggests that rising trade opposition should not necessarily be interpreted as a sign that the public is holding political leaders accountable for the economic effects of their trade policies. Likewise, increases in support for trade do not necessarily mean that trade is no longer taking a toll on American workers. Rising protectionism is simply a sign that people are fearful and anxious. A wide range of phenomena can be responsible for a collective sense of fear.

As part of "hunkering down," when people are fearful, they prefer that attention be focused on domestic affairs. As the Council on Foreign Relations describes this well-known reaction, "When the economy dips, so does the public's enthusiasm for activity abroad."[11] When things are bad, people become less enthusiastic about involvement in overseas activity in general. This line of thought predicts an increasing desire for isolationism of all kinds—not just economic isolation—when fear levels increase.

Turning inward definitely occurred in response to the Great Recession. Five questions tapped Americans' general desire to be involved in world affairs by asking for agreement or disagreement with statements such as, "The U.S. needs to play an active role in solving conflicts around the world," and "It is essential for the United States to work with other nations to solve problems, such as overpopulation, hunger, and pollution." This same index of isolationism, with no references to the economy whatsoever, was measured in 2007 and 2009. As expected, the recession led to a stronger preference for hunkering down on the world stage. And, as it turns out, quite a bit of the decline in support for trade during the recession was accounted for by changes in non-economic isolationism.[12]

When times are bad, Americans oppose international trade as a means of focusing their energies inward. In answering open-ended questions about trade, several survey respondents nicely articulated what I have dubbed the "oxygen mask theory" of trade support. Just as flight attendants tell their passengers that in cases of emergency they must secure their own oxygen masks before helping others, many respondents offered an eerily similar rationale for trade opposition, even during a period of strong economic growth and low unemployment in the US:

We need to support our own country before assisting others. Once we are working and supporting our families then we should help the less fortunate.

What comes to mind is the loss of family and jobs in the US. We need to take care of our own first, neighbors second. If we don't take care of our own first, how can we be expected to help our neighbors when we are in such need ourselves?

Our domestic policy in the United States of America should be take care of our own first, PERIOD! When there is no longer a line at the unemployment office or people living in homeless shelters or children going to bed hungry then Americans should consider a trade policy that benefits those that live outside our country.

Despite my want for global collaboration and the like, I'd really like to be able to see America take care of itself first, that way we can assist everyone else later.

In this line of thinking, "America First" has been recast as a necessary and logical first step with the best of intentions, as opposed to being a form of ingroup favoritism. Further, trade is portrayed as a form of foreign aid, something "we" do for "them," as opposed to something that we benefit from as well.

The theory that best fits what happened in 2016 is likewise based on prospective fears rather than economic damage that people had experienced in the run-up to the election. It bears similarities to what have been characterized as the "status anxiety"[13] and "cultural backlash"[14] explanations for why populist parties have gained support in recent decades. But there are some important differences worth noting. Where my theory differs from others who have emphasized prospective fears is that I believe the source of heightened threat need not be a personal economic threat. It certainly can be, as it was during the Great Recession. But any threat will do, so long as it is widely shared by one's ingroup members. It may have nothing to do with a specific event, and people may not even be able to put their finger on exactly what they are afraid of. Nonetheless, fear matters. For this reason, it is most accurately conceived of as *ingroup status threat*. All that is necessary is a sense that "we" are being threatened.

Why favor this explanation over the other theories described in Chapter 10? First, it better explains both what did and did not happen during The Great Recession. Protectionist views increased, but for the most part it was not a function of personal suffering due to the recession. In addition, people were no more likely to reduce their support for trade regardless of whether their immediate area was hit hard or spared. But prospective worry about the economy mattered a great deal to declining support for trade. Living through a recession creates anxiety, to be sure, but this theory does not require that people personally suffer in order to be affected.

This same theory also better fits what happened to racial attitudes in the US during The Great Recession. The cultural backlash/status anxiety explanation suggests that personal financial difficulties led people to take their economic frustrations out on minorities, and on immigrants in particular. But this "frustration-aggression" hypothesis has been examined at length over many decades, with mixed support and very little confirmatory evidence when macro-level conditions are the source of frustration.[15] Moreover, in the pre- to post-recession study, there was no increase in negative attitudes toward minority outgroups, despite the huge economic downturn.[16] If any financial hardship can produce a backlash against minorities, then the Great Recession should have done so. But it did not. Americans expressed no more or less negative assessments of racial outgroups in 2009 than they did in 2007 before the recession occurred.

Ingroup Status Threat in 2016

In 2016, two forms of ingroup status threat were prominent, one that was specific to white men, and the other based on threats perceived from abroad. Not long before the 2016 election, for the very first time since Europeans arrived in this country, white Americans were told that they would soon be the minority race.[17] Although the declining white share of the national population continues to be unlikely to change white Americans' status as the most economically well-off racial group, it nonetheless threatened some whites' sense of dominance in the United States.[18] Some whites feel threatened when exposed to evidence of racial progress.[19] Moreover, whites' perceptions of antiblack and antiwhite bias are widely believed to be zero-sum, just like their perceptions of trade's impact on jobs. The less antiblack bias that whites perceive, the greater the antiwhite bias that they perceive,[20] just as the more jobs they believe that trade produces overseas, the more jobs they believe it takes away from Americans.

In addition to ingroup status threat based on increasing racial diversity, Americans in 2016 also felt threatened by globalization and the increasing interdependence of the United States and other countries. As headlines warned, "The era of American global dominance is over."[21] Whether such headlines are true is debatable,[22] but the perception of a threat to US global dominance was very real. For example, in 2011, 38 percent of Americans endorsed the view that "[t]he US stands above all other countries in the world." By 2014, that same percentage was down to 28 percent.[23] This drop was most precipitous among Republicans.

Trump promised to rip up international trade agreements and "Make America Great Again," speaking directly to Americans' sense of declining status, and their fear that they were being taken advantage of by other countries. To the extent that the public in 2016 viewed the global economy in zero-sum, competitive terms, and thought they were "losing" at this competitive endeavor, it threatened the status of their national ingroup. And the more highly that national ingroup thought of itself, the more threatening this loss of status felt. Because China was the country depicted as the primary rival of the US, the "China threat" in particular loomed large in many American minds.[24] And Trump consistently portrayed China as a threat to America's dominant status.

While racial status threat and global status threat are technically separable, they are difficult to distinguish in practice. Because white male Christians are seen as most prototypically "American,"[25] they also have the most to lose psychologically if they perceive America and/or men and whites to be no longer dominant. Given that the 2016 election featured discussions of perceived threats from religious minorities, racial minorities, and foreigners, this generalized sense of threat is likely to have spilled over into multiple arenas. For white male Americans, the political consequences of racial and global status threat seemed to point in similar directions: resentment against groups who were achieving greater status in American society, rejection of international trade relationships that do not benefit us more than them, and branding China as a threat to American wellbeing.

The Increasing Perceptions of Threat from 2012 to 2016

One sign of increasing threat perception was evident in changes over time in social dominance orientation (SDO), a scale that taps individual differences in support for hierarchy over equality.[26] Although SDO is often viewed as a personality characteristic, levels of SDO are known to increase when people feel threatened,[27] and to decline when they feel less threatened.[28] Thus increasing levels of SDO would indicate increasing status threat. In a representative national panel of Americans, SDO significantly increased from 2012 to 2016. Because many associate high levels of SDO with racist attitudes, it is important to note that during the very same period of time and in the very same sample, negative racial stereotypes did not change, just as there was no increase in stereotyping of minorities in response to The Great Recession.[29] When one considers what these items measure, this is not so baffling. Stereotypes tap perceptions of minorities as lazy, untrustworthy, and so on—all characteristics that suggest they are not much of a threat if one considers one's ingroup to be more competent. Social dominance, on the other hand, taps one's sense that one's own group should rightfully dominate other groups.

Instead of thinking ill of minorities, white Americans became increasingly threatened by the successes of typically low-status groups. Obama's presidency stands as a very high-profile case in point. With a Black president in office, it would be difficult for whites not to notice some of the gains made by African-Americans and Hispanics. What made Trump voters stand out was not that they held increasingly negative stereotypes about minorities; it is that they perceived the accomplishments of traditionally lower status groups to have been at their own group's expense.

By 2016, being a white male in America no longer conveyed the same status and advantages that it once had. Some majority group members felt their ingroups were now being treated unfairly, and that they were being discriminated against more so than minority groups. Figure 11.1 shows how much discrimination Trump voters perceived against traditionally dominant majority groups such as whites, Christians, and men, relative to how much discrimination they perceived against lower-status groups.[30] What is striking about Figure 11.1 is that without exception, Trump voters perceived the high-status majority group to be discriminated against *more than* the subordinate minority group. According to Trump voters, men, whites, and Christians were being discriminated against significantly more than women, minorities, and Muslims. For those who voted for someone other than Trump, these numbers were reversed, with lower-status groups seen as the main targets of discrimination.

Given that the status of women and minorities was simply moving toward greater equality, one might wonder why so many Trump voters felt this way. Just ask some Philadelphia Eagles fans after they lose a big game and fall in the rankings whether or not the game was fair and they actually *deserved* to decline in the standings. Of course not! When home teams lose, the fans rarely believe it is because they were outplayed. Instead, the rallying cry is that the other team broke the rules or got away with something illegitimate. Ingroups with declining status feel themselves to be victims, not rightful losers. Thus, it is not the perceived failures of minority groups that are being held against them, but rather their perceived successes. Threat triggers a desire for the "normal" hierarchy of the past.

Likewise, The United States was accustomed to being top dog, a dominant "superpower" as we are often described. But by 2016, China had come to be viewed as a worthy opponent and competitor on the world economic stage, much as Japan was in the 1980s. When China is consistently described as an arch-rival, it suggests that any "wins" for China must mean losses for

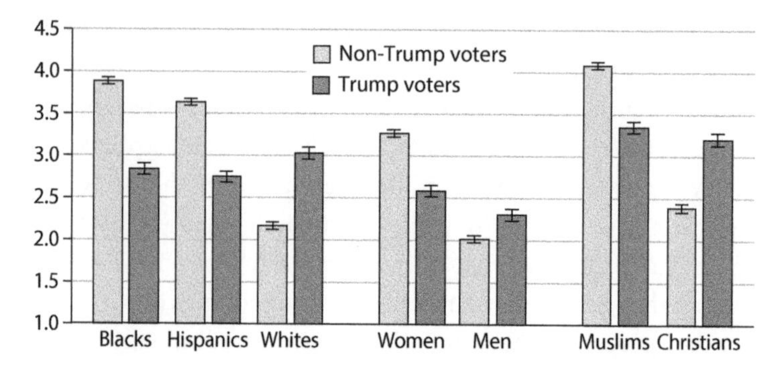

FIGURE 11.1. Extent of Perceived Discrimination Against Racial, Religious, and Gender Groups, by Trump Voter or Not
Source: ISCAP Panel Surveys 2016–2019 (Amerispeak/NORC).
Note: Differences between Trump voters and non-voters are consistently significantly different ($p < .001$).

Americans. As illustrated by the experimental findings in Chapter 4, even if the US had an agreement with China that was on ostensibly equal footing, for those with a competitive mindset, or those high in social dominance, this would not be enough. Sharing power is unacceptable to citizens of a country that is accustomed to being the dominant superpower. China, more than any other country, embodied the sense of threat Americans felt from globalization in 2016.

Opinions on international trade and China both potentially tap the extent to which people feel threatened by the world beyond national borders. But is there any evidence that voters in 2016 were experiencing a greater sense of threat from China or trade than usual? Figure 11.2 shows Americans' opinions on trade, immigration, and China in 2012 and in 2016. The average citizen opinion is designated on the opinion spectrum (S). For each issue, Figure 11.2 also shows where voters perceived the Republican (R) and Democratic (D) candidates to be located on these issues. As pointed out in the previous chapter, before the 2012 election, voters perceived no differences between the Republican and Democratic candidates and also located themselves smack in the middle of the scale on international trade.

By 2016, their own opinions were more opposed to trade, but the magnitude of this shift was modest. More obviously, the two parties had diverged greatly by 2016 in the views the public attributed to them, with the Republican candidate now much closer to where Americans were on average. Trump effectively moved the Republican party into the anti-trade camp, closer to where average Americans stood. The truly impressive change between 2012

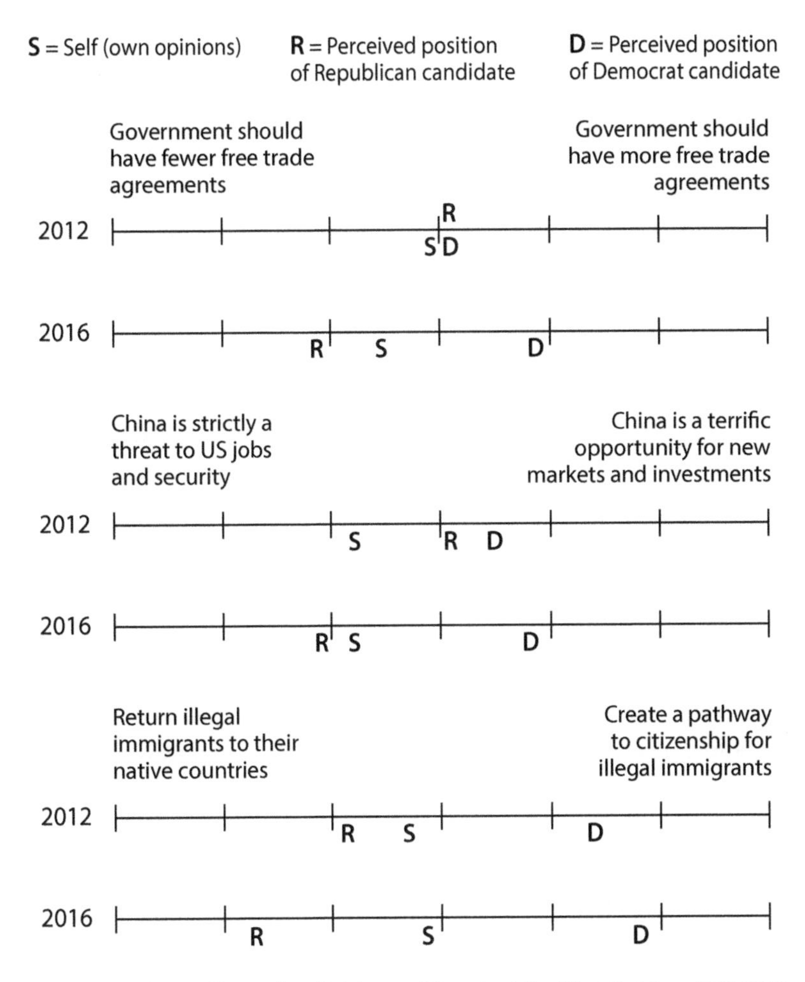

FIGURE 11.2. Average Respondent Opinions and Perceived Candidate Opinions, 2012–2016
Source: ISCAP Panel Surveys, 2012–2016 (GfK Ltd.).

and 2016 was not in public opinion, but in the public's perceptions of which party stood where.

However, as shown in the second panel in Figure 11.2, average opinions about the extent to which China was a threat did not change at all from 2012 to 2016. In 2012, the American public already felt that both Republican and Democratic leaders were under-estimating the threat posed by China. But by 2016, the Republican candidate came to share their level of concern. Again, as with opinions on trade, the dramatic shift was not in mass opinion so much as it was in where the parties were perceived to stand on issues tied to a sense of international threat.

Notably, as shown in the bottom panel of Figure 11.2, Trump actually lost ground in mirroring the public on immigration. The position he staked out was far more extreme than most voters, and Romney in 2012 better represented their views than Trump did in 2016. Surprisingly, even among Republicans, between 2012 and 2016 the distance between the Republican candidate's perceived position on immigration and that of the average Republican voter increased, suggesting that Trump's views were too harsh on immigration even for most Republicans. These 2016 patterns parallel reactions to threat during the Great Recession.

The Role of Attitudes Toward Trade and China in 2016

By 2016 it was at least far more plausible that Americans could evaluate presidential candidates based on where they stood on trade or China. The key conditions for issue-based voting were met. Voters perceived differences between Trump's stance and Hillary Clinton's position. Even though Clinton disavowed both the TPP and the NAFTA during the campaign, both Democratic and Republican voters perceived her to be more pro-trade than Donald Trump. Further, they perceived clear differences in how the two candidates would approach the threat from China as well, with the Republican candidate perceived to be more likely to treat China as a threat to US jobs and security.

Using this nationally representative panel of voters interviewed immediately before the 2012 election and again immediately before the 2016 election, I examined whether changes over time in attitudes toward trade or China made any difference to candidate evaluations and vote choice. The advantages of a panel study are tremendous when studying American electoral behavior because most voters' preferences are known in advance from their preference four years earlier. One need not explain why 90+ percent of voters vote consistently along party lines; one need only explain why a relatively few people occasionally change from their previous pattern of voting. What we really want to know is what changed to increase the likelihood that voters in 2016 voted for the Republican candidate?

Was the high profile of trade and China in 2016 enough for these issues to *change* people's preference for Trump versus Clinton? Party loyalty in the US is so strong that few single issues are able to flip voters from supporting a candidate of one party to another. Moreover, before 2016, foreign policy issues seemed particularly unlikely to do so.

To answer this question, I created measures of the absolute value of the difference between each individual's self-placement and his or her candidate placement in both 2012 and 2016. This allowed the over-time analysis simultaneously to take into account changes in individuals' issue opinions from 2012 to 2016, as well as shifts in where the Republican and Democratic candidates stood on these same issues.

When issue placements of this kind are analyzed at a single point in time, there is a risk that respondents will project their own issue positions onto the candidate they prefer, and/or contrast them with the views of the opponent.[31] Projection, also known as assimilation effects,[32] suggest that a respondent may report that a candidate she likes has views closer to her own views than is actually the case, thus creating a relationship between perceptions of a candidate's issue positions and vote choice, but not a relationship that reflects an issue position that influenced vote choice.[33]

Fortunately, this problem is less worrisome with fixed effects analyses of panel data.[34] Because each respondent's closeness to a candidate's position is compared to the same person's closeness at a previous point in time, any tendency to project one's views onto a liked candidate or to contrast them with a disliked candidate will occur at *both* points in time, in 2012 and 2016, thus canceling itself out of the model when looking at the *difference* in individual distances from candidates in 2012 relative to 2016. Because the fixed effects analyses represent the effects of *change* in an individual's perceived distance from the candidate in 2012 relative to the perceived distance in 2016, any individual differences in the propensity to project should be cancel out in the analysis predicting individual vote choice.[35]

Opinions on trade and China as a threat both capture global status threat. Trade opposition captures Americans' fear of takeover by more dominant economic powers, as well as racial opposition based on resentment of "others," including foreigners and businesses in countries that are racially different.[36] Moreover, China can be considered an outgroup threat both racially and with respect to threatening America's global dominance.

In order to determine if these issues changed the party that a voter supported between 2012 and 2016, I conducted two analyses. One used as an outcome the difference in Republican and Democratic candidates' thermometer ratings as rated by the same people in 2012 and 2016, since higher thermometers ratings are known to be the best proxy for vote choice. A second analysis used the vote preference expressed in October 2012 and 2016, strictly among voters who were externally validated to have turned out to vote.[37] The results are virtually identical in what they suggest, leaving little doubt about what changed that helped and hurt Trump.

My results indicate that the public's own changing opinions on these issues had little to do with their changes in vote choice. What mattered most were changes in the *candidates'* positions. For example, by shifting toward a more negative stance on trade and China, Trump capitalized on pre-existing public views that were already more anti-trade. Likewise, attitudes toward China were more negative among the mass public as far back as 2012, as shown in Figure 11.2. What Trump did was to reposition the Republican party to where voters already were by 2016.

In order to estimate whether these changes between 2012 and 2016 brought about changes in voting, I used fixed effects analysis. This allowed me to avoid many model specification issues, as well as to take into account both the amount and direction of over-time change in a given variable. To assess net effects, I computed the predicted probabilities of change using the fixed effects model, and then evaluated the impact of the average extent of change between 2012 and 2016 in each of these independent variables, while holding all other variables at their 2012 means. The difference between the 2012 and 2016 probabilities provides the marginal impact of each variable, taking into account both the extent of change in that variable that occurred on average, and the extent to which change in a variable predicts change in Republican Vote Choice.[38]

As shown in Figure 11.3, the candidates' changing positions on trade account for the greatest net impact on Trump support, followed by China. By 2016, the Democratic candidate had become much further away from the average American on these issues. However, as noted in Figure 11.3, contrary to many pundits' assumptions, Trump's more extreme position on immigration hurt him more than it helped. It moved him further away from where most Americans were on this issue and thus alienated some potential voters with more moderate positions on this issue.

Rising social dominance orientation also accounted for a small increase in the probability of voting for the Republican candidate. People who increasingly eschewed equality in favor of dominance were drawn to Trump's message. A nostalgic return to America of days gone by, including the status hierarchies of the past, is attractive when one's own groups feel under siege. Given that social dominance also impacts trade opposition, its indirect effects may mean it accounts for even more than this small change in the predicted probability of voting Republican.

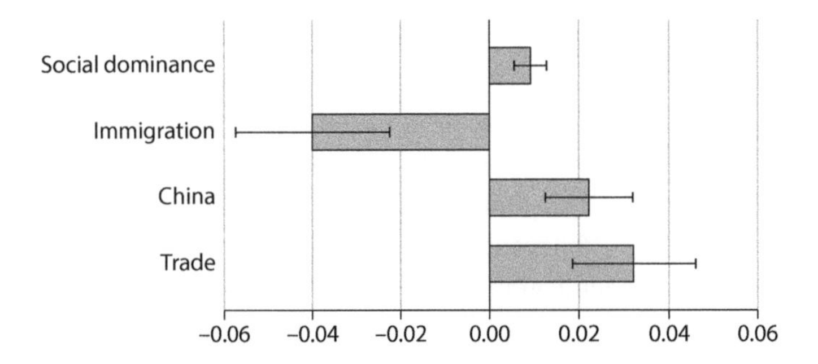

FIGURE 11.3. Net Change in Predicted Probability of Republican Vote for President, 2012–2016, Among Validated Voters Only
Source: ISCAP Panel Surveys, 2012–2016 (GfK Ltd.). See Mutz (2018) for details.
Note: Social Dominance Orientation, Issue Distance on China and on Trade all had significant positive effects, increasing the probability of voting for the Republican. Issue Distance on Immigration had a net negative effect on the probability of voting for the Republican.

I repeated this same analysis using Feeling Thermometer ratings for the two candidates, the best measures for predicting vote choice, with exactly the same results. Trump's shift to a more extreme stance on immigration relative to his predecessor cost him support, whereas rising levels of social dominance and better reflecting the public's increased opposition to trade both produced higher levels of support relative to Romney in 2012.[39]

To summarize, perceptions of the Republican candidate's issue positions in 2016 changed in what were more appealing, status threat defensive directions for the average voter. Trump's shift toward an anti-trade stance was a particularly effective strategy for capitalizing on a public experiencing ingroup status threat due to racial progress as well as globalization. The 2016 election was thus a result of anxiety about dominant groups' *future* status rather than a result of economic disadvantage that came from being overlooked in the past.

Based on these results, it would be a mistake for people to understand the 2016 election as resulting from the frustration of those left behind economically by globalization. Economic indicators at the individual level improved throughout this period, and thus predicted greater support for the incumbent party. Nonetheless, the popularity of the left-behind thesis continues to focus attention on economically beleaguered victims of trade-related job loss. Most people were experiencing improvements in their personal financial circumstances during this time period, and Trump's supporters were not disproportionally losing jobs or experiencing stagnant incomes.

Political uprisings are often about downtrodden groups rising up to assert their right to better treatment and more equal life conditions relative to high-status groups. That interpretation hews closely to the idea that Democrats lost in 2016 because the public was holding them accountable for the negative impact of globalization. Instead, my evidence suggests that the 2016 election was an effort by members of already dominant groups to assure their continued dominance, and by those in an already powerful and wealthy country to assure its continued dominance. Most importantly, it would be a mistake to read this election as evidence of political accountability for the negative effects of trade. Trade has in the past and will continue to produce job losses, and it makes sense for government leadership to be expected to address job dislocation due to trade. But there is little evidence that the electoral process is capable of producing that kind of accountability. Those threatened by loss of status whether domestic or global may react at the ballot box, but this does not represent electoral accountability for the economic impact of trade.

Is This an Anomaly?

Based on my analyses of 2016, I have suggested that people's views on globalization-related issues and their perceptions of the candidates' positions can, indeed, matter to election outcomes. But is this likely to be an anomaly specific to an unusually anti-trade candidate who made trade a salient campaign issue? In recent history, such issues have rarely been as salient as they were during the 2016 election, so this is certainly possible. On the other hand, problems due to globalization are not going away any time soon.

Until very recently, public opinion on international trade was seldom a means of differentiating between presidential candidates or of persuading the much-prized "swing voter" to support one candidate over another. Instead, this type of issue had several characteristics suggesting precisely the opposite; it is widely considered to be a "hard" issue, meaning that it is complex and difficult for experts, let alone ordinary Americans, to feel they have a firm grasp on it. The highly technical nature of international trade policy would not seem to make it a natural election issue. When studies from economics have suggested that trade is, indeed, an issue for which political leaders are held accountable by the mass public, they have argued that this occurs because people understand how they are personally affected by trade, a highly complex calculation.

But political scientists have highlighted the fact that voters need not be sophisticated or knowledgeable in order to engage in issue voting. Instead, citizens can form opinions on "easy" policy issues based on gut-level, symbolic feelings. These issues can be electorally relevant to potential voters of all levels of sophistication.[40]

But what kind of issue is trade? Trade is obviously a complex issue when understood as economists view it. The mass public has little information and limited understanding of how the international economy works and limited awareness of how it affects them as individuals. These characteristics make it unlikely that citizens would hold their leaders accountable for the effects trade has on their livelihoods. However, this does not mean citizens do not have opinions on trade or that their opinions are politically irrelevant. As highlighted in many of the chapters of this book, trade can be supported or opposed for highly symbolic, expressive reasons, without reference to its economic impact on one's self or family, and without knowledge of how it affects people in different occupations and industries. Indeed, most studies of trade opinion show little evidence of self-interest calculations based on industry of employment or level of skill as a worker.[41] Moreover, multiple studies now concur "that the effects of education on individual trade preferences are not primarily a product of distributional concerns linked to job skills."[42] Instead, protectionist attitudes in the US are driven largely by non-economic, symbolic beliefs. For example, domestic racial attitudes as well as perceptions of national superiority influence trade support.[43] Xenophobic attitudes toward other countries also drive opposition to trade.[44]

Using the well-known distinction in studies of electoral behavior between "easy" and "hard" policy issues,[45] I argue that trade is essentially an easy issue as viewed by much of the American public. Hard-issue voting "presumes that issue voting is the final result of a sophisticated decision calculus; that it represents a reasoned and thoughtful attempt by voters to use policy preferences to guide their electoral decision."[46] When voters instead use emotional, gut-level responses that require no conceptual sophistication, it is deemed "easy" issue voting. Importantly, the same issue can be reclassified as easy to hard or vice-versa, depending upon how voters come to decisions about it. Whereas hard issues are used more in decision making by the politically interested and highly educated, easy issues make it possible for anyone to engage in issue voting.

Despite the obvious complexity of international economic markets, trade policy meets all of the requirements for an "easy" issue as specified by the definition of this concept.[47] First, easy issues are symbolic rather than technical. Numerous scholars have demonstrated that mass trade opinions do not result from complex calculations of economic self-interest.[48] Instead, they result from highly symbolic attitudes such as high levels of nationalism,[49] racial prejudice,[50] competitiveness, and the general desire to dominate others.[51] As an extension of their simplicity, easy issues typically address normative ends rather than highly technical means. When trade opponents claim that "buying American" is a form of patriotism, or that jobs that have gone overseas are rightfully "ours," this normative emphasis is evident.

Finally, and perhaps most importantly, whether a given easy issue is used for political decision making "depends more crucially upon whether the choice was offered than upon the ability of the voter to make such a choice."[52] In 2016, the presidential candidates offered a clear choice on this issue that was not present in 2012, so the potential to use this in their decision calculus was available to all.

Does the empirical evidence back up my claim that trade should be viewed as an easy issue? This easy-hard distinction generally rests on whether an issue matters differently in the calculus of sophisticated versus unsophisticated voters. For example, the originators of the easy-hard distinction suggest that on hard issues such as healthcare, sophisticated voters will demonstrate stronger relationships between issue distance and candidate preferences. In the context of a panel study, this means they will exhibit stronger relationships between changes in issue distance and changes in candidate evaluations. For easy issues, by contrast, sophistication should make no difference.

I examined this question using opinions and perceived candidate positions on both trade, my hypothesized easy issue, and healthcare, a well established hard issue. I tested this hypothesis by incorporating the main effects of change in issue distance on change in candidate evaluations in a fixed effects model, as well as interactions between each issue variable and a dichotomous indicator of sophistication level. If healthcare policy is, indeed, a hard issue, then its impact should be greater among sophisticated voters. Likewise, if trade opinions are formed from gut-level responses rather than sophisticated calculations, then this policy's impact should be the same among voters with low and high levels of sophistication.

As shown in the left column of Table A11.2 in the online appendix, the main effects of changes in healthcare policy preferences and changes in trade opinions were as before; the greater the reduction in Relative Closeness of the Republican candidate from 2012 to 2016, the more a person's evaluation of the Republican candidate improved from 2012 to 2016. This same pattern is observed for both issues. The key coefficients for purposes of evaluating whether the politically sophisticated are more likely to engage a given policy issue in forming candidate preferences are shown in the right-hand column of Table A11.2 in the online appendix. The size of the positive coefficient for the Relative Closeness of the Republican candidate on healthcare more than doubles among Sophisticated respondents. For trade opinions, in contrast, both Sophisticated and Less Sophisticated Voters used the Relative Closeness of the Republican on Trade equally in forming their views. This pattern is consistent with the notion that healthcare policy is a hard issue and trade policy is an easy issue. In other words, people respond at a gut level to trade as a policy issue. Its technical complexity does not limit its potential impact as an election issue. Thus I would predict that its impact can occur in any election where people perceive a clear distinction between candidates on these issues. But thus far, the low profile of this issue has meant that this has seldom occurred.

Trade and Voting Revisited

This evidence suggests that mass opinion on trade has the potential to alter vote choice, even among those who know little to nothing about trade. But my interpretation of this evidence is different from what has typically been proposed as an explanation by economists who have found that areas heavy in manufacturing ended up more likely to support Trump. Given the state of the economy in 2016, most of those workers reported that they were doing better economically in 2016 than they were in 2012, thus making it difficult to argue that they were reacting to negative effects of globalization. While Trump clearly better represented those who opposed trade, I find no evidence that economic hardship led people to become more anti-trade. Instead, as suggested in various chapters throughout the book, less-educated white males supported Trump because they felt threatened by the changing nature of America. They viewed trade as a competition that their country was not winning when they thought it rightfully should be. This same group was higher in levels of social dominance, higher in competitiveness, more negative toward minorities, and more authoritarian in orientation than other citizens. Trade is naturally tied to levels of ingroup status threat because it is understood to be an "us versus them" issue. Status threat can be a powerful motivator even when one's economic status is not declining. Loss of a formerly privileged status is still a loss, even if it is in the name of greater equality.

My findings also suggest that economic downturns do not necessarily bring about more negative attitudes toward outgroups. In trying to connect patterns of political change around the globe, social scientists may have gone too far in assuming that all such changes must be part of a single phenomenon. For example, in the United States, there is no evidence of which I am aware that American attitudes toward immigration have become more negative although there is such evidence in Europe. Because Trump won the election, many inferred that all of his issue positions must have resonated with the mass public. More likely, any given candidate is going to have some issues that are favorable to his prospects, and others that hurt rather than help. The election outcome simply represents the net impact of these forces. Immigrants, who are generally conceived of as poor and powerless, do not pose as much of a threat as does rising power from China, or as do American minorities who have by now made their way into some highly visible echelons of American power. Because many Americans perceive racial groups as zero-sum in the same way they view trade as zero-sum, they believe improvement in a minority group's status must come at the expense of whites.

Finally, these results also speak to the issue of holding leaders accountable for the impact of their trade policies. Economists' aggregate-level studies have been used to suggest that the relationships they identify represent payback for politicians who have ignored the real-world impact of trade's policies on American workers. Certainly, the US does far less for displaced workers than most other western democracies, so there is ample reason for such a reaction. Moreover, perceiving one's country as having a stronger safety net predicts greater support for trade, as shown in Chapter 7.

But this evidence calls into serious question whether voting patterns based on local trade exposure represent accountability for the personal impact that trade has had on individuals' lives and communities. Scholars have found little evidence that those with declining incomes or those who have lost jobs punish politicians accordingly. Further, people do not always understand whether their job has been lost due to trade or other economic forces. Even when they do, they are unlikely to know which party to blame. Instead, trade seems to have borne the blame for economic decline more generally, and outgroup anxiety more generally, even when such change is not trade-related.

12

Shaping Opinions on Trade

WHAT WORKS AND WITH WHAT CONSEQUENCES

Opinions on political issues are often extremely difficult to change in the US because they are firmly anchored in partisanship. However, as reviewed in Chapter 3, partisan cues are extremely confusing when it comes to trade. For example, Republicans are more likely to believe in unfettered markets, which is connected to greater support for free trade. But Republicans also tend to have more negative views of foreigners, thus limiting their desire to interact with entities overseas, especially those who do not necessarily share American customs and values. Traditionally, Democrats have been aligned with unions that vigorously oppose trade. On the other hand, Democrats are more favorable toward promoting economic development in other countries, where trade can play an especially important role.

All of these confusing cues and competing considerations should make it relatively easy to change people's minds on trade. But many studies that have tried to do so have not been very successful. I suspect that these efforts often fail because they take as their starting point the assumption that positive attitudes toward trade are encouraged by emphasizing personal financial self-interest. They assume that people can be swayed simply by pointing out how much more expensive their consumer goods will be if they are American-made. In one of my Penn classes, this is exactly where my undergraduates started when tasked with trying to change views about trade. They believed that people's pocketbooks would ultimately convince them of the merits of international trade. As part of a class project that illustrated how difficult it is to change public opinion on political issues, they set out to change opinions on trade by borrowing a story from the *New York Times* showing that if a person were to buy blue jeans, a white t-shirt and work boots that were all made in the US, it would cost around $421. If those exact same products were imported from overseas, they would instead cost $99 in total. They added a colorful graphic calling attention to the cost difference for each item of clothing to further drive home their point.

A second experimental treatment emphasized reducing tariffs as a way to save Americans money. Respondents were told about a new international trade agreement that would lower tariffs on clothing and thus save the average American family 21 percent of their annual clothing costs. Respondents were randomly assigned to one of the two treatment groups or to a control group that read an unrelated story. Buoyed by over-confidence in the power of media to change opinions, as well as the widespread belief that people can surely be persuaded by economic self-interest, they chose these two approaches as most likely to produce the desired result.

Their experiment did not succeed. Although the manipulation checks confirmed that people understood the information and believed it, neither experimental condition differed significantly from the control group in levels of trade support. Instead, people appeared to favor or oppose trade for reasons that had little to do with their pocketbooks. Some even explicitly rejected appeals to self-interest in their comments. This raises the question: If appealing to people's economic self-interest is not sufficient to change opinions, then what is?

Some hints come from other failed experiments that produced unexpected results. For example, one survey-experiment primed people to think about cultural issues or government interference before being asked about trade. Those primed with libertarian questions about government interference did not change opinions. The opinions of those primed with questions such as whether it should be okay to sing "The Star-Spangled Banner" in other languages were not affected either overall. But those with lower levels of education who were exposed to cultural threat, that is, the idea of hearing the national anthem sung in another language, expressed less supportive views of trade.[1] This result is consistent with the theory of ingroup status threat described in Chapter 11, as well as the findings in Chapter 9.

Less-educated Americans are more sensitive to status threat, and thus respond by battening down the international hatches.

Another experiment exposed Americans to a pro-trade advertisement by John McCain. Counterintuitively, the ad produced more negative views of trade among women, but more positive views among men.[2] Another study executed across three different countries investigated interest group appeals to change trade preferences, experimenting with twelve different persuasive appeals, all designed to alter people's trade opinions.[3] Results suggested that interest group endorsements mattered little, but strong claims about how the trade agreement would allow foreign companies to sue their home country for billions of dollars in compensation shifted people against the Transatlantic Trade and Investment Partnership (TTIP).

If my theory about the underlying basis for wanting to trade with some countries but not others is correct, then cultivating more positive attitudes toward international trade requires improving Americans' attitudes toward foreign people and countries. Thus far, some of the most high-quality, professional efforts to do this have come not from within the US, but from those with perhaps the most at stake in improving Americans' attitudes toward other countries: foreign governments. China, for example, is extremely concerned about how it is viewed internationally. For this reason, the Chinese government has expended tremendous energy on soft power, in this case, efforts to change negative impressions of China among international audiences.[4]

American attitudes toward China have been described as "at best tepid" and significantly lower than their assessments of Japan, India, and Russia.[5] Thus soft power efforts "have taken on a new level of assertiveness, confidence, and ambition" since Xi Jinping came to power.[6] Soft power, according to Joseph Nye (2008: 95), "rests on the ability to shape the preferences of others." Yet there is surprisingly little empirical research documenting what actually works and what does not.

One exception was a study in which participants were randomly assigned to watch a sixty-second advertisement featuring the contributions of Chinese citizens. The video was produced by the Chinese government and was shown extensively on a large screen in Times Square in New York City. Those assigned to watched the video evaluated China more positively than those randomly assigned not to watch it.[7] Another study involved a longitudinal survey in a university community immediately before and after the 2008 Beijing Olympics, an event that was widely seen as a major opportunity for China to improve its international image.[8] However, no such beneficial effects were found from pre- to post-Olympics, regardless of people's viewing of the games.

To further understand how to successfully change attitudes toward China and potentially, in turn, to change attitudes toward trade, Kecheng Fang and I conducted two survey-experiments in the US. We examined the effects of two short online videos released online by the Communist Party of China (CPC).[9] The videos were in English and were said to be produced by "The Road to Rejuvenation Studio" (*fuxing lushang gongzuoshi*). One video focused on how Chinese foreign direct investment benefitted employment in the American south. The main purpose of this video appeared to be encouraging positive attitudes toward Chinese foreign direct investment, but it did so indirectly by emphasizing the similarities and friendships between Americans and Chinese people. A second video focused on explaining China's political system and how it compares to the US system. The videos were professionally made and went viral on YouTube with millions of clicks. The producers also hired local marketing specialists to promote the videos and attracted a large amount of media attention.[10,11] Although the Communist Party of China has never explicitly acknowledged its relationship with the Rejuvenation Studio, the videos were reported to be produced under the direction of the CPC and outsourced to professional firms.

One video entitled, "When China Met Carolina" featured many Carolinians explaining how China and the US have a lot in common, such as a hard work ethic and family values.[12] It also describes two local companies that went out of business, which were then bought by Chinese companies. The American employees interviewed in the video emphasize how the investment from China created new jobs and how much they enjoy working for a "Chinese boss man" who treats them like family. It concludes by highlighting the similarity and collaboration between Chinese and Americans: "We all have a dream. Whether it is an American dream or a China dream. . . . It doesn't matter where you're from. If we're working together and we're talking about what our goals are, we have a chance of getting there together."

In contrast to this warm and fuzzy appeal, the second video was humorous and entitled, "So You Want to be President."[13] This cartoon animation compared the ways in which one becomes a national leader in the US, the UK, and China. It featured animated versions of Barack Obama, David Cameron, and Xi Jinping. In praise of the Chinese system, it mentions the fact that Chinese political leaders undergo "decades of selections and tests" in order to work their way up the ladder, and it mentions the large role of money in politics in the US. As the narrator concludes, "Many roads lead to national leadership and each country has one for itself. Whether by a single ballot that gets the whole nation out to vote, or a meritocratic screening that requires years of hard work like the making of a Kung Fu Master, as long as people are satisfied and the country develops and progresses as a result, it's working." The video stops short of claiming Chinese superiority, and it is careful to point to positive aspects of both systems. The control group watched a three-minute abstract animation video, which was chosen because it was unrelated to China or politics, yet it was upbeat and generated a positive mood as did both of the two treatment videos.

After viewing their assigned video, respondents were asked about their attitudes toward the US government and the Chinese government, as well as how they felt about the people in both countries. They also answered a series of six questions about the extent to which Americans and Chinese people were similar or different in various ways. They were asked to agree or disagree with items such as "Americans and Chinese people see things in much the same way," or "Americans and Chinese share more similarities than differences."

With respect to policies, respondents were asked about their attitudes toward foreign direct investment from China in the US by indicating agreement or disagreement with statements such as "Chinese companies should be forbidden from buying American companies." Finally, using three separate questions, they were asked their opinions about general support for international trade, a topic that was not addressed at all in either one of the videos.

While both of these videos aimed to improve American attitudes toward China, they were notably different in emphasis. "When China Met Carolina" focused on warm personal relationships, showing Americans line dancing and sharing cake with the Chinese. Americans in the video repeatedly gave testimony to how much their Chinese boss treated them like family, and how their two cultures were more alike than different. In contrast, "So You Want to be President" focused explicitly on the Chinese and US forms of government and their institutional similarities and differences. Its tone was positive toward both systems, without explicit criticism of either system.

Given the personal emphasis of "When China Met Carolina," we anticipated effects from the video on how warmly Americans would feel toward the Chinese. Indeed, those randomly assigned to view the video reported attitudes toward Chinese people that were 5 percent more positive than those assigned to view the control video.[14] Attitudes toward the *people* of another country are typically far more positive than attitudes toward the government of the same country, and the same was true in this case. Attitudes toward the government in China averaged in the 30s and 40s on a 100 point feeling thermometer, while warmth toward Chinese people produced means in the high 60s to low 70s on the same scales.

Did "When China Met Carolina" affect attitudes toward the Chinese government as well? Although the video never mentions the Chinese government at all, as shown in Figure 12.1, relative to the control condition, attitudes toward the Chinese government improved, while attitudes toward the US government were unaffected. What is perhaps most surprising is that although evaluations of China start out much lower, among those viewing the treatment video, evaluations of the two countries' governments converge to the point that they are almost (though not quite) indistinguishable after viewing "When China Met Carolina."

I had expected perceived similarity to drive people's willingness to trust foreigners, and as shown in Figure 12.2, the extent of perceived similarity between Americans and Chinese was significantly increased by viewing "When China Met Carolina." To the extent that perceived similarity drives Americans' willingness to engage in trade or foreign direct investment, the experimental treatment brought about the required conditions to witness such an effect.

The rest of Figure 12.2 illustrates the impact of the video on attitudes toward Chinese foreign direct investment in the US, and on support for international trade. The video directly addresses foreign direct investment, though not in those specific terms. The Americans in the video talk repeatedly about how happy they are to have the jobs provided by Chinese companies. International trade, on the other hand, is not mentioned at all, making it more of a stretch to identify such effects. However, as shown in Figure 12.2, both attitudes toward Chinese FDI and attitudes toward trade with China improved significantly. It is worth noting that the sole economic argument in the video is that the Chinese companies created jobs for people in the US. Here, as in other analyses, I have described how attitudes toward FDI and trade are positively related even though one is feared to cause jobs to leave, while the other creates more domestic employment. Nonetheless, a single video emphasizing perceived similarities between Chinese and Americans encouraged Americans to become more supportive of both. The increase in perceived similarity between Americans and Chinese appears to account for the experimental effects on policy attitudes. If one controls for effects on the

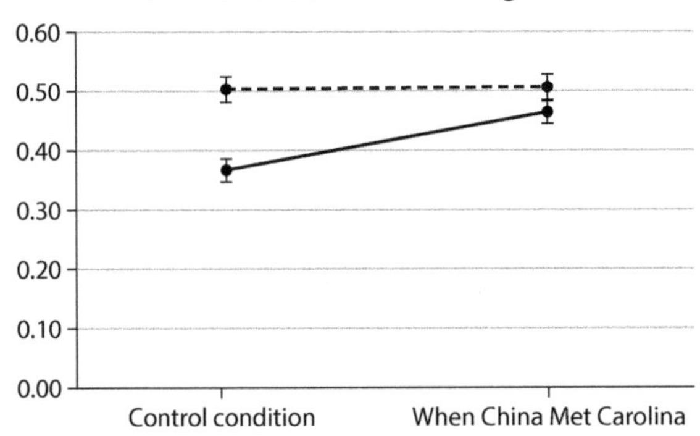

FIGURE 12.1. Effects of "When China Met Carolina" on American Attitudes Toward the US and Chinese Governments
Source: Changing Attitudes Toward China and Trade, 2016 (Experiment with Kecheng Fang).
Note: The interaction between Attitudes Toward Government (US versus China) and Experimental Treatment was significant ($F = 30.12$, $p < .001$).

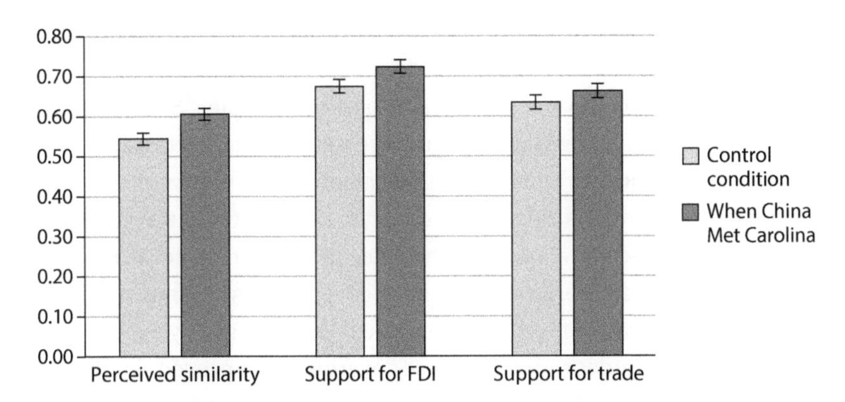

FIGURE 12.2. Effects of "When China Met Carolina" on the Extent of Perceived Similarity Between Americans and Chinese, Support for Chinese Foreign Direct Investment in the US, and International Trade
Source: Changing Attitudes Toward China and Trade, 2016 (Experiment with Kecheng Fang).
Note: The experimental treatment video raised levels of Perceived Similarity ($F = 32.99$, $p < .001$), levels of Support for Chinese Foreign Direct Investment in the US ($F = 15.70$, $p < .001$) and Support for International Trade ($F = 4.66$, $p < .05$).

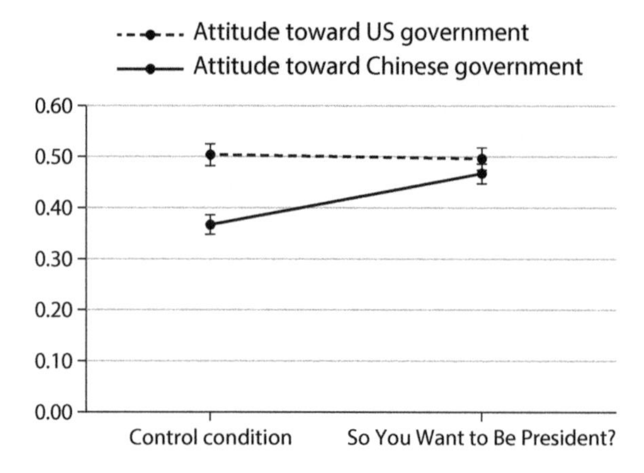

FIGURE 12.3. Effects of "So You Want To Be President" on American Attitudes Toward American and Chinese Governments
Source: Changing Attitudes Toward China and Trade, 2016 (Experiment with Kecheng Fang).
Note: The interaction between Attitudes Toward Government (US versus China) and Experimental Treatment was significant ($F = 33.02, p < .001$).

direct extent of perceived similarity, the direct effects of the experimental treatment on attitudes toward China disappear.

Because of its focus on institutions rather than people, "So You Want to be President" seemed less likely to produce more positive attitudes toward Chinese people. Indeed, I found no significant difference between those who did and did not view this video with respect to their attitudes toward American and Chinese people. However, the video did have its anticipated effects on attitudes toward American and Chinese governments. As shown in Figure 12.3, attitudes toward American government did not vary by experimental condition, but attitudes toward Chinese government improved significantly. In fact, Figure 12.3 looks almost identical to the results in Figure 12.1, even though the results reflect a different group of experimental subjects reacting to a completely different video.

Were more positive attitudes toward the Chinese government enough to make trade more palatable to Americans? Since the topic of trade was never brought up, this might seem unlikely. Although more positive attitudes toward the Chinese government did not contribute to more positive predispositions toward having Chinese companies locate in the US, the video emphasizing institutional similarities altered levels of support for international trade. The percentage of people favoring international trade in the treatment condition was around 4 percent higher than in the control condition. Given that trade involves countries doing business with other countries, one can see why trade might be more closely linked to positive feelings about a foreign government than FDI, which involves personal contact between Chinese and Americans. Foreign direct investment attitudes were more tightly linked to feelings about Chinese people.

Overall, it appears that these efforts by the Chinese government could be expected to produce their desired effects if they were widely viewed by American audiences. But this raises the important question of whether Americans would simply view these videos as Chinese propaganda, thus undermining any potential effects they might have. If a person viewed them online where we found them, both advertisements ended with a screen showing Chinese characters that one assumes most Americans could not read. Even if they could read the characters, the writing revealed only the name of the studio that produced the ads, not that they were created by the Communist Party of China.

But if properly identified, would these messages have been as effective? If people had known that the Communist Party of China was behind them, surely they would have been less effective, or so I thought. In the two experiments described above, we showed the same ads with three different final images. One indicated very clearly in bold English, "Produced by the Communist Party of China." A second version indicated that the video was produced by a media group in Melbourne, Australia. The remaining third of the sample was shown the same Chinese characters as shown at the end of the original videos. These same three sources were also included on the control versions of the videos. I had assumed that if the source was more clearly identified as the Communist Party, it would create a strong backlash against the message. However, I was wrong. Surprisingly, we found no evidence of significant interactions between exposure to treatment and the Communist Party as the source of the message. This was true in analyses of the effectiveness of both "When China Met Carolina" and "So You Want to be President." Opinions were moved in the intended directions regardless of the source indicated at the end of the video.

I can only speculate as to why this was the case. It was notable that neither advertisement relied on Chinese sources within the ad itself. In "When China Met Carolina," most of the people interviewed were Americans talking about how much American and Chinese cultures were similar. "So You Want to be President" had the flavor of a *Schoolhouse Rock* educational video that many Americans see as kids. Neither came across as heavy-handed propaganda from a pro-Chinese source.

Based on the evidence offered thus far in this chapter, trade attitudes are indeed malleable—perhaps not based on personal economic self-interest, but on the basis of increased perceptions of similarity between Americans and Chinese people, or similarities between American and Chinese governments.

The Unintended Consequences of Using Trade as a Campaign Weapon

Thus far the persuasion efforts that I have presented have all been expected to produce more trade-supportive views. By improving opinions about the trustworthiness of foreigners and their governments, it is possible to increase support for international trade. This is consistent with previous evidence that distrust of foreigners influences trade preferences, even when it is only products, not people, crossing borders.

But what about the more common type of persuasion in the US, that is, campaign advertisements attacking candidates for not being sufficiently opposed to trade or hard enough on China? Indeed, most persuasive communications that Americans see addressing trade as an issue are not like the ones from the Communist Party. They are instead political advertisements produced by candidates running for office. In her extensive analysis of trade-related political advertising in congressional, gubernatorial, and presidential races, Guisinger noted that candidate advertising is overwhelmingly protectionist, emphasizing the loss of jobs due to foreign competition.[15] At election time, few candidates risk publicly advocating trade. The cartoon in Figure 12.4 aptly illustrates candidates' impulses during election campaigns: Who can appear toughest of all on trade?

By linking themselves to protectionism through their advertising, candidates try to garner additional votes, but in so doing they may also discourage public support for trade by making it clear that trade is a bad thing. Since both Republicans and Democrats have run trade-bashing ads, this further encourages the view that all right-thinking and decent people—regardless of partisanship—should want to protect America from the ravages of trade. This common type of ad could simply capitalize on people's pre-existing views for political gain, but it could also encourage more protectionist views.

Broader concerns, however, stem from some of the findings in Chapter 9. A newspaper article attributing a single individual's job loss to outsourcing to China as opposed to automation convinced a random sample of Americans that it was more socially acceptable to badmouth Asians. The fact that people's attitudes toward foreigners influence their attitudes toward trade implies that encouraging trade opposition may also change attitudes toward foreigners, or perhaps even toward foreign-seeming Americans.

FIGURE 12.4. Mine is Taller: Out-Toughing the Opposition on Trade

Encouraging trade opposition is likely to foment negative outgroup views, just as negative views of outgroups discourage support for trade.

Although it is an extreme example, the death of Vincent Chin described in Chapter 9 provides a case in point. Negative coverage of Japan flooded American media during the 1980s and 1990s, along with extensive coverage suggesting that America's trade imbalance with Japan was responsible for factory closures. Many fixated on Japan's "unfair" trade practices, and how America was losing and falling behind.[16] It was in this context that Vincent Chin was bludgeoned to death with a baseball bat by a Chrysler plant supervisor and a laid-off autoworker, both yelling racial slurs and accusing him of harming the local auto industry.[17] Chin was assumed to be Japanese by his attackers, but was actually a twenty-two-year-old Chinese-American.[18] Regardless, the implications are clear. Whether intentional or not, those who use trade-bashing for electoral gain may also be compromising race relations in an increasingly diverse America.[19]

One of my former graduate students, Laura Silver, vividly illustrated this problem in her dissertation research using a clever experimental design.[20] Real-world political ads from the 2012 presidential campaign were used as experimental treatments. Both Barack Obama and Mitt Romney ran China-bashing advertisements in 2012, each trying to accuse the other of being "soft on China." These two ads served as the "China-bashing" treatment videos.

Both were thirty-second long television ads featuring ominous background music, images of American factories closing, and images of Chinese factories. For example, in Obama's advertisement, entitled "The Cheaters," he says, "Mitt Romney has never stood up to the cheaters in China. All he's done is send them our jobs." In Romney's advertisement entitled, "Stand up to China," China is presented as "stealing American ideas and technology" and the focus is on which candidate would be tougher on China: Romney or Obama. As one China-watcher noted, in 2012, the candidates "outdid each other on promises to get (or stay) tough."[21]

The control condition videos—another from each candidate's actual repertoire of ads—focused on each candidate's positions on women's issues. These videos were chosen because they supported the same candidate, but featured no discussion of foreign countries nor any images of Asians. Those who voted for Romney saw Romney-sponsored ads (either a treatment ad or a control), and those who voted for Obama saw one of the two Obama-sponsored ads. The candidates' supporters were randomly assigned to view either the China-bashing ad or the ad emphasizing women's issues from each candidate's campaign.

As shown in Figure 12.5, the China-bashing ads significantly raised respondents' levels of anxiety relative to watching the ads on women's issues. Respondents reported feeling greater anxiety at the time, as well as feeling more threatened by China in particular, and believing that ordinary Americans like themselves would be hurt by China. Those randomly assigned to view the China-bashing ads also reported significantly less positive attitudes toward China as shown in Figure 12.5. This is somewhat surprising since attitudes toward China were already so negative among control group participants that there was relatively little room to decline.

Consistent with the Vincent Chin tragedy, exposure to the China ads also lowered Americans' opinions of Japan, which was not mentioned in any of the ads. In fact, findings were virtually identical when asking about attitudes toward the people of China and Japan. As illustrated in Figure 12.6, when respondents were assigned to the trade-bashing advertisements rather than the advertisements addressing women's issues, Chinese and Japanese people were evaluated more negatively, but Brazilians and Indians were not.

There is thus a circularity built into the way that candidates interact with trade as an issue. They are convinced that their constituents oppose trade, so they run trade-bashing ads at election time to reassure the public that they are on the same side. These ads, in turn, create still more negative attitudes toward these groups. Then, unsurprisingly, they encounter public resistance

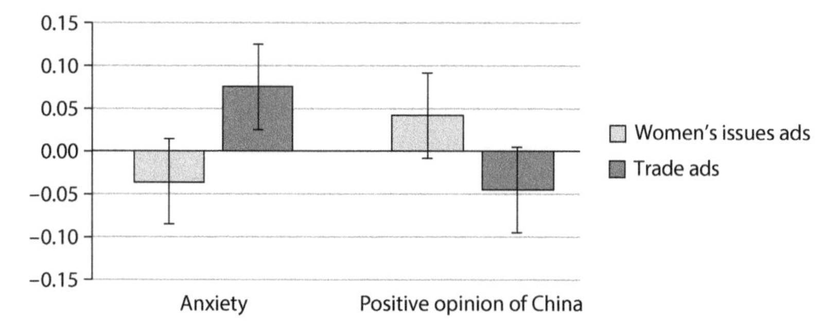

FIGURE 12.5. Effects of Obama and Romney China-Bashing Ads on Respondent Anxiety Levels and Attitudes Toward China
Note: Anxiety was an index comprised of items tapping personal feelings of anxiety after viewing. The index of Positive Opinions of China included questions tapping See Silver (2016), for details. Levels of anxiety were significantly different by treatment, $t=2.82$, $p<.01$. Opinions of China also differed, $t=2.00$, $p<.05$.

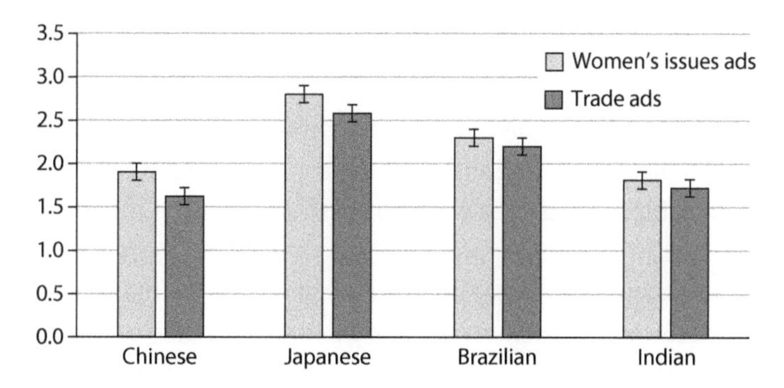

FIGURE 12.6. Effects of Obama and Romney China-Bashing Ads on Attitudes toward Foreigners
Source: China in the Media: Effects on American Opinion, 2016 (Dissertation of Laura Silver, University of Pennsylvania). Mechanical Turk experiment, N=1,629. Means for ratings of Chinese and Japanese people in the Control and Treatment conditions were significantly different ($p<.05$).

when championing trade agreements as Obama did when later championing the Trans-Pacific Partnership (TTP). It is difficult for politicians to have things both ways when they provide inconsistent public messages about whether reducing tariffs and encouraging international trade is a good idea or not.

As with most forms of threat, some people are more sensitive than others. In the study of China-bashing political ads, an index of authoritarianism made it possible to see if this remained true in the context of threat from a political ad as well. If increased outgroup bias can indeed be "activated" by threat, then that is precisely what one would expect the "China bashing" ads to do. When we examined the treatment and control groups by low versus high levels of authoritarianism,[22] this is precisely what we saw. Those with low levels of authoritarianism were roughly the same in negativity toward China whether they viewed the trade-bashing ad or the women's issues ad. But among those with more authoritarian tendencies, the anxiety induced by viewing one China-bashing candidate ad was enough to have significant effects on their attitudes toward China. China-bashing ads thus triggered an underlying sensitivity to threat in those high in sensitivity to threat.[23] Heightened anxiety was mainly driven by those with higher levels of authoritarianism. Watching the trade-bashing ads also triggered greater negativity toward China among those with authoritarian tendencies. The authoritarian's defensive arsenal involves defending "us" in conditions that appear threatening by discriminating against "them."[24]

Like it or not, we have a two-way street. Negative attitudes toward foreign outgroups make people more negative toward trade, and trade bashing triggers greater outgroup hostility. Based on my initial theory, this should have been obvious, although I confess it was not to me. If people think about international trade the same way they think about with whom to trade sandwiches, then of course liking and trusting one another is an essential part of any "relationship." We may establish formal bodies such as the World Trade Organization to arbitrate disputes among countries, but most of this is invisible to ordinary people. What ultimately matters to the public is whether they think our trading partners are good people that they can trust. When large-scale international organizations are conceived of largely in interpersonal terms, one cannot expect to change attitudes toward trade without changing attitudes toward foreign others.

Effects of Trade-Bashing on Discrimination in College Admissions

A second experiment used these same advertisements to expose people to China-bashing rhetoric in order to examine a related, but distinct question: Does China-bashing encourage discriminatory behavior against Asians and potentially Asian-Americans? After viewing their assigned ad and answering a few questions consistent with the cover story in the study, respondents were offered the opportunity to participate in a second study that involved evaluating a collection of student applications for admission to a college.

Using university admissions as the context for evaluations was ideal because rather than directly asking about people of different races, each respondent evaluated many different applications, each of which was unique. This made it possible to use subtler measures. For example, rather than directly asking people whether they would like to limit the number of Chinese or Asians who can attend US colleges, their task was to evaluate the quality of applicants, one by one, without drawing attention to race or nationality.

Respondents were asked to think of themselves as admissions officers at an elite university who must rate the quality of applicants who have applied to join next year's freshman class, on a scale ranging from 0 (very poor) to 10 (excellent). Each respondent was presented with student files, one at a time. Among many other pieces of information, two characteristics of the candidate were randomly assigned to these profiles: race (Asian/White) and nationality (Chinese/American). Race was manipulated via a photograph, and nationality was stated in the student's profile.

The photographs used to manipulate race were chosen to maximize comparability. All were headshots of college-aged men wearing suits in front of the same background. The photos were pretested in advance to confirm no difference in their perceived attractiveness. Figure A12.1, in the online appendix provides a sample profile for one of the students rated by respondents.[25,26]

Underneath all of the trappings that disguised the purpose of the study, this was an experimental design manipulating both the race of the applicant (Asian versus Caucasian) and their nationality (American versus Chinese), providing four unique combinations.[27] All respondents evaluated all four possible combinations, embedded in a larger pool of applicants. Thus each individual was asked to evaluate *multiple* profiles that included all possible race by nationality combinations as well as other applicants. Each subject's evaluation of each candidate for admission could be compared to that same person's judgments of other applicants, providing a subtle manipulation. Using a within-subject design allowed me to identify even small differences in evaluations of the prospective students. In addition to the four profiles of interest representing all four race by nationality combinations, the other profiles evaluated included one of an African-American student and one of a Caucasian-looking Brazilian student. As participants were advised,

> Admissions officers routinely have to make tough decisions, choosing between very strong candidates. Thinking back on the six profiles that

> you evaluated, please rank the students in order, from the one you would most like to admit (1) to the one you would least like to admit (6).

The respondent then dragged the profile pictures—which were presented in a random order—into their preferred order.

The experimental design was set up so that the student descriptions rotated several student characteristics including a GPA, an intended major, and a brief description of the student's extracurricular activities, so that the quality of the applicant profile shifted from one race-ethnicity to another, thus making the applicants impossible to distinguish collectively based on their considerable achievements. Indeed, they were all well qualified.

Did the thirty-second China-bashing ads encourage people to discriminate against Chinese citizens applying for college admission? Evaluations of the quality of each application showed that those listed as having Chinese nationality were indeed evaluated significantly lower by people in the treatment condition relative to those who viewed an ad involving women's issues.[28] Individuals were less willing to ascribe positive characteristics to Chinese nationals, even though these candidates were, on average, assigned the exact same student profiles as were American applicants. It is possible that the same credentials coming from overseas would be viewed less favorably by a college because of concerns about the validity of test scores coming from China. For this reason, the student profiles did not include test scores. Instead the profiles listed their school activities and leadership roles in high school, along with a GPA.

How far-reaching was the outgroup bias triggered by the China-bashing ads? Interestingly, even the Brazilian college applicant was evaluated systematically less favorably by those who saw the trade-bashing ad compared to those who saw the control ad.[29] This is a notable decrease given that the treatment was exclusively about China and had *no* reference to Brazil or Brazilians. This suggests that bashing foreigners may possibly have negative consequences even for foreign publics who are *not* of the nationality targeted in the ad.

Finally, we also examined whether race had a similar impact. Did the China-bashing ads encourage people to discriminate against Asians—regardless of their citizenship? Again, the results are consistent with this expectation: evaluations of the quality of Asian applicants were systematically lower among individuals who were exposed to the China-bashing ad relative to those who saw the political advertisement about women's issues. This is the case despite the fact that one of the two Asian students evaluated was clearly described as an *American* citizen and his race was primed solely via photo (meaning he could have been perceived by Americans to be Korean-American, Japanese-American, or any other Asian-American background). Even though Asians are widely viewed as the "model minority," ads encouraging negative views of trade also encourage discrimination against Asians and Asian-Americans. The size of these effects was quite small, yet statistically significant. Of course, it is also difficult to say precisely how much of a difference would actually matter in college admissions given the dichotomous nature of the final outcome. But the fact that exposure to a single thirty-second ad made any difference at all is surprising.

These results foreshadow what the cumulative consequences of encouraging economic isolationism might look like for Americans, particularly non-white Americans. The more that politicans and interest groups fan the flames of economic nationalism, the more individual citizens may be discriminated against, regardless of nationality. There is simply no way to attack foreign countries with populations that look different from white Americans without also encouraging discrimination. Some commentators have suggested that inflammatory comments about trade point to the fundamentally racial roots of protectionism.[30] Whether one buys into that argument or not, it seems clear that protectionism encourages the idea that foreigners are threatening and dangerous, and thus fans the flames of racism and xenophobia.

The Social Consequences of Trade Bashing

Overall, the results in this chapter paint a pessimistic picture of how globalization will influence American social life. Politicians eager to utilize American anxieties about globalization for electoral advantage will emphasize the need for protectionism and the threatening nature of those outside our national boundaries. The social acceptability of trade-bashing is already far greater than the social acceptability of expressing explicitly racist views, mainly because one seems like an economic preference rather than a racist position. And yet, the two go hand in glove.

Attitudes toward Asians may be most susceptible to this impact at the moment, but as happened with Japan and China, one country may replace another as the biggest perceived threat. Trade helps justify as an economic matter what ultimately appears to be racial discrimination. The negative impact of trade-bashing on attitudes toward outgroups is likely to be greater among Republicans than Democrats. This is because threat-sensitivity and authoritarianism, the characteristics that cause people to react more strongly against perceived threats by increasing their negativity toward outsiders, are much more common among Republicans.[31]

The danger is that by emphasizing threatening "others," Americans will unwittingly be led by politicians to discriminate even against other Americans. White discomfort with racial diversity and opposition to trade with foreigners are natural allies. They are "a self-reinforcing package."[32] Further, they suggest that the US will probably need more than additional trade adjustment assistance and stronger safety nets in order to become a willing participant in the international economy.

13

The Future of Mass Support for International Trade

The 2016 presidential election is destined to be the most over-interpreted event of the decade, with claims arguing that it represents the rise of mass support for populism, for fascism, for authoritarianism, as well as for isolationism and trade opposition. Trump's election victory was widely interpreted as an indicator of a sea change in attitudes toward globalization. Indeed, some claimed that opposition to globalization is what made Trump's election possible (Judis 2018).

But elections are a notoriously crude means for the public to speak its mind. With the benefit of a few years of hindsight, claims of this kind are difficult arguments to make. As the 2020 election approached, levels of support for international trade were among the highest on record. Both Republicans and Democrats expressed enthusiasm for trade, although for entirely different reasons. This state of affairs was all the more surprising because the economy was in shambles due to a recession and high unemployment brought on by the COVID19 pandemic.[1]

As of 2020, Republicans are the most enthusiastic trade supporters, despite the fact that the trade balance—the supposed focus of their concern—has worsened a great deal during the Trump administration.[2] As the cartoon in Figure 13.1 points out, if one believes that trade deficits are a bad thing, then one should not be happy with the current state of affairs. And yet Republican support for trade soared, nonetheless. Clearly people

FIGURE 13.1. Trump and the Trade Deficit

didn't change their minds about trade due to an improved balance of trade. And what about manufacturing workers? The huge losses in manufacturing jobs that occurred in the late 1990s through 2010 and then abated were supposedly the cause of a public backlash against globalization in 2016. But there has been no renaissance in manufacturing, and the number of manufacturing jobs has not rebounded.[3] Nonetheless, Republican enthusiasm for trade has more than recovered.

Why such a large shift in opinions when all of these problems persist? Most likely because these were never the actual causes of trade opposition to begin with. Instead of a fundamental rejection of globalization, white voters in 2016 were expressing a fear that their status in the world as well as their status within the country was suffering. On more than one front, it no longer felt like their ingroup was winning. When people feel threatened, asserting dominance and flexing of muscles is a predictable response.

Just as one should not interpret the current groundswell of mass support for globalization as evidence that the problems of globalization have been fixed, likewise it was imprudent to attribute Trump's rise in 2016 to public frustration with the negative economic effects of international trade on American citizens. Negative economic effects occurred, to be sure, but most were far earlier than 2016. Moreover, the people who elected Trump were not responding to manufacturing job loss so much as loss of ingroup status.

The studies in this book also collectively suggest that Trump's election did not represent a fundamental change in American attitudes toward trade and globalization. Nor was there any evidence that he exercised opinion leadership on this issue once in office.[4] Trump himself foreshadowed the idea that he did not think trade per se was so bad. As he put it in one of his infamous tweets, "Free trade is terrible. Free trade can be wonderful if you have smart people. But we have stupid people."[5] And thus by taking trade out of the hands of "stupid people" and putting it in Trump's hands, it could be a new-better-different form of trade, just as predicted by party-in-power effects. Importantly, Trump also portrayed this version of trade as one that allowed the US to dominate and take advantage of other countries, an idea that suited Republicans favoring trade-as-dominance quite well.

Rumors of the death of mass support for trade and globalization have been greatly exaggerated.[6] Essays proclaiming the death of globalization and the end of the liberal international order were common on the pages of major newspapers and magazines during the Trump presidency. As early as 2016, long before any of Trump's policies had gone into effect, globalism was claimed to have "collapsed under the weight of its own hubris."[7] Trump's policies undoubtedly have damaged US relations with other countries.[8] But if globalization is dead, it is not from lack of mass public support for trade. The huge swings in public opinion toward trade during this period illuminate the fact that the public is reacting more to how trade is framed than to what it actually does. Opinions toward trade and globalization are volatile, to be sure. But despite many ongoing complaints about globalization, the mass public shows no signs of having abandoned its commitment to international commerce.

Notably, this is not the story as foretold. For example, in 2018 foreign policy expert Robert Kagan argued that the three core elements of Trump's "America First" approach to the world—isolationism, protectionism, and immigration restrictions—were gaining popularity. He suggested that both Republicans and Democrats had lost faith in the domestic and international benefits of international engagement. Elected officials therefore needed to accommodate an increasingly isolationist public. I find no evidence that such shifts in mass opinion have occurred since Trump was elected, whether by 2018 or by 2020. The change that allowed Trump to capitalize on anti-trade sentiment in 2016 was a shift in the Republican party's position on trade. He did not lead public opinion toward protectionism so much as exploit an issue where the mass public already tended to be more protectionist than its elite representatives.

Did this change represent a rising tide of populism in America as has often been claimed? I have avoided this term in part because there appear to be as many definitions of populism as people writing about it. Trade opposition and economic nationalism have been widely linked to surges in populism around the world, including within the United States. Although the Republican party under Donald Trump certainly sounded populist in many of its slogans, in its desire for strong leadership, and in its racially inflammatory language, I have doubts about the role of populism in US trade preferences. Populism is fundamentally about the relationship between an authentic common people and an elite that is viewed as corrupt. It involves distrust in government and a desire for more direct democracy.

Trade opposition in the US does not easily fit this mold. Populist parties are supposed to be comprised of the "little guys," that is, the economic losers of globalization.[9] One could easily cast trade opposition in the US as a populist battle between the corporate elite and less powerful workers, but that is, perhaps surprisingly, not how Americans talked about trade. For most Americans, the "them" in the us-versus-them battle is powerful other countries and only occasionally the corporate elite.[10]

The immediate post-election shift among Republicans, both toward more trade-supportive preferences and toward very high levels of trust in government, suggests partisanship more than populism. So long as their own partisan leader is in power, international trade per se is not a grave concern to Republicans. Trade is fine when they have the impression that the playing field is tilted in our favor and allows the US to take advantage of others. And unlike in Europe, another element of populism—anti-immigration sentiment—has not surged among Americans, not even among Republicans.[11]

Strong partisanship in the US complicates citizens' abilities to hold leaders accountable for their trade policies. Evaluations of whether trade is helping or hurting the country as a whole are heavily influenced by partisanship. These "party in power" effects suggest that when one's own party is in the White House, trade is automatically viewed more positively than when one's party is out of power. Although this may appear to be mindless partisan enthusiasm, trade is a policy area over which the president has a fair degree of control. If one trusts the president in power, one automatically views trade relationships in rosier terms, even without any actual changes in trade agreements.

The Lingering Damage of The "Left Behind" Thesis

This brings me to a more general point, which is that it is dangerously misleading to simply impute economic arguments into the public mind as explanations for changes in mass opinion. Evidence simply does not support this interpretation. Many studies have looked for such effects without success. For example, those who lost jobs during the Obama administration were no more supportive of Trump than those who did not, and those whose incomes declined relative to others' were no more enthusiastic about Trump's presidency. Even those whose communities experienced greater job loss or economic decline were no more likely to support Trump. My evidence, as well as that of many other scholars, tells a different story about why people supported Donald Trump.[12]

If the left-behind thesis had turned out to be supported by empirical evidence, then the 2016 election could be seen as a tidy morality tale of political accountability. This is what happens when political leaders do not pay attention to the consequences of their policies! Those hurt by their policies will rise up to punish them for their inattention and pro-globalization views. Unfortunately, the only kind of evidence consistent with this narrative is aggregate-level data showing that less-educated whites, that is, whites concentrated in manufacturing areas, were more likely to vote for Trump. This relationship, like the relationship between low levels of education and trade opposition, is subject to many alternative interpretations.

When research failed to confirm the relationship between economic hardship and Trump support, scholars turned to other possible explanations. Maybe those supporting Trump were not people who were actually hurting due to trade, but instead people who were worried about the *future possibility* of losing their jobs due to the volatility induced by trade. As illustrated by the many theories in Chapter 10 linking trade to vote choice in aggregate-level studies, no one theory has amassed sufficient support to provide a consensus understanding of when and under what conditions the negative real-world impacts of trade alter individual voting behavior.

To be clear, there have been and continue to be many people who have been hurt by trade through job loss and wage stagnation, but these are not the same people clamoring to shut down the borders to foreign products.

Nor are Trump supporters advocating for stronger safety nets for those displaced by trade. In other words, trade preferences are not an example of policymakers being held accountable for the negative impact of their policies on the mass public. No new policies have enacted safeguards for those who lose jobs due to trade, and the safety nets for Americans are no stronger today than before Trump. Yet support for trade has surged among Trump supporters in particular. Most Republicans overwhelmingly say they favor international trade while also favoring increased tariffs on Chinese goods.[13] From this perspective, trade policy is simply another means of exercising dominance over those they find threatening.

The idea that the public holds political leaders accountable for individual issues at the ballot box is known to be highly unlikely.[14] In the case of trade in particular, empirical evidence does not support it. The romantic notion that globalization has provided a lesson in democratic accountability is simply inaccurate. Nonetheless, this continues to be the conventional wisdom used to interpret the 2016 election.

Accountability concerns aside, the "left-behind" thesis has produced even greater damage during the Trump administration because it has convinced many policymakers—those beyond Donald Trump—that the public is opposed to international trade and that their opposition is a result of personally experiencing its damaging effects. Because Trump won, people inferred that his policy positions must have been what the public wanted. In one sense, this is correct. By repositioning the Republican party closer to the average American on trade in 2016, Trump exploited this issue to his electoral advantage. The public's views changed very little.

More importantly, due to their belief in the power of the president's bully pulpit, both policymakers and the public appear to believe that his issue positions have become even more popular since then, perhaps due to the widespread media coverage his views have received.[15] There are widespread misperceptions of mass opinion on Trump's pet issues.[16] For example, our survey panelists were asked in both 2019 and 2020 for their perceptions of trends in mass opinion on both trade and immigration. On immigration, respondents were asked, "Since 2016, would you say that Americans have become more supportive of immigration, more opposed to immigration or haven't they changed their views much either way?" With respect to trade, respondents were asked, "What about the public's opinions on international trade? Since 2016, would you say that Americans have become more supportive of international trade, more opposed to international trade, or haven't they changed their views much either way?"

On immigration, the correct answer is that Americans on the whole have become *more* supportive of immigration since 2016. But only 16 percent of respondents thought the country had become somewhat or much more supportive of immigration, while 58 percent thought that people in the US had become somewhat or much more opposed to immigration since 2016. This distorted perception of public opinion led many journalists and policymakers to suggest that in 2020, immigration could serve as Trump's ace in the hole, encouraging still more support from those susceptible to nativist appeals (e.g., Olsen 2020; Nobles et al. 2020).

On trade, the correct answer is that Americans are overwhelmingly more supportive of trade now than they were in 2016. But based on our 2019 and 2020 panel waves, only around 25 percent thought that the country had become somewhat or much more supportive of international trade since 2016. These results suggest that presidential exhortations may shape *perceptions* of collective opinion even when they have little effect on individuals' actual opinions.

Candidates and policymakers may hold similarly mistaken perceptions.[17] For example, while President Trump and Democratic nominee Joe Biden agreed on very little, during the 2020 election Biden appeared, nonetheless, to have adopted Trump's "America First" agenda as his own policy agenda to some extent, advising Americans to "Buy American" and establishing government procurement policies with this in mind. Indeed, the phrases "Made in America" or "Buy American" appeared a total of 29 times in Biden's policy document, making it difficult to tell him apart from Donald Trump during the election.[18]

Economists suggest that such efforts will not be effective at saving US jobs.[19] In addition, my findings suggest that they may do harm to the kind of intergroup attitudes needed to sustain a diverse nation. Candidates who see themselves as doing little more than catering to pre-existing trade opposition are in reality making US participation in the global economy even more difficult. Fanning the flames of ingroup chauvinism can only increase international tensions as well as racial tensions here at home at a time when that is the last thing we need.

The emphasis on trade-as-competition in the US creates myriad problems. Ordinarily, mutual economic benefits might seem difficult to disparage as outcomes, yet among some Americans there is evidence that even this is not enough. For example, although American women are more likely to favor win-win, cooperative trade agreements, men are more likely to favor agreements if they give their home country a systematic advantage over its trading partners. Like Vladimir in the folktale, some Americans perceive the benefits to the home country to be less valuable when everyone gains, so they prefer agreements where their country gains at another's expense.[20] This is a clear sign of status threat. Those high in social dominance orientation—namely, white men and Republicans—are looking for opportunities not just to do well, but to dominate other countries. As the Canadian study illustrated, this is not universal human psychology. It is not inevitable that trade be viewed as an international competition. Canadians, unlike Americans, are more supportive of trade agreements that benefit everyone.

Ingroup bias in favor of the home team influences support for trade in both the US and Canada. But it is a much stronger force in the United States, even though the US is less dependent on trade than Canada. Americans perceive themselves to have been taken advantage of by others to such a degree that many see payback as fair and deserved. Even though the notion of "fair trade" originated in concerns about how trade may have adversely affected people in less powerful countries, ironically it has been usurped as a rallying cry by those who want the US to gain more than other countries from trade agreements.

Approaching Trade as the Public Understands It

For those who feel that trade is under-appreciated by the mass public despite its many shortcomings, it is important to contemplate how political leaders might better communicate with the public about this important issue. Trump's failures of opinion leadership notwithstanding, the volatility in trade support witnessed over the last two decades suggests that relative to many issues, trade provides opportunities to shape public opinion if leaders can speak the same language as voters.

To the extent that political leadership harps on trade as economic competition, leaders will create still more mass anxiety about who is winning and losing and thus feel obligated to frame trade as a means of dominating other countries. If they want to champion public support for free trade, their chances are far better if they frame trade as cooperation. Once the element of competition is removed, ingroup-outgroup biases will de-escalate, although they will not disappear altogether.

Awareness of trade as a form of cooperation is already evident in the mass public, even if it is not in the form of an economic logic in which countries cooperate in order to maximize their economic gains. What is already intuitive to the mass public about trade is far simpler than Smith or Ricardo's logic; it is that entities who trade things with one another feel more warmly toward each other as a result. If one wanted to downplay the potential for great power competition and increase public support for international cooperation, trading conveys precisely this sense to the mass public. The idea that those who trade things with one another come to like and trust one another is an easy, more accessible argument in favor of trade than complex economic analyses. It essentially mirrors the way people understand and assess interpersonal relationships.

In Chapter 12, the kinds of persuasive appeals that successfully encouraged more positive attitudes toward trade and foreign direct investment were ones that emphasized basic human similarities and mutual trust. These were essentially warm fuzzy appeals rather than cold economic arguments. The results of these studies suggest that it is not naïve to think such appeals can be effective.

Belief in various economic fallacies has been well documented,[21] so it not surprising that when Trump raised these same themes, they resonated with the public. For example, when Trump asserted that a trade deficit is like a business that is losing money, this analogy made sense to people, even though a trade deficit is not really akin to a business's failing bottom line. A company cannot lose money indefinitely without going under. But the US can run a trade deficit indefinitely without compromising its economy.[22] And running a trade deficit does not mean that the US is losing more jobs as a result of imports than the jobs it creates due to exports. As economists have taken pains to explain, "the trade deficit usually increases when the economy is growing and creating jobs and decreases when it is contracting and losing jobs."[23]

None of this is very intuitive. Rather than try to convey an economist's understanding to the public, policymakers would be better off speaking the public's language on this issue. We know, for example, that public perceptions of how trade affects the nation play a critical role in shaping trade policy support. Given that media coverage follows the regular release of key economic statistics, why not create a statistic that does not mislead and that more accurately reflects how well the US is doing with respect to international trade? If trade is essentially a competition for the cooperation of others, how well are we doing? It would seem far easier to create a better statistic than to re-educate the public about a highly misleading one.

It is easy to chastise Americans for not better understanding trade.[24] but the idea that free trade is mutually beneficial for countries is admittedly counter-intuitive. When a mathematician, Stanislaw Ulam, challenged Paul Samuelson, then-president of the International Economic Association, to name an economic proposition that was true, non-trivial, and not obvious, Samuelson suggested Ricardo's theory of comparative advantage.[25] This theory is not at all obvious because it suggests that even when a country has an absolute advantage over another country in all areas (for example, they are better at producing widgets of all kinds), it is still beneficial for the two countries to cooperate and trade with one another by having each contribute in the area in which their comparative disadvantage is least. But I doubt a lesson in comparative advantage would be likely to change levels of public skepticism. After all, levels of knowledge are just as low in more trade-supportive countries such as Canada, but their lesser emphasis on competitiveness makes them more open to mutually beneficial agreements.

Race, Trade and Identity Politics

Domestic racial attitudes turn out to play a surprising role in shaping attitudes toward trade, particularly trade with countries whose populations appear different from the average white American by virtue of different races, religions, or systems of government. So long as dissimilarity breeds distrust, it will remain challenging to maintain international relationships with dissimilar entities. Although few people may mention reducing racial prejudice and promoting free trade in the same breath, they are closely linked. It is not just that opinions on foreign trade are influenced by people's attitudes toward those who are racially dissimilar. The reverse is also true. When political candidates and politicians engage in China-bashing, for example, they also encourage prejudice and discrimination.

I am not suggesting that candidates have a specific intent to encourage more xenophobic or racist views among Americans when they try to use trade to their political advantage. The belief that China-bashing buys votes makes it seem a natural issue at election time. But it should come as a surprise to no one that anti-trade ads portraying menacing foreigners encourage ethnocentric views. Asian-Americans as well as foreign nationals are harmed by this common practice.

The potential to instead take pride in the diversity of one's nation was highlighted most clearly in the Canadian comparison where those most positive toward immigration and trade were also most positive about their nation. Because the Canadian national identity is defined by its openness, it was not surprising to see positive feelings about Canada go hand in hand with supportive attitudes toward trade and immigration. But this also implies that we may not be able to address Americans' aversion to international trade without also addressing the American tendency to distrust those who are different from the white American majority.

The obsession with "birtherism" in the US is an excellent illustration of why domestic racial attitudes and attitudes toward foreign trade are intertwined.[26] Race and nationality are obviously not the same thing. Nonetheless, non-white candidates such as Barack Obama and, more recently, Kamala Harris, are more readily accused of not being "real" Americans. Both Obama and Harris are native-born Americans, but their skin color makes them suspect in some Americans' eyes. In other words, being non-white is akin to being a "foreigner." It suggests to many white Americans that a person should not be trusted, just as foreigners are deemed less trustworthy than other Americans. This fact is, of course, ironic in a nation whose origin story suggests that we are all immigrants, native Americans excepted.

The link between foreignness and distrust is at one level obvious, even in the context of trade. Interstate trade is not controversial, even when the Americans in one state are clearly moving jobs and factories to another state. But foreign trade is another matter. In fact, the reason I wanted this book's title to include the phrase "foreign trade" rather than "international trade" is because I wanted to emphasize that opinions are not just about the concept of international commerce, they are about how people react to foreignness. Trade is opposed or favored not only due to the job loss or economic growth that it is perceived to produce. Trade preferences also embody how people feel about people and cultures different from their own. Trade is thus inextricably related to diversity. The foreignness of the other in international trade makes it all too easy for Americans to react as mere ingroup members rather than as fellow human beings.

Nations that have already dealt successfully to some degree with population diversity are in a better position to take advantage of the benefits of international trade. For example, the fact that trade deals in which both countries benefit are the kind most popular in Canada suggests that the Canadian population lacks the competitive desire to dominate their trade partners that Americans demonstrate. To the extent that trade agreements are not hampered by sentiments that are unrelated to the mutual economic benefits that can be gained, countries will ultimately benefit more economically from the process.

The Canadian experience suggests that it is possible to make national and international diversity a point of national pride. As the US becomes a majority minority nation, the challenge for white Americans will be taking pride in the diverse status of their nation rather than seeing it as a threat to the core identity of the country. Identities can change. Integrating into a global economic system and integrating diverse populations have more in common than is immediately obvious. It is unlikely that either project can proceed successfully without the other.

Trade as Cooperation

What generates enthusiasm for trade and trade agreements is the belief that trade encourages better relationships. This belief is frankly widespread. Recall that when Americans opposed to trade were asked why, there was a high degree of consensus about why trade was bad for America: loss of jobs. But those who favored trade were all over the map with respect to why trade was a good idea. This is because political leaders and interest groups to date have failed to offer a coherent justification of the need to participate in international trade—at least not one that resonates with the mass public.

Once I realized how much people thought of trade as a signifier of positive relationships, I began asking a new question in subsequent surveys, "Is increasing the amount of international trade good or bad for our relationships with other countries?" Fully 80 percent of Americans said trade was good or very good for our relationships with other countries. Even more surprising, as illustrated in Figure A13.2 in the online appendix, there was absolutely no partisan difference in this belief. Both Republicans and Democrats were equally enthusiastic about the impact of trade on international relationships.

Given this high level of bipartisan consensus, one would not necessarily expect it to predict differences in people's trade policy preferences to any large degree. But when I compared its ability to predict people's trade policy preferences to a parallel measure asking people whether international trade helps or hurts jobs in the US, the results of this analysis suggested that trade's perceived effects on international relationships are a much stronger predictor than the extent to which people think trade increases or decreases the availability of jobs in the US.[27] This finding is worth repeating: Support for trade is more closely tied to whether people believe trade improves international relationships than to whether they believe trade increases or eliminates jobs.

The perceived positive impact of trade on international relationships is already a boon to trade support. The fact that this belief is non-partisan makes it potentially even more influential as a unifying argument. Drawing on this logic, elites' leadership could make a case that is both intuitive and already embedded in the minds of many. The desire to establish and maintain strong relationships with other countries is, in itself, a powerful argument for trade. Despite partisan effects on trade support from whoever the party in power is at any given point in time, Republicans and Democrats alike will widely endorse the idea that trade is a positive force for the United States' relationships with other countries. Given this seemingly natural understanding of the value of trade, those advocating globalization would be wise to emphasize the value of trade for international relationships, rather than as a means to prosperity. Good will and friendly relationships are non-partisan values.

Comparable insights into what is most likely to change trade preferences were provided in Chapter 12. The kind of appeal most likely to convince the American mass public that trade is worthwhile is one that persuades them that dissimilar others are fundamentally just like them. A strong emphasis on cross-national similarity among people of different countries may draw sarcasm for producing little more than a kumbaya moment, but demonstrations of cross-national unity and similarity are things that people easily understand. To the extent that foreigners are seen as having the same underlying motivations and desires that Americans do—as the narrator in the ad in Chapter 12 put it, "whether it is a China dream or an American dream"—then Americans will trust them and be more willing to engage in trade with them. It is the job of policymakers and politicians to oversee the details enough to ensure that these arrangements do, in fact, benefit Americans economically, and that safeguards are in place for trade's negative externalities. Mass support for trade should not automatically be interpreted as evidence of how well leadership has accomplished these ends, nor should mass opposition be interpreted as a reaction among those who have been harmed.

Threats that currently cross national borders highlight the importance of the international relationships that are necessary to control global problems. Before 2020, the highest-profile issue of this variety was probably climate change, since climates obviously do not honor national borders. But neither do infectious diseases. Maintaining an us-versus-them, zero-sum mentality makes little sense to people when there are problems that cannot be addressed by any one country alone. Trade wars hinder America's ability to benefit from the global marketplace. But they also hinder the trust and cooperation needed to address other global issues.

APPENDIX

Descriptions of Sources of Data

I. Mansfield-Mutz Survey 2007–2009 (GfK Ltd.)

Representative national probability sample of Americans interviewed online. Sample Size: 1,964. In 2009, 923 were recontacted and reinterviewed. The 2007 field period was June 29 through August 16, 2007. The 2009 field period was June 24 through July 10, 2009.

II. ISCAP Panel Surveys, 2012–2016 (GfK Ltd.)

Representative national probability sample of Americans interviewed online. Samples sizes and dates as indicated:

Survey	Dates	Sample size
Post-election, 2012 presidential election	Nov. 14, 2012–Jan. 29, 2013	2,471
Pre-election, 2014 midterm elections	Oct. 17–Oct. 31, 2014	1,693
Post-election, 2014 midterm elections	Nov. 19, 2014–Jan. 14, 2015	1,493
Primary period, 2016 presidential election	Jan. 22, 2016–Feb. 8, 2016	1,562
Pre-election, 2016 presidential election	Oct. 14, 2016–Oct. 24, 2016	1,227
Post-election, 2016 presidential election	Nov. 28, 2016–Dec. 7, 2016	1,075

III. ISCAP Panel Surveys 2016–2019 (Amerispeak/NORC)

Representative national probability sample of Americans interviewed online or by phone. Sample sizes and dates as indicated:

October 2016	3214
August 2017	3152
October 2018	3202
June 2019	3419

IV. Fortune Magazine 2008 (Abt SRBI, Inc.)

Telephone survey conducted January 14–16, 2008, Sample size = 1000.

V. National Annenberg Election Survey Panel Study 2008 (Knowledge Networks)

Representative national probability sample of Americans interviewed online or via provided WebTV. Sample Size, Wave 1: 19,190; Wave 2: 17,747; Wave 3: 20,052; Wave 4: 19,241; Wave 5: 19,234.

VI. Chicago Council on Global Affairs Surveys, 1998–2017

Representative national probability samples. Interview mode varies based on survey year as indicated below.

Chicago Council 98 (Attitudes of the American Public Related to Foreign Policy 1998)
Survey Organization: The Gallup Organization
Sample Size: 1,507
Interview Method: Personal in-home interview

Chicago Council 02 (American Public Opinion and Foreign Policy 2002)
Survey Organization: The Gallup Organization
Sample Size: 3,262
Interview Method: Personal and phone

Chicago Council 04 (Global Views 2004: American Public Opinion and Foreign Policy)
Survey Organization: Knowledge Networks
Sample Size: 1,195
Interview Method: Online and phone

Chicago Council 06 (Global Views 2006: American Public Opinion and Foreign Policy)
Survey Organization: Knowledge Networks
Sample Size: 1,227
Interview Method: Online

Chicago Council 08 (Global Views 2008: American Public Opinion and Foreign Policy)
Survey Organization: Knowledge Networks
Sample Size: 1,505
Interview Method: Online

Chicago Council 14 (2014 Biennial American Survey)
Survey Organization: GfK/Knowledge Networks
Sample Size: 2,108
Interview Method: Online

Chicago Council 16 (2016 Biennial American Survey)
Survey Organization: GfK
Sample Size: 2,061
Interview Method: Online

Chicago Council 17 (2017 Biennial American Survey)
Survey Organization: GfK
Sample Size: 2,760
Interview Method: Online

VII. US Trade Survey-Experiment, 2013–2014 (GfK Ltd.)

Representative national probability sample of Americans interviewed online. Sample size = 3170.

VIII. Canadian Trade Survey-Experiment 2015 (YouGov)

National sample of Canadians who opted into being interviewed, matched down to a demographically-representative sample of Canadians. Interviews conducted online in both French and English. Sample Size = 3002; Field Period: October 22 to November 3, 2015.

IX. Trade with Whom Survey-Experiment 2015 (YouGov)

National sample of Americans who opted into being interviewed, matched to a demographically-representative sample of Americans. Interviews conducted online. Sample size = 2500.

X. China in the Media: Effects on American Opinion, 2016 (Dissertation of Laura Silver, University of Pennsylvania)

Experiment participants were recruited via Amazon Mechanical Turk in 2015. Sample size = 1629.

XI. Changing Attitudes toward China and Trade, 2016 (Experiments with Kecheng Fang).

Experiment participants were recruited via Amazon Mechanical Turk, February 2016. Sample size = 1504.

XII. Attributing the Causes of Job Loss, (TESS, Amerispeak/NORC)

Representative national probability sample of Americans interviewed online. Sample size = 2549.

XIV. National Annenberg Election Survey 2004

Cross-sectional sample (described in Mansfield and Mutz 2009). Sample size = 1706.

NOTES

Preface

1. Milanovic (2012); Economist (2017b, March 30).

Chapter 1. Beyond the Conventional Wisdom

1. Kevin was interviewed as part of The Daily, a *New York Times* podcast entitled, "Caught in the Middle of the Trade War," on Thursday, May 16, 2019.

2. For example, when asked about the effect of trade on their family's financial situation, over 60 percent of Americans in 2004 reported that it had no effect (see Mansfield and Mutz 2009). Surprisingly, by 2019, after massive amounts of news coverage of Trump's trade war had brought the issue to the forefront of public attention, little had changed. When a representative national sample was asked, "Are you and your family better off financially or worse off financially when the US engages more in trade with other countries, or doesn't it make much of a difference either way?" 56 percent said it made no difference either way.

3. These two ideas are outlined for lay readers in Buchanan and Yoon (2002).

4. Smith (2011).

5. For example, by targeting high-technology counties, Malhotra, Margalit, and Mo (2013) find evidence of self-interested immigration attitudes in high-tech workers' attitudes toward the H-1B visa. Anti-smoking policies are likewise more opposed by smokers than non-smokers (Green and Gerken 1989). But these studies are noteworthy because they are exceptions to the usual findings.

6. Rho and Tomz (2017: S105).

7. In trade coverage, for example, farmers who continue to support Trump despite knowing the negative effects of the trade war on their personal finances are presented as if they are anomalies (see, e.g., *The Daily* 2019).

8. Miller and Ratner (1998).

9. E.g., Beaulieu (2002); Mayda and Rodrik (2005); O'Rourke and Sinnott (2001); Scheve and Slaughter (2001).

10. See, e.g., Rho and Tomz (2017); Mansfield and Mutz (2009); Hainmueller and Hiscox (2006); Sabet (2016); Kuo and Naoi (2015); Wolfe and Mendelsohn (2005).

11. See Blonigen (2011).

12. Rho and Tomz (2017).

13. Kinder and Kiewiet (1981) first applied this logic applied to the economy as a whole.

14. Trade preferences are clearly influenced by whether trade is perceived to be good for the country as a whole. This has been demonstrated both observationally (Mansfield and Mutz 2009) and experimentally (Mutz and Kim 2017).

15. Brody and Sniderman (1977); Sniderman and Brody (1977); cf. Mansfield, Mutz, and Brackbill (2019).

16. Rho and Tomz (2017: S86).

17. See Sears and Funk (1990a,b) for an overview.

18. It is often unclear to workers which jobs were lost due to trade versus due to other factors (Hai 2019).

19. Rankin (2001).

20. Kiewiet (1983: 5).

21. Feldman (1982).

22. A study by Rho and Tomz (2017) illustrates this same progression in studies of trade preferences. By giving people information about the interests of those with differing levels of education in an experimental study, they induce group-based preferences based on education level.

23. This has been demonstrated both observationally (Mansfield and Mutz 2009) and experimentally (Mutz and Kim 2017).

24. Coyle (2014); Karabell (2014).

25. See Calhoun (1988). As Kyvig (1995) points out, this analogy ignores the fact that long-term mortgages are a regular part of family economies.

26. See Shiller (2019) on the importance of viral narratives.

27. Boyer and Petersen (2018) call these "folk economic beliefs."

28. Shakespeare (2005).

29. If you have the misfortune to be too young to remember this advertisement and also missed its revival on *Mad Men*, you can still see it at https://www.youtube.com/watch?v=-IBqfqNhDqg, along with the even more heart-warming version filmed 20 years later with the same people gathered again on the same Italian hilltop, this time with their young children.

30. Rubin (2014).

31. The search purposely eliminated most references to trade in other contexts. For example, if trade was mentioned in the context of a sport such as baseball, basketball, or football, it was automatically eliminated.

32. Rubin (2014).

33. Rubin (2014).

34. Brilliant (2014).

35. Here the competition is *against* their trading partners, not a competition to have trading partners, as economists might view it (Rubin 2014).

36. *Animal Face-Off* now has several spin-offs including *Monster Bug Wars, Death Battle, Jurassic Fight Club*, and *Deadliest Warrior*.

37. Duina (2010).

38. This statement comes from the 2012 Democratic Platform, available at https://www.presidency.ucsb.edu/documents/presidential-documents-archive-guidebook/national-political-party-platforms.

39. 2012 Republican party platform, available at https://www.presidency.ucsb.edu/documents/presidential-documents-archive-guidebook/national-political-party-platforms.

40. Schneider (1991).

41. See http://freerepublic.com/focus/f-news/3173627/posts.

42. Salama, Ballhaus, Restuccia, and Bender (2019).

43. Liptak (2020).

44. For the full play-by-play, see "Sperm Whale vs Giant Squid," Animal Face Off Wiki, https://animalfaceoff.fandom.com/wiki/Sperm_Whale_vs_Giant_Squid.

45. See Pratto et al. (1994; 2013).

46. Duriez and Van Hiel, (2002).

47. Johnston (2013).

48. Margalit (2012); Mayda and Rodrick (2005); Rankin (2001); O'Rourke and Sinnott (2001).

49. Haidt (2017).

50. Feldman and Stenner (1997); Hibbing (2017).

51. Mayda and Rodrik (2005); Herrmann, Tetlock, and Diascro (2001).

52. Rho and Tomz (2015, 2017).

53. O'Rourke et al. (2001).

54. Mansfield and Mutz (2009); Sabet (2013).

55. Mansfield et al. (2014).

56. Mutz and Kim (2017).

57. Being "better" at producing something in this context means that the ratio of the cost of producing A versus B is lower for that country than for the trading partner country.

58. See, e.g., Hicks and Devaraj (2017); Irwin (2016); Rose (2018); Acemoglu et al. (2016); Cocco (2016).

Chapter 2. At Face Value: What Americans Say They Like and Dislike about Trade

1. Egan (2015).

2. Smeltz et al. (2016).

3. As with any survey question, offering "don't know" as an option increases the number of people who will choose it. But it is unclear if this means people truly have no views, or that they are not sure they understand the question. After all, many voters refuse to choose a party identification, although it is well documented that if pushed to answer which way they "lean," this party choice predicts their opinions just as well as having chosen a label up front.

4. See Chicago Council on Global Affairs (2017).

5. Ongoing concerns about the difficulty of the ANES import/export question on trade led the organization to ask an additional question in 2016, one that more straightforwardly asks respondents for their views on trade by asking whether "increasing amounts of trade with other countries has been good for the United States, bad for the United States, or neither good nor bad." By comparing individuals' answers to this question to their answers to the ongoing question asking about favoring or opposing limits on imports, it is possible to assess the extent to which non-responses with respect to limiting imports indicate a lack of opinion on trade.

In 2016, the standard question about whether one favors or opposes limits on imports produced its usual high rate of non-responses at 45 percent. However, when those same people were asked whether "increasing amounts of trade with other countries has been good for the United States, bad for the United States, or neither good nor bad," under 2 percent provided "Don't know" answers. One would expect that the "Don't knows" from the import question would be driven into the "neither good nor bad" category when "don't know" was not explicitly offered. But this was not the case. Of those who could not answer whether they favored or opposed limits on imports, 53 percent of them had no problem answering whether trade was either good or bad for the US. In other words, they could express opinions on trade when the question was asked in a simpler fashion. Instead of having no real opinions on trade, non-responses often reflect the nature of the survey question.

6. See surveys of the International Social Survey Programme (ISSP), http://w.issp.org/menu-top/home/.

7. The Trade Support index produced a Cronbach's alpha of .83, and dropping any one item did not increase the alpha.

8. Those reluctant to offer their ideas in their own words were further probed, "Please take a minute to tell us why you think trade should be [encouraged/discouraged]. Anything else?"

9. For these ten categories, two independent coders reached an agreement level of 97 percent on the number of decisions classified identically among those who gave anti-trade reasons.

Pro-trade reasons were less concentrated in a few categories and thus also produced a lower reliability. Among those giving reasons in favor of trade there was 83 percent agreement on the top ten categories.

10. Because open-ended statements often include spelling errors and the like which can distract from their content, I have taken the liberty of correcting minor errors rather than using the "sic" designation throughout. To mark where one statement begins and another ends, I also insert capitalizations at the beginning of individual statements, and periods at the end.

11. Lake (1992).

12. Szayna et al. (2001).

13. Pettigrew (1998).

14. For a recent review, see Pettigrew and Tropp (2006).

15. See Miller and Ratner (1998) for five demonstrations of this tendency to exaggerate the impact of self-interest on human behavior.

16. Cohen's Kappa ranged from .37 to .50. See online Chapter 3 Appendix, Table A.21

17. Cohen's Kappa was .50.

18. As continuous measures, these are correlated at r = .71.

19. r = .45.

20. r = .19.

21. r = .07.

22. r = .30.

23. Hainmueller and Hiscox (2006); Rho and Tomz (2015).

24. Mansfield and Mutz (2009).

25. Further, believing that trade is favored by economists could be projecting one's views onto economists rather than being influenced by their expertise, thus tilting the scale toward finding strong relationships, which we did not ultimately find.

26. See online Chapter 2 Appendix, Table A2.1.

27. See online Chapter 2 Appendix, Table A2.2

28. Perry (2017).

29. Stasi (2015).

30. Perry (2017).

31. McBride and Chatzky (2019).

32. Froman (2017).

33. Irwin (2019).

34. See Table A2.3 in the online appendix.

35. Rho and Tomz (2015, 2017).

36. Herrmann (2017).

Chapter 3. Partisan Trends in Mass Opinion on Trade

1. Milner and Judkins (2004).

2. Irwin (2017) provides an excellent history of political conflicts over trade throughout American history.

3. Kucik and Moraguez (2017).

4. Guisinger (2017).

5. Williamson (2004–2005).

6. That is, if they were looking at all. In October 2018, when a representative national sample was asked if the new trade agreement was better or worse or about the same as NAFTA, over 40 percent of Americans said they did not know. Another 30 percent said it was no different from NAFTA or was worse than NAFTA. Even among Republicans, who would be predisposed

to favor the USMCA since it was Trump's trade agreement, 33 percent said they had no opinion, and another 13 percent said it was no different or worse than NAFTA (ISCAP Panel Survey, October 2018).

7. 1988 Republican party platform, available at https://www.presidency.ucsb.edu/documents/presidential-documents-archive-guidebook/national-political-party-platforms.

8. 2012 Republican party platform, available at https://www.presidency.ucsb.edu/documents/presidential-documents-archive-guidebook/national-political-party-platforms.

9. Brady, Ferejohn, and Parker (2019); Mutz and Kim (2017).

10. Morisi, Jost, and Singh (2019).

11. The analyses presented in Tables A3.1 to A3.5 in the online appendix summarize all of the results pertaining to the discussion of party-in-power effects.

12. See Table A3.1 in the Chapter 3 Appendix for detailed analyses confirming the interaction between change over time and party.

13. It is possible that question wording might be driving the sharp increase in the positivity of Republicans and Trump supporters after Trump's election. For example, those responding to the question on trade might be answering based on their confidence in the "federal government in Washington" that the question references rather than on their interest in seeing more free trade agreements negotiated. However, it is worth noting that several other national surveys using different question wordings, such as those conducted by the Chicago Council on Global Affairs and by the Pew Foundation have identified similarly large upticks in Republican support for trade since Trump's election (Helm, Smeltz, and Hitch 2019; Jones 2018).

14. Table A3.2 in the online appendix confirms the significant difference in change by party in 2008 as well as the null effect in 2012.

15. The statistical analyses corresponding to these tests are shown in Table A3.3 in the online appendix.

16. The analyses supporting these conclusions are shown in Tables A3.1 to A3.5 in the online appendix.

17. Morisi, Jost, and Singh (2019).

18. Zaller (1992).

19. Kernell (2007).

20. See, e.g., Lenz (2012).

21. Edwards (2003); Canes-Wrone (2006).

22. Gabel and Scheve (2007); Gilens and Murakawa (2002).

23. Tedin, Rottinghaus, and Rodgers (2011).

24. Bodet et al. (2020).

25. Skelley (2019).

26. Page, Shapiro, and Dempsey (1987).

27. See Table A3.6 in the online appendix for details.

28. This group was defined as those who were in the top 25 percent of Trump thermometer ratings.

29. Martin and Mutz (2019).

30. See Tables A3.6 and A3.7 in the online appendix for the statistical analyses of panel data corresponding to this conclusion.

31. See Table A3.9 in the online appendix for details of this analysis.

32. Mansfield and Mutz (2009); O'Rourke et al. (2001).

33. Perceived US standing relative to other countries was assessed by asking panel respondents on a 5-point scale ranging from much better to much worse, "Compared to twenty-five years ago, do you think that the United States' standing in the world today is better, worse or about the same?"

34. Radu (2019); Ellyatt (2020); Drew (2020).

Chapter 4. How Much Is One American Worth?

1. Brewer (1979).

2. E.g., Campbell (1965); Rabbie et al. (1974); Sherif and Sherif (1953); Pratto and Glasford (2008).

3. Policies requiring vaccinations serve as another example of a policy where a small number of people are known to be adversely affected, but it still makes collective sense to have vaccination requirements because they benefit society as a whole. These policies are also quite politically controversial these days.

4. Armstrong et al. (2019).

5. Friesdorf et al. (2015).

6. Gleichgerrcht and Young (2013).

7. Cikara et al. (2010); Swann et al. (2010).

8. Mutz and Kim (2017).

9. Bartlett and Steele (2012

10. Freeland (2011).

11. Bartlett and Steele (2012: 9).

12. E.g., Lyman (2018).

13. Johnston (2013).

14. Mansfield and Mutz (2009).

15. Margalit (2012); Mayda and Rodrick (2005); Rankin (2001); O'Rourke and Sinnott (2001).

16. Hoffman (2005); Lan and Li (2012); Margalit (2012); Mayda and Rodrik (2005); Merolla et al. (2005).

17. Huddy and Khatib (2007).

18. Sabet (2013).

19. Margalit (2012).

20. Sidanius and Pratto (1999); Kinder and Kam (2010).

21. Sapolsky (2019).

22. Theiss-Morse (2009).

23. For reviews, see Brown (2000) or Huddy (2001).

24. Mutz and Kim (2017).

25. Kinder and Mebane (1983).

26. See Figure A4.1 in the online appendix for the full design.

27. If interpreted literally, ratio statements of this kind do not say anything definitive about the total number of jobs gained or lost. However, based on a pretest using subjects from MTurk, it became clear that this was the most effective way to manipulate perceptions of which country was gaining/losing due to the agreement.

28. See Mutz and Kim (2017), Appendix B.

29. See Mutz and Kim (2017) for details.

30. This interaction is illustrated in Mutz and Kim (2017), Figure 2.

31. See Mutz and Kim (2017) for a full description of open-ended comments.

32. Figure A4.1 in the online appendix diagrams all 21 fully-crossed conditions in this factorial experimental design.

33. E.g., Brewer (1979); Mutz and Kim (2017); Tajfel et al. (1971).

34. Caporael et al. (1989).

35. Batson and Ahmad (2009); Cikara et al. (2011).

36. Caporael et al. (1989).

37. Opotow (1990 : 1).

38. McFarland, Brown, and Webb (2013).

39. Hermann et al. (2001); Rousseau (2002).

40. Sidanius et al. (2007).

41. E.g., Hogg and Abrams (1990); Tajfel and Turner (1986); Turner (1975); Turner et al. (1987).

42. Sidanius et al. (2007, 258).

43. Ibid.

44. Sidanius et al. (2007: 259).

45. See Sidanius and Pratto (1999).

46. $r = -.03$, $p = .10$.

47. See Mutz and Kim (2017), Table 2.

48. See Tables A4.2 and A4.3 in the online appendix.

49. The remaining 30 percent of the population thought either that trade neither helped nor hurt the US or trading partner countries.

50. Baron, Ritov, and Greene (2013).

51. Miller (2005).

52. Hogg, Fielding, and Darley (2005); Theiss-Morse (2009).

53. See Theiss-Morse (2009) for a full discussion.

54. See, e.g., Gilens (1999).

55. Theiss-Morse (2009).

56. See Rueda and Stegmueller (2019).

57. Rousseau (2002).

58. DeLamater, Katz, and Kelman (1969).

59. Pascarella, Ethington, and Smart (1988).

60. Ishay (2004).

61. Iacoviello and Spears (2018).

Chapter 5. Trade with Whom?

1. The Linder hypothesis is an important exception in that it predicts greater trade among countries with similar per capita incomes because these countries will produce and consume similar, but differentiated, kinds of products (see Linder 1961).

2. Isard (1954); Tinbergen (1962).

3. Mansfield, Milner, and Rosendorff (2002); Polachek (1997).

4. Milner (1999).

5. Rauch and Trindade (2002); Tongberg (1972); Wang and Lamb (1980).

6. Guo (2004).

7. Helpman and Krugman (1985).

8. Giuliano et al. (2006).

9. Chaney (2014).

10. "Reports and Statistic," U.S. Department of State—Bureau of Consular Affairs, https://travel.state.gov/content/passports/en/passports/statistics.html.

11. McNamara (1986).

12. Berti and Frassinetti (2000).

13. Trope and Liberman (2010).

14. O'Grady and Lane (1996).

15. Vahlne et al. (1992).

16. O'Grady and Lane (1996: 315).

17. Nagashima (1970); Nagashima (1977); Bannister and Saunders (1978); Lillis and Narayana (1974).

18. Anderson and Cunningham (1972); Peterson and Jolibert (1995); Wang and Lamb (1983); Watson and Wright (2000).

19. Lantz and Loeb (1996).

20. Gokcekus et al. (2012).

21. Loughlin (2003).

22. Pandya and Venkatesan (2015).

23. Shimp and Sharma (1987).

24. Mutz and Rao (2018).

25. Greene (2008).

26. Noland (2005).

27. Nowak, Vallacher, and Miller (2003).

28. Byrne and Clore (1971); Newcomb (1961).

29. Messick and Kramer (2001); Putnam (2007); Stolle, Soroka, and Johnston (2008).

30. LaFrance (1985); Locke and Horowitz (1990); Woodside and Davenport (1974).

31. Emswiller, Deaux, and Willits (1971).

32. See Chen, Pevehouse, and Powers (2019); Strezhnev (2013).

33. Guiso, Sapienza, and Zingales (2009).

34. Jensen and Lindstädt (2012).

35. DeBruine (2002).

36. Bailenson et al. (2008) (2008); DeBruine (2002).

37. Kaltenthaler and Miller (2013); Spilker, Schaffer, and Bernauer (2012).

38. Nguyen and Bernauer (2014).

39. As anticipated, these questions formed a highly reliable index (Cronbach's alpha = .88), thus making it clear that respondents had formed opinions toward trading with the country.

40. In order to test all five hypotheses simultaneously, I used an analysis of variance model including each of the five two-level factors in a full factorial design in order to ascertain which treatments produced differences in the predicted directions. In order to increase the efficiency of the model, the pre-experimental battery of items tapping general trade support was used as a covariate. Respondents had well-formed preferences on trade, countries notwithstanding. The items formed a highly reliable index (Cronbach's alpha = .82) indicating that, as predicted, these general preferences influenced their levels of support for trade, regardless of country, thus improving the efficiency of the analyses.

41. Byrne (1971); Rokeach (1960).

42. Tajfel and Turner (1986).

43. Carnegie and Gaikwad (2017).

44. Although a few respondents directly questioned whether there was a country with a superior military, this was less than 1 percent of respondents, and omitting them from the sample did not affect the results.

45. Reid (2017).

46. Aarøe, Petersen, and Arceneaux (2017).

47. Dawsey (2018).

48. Mansfield and Mutz (2009); Mutz and Kim (2017); Sabet (2013).

Chapter 6. How Racial Attitudes Affect Support for International Trade

1. See, e.g., Guisinger (2017).

2. Mansfield and Mutz (2009).

3. Mutz, Mansfield, and Kim (forthcoming).

4. Leamer (1984); Mayda and Rodrik (2005); O'Rourke and Sinnott (2001).

5. Guisinger (2017); Jensen et al. (2017).

6. Bohara and Kaempfer (1991); Bown and Crowley (2013); Irwin (2005).

7. Hainmueller and Hiscox (2006).

8. Guisinger (2017).

9. Mansfield and Mutz (2009); Mutz and Kim (2017); Sabet (2013).

10. Mansfield and Mutz (2009).

11. Tajfel (1982).

12. Brewer (2007).

13. Kinder and Kam (2010).

14. Davenport (2018).

15. Farley, Fielding, and Krysan (1997).

16. Sidanius et al. (1997).

17. From "Let America be America Again," in *The Collected Poems of Langston Hughes*, ed. Arnold Rampersad (New York: Vintage, 1991), 1899–91.

18. Citrin et al. (2007); Huddy and Khatib (2007); Harlow and Dundes (2004); Sidanius et al. (1997); Stempel (2006).

19. Minorities in general report feeling less national superiority, both in the US and elsewhere. Carter and Pérez (2015); Cebotari (2015); Elkins and Sides (2007); Theiss-Morse (2009).

20. Carter and Pérez (2015); Cebotari (2015); Elkins and Sides (2007); Theiss-Morse (2009).

21. These categories are designated in The Higher Education Act used by NSF and NIH, for example. In practice, however, the number of other minorities is low enough that broadening this definition does not affect any of the findings shown here.

22. Lantz and Loeb (1996).

23. Sidanius and Pratto (1999).

24. Mutz and Kim (2016).

25. McFarland et al. (2013).

26. Bhagwati (2007).

27. Coding of countries was highly reliable, with over 95 percent agreement. The countries that lacked agreement were those in the Middle East (e.g., Lebanon, Jordan, and Saudi Arabia). Given high levels of uncertainty, they were not counted as dark-skinned or light-skinned countries.

28. See Table A6.1 in the online appendix for details.

29. Main effect of light versus dark countries, $F = 94.70$, $p < .001$.

30. As predicted, there is a significant interaction effect between evaluations of the desirability of imports from light-skinned and dark-skinned countries among white versus non-white respondents ($p = F = 12.77$, $p < .001$).

31. Rogers and Fandos (2019).

32. See Mutz, Mansfield, and Kim (forthcoming).

33. See Mutz, Mansfield, and Kim (forthcoming) for details of this analysis.

34. Ibid.

35. Mutz (2017).

36. See Mutz, Mansfield, and Kim (forthcoming).

Chapter 7. Is This Inevitable? A Cross-National Comparison

1. Duina (2010).

2. Hiscox (2006); Slaughter (1999). This was further confirmed in Canadian and US open-ended explanations for trade support and opposition in these original surveys. Jobs was the number one reason cited for opposing trade in both countries.

3. Lipset (1989).
4. Lipset (1989: 1).
5. Pratto and Glasford (2008).
6. Bloom (2005).
7. Herrmann et al. (2001).
8. Trump (2017a).
9. BBC (2016).
10. Results demonstrated a significant interaction between country and experimental condition in the expected direction. See Table A7.1 in the online appendix for details.
11. The mean SDO level in the US is 4.24, significantly higher than in Canada where it is 3.94 ($p < .001$).
12. E.g., Mansfield and Mutz (2009).
13. Caporael et al. (1989).
14. Rios, Finkelstein, and Landa (2015).
15. See Brilliant (2014).
16. There was a significant interaction between country and experimental condition. See Table A7.4 in the online appendix for details.
17. Tajfel et al. (1971: 172).
18. Baron (2012).
19. Washington Post (2015).
20. Schwartz (2015).
21. Wave 2 of the US sample experienced differential attrition by age, education, and income, but these characteristics were not associated with the size-of-treatment effects and thus did not bias effect size.
22. Popper (2016), quoting Autor.
23. Green (1992).
24. Green and Blair (1995).
25. See Pratto and Glasford (2008). Based on prospect theory, one might expect the magnitude of losses to play a greater role in influencing preferences than the magnitude of gains. However, prospect theory applies to choices made under conditions of uncertainty; that is, when participants choose between certain and probabilistic options. Policy options are seldom described to the public in probabilistic terms, and mass publics tend to have limited understanding of probabilities in any case (Pelham et al. 1994).
26. O'Rourke et al. (2001); Mayda and Rodrik (2005).
27. Elkins and Figueiredo (2003).
28. E.g., Johnston et al. (2010).
29. For a discussion of how this came about, see Uberoi (2008; 2016).
30. E.g., Wright and Bloemraad (2012).
31. Kazemipur (2009).
32. Citrin, Johnston, and Wright (2012).
33. Kymlicka (2010: 263) citing Sides and Citrin (2007).
34. Kymlicka (2010: 263).
35. Laczko (2007).
36. Gordon (2016).
37. Breton (2015) makes this point in the context of Canadian support for immigration.
38. Christiansen and Loeschcke (1990).
39. Hayward and Kemmelmeier (2007).
40. Mayda and Rodrik (2005).
41. Actually, soccer does have ties, but it remains less popular in the US.
42. Cornell (2018).

43. Milanovic (2012).
44. World Bank (2017).
45. Uberoi (2008).
46. Tocqueville (1835).

Chapter 8. Media Coverage of Trade: The Vividness of Losers

1. Mutz (1998).
2. As described in Chapter 1, I use this term in the sense that it is defined by Carmines and Stimson (1980).
3. See Mullainathan and Shleifer (2002; 2005).
4. See Baum and Groeling (2008); Groeling (2013); Larcinese, Puglisi, and Snyder (2011).
5. See Galician and Vestre (1987); Blood and Phillips (1995), Broome (2006); Fogarty (2005); Hagen (2005); Harrington (1989); Kepplinger (2002); Nadeau et al. (1999); Nadeau, Niemi, and Amato (2000); Sanders and Gavin (2004); Shah et al. (1999); Heinz and Swinnen (2015).
6. Doms and Morin (2004); Goidel and Langley (2010); Lamla and Lein (2008); Shah et al. (1999).
7. See Hetherington (1996); Goidel et al. (2010).
8. Guisinger (2017).
9. Guisinger (2017).
10. Guisinger (2017).
11. Kim (2018: 954).
12. Kaniss (1991).
13. Kim (2018).
14. Brutger and Strezhnev (2018).
15. Kaniss (1991).
16. Johnson (2011).
17. Hallin (1984).
18. Clifford (2013).
19. Frank (1999).
20. O'Hanlon (2018).
21. Frank (1999).
22. Frank (2002).
23. Dana Frank as quoted in Chris Brooks (2017, May 16). *In These Times.* https://inthesetimes.com/article/the-slippery-slope-of-buy-american-campaigns.
24. Johnson (2011).
25. Mansfield and Mutz. (2006).
26. The newspapers are the *Arizona Republic, Atlanta Constitution, Baltimore Sun, Boston Globe, Chicago Tribune, Dallas Morning News, Denver Post, Detroit Free Press, Houston Chronicle, Los Angeles Times, New York Daily News, New York Times, Oregonian, Philadelphia Inquirer, San Diego Union-Tribune, San Francisco Chronicle, USA Today, Wall Street Journal,* and *Washington Post.*
27. Articles qualified for our content analysis based on a Nexis search using keywords "free trade" or "open trade" or "trade liberalization" or "trade reform" during the first six months of 2004.
28. A coding reliability estimate was obtained by having two independent readers code 40 overlapping news stories. The correlation between the extent of support/opposition to trade between the two coders was .80, suggesting a relatively high level of agreement with respect to which stories were neutral, pro-trade, or anti-trade. Individuals who reported no newspaper reading or television news viewing were coded as 0 (neutral) on the print and television measures, respectively.
29. Mansfield, Mutz and Brackbill (2019).
30. Leiser and Aroch (2009).

31. Brady, Ferejohn, and Parker (2019).

32. Dilliplane, Goldman, and Mutz (2013); Adams (2000).

33. $t=58.9$, $p<0.000$.

34. Mutz (1998); Goidel and Langley (1995); Funk and Garcia-Monet (1997); Books and Prysby (1999); Nadeau et al. (1999); Duch, Palmer, and Anderson (2000).

35. Lippmann (1922: 13).

36. Aarøe and Petersen (2014).

37. Amit and Greene (2012).

38. Amit and Greene (2012).

39. For this analysis I limited the sample to those receiving scenarios involving both job gains and job losses. For those assigned to the "win-win" trade policy, there was obviously no reason for them to visualize anyone suffering loss.

40. Popper (2016); Autor et al. (2016).

41. Lakner and Milanovic (2016).

42. As quoted in Popper (2016).

43. Reese, Daly, and Hardy (1987); Guisinger (2017).

44. Small and Loewenstein (2005); Fetherstonhaugh et al. (1997); Kogut and Ritov (2005); Lyon and Slovic (1976); Small (2010); Small and Lerner (2008); Small and Loewenstein (2003); Small, Loewenstein, and Slovic (2007).

45. See Loewenstein and Small (2007).

46. Gross (2008).

47. Liberman, Trope, and Stephan (2007).

48. Gowen (2019).

49. Smialek (2019).

50. Mankiw (2018, Oct. 5).

51. Stockman (2017).

52. Hallin (1984).

53. Hallin (1984).

54. Kernell (2007).

55. Harwood (2019).

Chapter 9. Attributing Responsibility for Job Loss

1. E.g., Porter (2016).

2. Petri (2017).

3. Wolcott (2018).

4. Cooper (2017).

5. Muro and Kulkarni (2016).

6. Wlezien (2015).

7. See Hicks and Devaraj (2017); Irwin (2019); Rose (2018).

8. Acemoglu et al. (2016); Cocco (2016); Miller (2016).

9. Estimating what proportion of manufacturing jobs have been lost due to trade versus automation is not as simple as it may sound. Thus, this claim has not been without controversy, even among economists. For example, one analysis disaggregating trends in computer and non-computer-related manufacturing challenges the claim that manufacturing job loss is primarily due to automation (Houseman 2018). But this has not been the dominant view.

10. Irwin (2017).

11. Iyengar (1989); Iyengar (1990); Iyengar (1991); Hameleers, Bos, and de Vreese (2017).

12. Aarøe and Petersen (2014).

13. To characterize public discourse on a large scale, I used all "Major US Newspapers" from the Nexis-Uni database, searching from 2000 to the present. Using a special license that allows large-scale bulk downloads of media content on weekends only, I downloaded all articles mentioning job loss or (un)employment and automation or trade. The exact search within Major US Newspapers was: ((job* w/10 (loss or declin*)) or unemployment) and (automat* or trad*). This search identifies any variant of the word job within ten words of loss or decline, or a reference to unemployment, but only those also mentioned in conjunction with trade or automation. I used a second program to search the downloaded collection of articles for those mentioning job loss along with automation-related terms, and a second search for those mentioning job loss along with references to trade. An article could thus include linkages to one or both topics at the same time. These counts were quantified by date. The specifications that created the two lines were:

Automation: (({job*} 50 ({loss}+{declin*}))+{unemployment}) & {automat*}
Trade: (({job*} 50 ({loss}+{declin*}))+{unemployment}) & {trad*}

14. Heider (1958); Kelley and Michela (1980).
15. Mansfield and Mutz (2013).
16. Tajfel and Turner (1979).
17. Blumer (1958); Bobo and Hutchings (1996).
18. E.g., Hutchings et al. (2011).
19. Jang (2013).
20. Tajfel and Turner (1986).
21. Data were collected through National Science Foundation Grant # SES-1628057, Time-sharing Experiments for the Social Sciences.
22. The sample was limited to non-Hispanic white respondents because minorities introduce heterogeneity in terms of the extent to which they identify with the American ingroup. Moreover, the issue of manufacturing job loss has been a concern among white Americans in particular.
23. Goodman (2016).
24. A manipulation check question was included at the very end of the study to assess whether respondents read the article carefully enough to notice the cause of job loss that was suggested. Respondents were asked why the man in the story lost his job, and given four options: a) his job was sent to China, b) he was replaced by new technology/robots, c) his company merged with another company so he was no longer needed, and d) the article said nothing about why he lost his job. Most respondents processed the experimental treatment as intended. For example, 97 percent of respondents recalled that technology was the cause of the man's job loss in the automation condition, whereas only 75 percent correctly answered in the trade condition. Those who erred said it was due to a merger instead of overseas competition. All subjects were retained in the analyses in order to preserve random assignment.
25. See Mutz (2021) for details on measures and results.
26. Hameleers, Bos, and de Vreese (2017); Han, Lerner, and Keltner (2007).
27. See Table A9.1 in the online appendix.
28. See Table A9.1 in the online appendix.
29. See Mutz (2021) for details on measures and results.
30. See Table A9.1 in the online appendix.
31. Hiscox (2006).
32. See Mutz (2021) for full question wording.
33. National Sample Cronbach's alpha = .85.
34. See Mutz (2021) for detailed analyses.
35. Hai (2019).
36. E.g., Rodrik (2018).

37. Nisbett and Ross (1980).
38. Langer (1975).

Chapter 10. The Impact of Trade on Elections

1. Guisinger (2017).
2. Publicly available records allow access to whether people actually voted, but *which candidate* received an individual's vote must be self-reported in surveys.
3. See, e.g., Sides, Tesler, and Vavreck (2018).
4. Guisinger (2009).
5. Sides, Tesler, and Vavreck (2018); Schaffner, MacWilliams, and Nteta (2017).
6. Mughan and Lacy (2002).
7. Che et al. (2016).
8. Gidron and Mijs (2019).
9. Inglehart and Norris (2017).
10. Cerrato, Ferrara, and Ruggieri (2018).
11. Inglehart and Norris (2016).
12. Cerrato, Ferrara, and Ruggieri (2018).
13. In this study Cerrato, Ferrara, and Ruggieri (2018) suggest that attitudes toward trade were unaffected by trade shocks, and instead that attitudes toward immigration were driven in a conservative direction by trade shocks, similar to the cultural backlash theory.
14. Inglehart and Norris (2017: 446) acknowledge the lack of a relationship between economic indicators and changes in voter preferences, noting that "Economic factors such as income and unemployment rates are surprisingly weak predictors of the populist vote." But they still maintain that "although the proximate cause of the populist vote is cultural backlash, its high present level reflects the declining economic security and rising economic inequality that many writers have emphasized" (p. 447).
15. Gidron and Hall (2017).
16. See Radford (2019); Martin and Mutz (2019).
17. For example, in 1998, 56 percent of Americans felt that "large numbers of immigrants and refugees coming into the United States" was a "critical threat to America's vital interests," whereas only 36 percent felt they were a critical threat by 2017. Again, although people are more divided by party on this issue, there is no sign of a groundswell of support for more severe immigration restrictions as suggested by the cultural backlash theory. See Radford (2019); Chicago Council on Global Affairs (2017); and Sargent (2019).
18. Mutz (2018); Martin and Mutz (2019).
19. A representative national panel study conducted for the Institute for the Study of Citizens and Politics (ISCAP) documents this same pattern. The average American became slightly more supportive of creating a path to citizenship for illegal immigrants from October 2012 to October 2016, consistent with the other surveys reviewed.
20. Autor et al. (2016a).
21. Autor et al. (2016a).
22. Margalit (2011).
23. Margalit (2011).
24. Hai (2019).
25. Ehrlich and Hearn (2014).
26. Jensen, Quinn, and Weymouth (2017).
27. Jensen, Quinn, and Weymouth (2017: 429).
28. DiTella and Rodrik (2019).

29. Mutz (2018).

30. Guisinger (2017).

31. See, e.g., Feigenbaum and Hall (2015).

32. See, e.g., Tsfati (2017).

33. See Mansfield and Mutz (2009) for a discussion of this problem.

34. Scheve and Slaughter (2001).

35. These numbers are from Sides, Tesler, and Vavreck (2018), and they are consistent with those from other sources, such as the panel study described in this chapter.

36. Erikson and Wlezien (2012).

37. See, e.g., Singer (2011).

38. See Anderson (2007).

39. Singer and Carlin (2013).

40. Anderson (2007).

41. Anderson (2007: 275)

42. Paldam (1991).

43. Anderson and O'Connor (2000).

44. Sanders and Gavin (2004); Nadeau et al. (1999).

45. Duch, Palmer, and. Anderson (2000).

46. Bartels (2002); Erikson (2004); Gerber and Huber (2009).

47. Lewis-Beck, Martini, and Kiewiet (2013).

48. Brady, Ferejohn, and Parker (2019).

49. Rudolph (2003).

50. Bisgaard (2015).

51. McDonald and Budge (2005).

52. Anderson (2007: 286).

53. E.g., Larcinese, Puglisi, and Snyder (2011); Groeling (2013); Baum and Groeling (2008); Mutz and Kim (2016).

54. Thirteen percent more of those people favoring NAFTA thought the Republican candidate agreed with their views than disagreed. Only 2 percent more of those who favored NAFTA thought the Democratic candidate agreed with them than disagreed, thus suggesting that NAFTA supporters felt more supported by Republicans than Democrats.

55. See, e.g., NBC News/Wall Street Journal poll, December 4–8, 2008. Accessible as USNBCWSJ.08DEC.R29 at the Roper Center Archive. Eight percent said the economy had "stayed about the same."

56. Before the recession, when a representative sample of Americans was asked who or what they thought should get most of the blame if a recession occurred, President George W. Bush was at the top of the list, the risky loans of mortgage lenders were second, and the third most popular target of blame was Congress (Los Angeles Times/Bloomberg Poll 2008). After the recession, a September 2009 survey indicated that Americans primarily blamed government institutions that did not do enough to regulate banks and financial companies, and financial companies that made risky loans or investments (Allstate/National Journal Heartland Monitor Poll 2009). In another survey, Americans were asked to what extent they blamed each of a long list of possible causes of the recession, and the most popular targets of blame were the banks and lenders that made risky loans, followed by the federal government and people who borrowed money that they could not afford to repay (Associated Press 2009; see also, Kenworthy and Owens 2011).

57. Nonetheless, some trade opponents tried to exploit the Great Recession to encourage anti-trade views. For example, union communications capitalized on the recession to encourage members to blame trade. For example, as one AFL-CIO-sponsored advertisement suggested, "25 million Americans are still searching for full-time jobs. Yet Congress is considering three new

trade agreements. . . . Tell your members of Congress to stop these dangerous trade deals and start putting Americans back to work" (AFL-CIO 2011).

58. This possibility is discussed in Mansfield, Mutz, and Brackbill (2019).

59. Although increased unemployment did not affect the trade preferences of most Americans, individuals working in import-competing industries who lost their jobs during the Great Recession did grow more hostile to trade. However, even greater increases in hostility to trade stemmed from a variety of non-material factors. Most importantly, increasing anxiety that foreign commerce would harm people in the *future*, even if it had not done so thus far, contributed to mounting opposition to trade among the American public. See Mansfield, Mutz, and Brackbill (2019) for details.

60. See Table 2 in Mansfield, Mutz, and Brackbill (2019).

61. Ehrlich and Maestas (2010).

Chapter 11. The Role of Trade in the 2016 Election

1. Lerner and Keltner (2000, 2001).

2. For example, Karlgaard (2009); Stokes (2012).

3. Seib (2010).

4. Cassar, Healy, and von Kessler (2011).

5. Malmendier and Nagel (2011).

6. Guiso, Sapienza, and Luigi Zingales (2013: 2).

7. Huddy and Feldman (2011).

8. Guiso, Sapienza, and Gonzales (2013).

9. Huddy and Feldman (2011). Likewise, personality studies suggest that those who feel they do not control their own lives as much as external agents do are more protectionist (e.g., Bastounis, Leiser, and Roland-Levy 2004).

10. Cassar et al. (2011).

11. Lindsay (2009).

12. See Mansfield, Mutz, and Brackbill (2019), Table 2.

13. Gidron and Hall (2017).

14. Inglehart and Norris (2017).

15. Feierabend and Feierabend (1966: 250) call this "systemic frustration," which has been less well studied.

16. Whites, blacks, and Hispanics assessed both positive and negative characteristics of their own ingroup as well as toward the other two groups. Subtracting outgroup favoritism from ingroup favoritism provides a measure of how much more positively a person regards their racial ingroup relative two racial outgroups.

17. Wazwaz (2015).

18. A large number of studies have documented white status threat (e.g., Craig and Richeson (2014a; 2014b); Danbold and Huo (2015); Major, Blodorn, and Blascovich (2016); Prislin, Limbert, and Bauer (2000).

19. Wilkins and Kaiser (2014); Schlueter and Scheepers (2010).

20. Norton and Sommers (2011).

21. Fuller (2016); Kupchan (2012).

22. Kiersz (2015).

23. Tyson (2014).

24. Pew Research Center (2014).

25. Theiss-Morse (2009)

26. Sidanius and Pratto (1999).

27. Sibley, Wilson, and Duckitt (2007); Liu et al. (2008); Morrison and Ybarra (2008).

28. Shook, Hopkins, and Koech (2016).

29. Hopkins and Washington (2019).

30. Respondents reported how much discrimination they thought each group was experiencing on a 1 to 7 scale.

31. Brody and Page (1972).

32. King (1977).

33. Brody and Page (1972).

34. See Allison (2009); Bellemare, Masaki, and Pepinski (2017).

35. Some have argued that to eliminate potential projection effects (perceiving the preferred candidate's issue position as closer than he/she actually is), one should substitute the mean perception of the candidate's position for all respondents (see Alvarez and Nagler 1995). I have not done so here because a) the statistical consequences of doing so are problematic, and b) projection is not problematic to begin with when using panel data and within-person fixed effects models. I explain both points further below.

(a) Assigning the mean perception of the candidate for purposes of establishing the distance between the respondent and the candidate produces multiple problems. If one assigns the same identical candidate position for all respondents, the distance to the candidate is entirely a function of each respondent's own position on this issue since candidate placement is now a constant. This makes it impossible to distinguish the impact of change over time in placement of the Republican candidate (such as Trump becoming perceived as a more strongly anti-trade candidate than Romney) from change in respondents' own opinions over time. In addition, the more variance that exists in a given candidate's perceived position, the more the candidate's distance to respondents' positions will be underestimated when the population average is substituted for the individual's actual perception of the candidate's position.

(b) In a fixed effects panel analysis, each individual is compared strictly to himself or herself over time. So the distance between a respondent's position and the Republican candidate's perceived position in 2012 is compared to the same person's perceived distance from the Republican candidate in 2016. Change in this distance is used to predict change in vote choice. Any projection effects that are registered in a person's perceptions of the candidates will be registered at both points in time, and thus will cancel out of the analysis. The only problem that could arise is if the same individual projects their position onto the candidate in one election year, but not in the next election. To evaluate this possibility, I also looked across four different issues to see if certain people—such as Trump supporters—were simply locating Trump close to themselves on issue scales across all possible issues. They did not. This pattern is illustrated in Republicans' views of immigration, in particular, where they perceived Trump as too extreme.

36. Sabet (2013).

37. See Mutz (2018). For the sake of simplicity in the presentation here I have combined the variables related to issue distances for Republicans and Democrats so that there is a single measure of the relative distance to the Republican versus the Democratic candidate. Otherwise, these analyses are identical.

38. See Mutz (2018) for details on these analyses.

39. The parallel results using Relative Thermometer Ratings as the dependent variable are shown in Table A11.1 in the online appendix.

40. Carmines and Stimson (1980).

41. Hafner-Burton et al. (2017); Mansfield and Mutz (2009).

42. Hainmueller and Hiscox (2006); see Rho and Tomz (2015) for a review.

43. Mansfield and Mutz (2009).

44. See Sabet (2013).

45. Carmines and Stimson (1980).
46. Carmines and Stimson (1980: 78)
47. Carmines and Stimson (1980).
48. Rho and Tomz (2015).
49. O'Rourke et al. (2001).
50. Mansfield and Mutz (2009); Sabet (2013).
51. Mutz and Kim (2017).
52. Carmines and Stimson (1980: 80); Prewitt and Nie (1971).

Chapter 12. Influencing Opinions on Trade: What Works and with What Consequences

1. Margalit (2012).
2. See Guisinger (2017), Table A8.1, page 229.
3. Dür (2015).
4. Entman (2008); Nye (2008).
5. Aldrich, Lu, and Kang (2015).
6. Brady (2015: 55).
7. Aldrich et al. (2012).
8. Gries, Crowson, and Sandel (2010).
9. Participants in these studies were recruited through Amazon Mechanical Turk (MTurk) in late February 2016. The experiments were only open to MTurk workers located in the US who were highly rated as workers.
10. E.g., Huang (2015); Ramzy (2013); Wong (2015).
11. Sources suggest that The Road to Rejuvenation Studio is affiliated with the International Department of the CPC, which is the CPC's diplomacy department. According to Shambaugh (2007), one important aspect of the International Department's work is publicizing China's policies and achievements overseas. In fact, the International Department has presented this series of videos at overseas conferences.
12. See Sonmez (2015).
13. Both original videos were shortened to three minutes for the sake of experimental control.
14. $F = 16.27$, $p < .001$.
15. Guisinger (2017).
16. Cummings (1989); Morris (2011).
17. Wu (2012).
18. Most Americans cannot differentiate Asians from different countries (Hourihan, Benjamin, and Liu 2012). This is not a new phenomenon; *TIME* and *Life* magazines in the 1940s published articles such as "How to Tell Your Chinese Friends from the Japs" (Wang 2015). Surveys suggest that this "lumping"—as it is sometimes called—persists today (Larson 2009; Kuo 2016; Lipin 2014).
19. See also Cummings (1989); Morris (2011); Iino (1994).
20. Silver (2016).
21. Osnos (2012).
22. The same scale for authoritarianism used here was also used in Hetherington and Suhay's (2011) study of terrorist threat.
23. Stenner (2005, 2009).
24. Haidt (2016).
25. While the white Chinese combination may seem odd, it has several advantages. First, this type of individual is increasingly common in a globalized world. Children of academics, reporters, diplomats, and the like may be raised overseas and apply to US universities with non-American

citizenship and a phenotype that appears closer to Caucasian Americans. Second, it is worth noting that no race is specified; rather, the manipulation is solely based on the photograph. While it is unlikely that any respondents were thinking in these terms, there are, in fact, millions of Chinese who identify as one of the 55 ethnic minority groups in the country—including the Uyghurs, who are regularly described as having "Western" or "Caucasian" features (Rudelson 1997). Third, it allows for a fully-crossed design in terms of race and nationality. By design, I can *separate* the effects of race and nationality—determining the degree to which Asian race and Chinese nationality—or both—are affecting perceived candidate quality.

26. Although profiles were pre-tested to be equally strong, and the pictures equally attractive, this Latin Square design allows me to look at the effects of the manipulated factors—race and nationality—while removing the extra variation that comes due to any residual differences in the profiles.

27. Each one of these "combinations" has three characteristics, which rotate together: a photograph (the race manipulation), a stated nationality (the nationality manipulation), and a name. These composites (name, photo to manipulate race, and text to manipulate nationality) then rotate across the profiles (that is, the stable characteristics of GPA, intended major, and activities) to form a Latin Square.

28. $F = 9.00$, $p < 0.05$.

29. Between-subjects analysis of variance, $F = 6.80$, $p < 0.01$.

30. Zeitlin (2019).

31. Oxley et al. (2008); Lilienfeld and Latzman (2014).

32. Noland (2019).

Chapter 13. The Future of Mass Support for International Trade

1. Although most of my data predate COVID19, the 2020 Chicago Council Survey confirms that trade support remains high even after the effects of the pandemic-induced recession.

2. Zakaria (2020); Sumner (2020).

3. Although Trump claimed some improvement in manufacturing in the initial two years of his administration, ironically Trump's trade war had destroyed those gains by 2019 (Heeb 2019; White 2019; Trafecante 2020).

4. See Martin and Mutz (2019) for more detailed analyses.

5. https://twitter.com/nprpolitics/status/610830756080918528?lang=en.

6. Kenny (2018) is one of few observers making similar observations.

7. Li (2016).

8. Haass (2020).

9. Rooduijn (2018).

10. One can hear strains of actual populism more clearly in the pro-working-class rhetoric of 2020 Democratic presidential hopeful Bernie Sanders.

11. Mutz (2019).

12. Rothwell and Diego-Rosell (2016); Sides et al. (2018); Schaffner et al. (2017); Mutz (2018).

13. See, e.g., the 2020 Chicago Council on Foreign Affairs survey.

14. Achen and Bartels (2016).

15. Cohen, Tsfati, and Sheafer (2008).

16. Details on this evidence can be found in Martin and Mutz (2019).

17. E.g., Broockman and Skovron (2018).

18. "The Biden Plan to Ensure the Future is 'Made in All of America' by All of America's Workers." https://joebiden.com/made-in-america/.

19. Hufbauer and Jung (2020).

20. Actually, according to the original story, Vladimir would prefer trade agreements in which the US loses, but the trading partner country loses *even more*. Sadly, I did not include such an experimental condition in the study in Chapter 4, because I did not anticipate the attractiveness of such an option.

21. Caplan (2007); Boyer and Petersen (2018).

22. Irwin (2016).

23. Irwin (2016): 86.

24. Caplan (2007) is probably most representative of this approach.

25. Samuelson (1969). See also Deirdre McCloskey, "A Punter's Guide to a True but Non-Obvious Proposition in Economics." http://ifreetrade.org/article/a_punters_guide_to_a_true_but_non_obvious_proposition_in_economics.

26. Pham (2015).

27. Result of this analysis are detailed in Table A13.1 in the online appendix.

BIBLIOGRAPHY

Note: Bibliographic entries are followed by parenthetical lists of the pages on which the entries are cited.

Aarøe, Lene, and Michael Bang Petersen. 2014. "Crowding Out Culture: Scandinavians and Americans Agree on Social Welfare in the Face of Deservingness Cues." *The Journal of Politics* 76 (3): 684–97. https://doi.org/10.1017/s002238161400019x. (Cited 174n36, 190n12.)

Aarøe, Lene, Michael Bang Petersen, and Kevin Arceneaux. 2017. "The Behavioral Immune System Shapes Political Intuitions: Why and How Individual Differences in Disgust Sensitivity Underlie Opposition to Immigration." *American Political Science Review* 111 (2): 277–94. https://doi.org/10.1017/S0003055416000770. (Cited 121n46.)

Acemoglu, Daron, David Autor, David Dorn, Gordon H. Hanson, and Brendan Price. 2016. "Import Competition and the Great US Employment Sag of the 2000s." *Journal of Labor Economics* 34 (S1): S141–98. https://doi.org/10.1086/682384. (Cited 22n58, 190n8.)

Achen, Christopher H., and Larry M. Bartels. 2016. *Democracy for Realists: Why Elections Do Not Produce Responsive Government.* Princeton: Princeton University Press. (Cited 268n14.)

Adams, William J. 2000. "How People Watch Television as Investigated Using Focus Group Techniques." *Journal of Broadcasting & Electronic Media* 44 (1): 78–93. https://doi.org/10.1207/s15506878jobem4401_6. (Cited 173n32.)

AFL-CIO. 2011. "AFL-CIO Runs Ads Opposing Korea, Panama and Colombia Trade Agreements." Common Dreams. 2011. https://www.commondreams.org/newswire/2011/10/04/afl-cio-runs-ads-opposing-korea-panama-and-colombia-trade-agreements. (Cited 223n57.)

Aldrich, J., L.L. Frankel, K. Liu, J. Lu, and J. Park. 2012, April. "U.S. Perceptions and Changing Opinions of China: Evaluations and Psychological Mechanisms." Paper delivered at the 70th Annual Meeting of the Midwest Political Science Association, Chicago, IL. April 12–15, 2012. (Cited 247n7.)

Aldrich, John, Jie Lu, and Liu Kang. 2015. "How Do Americans View the Rising China?" *Journal of Contemporary China* 24 (92): 203–21. https://doi.org/10.1080/10670564.2014.932148. (Cited 247n5.)

Allison, Paul D. 2009. *Fixed Effects Regression Models.* Los Angeles: Sage Publications, Inc. (Cited 237n34.)

Allstate/National Journal Heartland Monitor. 2009. Conducted by FD America, September 24–September 28, 2009, based on telephone interviews with a national adult sample of 1,200. [USFD.101009.R08]. Data provided by the Roper Center for Public Opinion Research, University of Connecticut. (Cited 223n56.)

Amit, Elinor, and Joshua D. Greene. 2012. "You See, the Ends Don't Justify the Means: Visual Imagery and Moral Judgment." *Psychological Science* 23 (8): 861–68. https://doi.org/10.1177/0956797611434965. (Cited 175n37, 175n38.)

Anderson, Christopher J. 2007. "The End of Economic Voting? Contingency Dilemmas and the Limits of Democratic Accountability." *Annual Review of Political Science* 10 (1): 271–96. https://doi.org/10.1146/annurev.polisci.10.050806.155344. (Cited 215n38, 215n40, 216n41, 217n52.)

Anderson, Christopher J., and Kathleen M. O'Conner. 2000. "System Change, Learning and Public Opinion about the Economy." *British Journal of Political Science* 30 (1): 147–72. https://doi.org/10.1017/S0007123400000077. (Cited 216n43.)

Anderson, W.T., and William H. Cunningham. 1972. "Gauging Foreign Product Promotion." *Journal of Advertising Research* 12 (1): 29–34. (Cited 99n18.)

Armstrong, Joel, Rebecca Friesdorf, and Paul Conway. 2019. "Clarifying Gender Differences in Moral Dilemma Judgments: The Complementary Roles of Harm Aversion and Action Aversion." *Social Psychological and Personality Science* 10 (3): 353–363. (Cited 73n4.)

Associated Press 2009. Conducted by Gfk Roper Public Affairs & Media September 3–September 8, 2009. Based on telephone interviews with a national sample of 1,001 adults. (Cited 223n56.)

Autor, David, David Dorn, Gordon Hanson, and Kaveh Majlesi. 2016. "Importing Political Polarization? The Electoral Consequences of Rising Trade Exposure." Working Paper 22637. Cambridge, MA: National Bureau of Economic Research. https://doi.org/10.3386/w22637. (Cited 180n40.)

Autor, David H., David Dorn, and Gordon H. Hanson. 2016. "The China Shock: Learning from Labor-Market Adjustment to Large Changes in Trade." *Annual Review of Economics* 8 (1): 205–40. https://doi.org/10.1146/annurev-economics-080315-015041. (Cited 210n20, 210n21.)

Bailenson, Jeremy N., Shanto Iyengar, Nick Yee, and Nathan A. Collins. 2008. "Facial Similarity between Voters and Candidates Causes Influence." *Public Opinion Quarterly* 72 (5): 935–61. https://doi.org/10.1093/poq/nfn064. (Cited 101n36.)

Bannister, J. P., and J. A. Saunders. 1978. "UK Consumers' Attitudes towards Imports: The Measurement of National Stereotype Image." *European Journal of Marketing*, August. https://doi.org/10.1108/EUM0000000004982. (Cited 99n17.)

Barlett, Donald L., and James B. Steele. 2012. *The Betrayal of the American Dream*. New York: Public Affairs. (Cited 73n9, 74n11.)

Baron, Jonathan, Ilana Ritov, and Joshua D. Greene. 2013. "The Duty to Support Nationalistic Policies. *Journal of Behavioral Decision Making* 26 (2): 128–38. (Cited 92n50.)

Baron, Jonathan. 2012. *Parochialism as a Result of Cognitive Biases*. Oxford: Oxford University Press. http://www.oxfordscholarship.com/view/10.1093/acprof:oso/9780195371895.001.0001/acprof-9780195371895-chapter-8. (Cited 148n18.)

Bartels, Larry M. 2002. "Beyond the Running Tally: Partisan Bias in Political Perceptions." *Political Behavior* 24 (2): 117–50. (Cited 217n46.)

Bastounis, Marina, David Leiser, and Christine Roland-Levy. 2004. "Psychosocial Variables Involved in the Construction of Lay Thinking about the Economy: Results of a Cross-National Survey." *Journal of Economic Psychology* 25 (2): 263–78. (Cited 228n9.)

Batson, C. Daniel, and Nadia Y. Ahmad. 2009. "Using Empathy to Improve Intergroup Attitudes and Relations." *Social Issues and Policy Review* 3 (1): 141–77. https://doi.org/10.1111/j.1751-2409.2009.01013.x. (Cited 83n35.)

Baum, Matthew A., and Tim Groeling. 2008. "New Media and the Polarization of American Political Discourse." *Political Communication* 25 (4): 345–65. https://doi.org/10.1080/10584600802426965. (Cited 163n4, 218n53.)

BBC. 2016, May 2. "China Accused of Trade 'Rape' by Trump." BBC News. https://www.bbc.com/news/av/world-us-canada-36185275/china-accused-of-trade-rape-by-donald-trump. (Cited 143n9.)

Beaulieu, Eugene. 2002. "Factor or Industry Cleavages in Trade Policy? An Empirical Analysis of the Stolper–Samuelson Theorem." *Economics & Politics* 14 (2): 99–131. https://doi.org/10.1111/1468-0343.00102. (Cited 4n9.)

Bellemare, Marc F., Takaaki Masaki, and Thomas B. Pepinsky. 2017. "Lagged Explanatory Variables and the Estimation of Causal Effects." *Journal of Politics*. 79(3): 949–963. (Cited 237n34.)

Bernstein, Jared. 2018, May 22. "What Governments Can Do for the Losers from Free Trade." *The Economist*. https://www.economist.com/open-future/2018/05/22/what-governments-can-do-for-the-losers-from-free-trade.

Berti, Anna, and Francesca Frassinetti. 2000. "When Far Becomes Near: Remapping of Space by Tool Use." *Journal of Cognitive Neuroscience* 12 (3): 415–20. https://doi.org/10.1162/089892900562237. (Cited 97n12.)

Bhagwati, Jagdish. 2007. *In Defense of Globalization: With a New Afterword*. Oxford; New York: Oxford University Press. (Cited 133n26.)

Bisgaard, Martin. 2015. "Bias Will Find a Way: Economic Perceptions, Attributions of Blame, and Partisan-Motivated Reasoning during Crisis." *The Journal of Politics* 77 (3): 849–60. https://doi.org/10.1086/681591. (Cited 217n50.)

Blonigen, Bruce. 2011. "Revisiting the Evidence on Trade Policy Preferences." *Journal of International Economics* 85 (1): 129–35. (Cited 5n11.)

Blood, Deborah J., and Peter C. B. Phillips. 1995. "Recession Headline News, Consumer Sentiment, the State of the Economy and Presidential Popularity: A Time Series Analysis 1989–1993." *International Journal of Public Opinion Research* 7 (1): 2–22. https://doi.org/10.1093/ijpor/7.1.2. (Cited 163n5.)

Bloom, Paul. 2005. *Descartes' Baby: How the Science of Child Development Explains What Makes Us Human*. Export Ed edition. New York: Basic Books. (Cited 142n6.)

Blumer, Herbert. 1958. "Race Prejudice as a Sense of Group Position." *The Pacific Sociological Review* 1 (1): 3–7. https://doi.org/10.2307/1388607. (Cited 192n17.)

———. 2016. "Race Prejudice as a Sense of Group Position:" *Pacific Sociological Review*, August. https://doi.org/10.2307/1388607.

Bobo, Lawrence, and Vincent L. Hutchings. 1996. "Perceptions of Racial Group Competition: Extending Blumer's Theory of Group Position to a Multiracial Social Context." *American Sociological Review* 61 (6): 951–72. https://doi.org/10.2307/2096302. (Cited 192n17.)

Bodet, Marc André, Yannick Dufresne, Joanie Bouchard, and François Gélineau. 2020. "Follow the (Issue) Leader? The Leader-Led Nexus Revisited." *Public Opinion Quarterly* 83 (4): 661–89 (Cited 65n24.)

Bohara, Alok K., and William H. Kaempfer. 1991. "A Test of Tariff Endogeneity in the United States." *The American Economic Review* 81 (4): 952–60. (Cited 124n6.)

Books, John, and Charles Prysby. 1999. "Contextual Effects on Retrospective Economic Evaluations: The Impact of the State and Local Economy." *Political Behavior* 21 (1): 1–16. https://doi.org/10.1023/A:1023371328591. (Cited 173n34.)

Bown, Chad P, and Meredith A Crowley. 2013. *Emerging Economies, Trade Policy, and Macroeconomic Shocks*. Policy Research Working Papers. The World Bank. Washington, DC. https://doi.org/10.1596/1813-9450-6315. (Cited 124n6.)

Boyer, Pascal, and Michael Bang Petersen. 2018. "Folk-Economic Beliefs: An Evolutionary Cognitive Model." *Behavioral and Brain Sciences* 41. https://doi.org/10.1017/S0140525X17001960. (Cited 9n27, 271n21.)

Brady, Anne-Marie. 2015. "Authoritarianism Goes Global (II): China's Foreign Propaganda Machine." *Journal of Democracy* 26 (4): 51–59. https://doi.org/10.1353/jod.2015.0056. (Cited 247n6.)

Brady, David W., John A. Ferejohn, and Brett Parker. 2019. "Partisan Cognition and the Growing Partisan Divide in Sociotropic Economic Perceptions." Unpublished manuscript, Stanford University. (Cited 59n9, 172n31, 217n48.)

Breton, Charles. 2015. "Making National Identity Salient: Impact on Attitudes toward Immigration and Multiculturalism." *Canadian Journal of Political Science* 48 (2): 357–81. https://doi.org/10.1017/S0008423915000268. (Cited 157n37.)

Brewer, Marilynn B. 1979. "In-Group Bias in the Minimal Intergroup Situation: A Cognitive-Motivational Analysis." *Psychological Bulletin* 86 (2): 307–24. https://doi.org/10.1037/0033-2909.86.2.307. (Cited 72n1, 82n33.)

———. 2007. "The Importance of Being We: Human Nature and Intergroup Relations." *The American Psychologist* 62 (8): 726–38. https://doi.org/10.1037/0003-066X.62.8.728. (Cited 125n12.)

Brewer, Mark D. 2016. "Populism in American Politics." *The Forum* 14 (3). https://doi.org/10.1515/for-2016-0021.

Brilliant, Myron. 2014, April 2. "U.S. Trade Agenda: Down a Dozen Points from the Tip Off?" U.S. Chamber of Commerce. https://www.uschamber.com/above-the-fold/us-trade-agenda-down-dozen-points-the-tip. (Cited 11n34, 147n15.)

Brinkley, John. 2019, April 8. "2020 Democratic Candidates Won't Find It So Easy To Be Anti-Trade." *Forbes*. https://www.forbes.com/sites/johnbrinkley/2019/04/08/2020-democratic-candidates-wont-find-it-so-easy-to-be-anti-trade/.

Brody, Richard A., and Benjamin I. Page. 1972. "Comment: The Assessment of Policy Voting." *American Political Science Review* 66 (2): 450–58. https://doi.org/10.2307/1957788. (Cited 237n31, 237n33.)

Brody, Richard A., and Paul M. Sniderman. 1977. "From Life Space to Polling Place: The Relevance of Personal Concerns for Voting Behavior." *British Journal of Political Science* 7 (3): 337–60. https://doi.org/10.1017/S0007123400001022. (Cited 6n15.)

Broockman, David E., and Christopher Skovron. 2018. "Bias in Perceptions of Public Opinion among Political Elites." *American Political Science Review* 112 (3): 542–63. https://doi.org/10.1017/S0003055418000011. (Cited 269n17.)

Brooks, David. 2017, June 2. "Donald Trump Poisons the World." *New York Times*, sec. Opinion. https://www.nytimes.com/2017/06/02/opinion/donald-trump-poisons-the-world.html.

Broome, André. 2006. "Setting the Fiscal Policy Agenda: Economic News and Election Year Tax." *Law in Context* 24 (2): 60–77. (Cited 163n5.)

Brown, Rupert. 2000. "Social Identity Theory: Past Achievements, Current Problems and Future Challenges." *European Journal of Social Psychology* 30 (6): 745–78. https://doi.org/10.1002/1099-0992(200011/12)30:6<745::AID-EJSP24>3.0.CO;2-O. (Cited 76n23.)

Brutger, Ryan, and Anton Strezhnev. 2018. "International Disputes, Media Coverage, and Backlash Against International Law." https://www.internationalpoliticaleconomysociety.org/sites/default/files/conference_files/IPES_Proposal_2018_Brutger_Strezhnev_0.pdf. (Cited 165n14.)

Buchanan, James M., and Yong J. Yoon. 2002. "Globalization as Framed by the Two Logics of Trade." *The Independent Review* 6 (3): 399–405. (Cited 2n3.)

Byrne, Donn, Gerald Clore, and George Smeaton. 1986. "The Attraction Hypothesis: Do Similar Attitudes Affect Anything?" *Journal of Personality and Social Psychology* 51 (December): 1167–70. https://doi.org/10.1037/0022-3514.51.6.1167. (Cited 100n28.)

Byrne, Donn Erwin. 1971. *The Attraction Paradigm*. New York: Academic Press. (Cited 109n41.)

Calhoun, Craig. 1988. "Populist Politics, Communications Media and Large Scale Societal Integration." *Sociological Theory* 6 (2): 219–41. https://doi.org/10.2307/202117. (Cited 8n25.)

Campbell, Ernest Q. 1965. "Introduction." *Sociological Inquiry* 35 (1): 3–7. https://doi.org/10.1111/j.1475-682X.1965.tb00586.x. (Cited 72n2.)

Canes-Wrone, Brandice. 2006. *Who Leads Whom? Presidents, Policy, and the Public*. Chicago: University of Chicago Press. (Cited 65n21.)

Caplan, Bryan. 2001. "What Makes People Think Like Economists? Evidence on Economic Cognition from the 'Survey of Americans and Economists on the Economy.'" *The Journal of Law and Economics* 44 (2): 395–426. https://doi.org/10.1086/322812.

———. 2007. *The Myth of the Rational Voter: Why Democracies Choose Bad Policies*. New ed. Princeton, NJ: Princeton University Press. (Cited 271n21, 271n24.)

Caporael, Linnda R., Robyn M. Dawes, John M. Orbell, and Alphons J. C. van de Kragt. 1989. "Selfishness Examined: Cooperation in the Absence of Egoistic Incentives." *Behavioral and Brain Sciences* 12 (4): 683–99. https://doi.org/10.1017/S0140525X00025292. (Cited 137n34, 137n36.)

Carmines, Edward G., and James A. Stimson. 1980. "The Two Faces of Issue Voting." *American Political Science Review* 74 (1): 78–91. https://doi.org/10.2307/1955648. (Cited 162n2, 241n40, 241n45, 241n46, 242n47, 242n52.)

Carnegie, Allison, and Nikhar Gaikwad. 2017. "Public Opinion on Geopolitics and Trade: Theory and Evidence." SSRN Scholarly Paper ID 2909761. Rochester, NY: Social Science Research Network. https://papers.ssrn.com/abstract=2909761. (Cited 110n43.)

Carter, Niambi M., and Efrén O. Pérez. 2015. "Race and Nation: How Racial Hierarchy Shapes National Attachments." *Political Psychology* 37 (4): 497–513. https://doi.org/10.1111/pops.12270. (Cited 126n19, 126n20.)

Cassar, Alessandra, Andrew Healy, and Carl von Kessler. 2011. "Trust, Risk, and Time Preferences After a Natural Disaster: Experimental Evidence from Thailand." *World Development* 94 (C): 90–105. (Cited 228n4, 228n10.)

Cebotari, Victor. 2015. "The Determinants of National Pride of Ethnic and Immigrant Minorities in Europe." *Nationalism and Ethnic Politics* 21 (3): 269–88. https://doi.org/10.1080/13537113.2015.1063911. (Cited 126n19, 126n20.)

Cerrato, Andrea, Federico Maria Ferrara, and Francesco Ruggieri. 2018. "Why Does Import Competition Favor Republicans?" SSRN Scholarly Paper ID 3147169. Rochester, NY: Social Science Research Network. https://papers.ssrn.com/abstract=3147169. (Cited 208n10, 208n12, 208n13.)

Chaney, Thomas. 2014. "The Network Structure of International Trade." *American Economic Review* 104 (11): 3600–3634. https://doi.org/10.1257/aer.104.11.3600. (Cited 97n9.)

Che, Yi, Yi Lu, Justin R. Pierce, Peter K. Schott, and Zhigang Tao. 2016. "Does Trade Liberalization with China Influence U.S. Elections?" Working Paper 22178. National Bureau of Economic Research. Cambridge, MA. https://doi.org/10.3386/w22178. (Cited 208n7.)

Chen, Frederick R., Jon C. W. Pevehouse, and Ryan M. Powers. 2019. "Great Expectations: The Democratic Advantage in Trade Attitudes." https://internationalpoliticaleconomysociety.org/sites/default/files/paper-uploads/2019-11-14-02_41_29-frederick.chenwisc.edu.pdf.

Chicago Council on Global Affairs. 2015, Feb. 1. "Chicago Council Survey Data." Chicago Council on Global Affairs. https://www.thechicagocouncil.org/publication/chicago-council-survey-data.

———. 2017, Sept. 26. "What Americans Think about America First." Chicago Council on Global Affairs. https://www.thechicagocouncil.org/publication/what-americans-think-about-america-first. (Cited 26n4, 209n17.)

———. 2018, Sept. 28. "America Engaged." Chicago Council on Global Affairs. https://www.thechicagocouncil.org/publication/lcc/america-engaged.

Christiansen, F. B., and V. Loeschcke. 1990. "Evolution and Competition." In *Population Biology: Ecological and Evolutionary Viewpoints*. Edited by K. Wöhrmann and S. K. Jain, 367–94. Berlin; Heidelberg: Springer Berlin Heidelberg. https://doi.org/10.1007/978-3-642-74474-7_13. (Cited 157n38.)

Cikara, Mina, Emile G. Bruneau, and Rebecca R. Saxe. 2011. "Us and Them: Intergroup Failures of Empathy." *Current Directions in Psychological Science* 20 (3): 149–53. (Cited 83n35.)

Cikara, Mina, Rachel A. Farnsworth, Lasana T. Harris, and Susan T. Fiske. 2010. "On the Wrong Side of the Trolley Track: Neural Correlates of Relative Social Valuation." *Social Cognitive and Affective Neuroscience* 5 (4): 404–13. (Cited 73n7.)

Citrin, Jack, Richard Johnston, and Matthew Wright. 2012. "Do Patriotism and Multiculturalism Collide? Competing Perspectives from Canada and the United States." *Canadian Journal of*

Political Science/Revue Canadienne de Science Politique 45 (3): 531–52. https://doi.org/10.1017/S0008423912000704. (Cited 155n32.)

Citrin, Jack, Amy E. Lerman, Michael Hughes Murakami, and Kathryn L. Pearson. 2007. "Testing Huntington: Is Hispanic Immigration a Threat to American Identity?" *Perspectives on Politics* 5 (1): 31–48. https://doi.org/10.1017/s1537592707070041. (Cited 126n18.)

Clifford, Stephanie. 2013, Nov. 30. "That 'Made in U.S.A.' Premium." https://www.nytimes.com/2013/12/01/business/that-made-in-usa-premium.html. (Cited 166n18.)

Cocco, Federica. 2016. "Most US Manufacturing Jobs Lost to Technology, Not Trade." *Financial Times*. https://www.ft.com/content/dec677c0-b7e6-11e6-ba85-95d1533d9a62. (Cited 22n58, 190n8.)

Cohen, J., Y. Tsfati, and T. Sheafer. 2008. "The Influence of Presumed Media Influence in Politics: Do Politicians' Perceptions of Media Power Matter?" *Public Opinion Quarterly* 72 (2): 331–44. https://doi.org/10.1093/poq/nfn014. (Cited 268n15.)

Committee of 100. 2009. "Still the 'Other'? Are Chinese and Asian Americans Still Seen as Perpetual Foreigners by the General Public?" 2009. https://committee100.typepad.com/committee_of_100_newslett/2009/04/still-the-other-are-chinese-and-asian-americans-still-seen-as-perpetual-foreigners-by-the-general-pu.html. (Cited 255n18.)

Cooper, Ryan. 2017, Dec., 28. "The Media Is Blinded by Its Obsession with Rural White Trump Voters." The Week. https://theweek.com/articles/745394/media-blinded-by-obsession-rural-white-trump-voters. (Cited 189n4.)

Cornell, Nicolas. 2020. "Competition Wrongs." *Yale L.J.* 129 (7). (Cited 158n42.)

Coyle, Diane. 2014. *GDP: A Brief but Affectionate History*. Rev. and expanded ed. Princeton: Princeton University Press. (Cited 7n24.)

Craig, Maureen A., and Jennifer A. Richeson. 2014a. "More Diverse yet Less Tolerant? How the Increasingly Diverse Racial Landscape Affects White Americans' Racial Attitudes." *Personality and Social Psychology Bulletin* 40 (6): 750–61. (Cited 231n18.)

———. 2014b. "On the Precipice of a 'Majority-Minority' America: Perceived Status Threat from the Racial Demographic Shift Affects White Americans' Political Ideology." *Psychological Science* 25 (6): 1189–1197. (Cited 231n18.)

Cummings, William K. 1989. "The American Perception of Japanese Education." *Comparative Education* 25 (3): 293–302. (Cited 255n16, 255n19.)

Danbold, Felix, and Yuen J. Huo. 2015. "No Longer 'All-American'? Whites' Defensive Reactions to Their Numerical Decline." *Social Psychological and Personality Science* 6 (2): 210–18. (Cited 231n18.)

Daily, The (New York Times podcast). 2019, May 16. https://www.nytimes.com/2019/05/16/podcasts/the-daily/trump-tariffs-china-trade-war.html (Cited 1n1, 4n7.)

Davenport, Lauren D. 2018. *Politics beyond Black and White*. New York: Cambridge University Press. (Cited 125n14.)

Dawsey, Josh. 2018, Jan. 12. "Trump Derides Protections for Immigrants from 'Shithole' Countries." *Washington Post*, sec. Politics. https://www.washingtonpost.com/politics/trump-attacks-protections-for-immigrants-from-shithole-countries-in-oval-office-meeting/2018/01/11/bfc0725c-f711-11e7-91af-31ac729add94_story.html. (Cited 122n47.)

DeBruine, Lisa M. 2002. "Facial Resemblance Enhances Trust." *Proceedings of the Royal Society of London. Series B: Biological Sciences* 269 (1498): 1307–12. https://doi.org/10.1098/rspb.2002.2034. (Cited 101n35, 101n36.)

DeLamater, John, Daniel Katz, and Herbert C. Kelman. 1969. "On the Nature of National Involvement: A Preliminary Study." *The Journal of Conflict Resolution* 13 (3): 320. (Cited 93n58.)

Dilliplane, Susanna, Seth K. Goldman, and Diana C. Mutz. 2013. "Televised Exposure to Politics: New Measures for a Fragmented Media Environment." *American Journal of Political Science* 57 (1): 236–48. https://doi.org/10.1111/j.1540-5907.2012.00600.x. (Cited 173n32.)

Di Tella, Rafael, and Dani Rodrik. 2020. Labour Market Shocks and the Demand for Trade Protection: Evidence from Online Surveys. *The Economic Journal* 130 (628): 1008–30. (Cited 212n28.)

Doms, Mark, and Norman Morin. 2004. "Consumer Sentiment, the Economy, and the News Media." Finance and Economics Discussion Series. Divisions of Research & Statistics and Monetary Affairs, Federal Reserve Board, Washington, D.C. https://www.federalreserve.gov/pubs/feds/2004/200451/200451pap.pdf. (Cited 163n6.)

Drew, Kevin. 2020, Jan. 15. "U.S. Suffers Greatest Global Decline in Trust." U.S. News. https://www.usnews.com/news/best-countries/articles/2020-01-15/us-trustworthiness-rating-dives-in-2020-best-countries-report. (Cited 71n34.)

Duch, Raymond M., Harvey D. Palmer, and Christopher J. Anderson. 2000. "Heterogeneity in Perceptions of National Economic Conditions." *American Journal of Political Science* 44 (4): 635–52. https://doi.org/10.2307/2669272. (Cited 173n34, 216n45.)

Duina, Francesco. 2010. *Winning: Reflections on an American Obsession*. Princeton: Princeton University Press. (Cited 12n37, 141n1.)

Dür, Andreas. 2015. "Interest Group Influence on Public Opinion: A Survey Experiment on the Transatlantic Trade and Investment Partnership." https://www.academia.edu/12125112/Interest_group_influence_on_public_opinion_A_survey_experiment_on_the_Transatlantic_Trade_and_Investment_Partnership. (Cited 247n3.)

Duriez, Bart, and Van Hiel, Alain. 2002. "The March of Modern Fascism. A Comparison of Social Dominance Orientation and Authoritarianism" (pdf). *Personality and Individual Differences* 32 (7): 1199–1213. (Cited 13n46.)

Economist. 2016, Nov. 19. "League of Nationalists." *The Economist*. http://www.economist.com/news/international/21710276-all-around-world-nationalists-are-gaining-ground-why-league-nationalists.

———. 2017a, March 27. "The New Nationalism." *The Economist*. http://www.economist.com/news/leaders/21710249-his-call-put-america-first-donald-trump-latest-recruit-dangerous.

———. 2017b, March 30. "The World Has Made Great Progress in Eradicating Extreme Poverty." www.economist.com/news/international/21719790-going-will-be-much-harder-now-world-has-made-great-progress (Cited 12n1.)

———. 2017c, April 1. "How Donald Trump Thinks about Trade." *The Economist*. http://www.economist.com/news/united-states/21709921-americas-next-president-wants-pull-out-existing-trade-deals-and-put-future-ones.

———. 2017d, April 1. "Is China Challenging the United States for Global Leadership?" *The Economist*. http://www.economist.com/news/china/21719828-xi-jinping-talks-china-solution-without-specifying-what-means-china-challenging.

———. 2019a, Jan. 5. "What to Expect from the Second Half of Donald Trump's First Term—The Trump Show, Season Two," *The Economist*. https://www.economist.com/leaders/2019/01/05/what-to-expect-from-the-second-half-of-donald-trumps-first-term.

———. 2019b, Feb. 7. "Canada in the Global Jungle." *The Economist*. https://www.economist.com/the-americas/2019/02/09/canada-in-the-global-jungle.

Edwards, George C. 2003. *On Deaf Ears: The Limits of the Bully Pulpit*. New Haven: Yale University Press. (Cited 65n21.)

Egan, Patrick J. 2015, March 11. "What Do Americans Think about Free Trade? Not Much." *Washington Post*, sec. Monkey Cage. https://www.washingtonpost.com/news/monkey-cage/wp/2015/05/11/what-do-americans-think-about-free-trade-not-much/. (Cited 25n1.)

Ehrlich, Sean D., and Eddie Hearn. 2014. "Does Compensating the Losers Increase Support for Trade? An Experimental Test of the Embedded Liberalism Thesis." *Foreign Policy Analysis* 10 (2): 149–64. https://doi.org/10.1111/fpa.12001. (Cited 211n25.)

Ehrlich, Sean, and Cherie Maestas. 2010. "Risk Orientation, Risk Exposure, and Policy Opinions: The Case of Free Trade." *Political Psychology* 31 (5): 657–84. https://doi.org/10.1111/j.1467-9221.2010.00774.x. (Cited 225n61.)

Elkins, Zachary, and Rui J.P. de Figueiredo. 2003. "Are Patriots Bigots? An Inquiry into the Vices of In-Group Pride." SSRN Scholarly Paper ID 1920318. Rochester, NY: Social Science Research Network. https://papers.ssrn.com/abstract=1920318. (Cited 124n27.)

Elkins, Zachary, and John Sides. 2007. "Can Institutions Build Unity in Multiethnic States?" *American Political Science Review* 101 (4): 693–708. https://doi.org/10.1017/S0003055407070505. (Cited 126n19, 126n20.)

Ellyat, Holly. 2020, June 20. "Europeans' Trust in Trump's America 'Is Gone' after Coronavirus Pandemic, Poll Finds." CNBC. https://www.cnbc.com/2020/06/29/europeans-trust-in-trumps-america-is-gone-after-pandemic-poll.html. (Cited 71n34.)

Emswiller, Tim, Kay Deaux, and Jerry E. Willits. 1971. "Similarity, Sex, and Requests for Small Favors." *Journal of Applied Social Psychology* 1 (3): 284–91. https://doi.org/10.1111/j.1559-1816.1971.tb00367.x. (Cited 101n31.)

Entman, Robert M. 2008, March. "Theorizing Mediated Public Diplomacy: The U.S. Case:" *The International Journal of Press/Politics*. https://doi.org/10.1177/1940161208314657. (Cited 247n4.)

Erikson, Robert. 2004. "Macro vs. Micro-Level Perspectives on Economic Voting: Is the Micro-Level Evidence Endogenously Induced?" ResearchGate. https://www.researchgate.net/publication/237505529_Macro_vs_Micro-Level_Perspectives_on_Economic_Voting_Is_the_Micro-Level_Evidence_Endogenously_Induced. (Cited 217n46.)

Erikson, Robert S., and Christopher Wlezien. 2012. "The Objective and Subjective Economy and the Presidential Vote." SSRN Scholarly Paper ID 2110791. Rochester, NY: Social Science Research Network. https://papers.ssrn.com/abstract=2110791. (Cited 137n36.)

Ettachfini, Leila, and Diana Tourjée,. 2017, Sept. 6. "At Starbucks, Men Open Up About the Stigma of Pumpkin Spice Lattes." https://broadly.vice.com/en_us/article/qvvy87/at-starbucks-men-open-up-about-the-stigma-of-pumpkin-spice-lattes.

Farley, Reynolds, Elaine L. Fielding, and Maria Krysan. 1997. "The Residential Preferences of Blacks and Whites: A Four-Metropolis Analysis." *Housing Policy Debate* 8 (4): 763–800. https://doi.org/10.1080/10511482.1997.9521278. (Cited 125n15.)

Feierabend, Ivo K., and Rosalind L. Feierabend. 1966. "Aggressive Behaviors within Polities, 1948–1962: A Cross-National Study 1." *Journal of Conflict Resolution* 10 (3): 249–71. (Cited 231n15.)

Feigenbaum, James J., and Andrew B. Hall. 2015. "How Legislators Respond to Localized Economic Shocks." *Journal of Politics* 77 (4): 1012–30. (Cited 213n31.)

Feldman, Stanley. 1982. "Economic Self-Interest and Political Behavior." *American Journal of Political Science* 26 (3): 446–66. https://doi.org/10.2307/2110937. (Cited 7n21.)

Feldman, Stanley, and Karen Stenner. 1997. "Perceived Threat and Authoritarianism." *Political Psychology* 18 (4): 741–70. https://doi.org/10.1111/0162-895X.00077. (Cited 14n50.)

Fetherstonhaugh, David, Paul Slovic, Stephen M. Johnson, and James Friedrich. 1997. "Insensitivity to the Value of Human Life: A Study of Psychophysical Numbing." *Journal of Risk and Uncertainty* 14 (3): 283–300. (Cited 181n44.)

Fogarty, Brian J. 2005. "Determining Economic News Coverage." *International Journal of Public Opinion Research* 17 (2): 149–72. https://doi.org/10.1093/ijpor/edh051. (Cited 163n5.)

Froman, Michael. 2017, October 16. NAFTA Renegotiation: Renewal or Expiration? Council on Foreign Relations Symposium. https://www.cfr.org/event/nafta-renegotiation-renewal-or-expiration. (Cited 47n32.)

Frank, Dana. 1999. *Buy American: The Untold Story of Economic Nationalism*. Boston: Beacon Press. (Cited 166n19, 168n21.)

———. 2002. "Demons in the Parking Lot: Auto Workers, Buy American Campaigns, and the 'Japanese Threat' in the 1980s." *Amerasia Journal* 28 (3): 33–50. https://doi.org/10.17953/amer.28.3.p74875252957n722. (Cited 168n22.)

Freeland, Chrystia. 2011, Jan. 4. "The Rise of the New Global Elite." *The Atlantic*. https://www.theatlantic.com/magazine/archive/2011/01/the-rise-of-the-new-global-elite/308343/. (Cited 74n10.)

Friesdorf, R., P. Conway, and B. Gawronski. 2015. "Gender Differences in Responses to Moral Dilemmas: A Process Dissociation Analysis." *Personality and Social Psychology Bulletin* 41: 696–713. doi:10.1177/0146167215575731. (Cited 73n5.)

Froman, Michael. 2017, Oct. 16. "NAFTA Renegotiation: Renewal or Expiration?" Council on Foreign Relations Symposium. https://www.cfr.org/event/nafta-renegotiation-renewal-or-expiration. (Cited 47n32.)

Fuller, Graham E. 2016, Sept. 15. "The Era of American Global Dominance Is Over." *Huffington Post* (blog). http://www.huffingtonpost.com/graham-e-fuller/america-global-dominance-over_b_12011012.html. (Cited 231n21.)

Funk, Carolyn L., and Patricia A. Garcia-Monet. 1997. "The Relationship Between Personal and National Concerns in Public Perceptions About the Economy:" *Political Research Quarterly*. https://doi.org/10.1177/106591299705000204. (Cited 173n34.)

Gabel, Matthew, and Kenneth Scheve. 2007. "Estimating the Effect of Elite Communications on Public Opinion Using Instrumental Variables." *American Journal of Political Science* 51(4): 1013–28. (Cited 65n22.)

Galician, Mary-Lou, and Norris D. Vestre. 1987. "Effects of 'Good News' and 'Bad News' on Newscast Image and Community Image." *Journalism Quarterly* 64: 399. (Cited 163n5.)

Gerber, Alan S., and Gregory A. Huber. 2009. "Partisanship, Political Control, and Economic Assessments." *American Journal of Political Science* 54 (1): 153–73. https://doi.org/10.1111/j.1540-5907.2009.00424.x. (Cited 217n46.)

Gidron, Noam, and Peter A. Hall. 2017. "The Politics of Social Status: Economic and Cultural Roots of the Populist Right." *The British Journal of Sociology* 68 (S1): S57–84. https://doi.org/10.1111/1468-4446.12319. (Cited 209n15, 230n13.)

Gidron, Noam, and Jonathan J.B. Mijs. 2019. "Do Changes in Material Circumstances Drive Support for Populist Radical Parties? Panel Data Evidence from the Netherlands during the Great Recession, 2007–2015." *European Sociological Review* 35 (5): 637–50. https://doi.org/10.1093/esr/jcz023. (Cited 208n8.)

Gilens, Martin. 1999. *Why Americans Hate Welfare: Race, Media, and the Politics of Antipoverty Policy*. Chicago: University of Chicago Press. (Cited 92n54.)

Gilens, Martin, and Naomi Murakawa. 2002. "Elite Cues and Political Decision Making." In *Political Decision-Making, Deliberation and Participation*. Research in micropolitics. Edited by Michael X. Delli Carpini, 15–49. Amsterdam: Jai. (Cited 65n22.)

Giuliano, Paola, Antonio Spilimbergo, and Giovanni Tonon. 2006. "Genetic, Cultural and Geographical Distances." SSRN Scholarly Paper ID 936741. Rochester, NY: Social Science Research Network. (Cited 97n8.)

Gleichgerrcht E, and L. Young. 2013. "Low Levels of Empathic Concern Predict Utilitarian Moral Judgment." *PLoS ONE* 8 (4): e60418. https://doi.org/10.1371/journal.pone.0060418. (Cited 73n6.)

Goidel, Kirby, Stephen Procopio, Dek Terrell, and H. Denis Wu. 2010. "Sources of Economic News and Economic Expectations." *American Politics Research* 38 (4): 759–77. https://doi.org/10.1177/1532673X09355671. (Cited 163n7.)

Goidel, Robert K., and Ronald E. Langley. 1995. "Media Coverage of the Economy and Aggregate Economic Evaluations: Uncovering Evidence of Indirect Media Effects." *Political Research Quarterly* 48 (2): 313–28. https://doi.org/10.2307/449071. (Cited 163n6, 173n34.)

Gokcekus, Omer, Jessica Henson, Dennis Nottebaum, and Anthony Wanis-St John. 2012. "Impediments to Trade across the Green Line in Cyprus: Classic Barriers and Mistrust." *Journal of Peace Research* 49 (6): 863–72. https://doi.org/10.1177/0022343312452286. (Cited 99n20.)

Goodman, Peter S. 2016, Sept. 28. "More Wealth, More Jobs, but Not for Everyone: What Fuels the Backlash on Trade." *New York Times*, sec. Business. https://www.nytimes.com/2016/09/29/business/economy/more-wealth-more-jobs-but-not-for-everyone-what-fuels-the-backlash-on-trade.html. (Cited 193n23.)

Gordon, Stephen. 2016, Oct. 31. "Stephen Gordon: Why Canada Has Avoided an Anti-Trade, Anti-Immigration Backlash." *National Post*. https://nationalpost.com/opinion/stephen-gordon-why-canada-has-avoided-an-anti-trade-anti-immigration-backlash. (Cited 156n36.)

Gowen, Annie. 2019, Nov. 9. "'I'm Gonna Lose Everything.'" *Washington Post*. https://www.washingtonpost.com/nation/2019/11/09/im-gonna-lose-everything/?arc404=true. (Cited 184n48.)

Green, Donald P., and Irene V. Blair. 1995. "Framing and the Price Elasticity of Private and Public Goods." *Journal of Consumer Psychology* 4 (1): 1–32. https://doi.org/10.1207/s15327663jcp0401_01 (Cited 152n24.).

Green, Donald Philip. 1992. "The Price Elasticity of Mass Preferences." *The American Political Science Review* 86 (1): 128–48. https://doi.org/10.2307/1964020. (Cited 152n23.)

Green, Donald Philip, and Ann Elizabeth Gerken. 1989. "Self-Interest and Public Opinion Toward Smoking Restrictions and Cigarette Taxes." *The Public Opinion Quarterly* 53 (1): 1–16. (Cited 4n5.)

Greene, Joshua D. 2008. "The Secret Joke of Kant's Soul." In *Moral Psychology*, Vol. 3: *The Neuroscience of Morality: Emotion, Brain Disorders, and Development*. Edited by Walter Sinnott-Armstrong, 35–80. Cambridge: MIT Press. (Cited 100n25.)

Gries, Peter Hays, H. Michael Crowson, and Todd Sandel. 2010. The Olympic Effect on American Attitudes towards China: Beyond Personality, Ideology, and Media Exposure. Journal of Contemporary China, Volume 19, Issue 64, Pages 213–231. (Cited 248n8.)

Groeling, Tim. 2013. "Media Bias by the Numbers: Challenges and Opportunities in the Empirical Study of Partisan News." *Annual Review of Political Science* 16 (1): 129–51. https://doi.org/10.1146/annurev-polisci-040811-115123. (Cited 163n4, 218n53.)

Gross, Kimberly. 2008. "Framing Persuasive Appeals: Episodic and Thematic Framing, Emotional Response, and Policy Opinion." *Political Psychology* 29 (2): 169–92. (Cited 181n46.)

Guisinger, Alexandra. 2009. "Determining Trade Policy: Do Voters Hold Politicians Accountable?" *International Organization* 63 (03): 533–557. (Cited 206n4.)

———. 2017. *American Opinion on Trade: Preferences without Politics*. New York: Oxford University Press. https://www.oxfordscholarship.com/view/10.1093/acprof:oso/9780190651824.001.0001/acprof-9780190651824. (Cited 53n4, 123n1, 124n5, 125n8, 164n8, 164n9, 164n10, 181n43, 203n1, 212n30, 247n2, 254n15.)

Guiso, Luigi, Paola Sapienza, and Luigi Zingales. 2009. "Cultural Biases in Economic Exchange?" *The Quarterly Journal of Economics* 124 (3): 1095–1131. https://doi.org/10.1162/qjec.2009.124.3.1095. (Cited 101n33.)

———. 2013. "Time Varying Risk Aversion." Cambridge, MA: National Bureau of Economic Research. (Cited 228n6, 228n8.)

Guo, Rongxing. 2004. "How Culture Influences Foreign Trade: Evidence from the U.S. and China." *The Journal of Socio-Economics* 33 (6): 785–812. (Cited 96n6.)

Haass, Richard. 2020, Sept./Oct.. "Present at the Disruption: How Trump Unmade U.S. Foreign Policy." *Foreign Affairs*. https://www.foreignaffairs.com/articles/united-states/2020-08-11/present-disruption. (Cited 265n8.)

Hagen, L.M. 2005. *Economic News, Economic Confidence, and the Business Cycle.* Colonia: Herbert von Halem. (Cited 163n5.)

Hai, Zuhad. 2019. "Automation and the Salience of Protectionism." Working Paper. https://internationalpoliticaleconomysociety.org/sites/default/files/paper-uploads/2019-11-15-03_01_24-zuhadhai@stanford.edu.pdf. (Cited 6n19, 200n35, 211n24.)

Haidt, Jonathan. 2017, March 27. "How People's Sensitivity to Threats Illuminates the Rise of Donald Trump." *Washington Post.* https://www.washingtonpost.com/news/monkey-cage/wp/2016/12/23/how-peoples-sensitivity-to-threats-illuminates-the-rise-of-donald-trump/. (Cited 14n49.)

Hainmueller, Jens, and Michael J. Hiscox. 2006. "Learning to Love Globalization: Education and Individual Attitudes toward International Trade." *International Organization* 60 (2): 469–98. (Cited 5n10, 42n23, 124n7, 241n42.)

Hallin, Daniel C. 1984. "The Media, the War in Vietnam, and Political Support: A Critique of the Thesis of an Oppositional Media." *The Journal of Politics* 46 (1): 2–24. https://doi.org/10.2307/2130432. (Cited 166n17, 187n52, 187n53.)

———. 1986. *The Uncensored War: The Media and the Vietnam: The Media and Vietnam.* New York: Oxford University Press.

Hameleers, Michael, Linda Bos, and Claes de Vreese. 2017, Aug. "'They Did It' The Effects of Emotionalized Blame Attribution in Populist Communication." *Communication Research* 44. https://doi.org/10.1177/0093650216644026. (Cited 190n11, 194n26.)

Han, Seunghee, Jennifer S. Lerner, and Dacher Keltner. 2007. "Feelings and Consumer Decision Making: The Appraisal-Tendency Framework." *Journal of Consumer Psychology* 17 (3): 158–68. https://doi.org/10.1016/S1057-7408(07)70023-2. (Cited 194n26.)

Harlow, Roxanna, and Lauren Dundes. 2004. "'United' We Stand: Responses to the September 11 Attacks in Black and White." *Sociological Perspectives* 47 (4): 439–64. https://doi.org/10.1525/sop.2004.47.4.439. (Cited 126n18.)

Harrington, David E. 1989. "Economic News on Television: The Determinants of Coverage." *Public Opinion Quarterly* 53 (1): 17–40. https://doi.org/10.1086/269139. (Cited 163n5.)

Harwood, John. 2019, Sept. 20. "Bipartisan Support for Free Trade Has Been Left behind as the 2020 Race Barrels Ahead." CNBC. https://www.cnbc.com/2019/09/20/republicans-and-democrats-oppose-free-trade-in-2020-white-house-race.html. (Cited 188n55.)

Hayward, R. David, and Markus Kemmelmeier. 2007. "How Competition Is Viewed Across Cultures: A Test of Four Theories." *Cross-Cultural Research* 41 (4): 364–95. https://doi.org/10.1177/1069397107306529. (Cited 157n39.)

Heider, Fritz. 1958. *The Psychology of Interpersonal Relations.* Hoboken, NJ: John Wiley & Sons Inc. https://doi.org/10.1037/10628-000. (Cited 192n14.)

Heinz, Matthias, and Johan Swinnen. 2015. "Media Slant in Economic News: A Factor 20." *Economics Letters* 132 (C): 18–20. (Cited 163n5.)

Helm, Brendan, Dina Smeltz, and Alexander Hitch. 2019, October 9. "Record Number of Americans Say International Trade Is Good for the US Economy." Chicago Council on Global Affairs. https://www.thechicagocouncil.org/publication/lcc/record-number-americans-say-international-trade-good-us-economy (Cited 60n13.)

Helpman, Elhanan, and Paul R. Krugman. 1985. *Market Structure and Foreign Trade: Increasing Returns, Imperfect Competition, and the International Economy.* Cambridge: MIT Press. (Cited 97n7.)

Herrmann, Richard K. 2017. "How Attachments to the Nation Shape Beliefs About the World: A Theory of Motivated Reasoning." *International Organization* 71 (S1): S61–84. https://doi.org/10.1017/S0020818316000382. (Cited 51n36.)

Herrmann, Richard K., Philip E. Tetlock, and Matthew N. Diascro. 2001. "How Americans Think About Trade: Reconciling Conflicts Among Money, Power, and Principles." *International Studies Quarterly* 45 (2): 191–218. https://doi.org/10.1111/0020-8833.00188. (Cited 16n51, 143n7.)

Hetherington, Marc J. 1996. "The Media's Role in Forming Voters' National Economic Evaluations in 1992." *American Journal of Political Science* 40 (2): 372–95. https://doi.org/10.2307/2111629. (Cited 163n7.)

———. 2006. *Why Trust Matters: Declining Political Trust and the Demise of American Liberalism.* Princeton, NJ: Princeton University Press.

Hetherington, Marc, and Elizabeth Suhay. 2011. "Authoritarianism, Threat, and Americans' Support for the War on Terror." *American Journal of Political Science* 55 (3): 546–60. https://doi.org/10.1111/j.1540-5907.2011.00514.x. (Cited 258n22.)

Hibbing, John R. 2017, May 27. "How People's Sensitivity to Threats Illuminates the Rise of Donald Trump." *Washington Post.* https://www.washingtonpost.com/news/monkey-cage/wp/2016/12/23/how-peoples-sensitivity-to-threats-illuminates-the-rise-of-donald-trump/. (Cited 14n50.)

Hicks, Michael J., and Srikant Devaraj. 2017. "The Myth and Reality of Manufacturing in America." Center for Business and Economic Research. Ball State University. Muncie, IN. (Cited 22n58, 190n7.)

Hiscox, Michael, and Brian Burgoon. 2004. "The Mysterious Case of Female Protectionism: Gender Bias in Attitudes Toward International Trade."

Hiscox, Michael J. 2006. "Through a Glass and Darkly: Attitudes Toward International Trade and the Curious Effects of Issue Framing." *International Organization* 60 (3): 755–80. https://doi.org/10.1017/S0020818306060255. (Cited 141n2, 196n31.)

Hoffman, Michael E. S. 2005. "Politico-Economic Determinants of American Trade Policy Attitudes." 0510017. International Trade. University Library of Munich, Germany. https://ideas.repec.org/p/wpa/wuwpit/0510017.html. (Cited 75n16.)

Hogg, Michael A., and Dominic Abrams. 1990. *Social Identity Theory: Constructive and Critical Advances.* New York: Prentice-Hall. (Cited 85n41.)

Hogg, Michael A., K. Fielding, and J. Darley. 2005. "Fringe Dwellers: Processes of Deviance and Marginalization in Groups." In *The Social Psychology of Inclusion and Exclusion.* Edited by Dominic Abrams, Michael A, Hogg, and Jose M, Marques, 191–210. New York: Psychology Press. https://espace.library.uq.edu.au/view/UQ:71972. (Cited 92n52.)

Hopkins, Daniel J., and Samantha Washington. 2019. "The Rise of Trump, the Fall of Prejudice? Tracking White Americans' Racial Attitudes 2008–2018 via a Panel Survey." https://papers.ssrn.com/sol3/papers.cfm?abstract_id=3378076. (Cited 232n29.)

Hourihan, Kathleen L., Aaron S. Benjamin, and Xiping Liu. 2012. "A Cross-Race Effect in Metamemory: Predictions of Face Recognition Are More Accurate for Members of Our Own Race." *Journal of Applied Research in Memory and Cognition* 1 (3): 158–62. https://doi.org/10.1016/j.jarmac.2012.06.004. (Cited 255n18.)

Houseman, Susan N. 2018. "The Decline of U.S. Manufacturing Employment—Automation and Trade." *Employment Research* 25 (2): 1–4. https://doi.org/10.17848/1075-8445.25(2)-1. (Cited 190n9.)

Huang, Zheping. 2015, Sept. 21. "Working for a Chinese Boss Is Great, Ordinary Americans Explain in This Slick New pro-China Video." Quartz. https://qz.com/506651/working-for-a-chinese-boss-is-great-ordinary-americans-explain-in-this-slick-new-pro-china-video/. (Cited 248n10.)

Huddy, Leonie. 2001. "From Social to Political Identity: A Critical Examination of Social Identity Theory." Political Psychology 22 (1): 127–56. https://doi.org/10.1111/0162-895X.00230 (Cited 76n23.)

Huddy, Leonie, and Stanley Feldman. 2011. "Americans Respond Politically to 9/11: Understanding the Impact of the Terrorist Attacks and Their Aftermath." *American Psychologist* 66 (6): 455–67. https://doi.org/10.1037/a0024894. (Cited 228n7, 228n9.)

Huddy, Leonie, and Nadia Khatib. 2007. "American Patriotism, National Identity, and Political Involvement." *American Journal of Political Science* 51 (1): 63–77. https://doi.org/10.1111/j.1540-5907.2007.00237.x. (Cited 75n17, 126n18.)

Hufbauer, Gary Clyde and Euijin Jung. 2020, August 5. "The High Taxpayer Cost of "Saving" US Jobs through "Made in America." PIIE. https://www.piie.com/blogs/trade-and-investment-policy-watch/high-taxpayer-cost-saving-us-jobs-through-made-america#:~:text=We%20calculate%20that%20the%20annual,economy%20to%20the%20procurement%20sector. (Cited 65n19.)

Hutchings, Vincent, Hanes Walton, Robert Mickey, and Ashley Jardina. 2011. "The Politics of Race: How Threat Cues and Group Position Can Activate White Identity." ResearchGate. https://www.researchgate.net/publication/241640951_The_Politics_of_Race_How_Threat_Cues_and_Group_Position_Can_Activate_White_Identity. (Cited 192n18.)

Iacoviello, Vincenzo, and Russell Spears. 2018. "'I Know You Expect Me to Favor My Ingroup': Reviving Tajfel's Original Hypothesis on the Generic Norm Explanation of Ingroup Favoritism." *Journal of Experimental Social Psychology* 76 (May): 88–99. https://doi.org/10.1016/j.jesp.2018.01.002. (Cited 93n61.)

Iino, Masako. 1994. "Asian Americans Under the Influence of 'Japan Bashing.'" *American Studies International* 32 (1): 17–30. (Cited 255n19.)

Inglehart, Ronald F., and Pippa Norris. 2016. "Trump, Brexit, and the Rise of Populism: Economic Have-Nots and Cultural Backlash." SSRN Scholarly Paper ID 2818659. Rochester, NY: Social Science Research Network. https://papers.ssrn.com/abstract=2818659. (Cited 208n11.)

Inglehart, Ronald, and Pippa Norris. 2017. "Trump and the Populist Authoritarian Parties: The Silent Revolution in Reverse." *Perspectives on Politics* 15 (2): 443–54. https://doi.org/10.1017/S1537592717000111. (Cited 208n9, 209n14, 230n14.)

Irwin, Douglas A. 1996. *Against the Tide: An Intellectual History of Free Trade*. Princeton: Princeton University Press. https://www.amazon.com/Against-Tide-Intellectual-History-Trade/dp/0691058962.

———. 2005. "The Rise of US Anti-Dumping Activity in Historical Perspective." *The World Economy* 28 (5): 651–68. https://doi.org/10.1111/j.1467-9701.2005.00698.x. (Cited 124n6.)

———. 2016, July. "The Truth About Trade." *Foreign Affairs*. https://www.foreignaffairs.com/articles/2016-06-13/truth-about-trade. (Cited 22n58, 271n22, 271n23.)

———. 2017. *Clashing over Commerce: A History of US Trade Policy*. Chicago: University of Chicago Press. (Cited 53n2, 190n10.)

———. 2019, Aug. 15. "The False Promise of Protectionism." *Foreign Affairs*. https://www.foreignaffairs.com/articles/united-states/2017-04-17/false-promise-protectionism. (Cited 47n33, 190n7.)

Isard, Walter. 1954. "Location Theory and Trade Theory: Short-Run Analysis." *The Quarterly Journal of Economics* 68 (2): 305–20. https://doi.org/10.2307/1884452. (Cited 96n2.)

Ishay, Micheline. 2004. *The History of Human Rights: From Ancient Times to the Globalization Era*. Berkeley: University of California Press. (Cited 93n60.)

Iyengar, Shanto. 1989. "How Citizens Think about National Issues: A Matter of Responsibility." *American Journal of Political Science* 33 (4): 878–900. https://doi.org/10.2307/2111113. (Cited 190n11.)

———. 1990. "Framing Responsibility for Political Issues: The Case of Poverty." *Political Behavior* 12 (1): 19–40. https://doi.org/10.1007/BF00992330. (Cited 190n11.)

———. 1991. *Is Anyone Responsible? How Television Frames Political Issues*. Chicago: University of Chicago Press. https://doi.org/10.7208/chicago/9780226388533.001.0001. (Cited 190n11.)

Jang, S. Mo. 2013. "Framing Responsibility in Climate Change Discourse: Ethnocentric Attribution Bias, Perceived Causes, and Policy Attitudes." *Journal of Environmental Psychology* 36 (December): 27–36. https://doi.org/10.1016/j.jenvp.2013.07.003. (Cited 192n19.)

Jardina, Ashley. 2019. *White Identity Politics*. Cambridge; New York: Cambridge University Press.

Jensen, J. Bradford, Dennis P. Quinn, and Stephen Weymouth. 2017. "Winners and Losers in International Trade: The Effects on US Presidential Voting." *International Organization* 71 (3): 423–57. https://doi.org/10.1017/S0020818317000194. (Cited 124n5, 211n26, 211n27.)

Jensen, Nathan M., and René Lindstädt. 2012. "Leaning Right and Learning From the Left: Diffusion of Corporate Tax Policy Across Borders." *Comparative Political Studies* 45 (3): 283–311. https://doi.org/10.1177/0010414011421313. (Cited 101n34.)

Johnson, Kirk. 2011, Sept. 11. "All-American, Floor to Roof? Not So Simple." *New York Times*, sec. U.S. https://www.nytimes.com/2011/09/05/us/05american.html. (Cited 166n16, 169n24.)

Johnston, Christopher D. 2013. "Dispositional Sources of Economic Protectionism." *Public Opinion Quarterly* 77 (2): 574–85. https://doi.org/10.1093/poq/nft004. (Cited 14n47, 74n13.)

Johnston, Richard, Keith Banting, Will Kymlicka, and Stuart Soroka. 2010. "National Identity and Support for the Welfare State." *Canadian Journal of Political Science/Revue Canadienne de Science Politique* 43 (2): 349–77. https://doi.org/10.1017/S0008423910000089. (Cited 154n28.)

Jones, Jonathan. 2018, Jan. 26. "Why Would Trump Turn down a Golden Toilet? Because He Already Has One." *The Guardian*. https://www.theguardian.com/artanddesign/2018/jan/26/why-would-trump-turn-down-golden-toilet-white-house-guggenheim-maurizio-cattelan-america. (Cited 60n13.)

Jost, John T., Christopher M. Federico, and Jaime L. Napier. 2009. "Political Ideology: Its Structure, Functions, and Elective Affinities." *Annual Review of Psychology* 60 (1): 307–37. https://doi.org/10.1146/annurev.psych.60.110707.163600.

Kagan, Robert. 2018a. *The Jungle Grows Back: America and Our Imperiled World*. New York: Knopf.

———. 2018b, Sept. 23. "'America First' Has Won." *New York Times*. https://www.nytimes.com/2018/09/23/opinion/trump-foreign-policy-america-first.html.

Kaltenthaler, Karl, and William J. Miller. 2013. "Social Psychology and Public Support for Trade Liberalization." *International Studies Quarterly* 57 (4): 784–90. https://doi.org/10.1111/isqu.12083. (Cited 102n37.)

Kaniss, Phyllis. 1991. *Making Local News*. Chicago: University of Chicago Press. (Cited 164n12, 165n15.)

Karabell, Zachary. 2014. *The Leading Indicators: A Short History of the Numbers That Rule Our World*. New York: Simon & Schuster. (Cited 7n24.)

Karlgaard, Rich. 2009, April 17. "Will Americans Turn Inward? (Study The 1970s)." *Forbes*. https://www.forbes.com/sites/digitalrules/2009/04/17/will-americans-turn-inward-study-the-1970s/#625e816e3917. (Cited 227n2.)

Karp, David. 2018, March 13. "Most of America's Fruit Is Now Imported. Is That a Bad Thing?" *The New York Times*, sec. Food. https://www.nytimes.com/2018/03/13/dining/fruit-vegetables-imports.html.

Kazemipur, Abdolmohammad. 2009. *Social Capital and Diversity: Some Lessons from Canada*. Bern: Peter Lang. (Cited 155n31.)

Kelley, Harold H., and John L. Michela. 1980. "Attribution Theory and Research." *Annual Review of Psychology* 31 (1): 457–501. https://doi.org/10.1146/annurev.ps.31.020180.002325. (Cited 192n14.)

Kenny, Charles. 2018, Nov. 9. "The Bogus Backlash to Globalization." *Foreign Affairs*. https://www.foreignaffairs.com/articles/united-states/2018-11-09/bogus-backlash-globalization. (Cited 265n6.)

Kenworthy, Lane, and Lindsay A. Owens. 2011. "The Surprisingly Weak Effect of Recessions on Public Opinion." In *The Great Recession*. Edited by David B. Grusky, Bruce Western, and Christopher Wimer, 196–219. New York: Russell Sage Foundation. (Cited 223n56.)

Kepplinger, Hans Mathias. 2002. "Mediatization of Politics: Theory and Data." *Journal of Communication* 52 (4): 972–86. https://doi.org/10.1111/j.1460-2466.2002.tb02584.x. (Cited 163n5.)

Kernell, Samuel H. 2007. *Going Public: New Strategies of Presidential Leadership*. Washington, D.C: CQ Press. (Cited 65n19, 187n54.)

Kiersz, Andy. 2015. "16 Charts That Illustrate America's Global Dominance." Business Insider. May 20, 2017. http://www.businessinsider.com/charts-that-illustrates-americas-global-dominance-2015-7. (Cited 231n22.)

Kiewiet, Roderick. 1983. *Macroeconomics and Micropolitics : The Electoral Effects of Economic Issues*. Chicago; London: University of Chicago Press. (Cited 7n20.)

Kim, Eunji, Rasmus Pedersen, and Diana C. Mutz. 2016. "What Do Americans Talk About When They Talk About Income Inequality?" SSRN Scholarly Paper ID 2805330. Rochester, NY: Social Science Research Network. https://papers.ssrn.com/abstract=2805330.

Kim, Sung Eun. 2018. "Media Bias against Foreign Firms as a Veiled Trade Barrier: Evidence from Chinese Newspapers." *American Political Science Review* 112 (4): 954–70. (Cited 164n11, 165n13.)

Kinder, Donald R., Gordon S. Adams, and Paul W. Gronke. 1989. "Economics and Politics in the 1984 American Presidential Election." *American Journal of Political Science* 33 (2): 491. https://doi.org/10.2307/2111157.

Kinder, Donald R., and Cindy D. Kam. 2010. *Us Against Them: Ethnocentric Foundations of American Opinion*. Chicago:: University of Chicago Press. (Cited 76n20, 125n13.)

Kinder, Donald R., and D. Roderick Kiewiet. 1981. "Sociotropic Politics: The American Case." *British Journal of Political Science* 11 (2): 129–61. (Cited 6n13.)

Kinder, Donald R., and Walter R. Jr. Mebane. 1983. "Politics and Economics in Everyday Life." In *The Political Process and Economic Change. Edited by Kristi R. Monroe, 141–80. New York: Agathon Press.* (Cited 76n25.)

Kinder, Donald R., and Nicholas Winter. 2001. "Exploring the Racial Divide: Blacks, Whites, and Opinion on National Policy." *American Journal of Political Science* 45 (2): 439. https://doi.org/10.2307/2669351.

King, Michael. 1977. "Assimilation and Contrast of Presidential Candidates' Issue Positions, 1972." *Public Opinion Quarterly* 41 (4): 515–22. https://doi.org/10.1086/268411. (Cited 237n32.)

Kogut, Tehila, and Ilana Ritov. 2005. "The 'Identified Victim' Effect: An Identified Group, or Just a Single Individual?" *Journal of Behavioral Decision Making* 18 (3): 157–67. https://doi.org/10.1002/bdm.492. (Cited 181n44.)

Kucik, Jeffrey, and Ashley Moraguez. 2017. "Balancing Multiple Goals: Analyzing Votes on Free Trade Agreements in the U.S. House of Representatives." *Congress & the Presidency* 44 (1): 29–54. https://doi.org/10.1080/07343469.2016.1261964. (Cited 53n3.)

Kuo, Iris. 2016, Feb. 2. "Why Do My Co-Workers Keep Confusing Me with Other People? Because I'm Asian." *Washington Post*. https://www.washingtonpost.com/posteverything/wp/2016/02/12/why-do-my-co-workers-keep-confusing-me-with-other-people-im-asian/. (Cited 255n18.)

Kuo, Jason, and Megumi Naoi. 2015. "Individual Attitudes." In *The Oxford Handbook of the Political Economy of International Trade*. Edited by Lisa Martin, 99–181. Oxford: Oxford University Press. (Cited 5n10.)

Kupchan, Charles A. 2012, March 20. "The Decline of the West: Why America Must Prepare for the End of Dominance." *The Atlantic*. https://www.theatlantic.com/international/archive/2012/03/the-decline-of-the-west-why-america-must-prepare-for-the-end-of-dominance/254779/. (Cited 231n21.)

Kymlicka, Will. 2010. "The Rise and Fall of Multiculturalism? New Debates on Inclusion and Accommodation in Diverse Societies." *International Social Science Journal* 61 (199): 97–112. https://doi.org/10.1111/j.1468-2451.2010.01750.x. (Cited 155n33, 156n34.)

Kyvig, David E. 1995. "Refining or Resisting Modern Government: The Balanced Budget Amendment to the U.S. Constitution." *Akron Law Review* 28 (2): article 1. (Cited 8n25.)

Laczko, Frank. 2007. "Enhancing Data Collection and Research on Trafficking in Persons." In *Measuring Human Trafficking*. Edited by Ernesto U. Savona and Sonia Stefanizzi, 37–44. New York: Springer New York. https://doi.org/10.1007/0-387-68044-6_5. (Cited 156n35.)

LaFrance, Marianne. 1985. "Postural Mirroring and Intergroup Relations." *Personality and Social Psychology Bulletin* 11 (2): 207–17. https://doi.org/10.1177/0146167285112008. (Cited 101n30.)

Lake, David A. 1992. "Powerful Pacifists: Democratic States and War." *American Political Science Review* 86 (1): 24–37. https://doi.org/10.2307/1964013. (Cited 36n11.)

Lakner, Christoph, and Branko Milanovic. 2016. "Global Income Distribution: From the Fall of the Berlin Wall to the Great Recession." *The World Bank Economic Review* 30 (2): 203–32. https://doi.org/10.1093/wber/lhv039. (Cited 180n41.)

Lamla, Michael J., and Sarah M. Lein. 2008. "The Role of Media for Consumers' Inflation Expectation Formation." *KOF Working Papers* 201. https://www.research-collection.ethz.ch/handle/20.500.11850/124083. (Cited 163n6.)

Lan, Xiaohuan, and Ben Li. 2012. "Nationalism and International Trade: Theory and Evidence." Munich Personal RePEc Archive. https://mpra.ub.uni-muenchen.de/36412/. (Cited 75n16.)

Langer, Ellen J. 1975. "The Illusion of Control." *Journal of Personality and Social Psychology* 32 (2): 311–28. https://doi.org/10.1037/0022-3514.32.2.311. (Cited 201n38.)

Lantz, Garold, and Sandra Loeb. 1996. "Country of Origin and Ethnocentrism: An Analysis of Canadian and American Preferences Using Social Identity Theory." *ACR North American Advances* NA-23. http://acrwebsite.org/volumes/7985/volumes/v23/NA-23. (Cited 99n19, 130n22.)

Larcinese, Valentino, Riccardo Puglisi, and James M. Snyder. 2011. "Partisan Bias in Economic News: Evidence on the Agenda-Setting Behavior of U.S. Newspapers." *Journal of Public Economics* 95 (9): 1178–89. (Cited 163n4, 218n53.)

Larson, Jane Leugn. 2009. "Still the 'Other'? Are Chinese and Asian Americans Still Seen as Perpetual Foreigners by the General Public?" Committee of 100. https://committee100.typepad.com/committee_of_100_newslett/2009/04/still-the-other-are-chinese-and-asian-americans-still-seen-as-perpetual-foreigners-by-the-general-pu.html. (Cited 255n18.)

Leamer, Edward E. 1984. *Sources of International Comparative Advantage*. Cambridge: MIT Press. https://mitpress.mit.edu/books/sources-international-comparative-advantage. (Cited 124n4.)

Leiser, David, and Ronen Aroch. 2009. "Lay Understanding of Macroeconomic Causation: The Good-Begets-Good Heuristic." *Applied Psychology* 58 (July): 370–84. https://doi.org/10.1111/j.1464-0597.2009.00396.x. (Cited 172n30.)

Lenz, Gabriel S. 2011. "Understanding and Curing Myopic Voting." SSRN Scholarly Paper. Rochester, NY: Social Science Research Network. https://papers.ssrn.com/abstract=1901607.

———. 2012. *Follow the Leader? How Voters Respond to Politicians' Policies and Performance*. Chicago; London: University of Chicago Press. (Cited 65n20.)

Lerner, Jennifer S., and Dacher Keltner. 2000. "Beyond Valence: Toward a Model of Emotion-Specific Influences on Judgement and Choice." *Cognition & Emotion* 14 (4): 473–93. https://doi.org/10.1080/026999300402763. (Cited 227n1.)

———. 2001. "Fear, Anger, and Risk." *Journal of Personality and Social Psychology* 81 (1): 146–59. https://doi.org/10.1037/0022-3514.81.1.146. (Cited 227n1.)

Lewis-Beck, Michael S., Nicholas F. Martini, and D. Roderick Kiewiet. 2013. "The Nature of Economic Perceptions in Mass Publics." *Electoral Studies* 32 (3): 524–28. (Cited 217n47.)

Li, Eric X. 2016, Dec. 9. "The End of Globalism." *Foreign Affairs*. https://www.foreignaffairs.com/articles/united-states/2016-12-09/end-globalism. (Cited 265n7.)

Liberman, Nira, Yaacov Trope, and Elena Stephan. 2007. "Psychological Distance." In *Social Psychology: Handbook of Basic Principles*. 2nd ed. Edited by Arie W. Kruglanski and E. Tory Higgins, 353–81. New York: The Guilford Press. (Cited 142n47.)

Lilienfeld, Scott O., and Robert D. Latzman. 2014. "Threat Bias, Not Negativity Bias, Underpins Differences in Political Ideology." *Behavioral and Brain Sciences* 37 (3): 318–19. https://doi.org/10.1017/S0140525X1300263X. (Cited 262n31.)

Lillis, Charles M., and Chem L. Narayana. 1974. "Analysis of 'Made in' Product Images—An Exploratory Study." *Journal of International Business Studies* 5 (1): 119–27. https://doi.org/10.1057/palgrave.jibs.8490816. (Cited 99n17.)

Linder, Staffan Burenstam. 1961. *An Essay on Trade and Transformation*. Stockholm; New York: Almqvist & Wiksell; J. Wiley. (Cited 96n1.)

Lindsay, James. 2009, Dec. 4. "Poll Shows US Isolationist Sentiment Growing." Voice of America. Accessed February 1, 2020. https://www.voanews.com/archive/poll-shows-us-isolationist-sentiment-growing. (Cited 229n11.)

Lipin, Michael. 2014, Sept. 1. "Chinese Americans: Discrimination in US Still a Problem, but Improving." Voice of America. https://www.voanews.com/east-asia-pacific/chinese-americans-discrimination-us-still-problem-improving. (Cited 255n18.)

Lippmann, Walter. 1922. "The World Outside and the Pictures in Our Heads.," In Walter Lippmann, *Public Opinion*, 3–32. New York. MacMillan Co. https://doi.org/10.1037/14847-001. (Cited 174n35.)

Lipset, Seymour Martin. 1989. *Continental Divide: The Values and Institutions of the United States and Canada*. Canadian-American Committee. (Cited 141n3, 141n4.)

Liptak, Kevin. 2020, Aug. 11. "Trump Says Americans Will Have to Learn Chinese If Biden Wins But Offers Little Condemnation of Beijing. CNN.com. https://www.cnn.com/2020/08/11/politics/trump-china-biden-learn-chinese/index.html. (Cited 12n43.)

Liu, James H., Li-Li Huang, and Catherine McFedries. 2008. "Cross-Sectional and Longitudinal Differences in Social Dominance Orientation and Right Wing Authoritarianism as a Function of Political Power and Societal Change." *Asian Journal of Social Psychology* 11 (2): 116–26. https://doi.org/10.1111/j.1467-839X.2008.00249.x. (Cited 232n27.)

Locke, Kenneth D., and Leonard M. Horowitz. 1990. "Satisfaction in Interpersonal Interactions as a Function of Similarity in Level of Dysphoria." *Journal of Personality and Social Psychology* 58 (5): 823–31. https://doi.org/10.1037/0022-3514.58.5.823. (Cited 101n30.)

Loewenstein, George, and Deborah A. Small. 2007. "The Scarecrow and the Tin Man: The Vicissitudes of Human Sympathy and Caring." *Review of General Psychology* 11 (2): 112–26. https://doi.org/10.1037/1089-2680.11.2.112. (Cited 181n44, 181n45.)

Los Angeles Times/Bloomberg Poll. 2008. Based on telephone interviews with a national adult sample of 1,541 adults. [USLAT.012408.R47] Data provided by The Roper Center for Public Opinion Research, University of Connecticut. (Cited 223n56.)

Los, Bart, Philip McCann, John Springford, and Mark Thissen. 2017. "The Mismatch between Local Voting and the Local Economic Consequences of Brexit." *Regional Studies* 51 (5): 786–99. https://doi.org/10.1080/00343404.2017.1287350.

Loughlin, Sean. 2003, March 12. "House Cafeterias Change Names for 'French' Fries and 'French' Toast. http://www.cnn.com/2003/ALLPOLITICS/03/11/sprj.irq.fries/. (Cited 99n21.)

Lyman, Eric J. 2018, Feb. 22. "America's Obsession with Competition Is Making Our Lives Worse." *Pacific Standard*. https://psmag.com/economics/american-exceptionalism-and-our-eroding-quality-of-life. (Cited 74n12.)

Lyon, Don, and Paul Slovic. 1976. "Dominance of Accuracy Information and Neglect of Base Rates in Probability Estimation." *Acta Psychologica* 40 (4): 287–98. https://doi.org/10.1016/0001-6918(76)90032-9. (Cited 181n44.)

Major, Brenda, Alison Blodorn, and Gregory Major Blascovich. 2016. "The Threat of Increasing Diversity: Why Many White Americans Support Trump in the 2016 Presidential Election." *Group Processes & Intergroup Relations*, 1–10. (Cited 231n18.)

Malhotra, Neil, Yotam Margalit, and Cecilia Hyunjung Mo. 2013. "Economic Explanations for Opposition to Immigration: Distinguishing between Prevalence and Conditional Impact." *American Journal of Political Science* 57 (2): 391–410. https://doi.org/10.1111/ajps.12012. (Cited 4n5.)

Malmendier, Ulrike, and Stefan Nagel. 2011. "Depression Babies: Do Macroeconomic Experiences Affect Risk Taking?." *The Quarterly Journal of Economics* 126 (1): 373–416. (Cited 228n5.)

Mankiw, N. Gregory. 2018, Oct. 5. Surprising Truths About Trade Deficits. *New York Times*. (Cited 186n50.)

Mansfield, Edward D., Helen V. Milner, and B. Peter Rosendorff. 2002. "Why Democracies Cooperate More: Electoral Control and International Trade Agreements." *International Organization* 56 (3): 477–513. https://doi.org/10.1162/002081802760199863. (Cited 96n3.)

Mansfield, Edward D., and Diana C. Mutz. 2006. "What Determines Perceptions of Trade's Influence on the U.S. Economy?" Paper presented at the 102nd Annual Meeting of the American Political Science Association, August–September, Philadelphia. (Cited 169n25.)

———. 2009. "Support for Free Trade: Self-Interest, Sociotropic Politics, and Out-Group Anxiety." *International Organization* 63 (03): 425–57. (Cited 2n2, 5n10, 6n14, 7n23, 18n54, 42n24, 69n32, 74n14, 122n48, 123n2, 125n9, 125n10, 146n12, 213n33, 241n41, 241n43, 242n50.)

———. 2013. "US versus Them: Mass Attitudes toward Offshore Outsourcing." *World Politics* 65 (04): 571–608. (Cited 192n15.)

Mansfield, Edward D., Diana C. Mutz, and Devon Brackbill. 2019. "Effects of the Great Recession on American Attitudes Toward Trade." *British Journal of Political Science* 49 (1): 37–58. https://doi.org/10.1017/S0007123416000405.

Mansfield, Edward D., Diana C. Mutz, and Laura R. Silver. 2014. "Men, Women, Trade, and Free Markets." *International Studies Quarterly* 59 (2): 303–15. https://doi.org/10.1111/isqu.12170.

Margalit, Yotam. 2011. "Costly Jobs: Trade-Related Layoffs, Government Compensation, and Voting in U.S. Elections." *American Political Science Review* 105 (1): 166–88. https://doi.org/10.1017/S000305541000050X. (Cited 210n22, 211n23.)

———. 2012. "Lost in Globalization: International Economic Integration and the Sources of Popular Discontent." *International Studies Quarterly* 56 (3): 484–500. (Cited 14n48, 74n15, 75n16, 76n19, 246n1.)

Martin, Elizabeth, and Diana Mutz. 2019. "Trade and Immigration: Failures of Opinion Leadership in the Trump Presidency." Prepared for presentation at the American Political Science Association 2019 Annual Meeting, "Populism and Privilege," Washington, DC. (Cited 65n29, 209n16, 210n18, 265n4, 268n16.)

Mayda, Anna Maria, and Dani Rodrik. 2005. "Why Are Some People (and Countries) More Protectionist than Others?" *European Economic Review* 49 (6): 1393–1430. https://citeseerx.ist.psu.edu/viewdoc/download?doi=10.1.1.396.1224&rep=rep1&type=pdf. (Cited 4n9, 14n48, 16n51, 74n15, 75n16, 124n4, 154n26, 157n40.)

McBride, James, and Andrew Chatzky. 2019. "The U.S. Trade Deficit: How Much Does It Matter?" Council on Foreign Relations. March 8. https://www.cfr.org/backgrounder/us-trade-deficit-how-much-does-it-matter. (Cited 46n31.)

McDonald, Michael D., and Ian Budge. 2005. *Elections, Parties, Democracy: Conferring the Median Mandate*. Oxford University Press. (Cited 217n51.)

McFarland, Sam, Derek Brown, and Matthew Webb. 2013. "Identification With All Humanity as a Moral Concept and Psychological Construct." *Current Directions in Psychological Science* 22 (3): 194–98. https://doi.org/10.1177/0963721412471346. (Cited 131n25.)

McNamara, Timothy P. 1986. "Mental Representations of Spatial Relations." *Cognitive Psychology* 18 (1): 87–121. https://doi.org/10.1016/0010-0285(86)90016-2. (Cited 97n11.)

Merolla, Jennifer, Laura B. Stephenson, Carole J. Wilson, and Elizabeth J. Zechmeister. 2005. "Globalization, Globalización, Globalisation: Public Opinion and NAFTA." *Law and Business Review of the Americas* 11 (3–4): 573–96. (Cited 75n16.)

Messick, David M., and Roderick M. Kramer. 2001. "Trust as a Form of Shallow Morality." In *Trust in Society*. Edited by Karen Cook, 89–118. Russell Sage Foundation Series on Trust. New York: Russell Sage Foundation. (Cited 101n29.)

Milanovic, Branko. 2012. *The Haves and the Have-Nots: A Brief and Idiosyncratic History of Global Inequality*. Reprint edition. New York: Basic Books. (Cited xiin1, 159n43.)

———. 2016. *Global Inequality: A New Approach for the Age of Globalization*. Cambridge: Belknap Press: An Imprint of Harvard University Press. (Cited 180n41.)

Miller, Claire Cain. 2016, Dec. 21. "The Long-Term Jobs Killer Is Not China. It's Automation." New York Times. https://www.nytimes.com/2016/12/21/upshot/the-long-term-jobs-killer-is-not-china-its-automation.html?searchResultPosition=3. (Cited 190n8.)

Miller, D.T., and R.K. Ratner. 1998. "The Disparity between the Actual and Assumed Power of Self-Interest." *Journal of Personality and Social Psychology* 74 (1): 53–62. (Cited 4n8, 38n15.)

Miller, David. 2005. "Reasonable Partiality towards Compatriots." *Ethical Theory and Moral Practice* 8 (1/2): 63–81. (Cited 92n51.)

Milner, Helen V. 1999. "The Political Economy of International Trade." *Annual Review of Political Science* 2 (1): 91–114. https://doi.org/10.1146/annurev.polisci.2.1.91. (Cited 96n4.)

Milner, Helen V., and Benjamin Judkins. 2004. "Partisanship, Trade Policy, and Globalization: Is There a Left–Right Divide on Trade Policy?" *International Studies Quarterly* 48 (1): 95–119. https://doi.org/10.1111/j.0020-8833.2004.00293.x. (Cited 52n1.)

Milord, Joseph. 2018, Feb. 2. "Deflategate Is Still The Greatest NFL Controversy No One Can Agree On." Elite Daily. February 2, 2018. https://www.elitedaily.com/p/what-was-deflategate-a-refresher-of-the-patriots-greatest-controversy-8091290.

Morisi, Davide, John T. Jost, and Vishal Singh. 2019. "An Asymmetrical 'President-in-Power' Effect." *American Political Science Review* 113 (2): 614–20. https://doi.org/10.1017/S0003055418000850. (Cited 59n10, 63n17.)

Morris, Narrelle. `2011. *Japan-Bashing : Anti-Japanism since the 1980s*. New York: Routledge. https://doi.org/10.4324/9780203851654. (Cited 155n16, 155n19.)

Morrison, Kimberly Rios, Nathanael J. Fast, and Oscar Ybarra. 2009. "Group Status, Perceptions of Threat, and Support for Social Inequality." *Journal of Experimental Social Psychology* 45 (1): 204–10. https://doi.org/10.1016/j.jesp.2008.09.004.

Morrison, Kimberly Rios, and Oscar Ybarra. 2008. "The Effects of Realistic Threat and Group Identification on Social Dominance Orientation." *Journal of Experimental Social Psychology* 44 (1): 156–63. https://doi.org/10.1016/j.jesp.2006.12.006. (Cited 232n27.)

Mughan, Anthony, and Dean Lacy. 2002. "Economic Performance, Job Insecurity and Electoral Choice." *British Journal of Political Science* 32 (3): 513–33. https://doi.org/10.1017/S0007123402000212. (Cited 206n6.)

Mullainathan, Sendhil, and Andrei Shleifer. 2002. "Media Bias." Harvard Institute Research Working Paper No. 1981; MIT Department of Economics Working Paper No. 02–33.

———. 2005. "The Market for News." *American Economic Review* 95 (1): 1031–53. (Cited 163n3.)

Muro, Mark, and Siddharth Kulkarni. 2016, March 15. "Voter Anger Explained—in One Chart." Brookings Institution. *Brookings* (blog). https://www.brookings.edu/blog/the-avenue/2016/03/15/voter-anger-explained-in-one-chart/. (Cited 190n5.)

Mutz, Diana C. 1998. *Impersonal Influence: How Perceptions of Mass Collectives Affect Political Attitudes*. Cambridge: Cambridge University Press. (Cited 162n1, 173n34.)

———. 2017. "Changing Party Alignments in American Attitudes Toward Trade: Reflections on the Past, Implications for the Future." http://iscap.upenn.edu/studies/changing-party-alignments-american-attitudes-toward-trade-reflections-past-implications.———. 2018. "Status Threat, Not Economic Hardship, Explains the 2016 Presidential Vote." *Proceedings of the National Academy of Sciences* 115 (19): E4330–39. (Cited 137n35.)

———.2021. "(Mis)Attributing the Causes of American Job Loss: The Consequences of Getting It Wrong." *Public Opinion Quarterly*, forthcoming. https://doi.org/10.1073/pnas.1718155115. (Cited 194n25, 195n29, 197n32,197n34.)

Mutz, Diana C., and Eunji Kim. (2016, Sept.). "The Implications of Partisan Media for Economic Perceptions" Paper presented at the annual meeting of the American Political Science Association. Philadelphia. 1–4 September 2016,. (Cited 131n24, 218n53.)

———. 2017. "The Impact of In-Group Favoritism on Trade Preferences." *International Organization* 71 (4): 827–50. https://doi.org/10.1017/S0020818317000327. (Cited 73n8, 76n24, 77n28, 78n29, 78n30, 80n31, 82n33, 87n47, 122n48, 125n9, 242n51.)

Mutz, Diana C., Edward Mansfield, and Eunji Kim. 2021. The Racialization of International Trade. *Political Psychology.* (Cited 194n25, 195n29, 197n32,197n34.)

Mutz, Diana C., and Jeffery J. Mondak. 1997. "Dimensions of Sociotropic Behavior: Group-Based Judgments of Fairness and Well-Being." *American Journal of Political Science* 41 (1): 284–308.

Mutz, Diana C., and Jahnavi S. Rao. 2018. "The Real Reason Liberals Drink Lattes." *PS: Political Science & Politics* 51 (4): 762–67. https://doi.org/10.1017/S1049096518000574. (Cited 210n18, 212n29, 238n37, 238n38, 267n12.)

Nadeau, Richard, Richard G. Niemi, and Timothy Amato. 2000. "Elite Economic Forecasts, Economic News, Mass Economic Expectations, and Voting Intentions in Great Britain." *European Journal of Political Research* 38 (1): 135–70. https://doi.org/10.1023/A:1007071801646. (Cited 163n5.)

Nadeau, Richard, Richard G. Niemi, David P. Fan, and Timothy Amato. 1999. "Elite Economic Forecasts, Economic News, Mass Economic Judgments, and Presidential Approval." *The Journal of Politics* 61 (1): 109–35. https://doi.org/10.2307/2647777. (Cited 163n5, 173n34, 216n44.)

Nagashima, Akira. 1970. "A Comparison of Japanese and U.S. Attitudes toward Foreign Products." *Journal of Marketing* 34 (1): 68–74. https://doi.org/10.1177/002224297003400115. (Cited 99n17.)

———. 1977. "A Comparative 'Made in' Product Image Survey among Japanese Businessmen." *Journal of Marketing* 41 (3): 95–100. https://doi.org/10.2307/1250943. (Cited 99n17.)

National Conference on Citizenship. 2009. "Americans Are Turning Inward and Cutting Back Civic Engagement in Tough Economic Times." America's Civic Health Index: Civic Health in Hard Times. National Conference on Citizenship. https://ncoc.org/wp-content/uploads/2015/04/2009AmericasCHI.pdf.

Newcomb, Theodore M. 1961. "The Acquaintance Process as a Prototype of Human Interaction." In *The Acquaintance Process*, 259–61. New York: Holt, Rinehart & Winston. https://doi.org/10.1037/13156-015. (Cited 100n28.)

Nguyen, Quynh, and Thomas Bernauer. 2014. "Does Social Trust Increase Support for Free Trade? Evidence from a Field Survey Experiment in Vietnam." *World Trade Institute Working Paper.* https://www.wti.org/research/publications/743/does-social-trust-increase-support-for-free-trade-evidence-from-a-field-survey-experiment-in-vietnam/. (Cited 102n38.)

———. 2019. "Does Social Trust Affect Public Support for International Trade? Insights from an Experiment in Vietnam." *Political Studies* 67 (2): 440–58. https://doi.org/10.1177/0032321718773560.

Nisbett, Richard E., and Lee Ross. 1980. *Human Inference: Strategies and Shortcomings of Social Judgment.* Englewood Cliffs, NJ: Prentice-Hall. (Cited 207n37.)

Noland, Marcus. 2005. "Affinity and International Trade." *SSRN Electronic Journal.* https://doi.org/10.2139/ssrn.739884. (Cited 100n26.)

———. 2019. "Protectionism under Trump: The China Shock, Intolerance, and the 'First White President.'" Working Paper 19-10. PIIE. https://www.piie.com/publications/working-papers/protectionism-under-trump-china-shock-intolerance-and-first-white. (Cited 262n32.)

Nordström, Kjell A. and Jan-Erik Vahlne, 1994. "*Is the Globe Shrinking: Psychic Distance and the Establishment of Swedish Sales Subsidiaries during the Last 100 Years.*" In *International Trade: Regional and Global Issues*. Edited by M. Landeck. New York: St. Martin's Press.

Norton, Michael I., and Samuel R. Sommers. 2011. "Whites See Racism as a Zero-Sum Game That They Are Now Losing." *Perspectives on Psychological Science* 6 (3): 215–18. https://doi.org/10.1177/1745691611406922. (Cited 231n20.)

Nowak, Andrzej, Robin R. Vallacher, and Mandy E. Miller. 2003. "Social Influence and Group Dynamics." In *Handbook of Psychology*. Edited by Irving B. Weiner, 383–417. Hoboken, NJ: American Cancer Society. https://doi.org/10.1002/0471264385.wei0516. (Cited 100n27.)

Nye, Jr., Joseph S. 2008. "Public Diplomacy and Soft Power." *The Annals of the American Academy of Political and Social Science* 616 (1): 94–109. https://doi.org/10.1177/0002716207311699. (Cited 247n4.)

O'Grady, Shawna, and Henry W. Lane. 1996. "The Psychic Distance Paradox." *Journal of International Business Studies* 27 (2): 309–33. (Cited 98n14, 99n16.)

O'Hanlon, Michael. 2018, Dec. 2. "The New 'Buy American' Movement." The National Interest. https://nationalinterest.org/feature/new-buy-american-movement-37567. (Cited 168n20.)

Opotow, Susan. 1990. "Moral Exclusion and Injustice: An Introduction." *Journal of Social Issues* 46 (1): 1–20. https://doi.org/10.1111/j.1540-4560.1990.tb00268.x. (Cited 83n37.)

O'Rourke, Kevin H., and Richard Sinnott. 2005. "The Determinants of Individual Attitudes Towards Immigration." *European Journal of Political Economy*, 838–861.

O'Rourke, Kevin H., Richard Sinnott, J. David Richardson, and Dani Rodrik. 2001. "The Determinants of Individual Trade Policy Preferences: International Survey Evidence." *Brookings Trade Forum*, 157–206. (Cited 18n53, 69n32, 154n26, 242n49.)

O'Rourke, Kevin, and Richard Sinnott. 2001. "What Determines Attitudes towards Protection? Some Cross-Country Evidence." *Brookings Trade Forum*, 157–206. (Cited 4n9, 14n48, 74n15, 124n4.)

Osnos, Evan. 2012, Oct. 17. "Watching the Debate in China: The Panda Sluggers." *The New Yorker*. https://www.newyorker.com/news/evan-osnos/watching-the-debate-in-china-the-panda-sluggers. (Cited 256n21.)

Oxley, Douglas R., Kevin B. Smith, John R. Alford, Matthew V. Hibbing, Jennifer L. Miller, Mario Scalora, Peter K. Hatemi, and John R. Hibbing. 2008. "Political Attitudes Vary with Physiological Traits." *Science* 321 (5896): 1667–70. https://doi.org/10.1126/science.1157627. (Cited 262n31.)

Page, Benjamin I., Robert Y. Shapiro, and Glenn R. Dempsey. 1987. "What Moves Public Opinion?" *The American Political Science Review* 81 (1): 23–43. https://doi.org/10.2307/1960777. (Cited 65n26.)

Paldam, Martin. 1991. "How Robust Is the Vote Function? A Study of Seventeen Nations over Four Decades." In *Economics and Politics: The Calculus of Support*. Edited by Helmut Norpoth, Jean-Dominique Lafay, and Michael S. Lewis-Beck, 9–31. Ann Arbor: University of Michigan Press. (Cited 216n42.)

Pandya, Sonal S., and Rajkumar Venkatesan. 2015. "French Roast: Consumer Response to International Conflict—Evidence from Supermarket Scanner Data." *The Review of Economics and Statistics* 98 (1): 42–56. https://doi.org/10.1162/REST_a_00526. (Cited 99n22.)

Pascarella, Ernest T., Corinna A. Ethington, and John C. Smart. 1988. "The Influence of College on Humanitarian/Civic Involvement Values." *The Journal of Higher Education; Columbus* 59 (4): 412–37. (Cited 93n59.)

Pelham, B.W., T.T. Sumarta, and L. Myaskovsky. 1994. "The Easy Path From Many To Much: The Numerosity Heuristic." *Cognitive Psychology* 26 (2): 103–33. https://doi.org/10.1006/cogp.1994.1004. (Cited 152n25.)

Perry, Mark J. 2017, March 16. "Trade Deficits Don't Matter; Understanding Deficits Do." Foundation for Economic Education. https://fee.org/articles/trade-deficits-dont-matter-understanding-deficits-do/. (Cited 43n28, 45n30.)

Peterson, Robert A., and Alain J. P. Jolibert. 1995. "A Meta-Analysis of Country-of-Origin Effects." *Journal of International Business Studies* 26 (4): 883–900. https://doi.org/10.1057/palgrave.jibs.8490824. (Cited 99n18.)

Petri, Alexandra. 2017, April 4. "Every Story I Have Read about Trump Supporters in the Past Week." *Washington Post*. https://www.washingtonpost.com/blogs/compost/wp/2017/04/04/every-story-i-have-read-about-trump-supporters-in-the-past-week/. (Cited 189n2.)

Pettigrew, Thomas F. 1998. "Intergroup Contact Theory." *Annual Review of Psychology* 49 (1): 65–85. https://doi.org/10.1146/annurev.psych.49.1.65. (Cited 36n13.)

Pettigrew, Thomas F., and Linda R. Tropp. 2006. "A Meta-Analytic Test of Intergroup Contact Theory." *Journal of Personality and Social Psychology* 90 (5): 751–83. https://doi.org/10.1037/0022-3514.90.5.751. (Cited 36n14.)

Pew Research Center. 2014, July 14. "Chapter 2: China's Image." *Pew Research Center's Global Attitudes Project* (blog). http://www.pewglobal.org/2014/07/14/chapter-2-chinas-image/. (Cited 232n24.)

Pew Research Center. 2019, Jan. 4. "More Say Immigrants Strengthen U.S. as the Partisan Divide Grows." http://www.people-press.org/2017/10/05/4-race-immigration-and-discrimination/4_9-3/.

———. 2019b, May 14. "Changing Attitudes on Gay Marriage." Pew Research Center's Religion & Public Life Project (blog). http://www.pewforum.org/fact-sheet/changing-attitudes-on-gay-marriage/.

Pham, Vincent N. 2015. "Our Foreign President Barack Obama: The Racial Logics of Birther Discourses." *Journal of International and Intercultural Communication* 8 (2): 86–107. https://doi.org/10.1080/17513057.2015.1025327. (Cited 274n27.)

Plutarch, Lucius. 1957. *Moralia*. Volume 12. Translated by Harold Cherniss. Cambridge, MA: Loeb Classical Library.

Polachek, Solomon W. 1997. "Why Democracies Cooperate More and Fight Less: The Relationship Between International Trade and Cooperation." *Review of International Economics* 5 (3): 295–309. https://doi.org/10.1111/1467-9396.00058. (Cited 96n3.)

Popper, Nathaniel. 2016, Sept. 6. "How Much Do We Really Know About Global Trade's Impacts?" *New York Times*, sec. Magazine. https://www.nytimes.com/2016/09/11/magazine/how-much-do-we-really-know-about-global-trades-impacts.html. (Cited 152n22, 180n40, 180n42.)

Porter, Eduardo. 2016, Dec. 13. "Where Were Trump's Votes? Where the Jobs Weren't." *New York Times*. https://www.nytimes.com/2016/12/13/business/economy/jobs-economy-voters.html. (Cited 189n1.)

Pratto, Felicia, Atilla Çidam, Andrew L. Stewart, Fouad Bou Zeineddine, María Aranda, Antonio Aiello, Xenia Chryssochoou, et al. 2013. "Social Dominance in Context and in Individuals: Contextual Moderation of Robust Effects of Social Dominance Orientation in 15 Languages and 20 Countries." *Social Psychological and Personality Science* 4 (5): 587–99. https://doi.org/10.1177/1948550612473663.

Pratto, Felicia, and Demis E. Glasford. 2008. "Ethnocentrism and the Value of a Human Life." *Journal of Personality and Social Psychology* 95 (6): 1411–28. https://doi.org/10.1037/a0012636. (Cited 72n2, 142n5, 152n25.)

Pratto, Felicia, Jim Sidanius, Lisa M. Stallworth, and Bertram F. Malle. 1994. "Social Dominance Orientation: A Personality Variable Predicting Social and Political Attitudes." *Journal of Personality and Social Psychology* 67 (4): 741–63. https://doi.org/10.1037/0022-3514.67.4.741. (Cited 13n45.)

Pratto, Felicia, Lisa M. Stallworth, Jim Sidanius, and Bret Siers. 1997. "The Gender Gap in Occupational Role Attainment: A Social Dominance Approach." *Journal of Personality and Social Psychology* 72 (1): 37–53. https://doi.org/10.1037/0022-3514.72.1.37.

Pratto, Felicia, Deborah G. Tatar, and Sahr Conway-Lanz. 1999. "Who Gets What and Why: Determinants of Social Allocations." *Political Psychology* 20 (1): 127–50. https://doi.org/10.1111/0162-895X.00139.

Prewitt, K., and N. Nie. 1971. "Election Studies of the Survey Research Center." *British Journal of Political Science* 7: 479–502. (Cited 242n52.)

Prislin, Radmila, Wendy M. Limbert, and Evamarie Bauer. 2000. "From Majority to Minority and Vice Versa: The Asymmetrical Effects of Losing and Gaining Majority Position within a Group." *Journal of Personality and Social Psychology* 79 (3): 385–97. https://doi.org/10.1037//0022-3514.79.3.385. (Cited 231n18.)

Putnam, Robert D. 2007. "E Pluribus Unum: Diversity and Community in the Twenty-First Century." The 2006 Johan Skytte Prize Lecture. *Scandinavian Political Studies* 30 (2): 137–74. https://doi.org/10.1111/j.1467-9477.2007.00176.x. (Cited 101n29.)

Rabbie, Jacob M., Frits Benoist, Henk Oosterbaan, and Lieuwe Visser. 1974. "Differential Power and Effects of Expected Competitive and Cooperative Intergroup Interaction on Intragroup and Outgroup Attitudes." *Journal of Personality and Social Psychology* 30 (1): 46–56. https://doi.org/10.1037/h0036620. (Cited 72n2.)

Radford, Jynnah. 2019, June 17. "Key Findings about U.S. Immigrants." *Pew Research Center* (blog). https://www.pewresearch.org/fact-tank/2019/06/17/key-findings-about-u-s-immigrants/. (Cited 209n16, 209n17.)

Radu, Sintia. 2019, Feb. 28. "The World Continues to Disapprove of America's Leadership." US News. https://www.usnews.com/news/best-countries/articles/2019-02-28/the-world-continues-to-disapprove-of-americas-leadership. (Cited 71n34.)

Ramzy, Austin. 2013, Oct. 17. "Chinese Leader Gets a Cartoon Makeover." *Sinosphere Blog*. https://sinosphere.blogs.nytimes.com/2013/10/17/chinese-leader-gets-a-cartoon-makeover/. (Cited 248n10.)

Rankin, David M. 2001. "Identities, Interests, and Imports." *Political Behavior* 23 (4): 351–76. (Cited 6n19, 14n48, 74n15.)

Rauch, James E., and Vitor Trindade. 2002. "Ethnic Chinese Networks in International Trade." *The Review of Economics and Statistics* 84 (1): 116–30. https://doi.org/10.1162/003465302317331955. (Cited 96n5.)

Reese, Stephen D., John A. Daly, and Andrew P. Hardy. 1987. "Economic News on Network Television." *Journalism & Mass Communication Quarterly* 64 (1): *137–44*. https://journals.sagepub.com/doi/10.1177/107769908706400119. (Cited 181n43.)

Reich, Robert B. 1990, June 18. "Do We Want U.S. to Be Rich or Japan Poor?" *Wall Street Journal*, 1990.

Reid, Daniel. 2017. "10 Things You Should Never Say to a Canadian." *Reader's Digest* (blog). 2017. https://www.readersdigest.ca/travel/canada/10-things-you-cant-say-canada/. (Cited 119n45.)

Rho, Sungmin, and Michael Tomz. 2015. "Industry, Self-Interest, and Individual Preferences over Trade Policy." http://www.sungminrho.com/uploads/3/7/0/0/37006927/rhotomz-2015-04-01.pdf. (Cited 17n52, 42n23, 51n35, 241n42, 242n48.)

———. 2017. "Why Don't Trade Preferences Reflect Economic Self-Interest?" *International Organization* 71 (S1): S85–108. https://doi.org/10.1017/S0020818316000394. (Cited 4n6, 5n12, 6n16, 7n22, 17n52, 51n35.)

Rios, Kimberly, Stacey Finkelstein, and Jennifer Landa. 2015. "Is There a 'Fair' in Fair-Trade? Social Dominance Orientation Influences Perceptions of and Preferences for Fair-Trade Products." *Journal of Business Ethics* 130 (1): 171–80. (Cited 147n14.)

Rodrik, Dani. 2018. "Populism and the Economics of Globalization." *Journal of International Business Policy* 1 (1–2): 12–33. https://doi.org/10.1057/s42214-018-0001-4. (Cited 200n36.)

Rogers, Katie, and Nicholas Fandos. 2019, July 14. "Trump Tells Congresswomen to 'Go Back' to the Countries They Came From." *New York Times.* https://www.nytimes.com/2019/07/14/us/politics/trump-twitter-squad-congress.html. (Cited 136n31.)

Rogoff, Kenneth. 2017, Aug. 2. "Protectionism Will Not Protect Jobs Anywhere." Project Syndicate. https://www.project-syndicate.org/commentary/protectionism-saves-no-jobs-by-kenneth-rogoff-2017-08.

Rokeach, Milton. 1960. *The Open and Closed Mind.* Oxford: Basic Books. (Cited 109n41.)

Rooduijn, Matthijs. 2018. "What Unites the Voter Bases of Populist Parties? Comparing the Electorates of 15 Populist Parties." *European Political Science Review* 10 (3): 351–68. https://doi.org/10.1017/S1755773917000145. (Cited 266n9.)

Rose, Stephen J. 2018. "Manufacturing Employment: Fact and Fiction." Income and Benefits Policy Center. Urban Institute. Washington, DC. (Cited 22n58,190n7.)

Rothwell, Jonathan T., and Pablo Diego-Rosell. 2016. "Explaining Nationalist Political Views: The Case of Donald Trump." SSRN Scholarly Paper. Rochester, NY: Social Science Research Network. https://papers.ssrn.com/abstract=2822059. (Cited 267n12.)

Rousseau, David L. 2002. "Motivations for Choice: The Salience of Relative Gains in International Politics." *Journal of Conflict Resolution* 46 (3): 394–426. https://doi.org/10.1177/0022002702046003004. (Cited 84n39, 93n57.)

Rubin, Paul H. 2014. "Emporiophobia (Fear of Markets): Cooperation or Competition?" *Southern Economic Journal* 80 (4): 875–89. https://doi.org/10.4284/0038-4038-2013.287. (Cited 9n30, 10n32, 10n33, 10n35.)

Rudelson, Justin Jon. 1997. *Oasis Identities: Uyghur Nationalism Along China's Silk Road.* New York: Columbia University Press. https://www.biblio.com/book/oasis-identities-uyghur-nationalism-along-chinas/d/1155008339. (Cited 259n25.)

Rudolph, Thomas J. 2003. "Who's Responsible for the Economy? The Formation and Consequences of Responsibility Attributions." *American Journal of Political Science* 47 (4): 698–713. https://doi.org/10.1111/1540-5907.00049. (Cited 217n49.)

Rueda, David, and Daniel Stegmueller. 2019. Who Wants What?" Cambridge; New York: Cambridge University Press. https://doi.org/10.1017/9781108681339. (Cited 92n56.)

Sabet, Shahrzad. 2013. "What's in a Name? Isolating the Effect of Prejudice on Individual Trade Preferences." SSRN Scholarly Paper. Rochester, NY: Social Science Research Network. https://papers.ssrn.com/abstract=2301118. (Cited 18n54, 75n18, 122n48, 125n9, 237n36, 241n44, 242n50.)

———. 2016. "Feelings First: Non-Material Factors as Moderators of Economic Self-Interest Effects on Trade Preferences." Unpublished manuscript, Harvard University, Cambridge, MA. http://scholar.harvard.edu/files/ssabet/files/sabet_feelings_first_.pdf. (Cited 5n10.)

Salama, Vivian, Rebecca Ballhaus, Andrew Restuccia, and Michael C. Bender. 2019, Aug. 16. "President Trump Eyes a New Real-Estate Purchase: Greenland." *Wall Street Journal,* sec. Politics. https://www.wsj.com/articles/trump-eyes-a-new-real-estate-purchase-greenland-11565904223. (Cited 12n42.)

Samuelson, Paul A. 1969. "Presidential Address: The Way of an Economist." In *International Economic Relations: Proceedings of the Third Congress of the International Economic Association.* Edited by Paul A. Samuelson, 1–11. International Economic Association Series. London: Palgrave Macmillan UK. https://doi.org/10.1007/978-1-349-00767-7_1. (Cited 272n25.)

San Francisco Chronicle. 2017, Jan. 22. "Trump's Dark Portrayal of America." https://www.pressreader.com/usa/san-francisco-chronicle/20170122/282789241149450.

Sanders, David, and Neil Gavin. 2004. "Television News, Economic Perceptions and Political Preferences in Britain, 1997–2001." *The Journal of Politics* 66 (4): 1245–66. https://doi.org/10.1111/j.0022-3816.2004.00298.x. (Cited 163n5, 216n44.)

Sapolsky, Robert. 2019, Oct. 2. "This Is Your Brain on Nationalism." *Foreign Affairs*. https://www.foreignaffairs.com/articles/2019-02-12/your-brain-nationalism. (Cited 76n21.)

Sapolsky, Robert M. 2018. *Behave: The Biology of Humans at Our Best and Worst*. Reprint ed. New York: Penguin Books.

Sargent, Greg. 2019, Jan. 2. "The Walls around Trump Are Crumbling. Evangelicals May Be His Last Resort." *Washington Post*. https://www.washingtonpost.com/opinions/2019/01/02/walls-around-trump-are-crumbling-evangelicals-may-be-his-last-resort. (Cited 209n17.)

Schaffner, Brian F., Matthew MacWilliams, and Tatishe Nteta. 2017. "Hostile Sexism, Racism Denial, and the Historic Education Gap in Support for Trump." In *The 2016 Presidential Election: Causes and Consequences of a Political Earthquake*. Edited by Amnon Cavari, Richard J. Powell, and Kenneth R Mayer, chapter 6. 99–116. New York: Lexington Books. (Cited 206n5, 267n12.)

Scheve, Kenneth F., and Matthew J. Slaughter. 2001. "What Determines Individual Trade-Policy Preferences." *Journal of International Economics* 54(2): 267–292. (Cited 4n9, 213n34.)

———. 2018, Oct. 15. "How to Save Globalization." *Foreign Affairs*. https://www.foreignaffairs.com/articles/united-states/2018-10-15/how-save-globalization.

Schlueter, Elmar, and Peer Scheepers. 2010. "The Relationship between Outgroup Size and Anti-Outgroup Attitudes: A Theoretical Synthesis and Empirical Test of Group Threat- and Intergroup Contact Theory." *Social Science Research* 39 (2): 285–95. https://doi.org/10.1016/j.ssresearch.2009.07.006. (Cited 231n19.)

Schneider, Keith. 1991, January 4. "Lujan Softens Criticism of a Japanese Takeover at Yosemite." *New York Times*, sec. U.S. https://www.nytimes.com/1991/01/04/us/lujan-softens-criticism-of-a-japanese-takeover-at-yosemite.html. (Cited 12n40.)

Schwartz, Ian. 2015, Sept. 15. "Trump: 'We Will Have So Much Winning If I Get Elected That You May Get Bored With Winning.'" Real Clear Politics. http://www.realclearpolitics.com/video/2015/09/09/trump_we_will_have_so_much_winning_if_i_get_elected_that_you_may_get_bored_with_winning.html. (Cited 149n20.)

Sears, David, and Carolyn L. Funk. 1990. "The Limited Effect of Economic Self Interest on the Political Attitudes of the Mass Public." *Journal of Behavioral Economics* 19 (3): 247–71. (Cited 6n17.)

Sears, David O., and Carolyn L. Funk. 1990. "Self-Interest in Americans' Political Opinions." In *Beyond Self-Interest*. Edited by Jane J. Mansbridge, 147–70 Chicago: University of Chicago Press. (Cited 6n17.)

Seib, Gerald F. 2010, Aug. 17. "How Hard Times Prompt Americans to Turn Inward." *WSJ* (blog). https://blogs.wsj.com/capitaljournal/2010/08/17/how-hard-times-prompt-americans-to-turn-inward/. (Cited 228n3.)

Shah, Dhavan V., Mark D. Watts, David Domke, David P. Fan, and Michael Fibison. 1999. "News Coverage, Economic Cues, and the Public's Presidential Preferences, 1984–1996." *The Journal of Politics* 61 (4): 914–43. https://doi.org/10.2307/2647548. (Cited 163n5, 163n6.)

Shakespeare, Stephan. 2005, April 16. "They Seem to Be Campaigning for the Sake of It." *The Guardian*. https://www.theguardian.com/politics/2005/apr/17/uk.election20054. (Cited 9n28.)

Shambaugh, David L. 2007. "China's 'Quiet Diplomacy': The International Department of the Chinese Communist Party." *China: An International Journal* 5 (1): 26–54. https://doi.org/10.1353/chn.2007.0004. (Cited 248n11.)

Sherif, Muzafer, and Carolyn W. Sherif. 1953. *Groups in Harmony and Tension; an Integration of Studies of Intergroup Relations*. Groups in Harmony and Tension; An Integration of Studies of Intergroup Relations. Oxford, UK: Harper & Brothers. (Cited 72n2.)

Shiller, Robert J. 2019. *Narrative Economics: How Stories Go Viral and Drive Major Economic Events*. Princeton: Princeton University Press. https://doi.org/10.2307/j.ctvdf0jm5. (Cited 8n26.)

Shimp, Terence A., and Subhash Sharma. 1987. "Consumer Ethnocentrism: Construction and Validation of the CETSCALE." *Journal of Marketing Research* 24 (3): 280–89. https://doi.org/10.1177/002224378702400304. (Cited 100n23.)

Shook, Natalie J., Patricia D. Hopkins, and Jasmine M. Koech. 2016. "The Effect of Intergroup Contact on Secondary Group Attitudes and Social Dominance Orientation." *Group Processes & Intergroup Relations* 19 (3): 328–42. https://doi.org/10.1177/1368430215572266. (Cited 232n28.)

Sibley, Chris G., Marc S. Wilson, and John Duckitt. 2007. "Effects of Dangerous and Competitive Worldviews on Right-Wing Authoritarianism and Social Dominance Orientation over a Five-Month Period." *Political Psychology* 28 (3): 357–71. https://doi.org/10.1111/j.1467-9221.2007.00572.x. (Cited 232n27.)

Sidanius, Jim, Seymour Feshbach, Shana Levin, and Felicia Pratto. 1997. "The Interface Between Ethnic and National Attachment: Ethnic Pluralism or Ethnic Dominance?" *The Public Opinion Quarterly* 61 (1): 102–33. (Cited 147n16, 148n18.)

Sidanius, Jim, Hillary Haley, Ludwin Molina, and Felicia Pratto. 2007. "Vladimir's Choice and the Distribution of Social Resources: A Group Dominance Perspective." *Group Processes & Intergroup Relations* 10 (2): 257–65. (Cited 85n40, 85n42, 85n44.)

Sidanius, Jim, and Felicia Pratto. 1999. *Social Dominance: An Intergroup Theory of Social Hierarchy and Oppression.* New York: Cambridge University Press. (Cited 76n20, 85n45, 130n23, 232n26.)

Sidanius, Jim, Felicia Pratto, and Diana Brief. 1995. "Group Dominance and the Political Psychology of Gender: A Cross-Cultural Comparison." *Political Psychology* 16 (2): 381–96. https://doi.org/10.2307/3791836.

Sides, John, and Jack Citrin. 2007. "European Opinion about Immigration: The Role of Identities, Interests and Information." *British Journal of Political Science* 37 (3): 477–504. (Cited 126n19, 126n20, 155n33.)

Sides, John, Michael Tesler, and Lynn Vavreck. 2018. *Identity Crisis: The 2016 Presidential Campaign and the Battle for the Meaning of America.* Princeton, NJ: Princeton University Press. (Cited 206n3, 206n5, 214n35, 267n12.)

Silver, Laura R. 2016. "China in the Media: Effects on American Opinion." Dissertation submitted for PhD in Political Science and Communication, University of Pennsylvania. Philadelphia. (Cited 255n20.)

Silver, Nate. 2016, Nov. 22. "Education, Not Income, Predicted Who Would Vote For Trump." FiveThirtyEight (blog). https://fivethirtyeight.com/features/education-not-income-predicted-who-would-vote-for-trump/.

Singer, Matthew M. 2011. "Who Says 'It's the Economy'? Cross-National and Cross-Individual Variation in the Salience of Economic Performance." *Comparative Political Studies* 44 (3): 284–312. https://doi.org/10.1177/0010414010384371. (Cited 215n37.)

Singer, Matthew M., and Ryan E. Carlin. 2013. "Context Counts: The Election Cycle, Development, and the Nature of Economic Voting." *The Journal of Politics* 75 (3): 730–42. https://doi.org/10.1017/S0022381613000467. (Cited 215n39.)

Skelley, Geoffrey. 2019, April 19. "Trump's Approval Rating Is Incredibly Steady: Is That Weird or the New Normal?" *FiveThirtyEight.* https://fivethirtyeight.com/features/trumps-approval-rating-is-incredibly-steady-is-that-weird-or-the-new-normal. (Cited 65n25.)

Slaughter, Matthew J. 1999. "Globalisation and Wages: A Tale of Two Perspectives." *The World Economy* 22 (5): 609–29. https://doi.org/10.1111/1467-9701.00221. (Cited 141n2.)

Small, Deborah A. 2010. "Reference-Dependent Sympathy." *Organizational Behavior and Human Decision Processes* 112 (2): 151–60. https://doi.org/10.1016/j.obhdp.2010.03.001. (Cited 181n44.)

Small, Deborah A., and Jennifer S. Lerner. 2008. "Emotional Policy: Personal Sadness and Anger Shape Judgments about a Welfare Case." *Political Psychology* 29 (2): 149–68. https://doi.org/10.1111/j.1467-9221.2008.00621.x. (Cited 181n44.)

Small, Deborah A., and George Loewenstein. 2003. "Helping a Victim or Helping the Victim: Altruism and Identifiability." *Journal of Risk and Uncertainty* 26 (1): 5–16. https://doi.org/10.1023/A:1022299422219. (Cited 181n44.)

Small, Deborah A., George Loewenstein, and Paul Slovic. 2007. "Sympathy and Callousness: The Impact of Deliberative Thought on Donations to Identifiable and Statistical Victims." *Organizational Behavior and Human Decision Processes* 102 (2): 143–53. https://doi.org/10.1016/j.obhdp.2006.01.005. (Cited 181n44.)

Small, Deborah, and George Loewenstein. 2005. "The Devil You Know: The Effects of Identifiability on Punishment." *Journal of Behavioral Decision Making*. 18 (5): 311–18. https://doi.org/10.1002/bdm.507. (Cited 181n44.)

Smeltz, Diana. 2018, Oct. 31. "FOMO: Many Americans Want to Join the Revised TPP Agreement." Chicago Council on Global Affairs. https://www.thechicagocouncil.org/blog/running-numbers/fomo-many-americans-want-join-revised-tpp-agreement.

Smeltz, Dina, Ivo Daalder, Karl Friedhoff, and Craig Kafura. 2016. "America in the Age of Uncertainty." *Chicago Council on Global Affairs*. (Cited 25n2.)

Smialek, Jeanna. 2019, May 29. "This Boutique Bike Shop Shows How Trump's Tariffs Can Hit the Little Guy." *New York Times*, sec. Business. https://www.nytimes.com/2019/05/29/business/pello-bikes-china-tariffs.html. (Cited 185n49.)

Smith, Adam. 2011. *The Theory of Moral Sentiments*. Kapaau: Gutenberg Publishers. (Cited 2n4.)

Sniderman, Paul M., and Richard A. Brody. 1977. "Coping: The Ethic of Self-Reliance." *American Journal of Political Science* 21 (3): 501–21. https://doi.org/10.2307/2110579. (Cited 6n15.)

Sonmez, Felicia. 2015, Sept. 22. "'When China Met Carolina:' Chinese Firms Save U.S. Jobs, New Video Says." *WSJ* (blog). https://blogs.wsj.com/chinarealtime/2015/09/22/when-china-met-carolina-chinese-firms-save-u-s-jobs-new-video-says/. (Cited 248n12.)

Spilker, Gabriele, Lena Maria Schaffer, and Thomas Bernauer. 2012. "Does Social Capital Increase Public Support for Economic Globalisation?" *European Journal of Political Research* 51 (6): 756–84. https://doi.org/10.1111/j.1475-6765.2012.02058.x. (Cited 102n37.)

Stasi, Linda. 2015, Sept. 25. "Stasi: Donald Trump Blames China for Biggest Theft in U.S. History. *New York Daily News*. https://www.nydailynews.com/news/national/stasi-trump-blames-china-biggest-theft-u-s-history-article-1.2337306. (Cited 45n29.)

Steele, James B., and Donald L. Barlett, 2012. *The Betrayal of the American Dream*. New York: PublicAffairs. (Cited 73n9, 74n11.)

Stein, Arthur A. 1990. *Why Nations Cooperate: Circumstance and Choice in International Relations*. Ithaca, NY: Cornell University Press.

Stein, Jeff, and Andrew Van Dam. 2018, Feb. 6. "Trump Immigration Plan Could Keep Whites in U.S. Majority for up to Five More Years." *Washington Post*. https://www.washingtonpost.com/news/wonk/wp/2018/02/06/trump-immigration-plan-could-keep-whites-in-u-s-majority-for-up-to-five-more-years/.

Stempel, Carl. 2006. "Televised Sports, Masculinist Moral Capital, and Support for the U.S. Invasion of Iraq." *Journal of Sport and Social Issues* 30 (1): 79–106. https://doi.org/10.1177/0193723505282472. (Cited 126n18.)

Stenner, Karen. 2005. *The Authoritarian Dynamic*. New York: Cambridge University Press.

———. 2009. "Three Kinds of 'Conservatism.'" *Psychological Inquiry* 20 (2–3): 142–59. https://doi.org/10.1080/10478400903028615. (Cited 258n23.)

Stockman, Farah. 2017, Oct. 14. "Becoming a Steelworker Liberated Her. Then Her Job Moved to Mexico." *New York Times*. https://www.nytimes.com/2017/10/14/us/union-jobs-mexico-rexnord.html?action=click&module=RelatedCoverage&pgtype=Article®ion=Footer. (Cited 187n51.)

Stokes, Bruce. 2012, Sept. 7. "Have Americans Turned Inward?" *Pew Research Center's Global Attitudes Project* (blog). https://www.pewresearch.org/global/2012/09/07/have-americans-turned-inward/. (Cited 227n2.)

———. 2016, March 31. "Republicans, Especially Trump Supporters, See Free Trade Deals as Bad for U.S." Pew Research Center (blog). http://www.pewresearch.org/fact-tank/2016/03/31/republicans-especially-trump-supporters-see-free-trade-deals-as-bad-for-u-s/.

Stolle, Dietlind, Stuart Soroka, and Richard Johnston. 2008. "When Does Diversity Erode Trust? Neighborhood Diversity, Interpersonal Trust and the Mediating Effect of Social Interactions." *Political Studies* 56 (1): 57–75. https://doi.org/10.1111/j.1467-9248.2007.00717.x. (Cited 136n29.)

Strezhnev, Anton. 2013. "The Effect of Trading Partner Democracy on Public Attitudes Toward Preferential Trade Agreements." Working Paper. (Cited 101n32.)

Sumner, Scott. 2020, Jan. 15. "Trump's Policies Are Increasing, Not Decreasing, the Trade Deficit." The Hill. https://thehill.com/opinion/international/478226-trumps-policies-are-increasing-not-decreasing-the-trade-deficit (Cited 263n2.)

Swann, W., Á. Gómez, J. Dovidio, S. Hart, and J. Jetten. 2010. "Dying and Killing for One's Group." *Psychological Science* 21: 1176–83. (Cited 73n7.)

Szayna, Thomas S., Steven C. Bankes, and Robert E. Mullins. 2001. "The Emergence of Peer Competitors. A Framework for Analysis." Rand Corporation, Santa Monica, CA. https://apps.dtic.mil/docs/citations/ADA398471. (Cited 36n12.)

Tajfel, Henri. 1970. "Experiments in Intergroup Discrimination." *Scientific American* 223 (5): 96–102. https://doi.org/10.1038/scientificamerican1170-96.

———. 1982. "Social Psychology of Intergroup Relations." *Annual Review of Psychology* 33 (1): 1–39. https://doi.org/10.1146/annurev.ps.33.020182.000245.

Tajfel, Henri, M.G. Billig, R.P. Bundy, and Claude Flament. 1971. "Social Categorization and Intergroup Behaviour." *European Journal of Social Psychology* 1 (2): 149–78. https://doi.org/10.1002/ejsp.2420010202. (Cited 82n33.)

Tajfel, Henri, and John C. Turner. 1979. An integrative theory of inter-group conflict. In *The Social Psychology of Inter-group Relations.* Edited by W. G. Austin and S. Worchel 33–47. Monterey, CA: Brooks/Cole. (Cited 192n16.)

Tajfel, Henri, and John C. Turner. 1986. "The Social Identity Theory of Intergroup Behavior." In *Psychology of Intergroup Relations.* Edited by S. Worchel and W.G. Austin, 7–24. Chicago: Hall Publishers. (Cited 193n20, 85n41, 109n42.)

Tajfel, Henri, and John C. Turner. 2004. *The Social Identity Theory of Intergroup Behavior.* Political Psychology: Key Readings. New York: Psychology Press.

Tedin, Kent, Brandon Rottinghaus, and Harrell Rogers. 2011. "When the President Goes Public: The Consequences of Communication Mode for Opinion Change across Issue Types and Groups." *Political Research Quarterly* 64 (3): 506–519. https://doi.org/10.1177/1065912910370685. (Cited 65n23.)

Theiss-Morse, Elizabeth. 2009. *Who Counts as an American? The Boundaries of National Identity.* New York: Cambridge University Press. (Cited 76n22, 92n52, 92n53, 92n55, 126n19, 126n20, 232n25.)

Tinbergen, Jan. 1962. "An Analysis of World Trade Flows." In *Shaping the World Economy.* Edited by Jan Tinbergen, 27–30. New York: Twentieth Century Fund. (Cited 96n2.)

Tocqueville, Alexis de, and Henry Reeve. 1835. *Democracy in America.* London: Saunders and Otley. (Cited 161n46.)

Tongberg, Richard Carey. 1972. "An Empirical Study of Relationships between Dogmatism and Consumer Attitudes toward Foreign Products." Doctoral dissertation. Pennsylvania State University. (Cited 96n5.)

Trope, Yaacov, and Nira Liberman. 2010. "Construal-Level Theory of Psychological Distance." *Psychological Review* 117 (2): 440–63. https://doi.org/10.1037/a0018963. (Cited 98n13.)

Trump, Donald. 2017a, Jan. 20. "The Inaugural Address." The White House. https://www.whitehouse.gov/briefings-statements/the-inaugural-address/. (Cited 143n8.)

———. 2017b, March 27. "Trump: 'The System Is Totally Rigged and Broken.'" *Washington Post.* http://www.washingtonpost.com/video/politics/trump-the-system-is-totally-rigged-and-broken/2016/10/22/01a60a20-9867-11e6-9cae-2a3574e296a6_video.html.

Tsfati, Yariv. 2017, Aug. "Public and Elite Perceptions of News Media in Politics." *The Oxford Handbook of Political Communication.* https://doi.org/10.1093/oxfordhb/9780199793471.013.52. (Cited 213n32.)

Turner, John C. 1975. "Social Comparison and Social Identity: Some Prospects for Intergroup Behaviour." *European Journal of Social Psychology* 5 (1): 1–34. https://doi.org/10.1002/ejsp.2420050102. (Cited 85n41.)

Turner, John C., Michael A. Hogg, Penelope J. Oakes, Stephen D. Reicher, and Margaret S. Wetherell. 1987. *Rediscovering the Social Group: A Self-Categorization Theory.* Rediscovering the Social Group: A Self-Categorization Theory. Cambridge, MA: Basil Blackwell. (Cited 85n41.)

Tuschman, Avi. 2013. *Our Political Nature: The Evolutionary Origins of What Divides Us.* Amherst, New York: Prometheus.

Tyson, Alec. 2014, July 2. "Most Americans Think the U.S. Is Great, but Fewer Say It's the Greatest." Pew Research Center (blog). http://www.pewresearch.org/fact-tank/2014/07/02/most-americans-think-the-u-s-is-great-but-fewer-say-its-the-greatest/. (Cited 231n23.)

Uberoi, Varun. 2008. "Do Policies of Multiculturalism Change National Identities?" *The Political Quarterly* 79 (3): 404–17. https://doi.org/10.1111/j.1467-923X.2008.00942.x. (Cited 160n45.)

———. 2016. "Legislating Multiculturalism and Nationhood: The 1988 Canadian Multiculturalism Act." *Canadian Journal of Political Science/Revue Canadienne de Science Politique* 49 (2): 267–87. https://doi.org/10.1017/S0008423916000366. (Cited 155n29.)

Wang, Chih-Kang, and Charles W. Lamb. 1980. "Foreign Environmental Factors Influencing American Consumers' Predispositions toward European Products." *Journal of the Academy of Marketing Science* 8 (4): 345–56. (Cited 96n5.)

———. 1983. "The Impact of Selected Environmental Forces upon Consumers' Willingness to Buy Foreign Products." *Journal of the Academy of Marketing Science* 11 (1): 71–84. https://doi.org/10.1007/BF02721862. (Cited 99n18.)

Wang, Yanan. 2015, Dec. 8. "Muslims Are to Trump as the Chinese Were to President Arthur in 1882." *Washington Post.* https://www.washingtonpost.com/news/morning-mix/wp/2015/12/08/muslims-are-to-trump-as-the-chinese-were-to-president-arthur-in-1882/. (Cited 255n18.)

Washington Post. 2015, June 15. "Donald Trump Announces a Presidential Bid." *Washington Post.* https://www.washingtonpost.com/news/post-politics/wp/2015/06/16/full-text-donald-trump-announces-a-presidential-bid/. (Cited 149n19.)

Watson, John J., and Katrina Wright. 2000, Oct. "Consumer Ethnocentrism and Attitudes toward Domestic and Foreign Products." *European Journal of Marketing.* https://doi.org/10.1108/03090560010342520. (Cited 99n18.)

Wazwaz, N. 2015, July 6. It's Official: The U.S. is Becoming a Minority-Majority Nation: Census Data Shows There Are More Minority Children under Age 5 than Whites. *US News and World Report.* https://www.usnews.com/news/articles/2015/07/06/its-official-the-us-is-becoming-a-minority-majority-nation (Cited 231n17.)

Wilkins C.L., and C.R. Kaiser 2014. "Racial Progress as Threat to the Status Hierarchy: Implications for Perceptions of Anti-White Bias." *Psychological Science* 25(2) 439–45. (Cited 231n19.)

Williamson, John. 2004–2005. "The Strange History of the Washington Consensus." *Journal of Post Keynesian Economics* 27 (2): 195–206. (Cited 54n5.)

Wlezien, Christopher. 2015. "The Myopic Voter? The Economy and US Presidential Elections." *Electoral Studies* 39 (September): 195–204. https://doi.org/10.1016/j.electstud.2015.03.010. (Cited 190n6.)

Wolcott, James. 2018, Oct. "Twilight at the Diner." *Vanity Fair*. https://archive.vanityfair.com/article/2018/10/twilight-at-the-diner. (Cited 189n3.)

Wolfe, Robert, and Matthew Mendelsohn. 2005. "Values and Interests in Attitudes toward Trade and Globalization: The Continuing Compromise of Embedded Liberalism." *Canadian Journal of Political Science / Revue Canadienne de Science Politique* 38 (1): 45–68. (Cited 5n10.)

Wong, Chun Han. 2015, Sept. 22. "'When China Met Carolina:' Chinese Firms Save U.S. Jobs, New Video Says." *WSJ* (blog). https://blogs.wsj.com/chinarealtime/2015/09/22/when-china-met-carolina-chinese-firms-save-u-s-jobs-new-video-says/. (Cited 248n10.)

Woodside, Arch G., and J. William Davenport. 1974. "The Effect of Salesman Similarity and Expertise on Consumer Purchasing Behavior." *Journal of Marketing Research* 11 (2): 198–202. https://doi.org/10.1177/002224377401100212. (Cited 101n30.)

World Bank. 2017, April 1. "The World Has Made Great Progress in Eradicating Extreme Poverty." *The Economist*. April 1, 2017. http://www.economist.com/news/international/21719790-going-will-be-much-harder-now-world-has-made-great-progress. (Cited 159n44.)

Wright, Matthew, and Irene Bloemraad. 2012. "Is There a Trade-off between Multiculturalism and Socio-Political Integration? Policy Regimes and Immigrant Incorporation in Comparative Perspective." *Perspectives on Politics* 10 (1): 77–95. https://doi.org/10.1017/S1537592711004919. (Cited 155n30.)

Wu, Frank H. 2012, June 22. "Why Vincent Chin Matters." *New York Times*, sec. Opinion. https://www.nytimes.com/2012/06/23/opinion/why-vincent-chin-matters.html. (Cited 255n17.)

Zakaria, Fareed. 2020, Feb. 20. "The Trade Deficit Is Soaring under Trump—And That's A Good Thing." *Washington Post*. https://www.washingtonpost.com/opinions/the-trade-deficit-is-soaring-under-trump--and-thats-a-good-thing/2020/02/20/017c3e36-5428-11ea-9e47-59804be1dcfb_story.html. (Cited 263n2.)

Zaller, John R. 1992. *The Nature and Origins of Mass Opinion*. New York: Cambridge University Press. (Cited 64n18.)

Zeitlin, Matthew. 2019, July 3. "The Racial Roots of Trump's Anti-Trade Agenda." Vox. https://www.vox.com/2019/7/3/20681384/trump-trade-agenda-race-immigration. (Cited 261n20.)

INDEX

A NOTE ON THE TYPE

This book has been composed in Adobe Text and Gotham. Adobe Text, designed by Robert Slimbach for Adobe, bridges the gap between fifteenth- and sixteenth-century calligraphic and eighteenth-century Modern styles. Gotham, inspired by New York street signs, was designed by Tobias Frere-Jones for Hoefler & Co.

www.ingramcontent.com/pod-product-compliance
Ingram Content Group UK Ltd.
Pitfield, Milton Keynes, MK11 3LW, UK
UKHW042230130125
453571UK00003B/88

9 780691 203027